Complexities of Motion

Complexities of Motion

New Essays
on A. R. Ammons's
Long Poems

Edited and with an Introduction
by Steven P. Schneider

Madison ● Teaneck
Fairleigh Dickinson University Press
London: Associated University Presses

PS
3501
.M6
Z62
1999

Associated University Presses
440 Forsgate Drive
Cranbury, NJ 08512

Associated University Presses
16 Barter Street
London WC1A 2AH, England

Associated University Presses
P.O. Box 338, Port Credit
Mississauga, Ontario
Canada L5G 4L8

The paper used in this publication meets the requirements
of the American National Standard for Permanence of Paper
for Printed Library Materials Z39.48-1984.

Library of Congress Cataloging-in-Publication

Complexities of motion : new essays on A.R. Ammons's long poems /
    edited and with an introduction by Steven P. Schneider.
        p.   cm.
    Includes bibliographical references and index.
    ISBN 0-8386-3742-6 (alk. paper)
    1. Ammons, A. R., 1926– —Criticism and interpretation.
I. Schneider, Steven P.
PS3501.M6Z62   1999
811'.54—dc21   98-35303
                                                                     CIP

Contents

Acknowledgments

I am especially grateful to the Research Services Council and Dean Ken Nikels, Dean of Graduate Studies and Research at the University of Nebraska at Kearney (UNK) for their generous support of this book. A grant from the Research Services Council at UNK enabled me to complete this manuscript.

I am also fortunate to have benefited from the insights of many helpful individuals. I would especially like to thank my colleague William Melaney for his very useful criticism on the manuscript. A special note of thanks to Ed Folsom, good friend and teacher, who provided valuable advice about the structure of the book and helpful comments on my own essay.

Thanks to Willard Spiegelman and Alex Albright, with whom I discussed in Chicago in 1995 the original conception of this book. My thanks also to Roger Gilbert and Marjorie Perloff for making helpful suggestions. A note of appreciation to Robert Luscher and Dean Harold Nichols at UNK, who assisted me in finding the time and resources to complete this project.

My gratitude to each of the contributors to this volume, whose thoughtful and thorough work made my job as editor stimulating and rewarding.

A special note of thanks to Archie Ammons, who spent the better part of three days with me in the spring of 1996 in Ithaca, New York, patiently answering my many interview questions.

And finally, I wish to warmly thank my wife Rivca for her unflinching support, and our two sons, Aaron and Roni, who continue to be a great source of joy.

8   ACKNOWLEDGMENTS

Collected Poems 1951–1971, by A. R. Ammons, by permission of the author and W.W. Norton & Company, Inc. Copyright (c) 1972 by A. R. Ammons.

Sphere: The Form of a Motion, by A. R. Ammons, by permission of the author and W.W. Norton & Company, Inc. Copyright (C) 1974 by A. R. Ammons.

Diversifications, by A. R. Ammons, by permission of the author and W.W. Norton & Company, Inc. Copyright (C) 1975 by A. R. Ammons.

The Snow Poems, by A. R. Ammons, by permission of the author and W.W. Norton & Company, Inc. Copyright (C) 1977 by A. R. Ammons.

Selected Longer Poems, by A. R. Ammons, by permission of the author and W.W. Norton & Company, Inc. Copyright (C) 1980 by A. R. Ammons.

Sumerian Vistas, poems by A. R. Ammons, by permission of the author and W.W. Norton & Company, Inc. Copyright (C) 1987 by A. R. Ammons.

Garbage, by A. R. Ammons, by permission of the author and W.W. Norton & Company, Inc. Copyright (C) 1993 by A. R. Ammons.

Glare, by A. R. Ammons, by permission of the author and W.W. Norton & Company, Inc. Copyright (C) 1997 by A. R. Ammons.

Introduction

Steven P. Schneider

This collection gathers new essays on A. R. Ammons's long poems, by many of the most influential critics of contemporary American poetry. The long poem has always fascinated Ammons, and his career as a poet is distinguished in part by the recognition given to his longer poems. In 1975 he received the Bollingen Prize in Poetry for his book-length volume, *Sphere: The Form of A Motion.* More recently, in 1993, Ammons won the National Book Award for *Garbage,* a long meditation on nature and mutability.

Despite the recognition garnered by these and other major long poems, little serious critical attention has been given to them until now. A small number of critical articles have appeared on Ammons's individual long poems, and an even fewer number of articles have attempted to contextualize them as a group. This collection of essays then fills a vacuum in Ammons scholarship and will serve as an important critical text on a vast body of work by one of the most prolific and innovative practitioners of the long poem in post-World War II American poetry.

This volume began when I coordinated a special session on A. R. Ammons's long poems, entitled "Complexities of Motion: Chaos and Order in A. R. Ammons's Long Poems," at the MLA Convention in Chicago in 1995. Two of the contributors to this collection, Willard Spiegelman and Alex Albright, along with myself, presented papers at that session, papers that have grown into much longer essays for this book. As a result of our conversations in Chicago and the excitement of exploring Ammons's unusual processes and procedures in his long poems, often composed on rolls of adding machine tape, I contacted other scholars who might be interested in contributing to this volume. The response from critics around the country was overwhelmingly positive, and the current volume is the result. Many of the contributors to *Complexities of Motion* have written important essays about Ammons in the past. All of them saw this volume as an exciting opportunity to focus anew, this time exclusively on the long poems.

Complexities of Motion then, is a collection of new critical articles on the entire range of Ammons's longer poems, beginning with *Tape for the Turn of the Year* (1965) and culminating with *Glare* (1997). Over the course of four decades, Ammons would write five book-length long poems: *Tape for the Turn of the Year* (1965), *Sphere: The Form of A Motion* (1974), *The Snow Poems* (1977), *Garbage* (1993), and now *Glare* (1997). In addition, he has produced eight other "longer" poems that have found their way into such volumes as the *Collected Poems 1951–1971, Sumerian Vistas,* and *Diversifications.* Five of these poems, "Pray Without Ceasing," "Summer Session," "Essay on Poetics," "Extremes and Moderations," and "Hibernaculum," are published in a volume entitled *Selected Longer Poems* (Norton, 1980). For a complete chronology of Ammons's longer poems, please see the listing of them at the back of this collection.

Before considering the essays collected here, it will be useful to briefly look at the development of the long poem in Ammons's career. According to Roger Gilbert, "Ammons's first gesture in the direction of a long poem came in 1960 when he published a series of numbered 'Cantos' in magazines and in a privately printed chapbook. This rather brash emulation of Ezra Pound proved to be a false start, however, and the 'cantos' were later included under separate titles in Ammons's second book, *Expressions of Sea Level* (1963)."[1] The publication in 1965 of *Tape for the Turn of The Year,* a two-hundred-and-five-page verse journal written on a narrow roll of adding machine tape, represented a breakthrough for the poet. In discovering the roll of adding machine tape as a device that enabled him to keep typing down the "page," the poet found a medium he would return to again and again over the course of his career, typing many of his subsequent long poems on rolls of tape.

Having invented a new technique that literalized tendencies already present in American long poems since Pound and Olson, Ammons was faced with something of a dilemma if he wanted to produce more long poems. If the content of these poems was to be a transcription of life in process, then how was he to make his long poems distinguishable as unique artifacts rather than mere volumes in an ongoing verse diary? He poses this question in"Summer Session"—"the problem is / how / to keep shape and flow."

"One partial solution he developed," according to Gilbert, "was to impose arbitrary demarcations on the flux of his discourse, breaking the poem into uniform groups of lines and stanzas that regulate only its appearance, not its substance. Ammons first employed this device in three middle-length poems: 'Essay on Poetics,' arranged primarily in three-line strophes, 'Extremes and Moderations,' cast in groups of four lines, and 'Hibernaculum,' organized into numbered sections of three three-line stanzas."[2] These experiments culminated in Ammons's second book-length poem, *Sphere* (1974), made up of one hundred and fifty-five numbered sections of four three-line strophes.

Of all Ammons's longer poems, *Sphere* may have required the greatest amount of revision by the poet. Initially he had composed two hundred and fifty sections and ended up throwing out one hundred and fifty of these. Subsequently, he wrote approximately fifty new sections of the poem. The final result, *Sphere : The Form of A Motion*, represents the culmination of the mid-career long poem for Ammons, with its characteristic "lattice work" stanzas. Moreover, in *Sphere*, Ammons was able to resolve through sustained reflection on the image of the earth the One:Many philosophical problem that had been a nagging question for him, pursued up to that time with relentless energy in his lyrics.

After the publication of *Sphere*, the poet began to explore differences in the shapes his long poems would take, devising subtle new ways of organizing them. The use of numbered sections in *Sphere* represented one kind of departure from the diaristic structure of *Tape*. More radically, Ammons returned to the tape as a medium for *The Snow Poems* (1977)—which, despite its title, he regarded as a single poem—but shifted the paradigm not only by using two tapes of different widths, but by structuring the work as a series of semi–independent poems of varying lengths and formats, each titled after its first line. *The Snow Poems* marked a radical departure from Ammons's previous long poems. His ambition to limit the subject of the poem exclusively to the weather, along with his experiment in "simultaneity" by writing in double columns, upset and mystified a number of his most ardent supporters at the time of the volume's publication. Here it is worthy of note that two of the contributors to this collection, Helen Vendler and Alex Albright, present fascinating reassessments of *The Snow Poems* in their essays.

"The Ridge Farm," the thirty-eight page poem that opens Ammons's 1986 volume *Sumerian Vistas*, was also composed on a roll of tape, but its individual sections were then cut apart and reordered to produce fifty-one numbered sections in a more consciously shaped sequence. Ammons would include another long poem in *Sumerian Vistas*, entitled "Tombstones," composed of twenty-nine numbered sections.

With *Garbage,* Ammons returned to the regularity of strophes—airy two-liners this time, with an occasional tercet. This poem was also typed on a roll of tape, wider than that used for *Tape for the Turn of the Year,* but Ammons reports that after completing each section he would tear it from the roll, perhaps lending a stronger sense of autonomy to the poem's component parts. The first five sections of *Garbage* originally appeared in an issue of the *American Poetry Review* in March/April 1992. Despite the enthusiastic response to these first five sections of *Garbage,* the poet was surprised by the overwhelming critical acclaim and popularity of the book-length poem when it was published in eighteen sections in 1993. Perhaps the anti-poetic nature of the title struck a popular chord among readers. More likely, however, the poem has won such a large readership because of its integration of concerns both lowly ("garbage") and sacred. In *Glare,* Ammons's most recent long poem, he uses two tapes of different widths to compose what Roger Gilbert calls (in his essay in this volume) the poet's "most audaciously original" long poem.

It is appropriate that this collection of essays begins with Helen Vendler's article "*The Snow Poems* and *Garbage:* Episodes in an Evolving Poetics." Vendler has reviewed Ammons's work steadily now for over three decades in such journals as *The New Yorker* and *Poetry.* In this new essay, she examines key aspects of *The Snow Poems* that suggest principles in a poetics that will survive and be modified in *Garbage.* Her piece asks us both to reevaluate *The Snow Poems* and to see *Garbage* as a descendant of this earlier volume. In doing so, Vendler establishes for the reader of Ammons's long poems an extremely useful guide to what can be difficult terrain.

The next several essays in the volume continue an exploration of the poetics of the long poem. In his reading of *Garbage,* Willard Spiegelman suggests that the "compost heap," piled up so that it will break down, serves as an apt metaphor for Ammons's poetic processes and forms. Spiegelman traces *Garbage* to two major literary precursors, the Whitman of "This Compost" and Stevens's "The Man on the Dump."

Following Spiegelman's essay, Marjorie Perloff proposes that we consider Ammons's collection *Briefings: Poems Small and Easy* (1971) as one long poem rather than a miscellany of occasional lyrics. In making this claim, Perloff points out that the eighty-eight poems in the collection are arranged alphabetically by first lines. Her startling examination of their prosody reveals that Ammons's poetry "testifies to the fractal geometer's concern for the 'morphology of the amorphous.'" Perloff's provocative essay challenges us to rethink Ammons's Emersonianism and also to consider *Briefings*, with its unlikely title, as perhaps a sixth major book-length poem by Ammons.

The first section of the book concludes with Alex Albright's reflections on the ways in which Ammons's composing processes resemble those of the fiction writer Jack Kerouac. Albright's essay is the first extended piece of criticism on Ammons's use of rolls of adding machine tape to compose his long poems. The unlikely pairing of Kerouac and Ammons, Albright argues, is based upon each writer's use of these "scrolls." Albright elucidates a number of interesting parallels between Kerouac's conception of process in his essay "Essentials of Spontaneous Prose" and Ammons's compositional practices, especially in *Tape for the Turn of the Year* and *The Snow Poems*.

The second section of this book is concerned with elements of science in Ammons's long poems. From his very first collection of lyrics, *Ommateum*, Ammons's poems have drawn extensively on the language and discoveries of science. It is not surprising, then, to find such elements incorporated into the longer poems. Daniel Tobin offers a lively overview of the parallels between chaos theory and the texts of *Sphere* and *Garbage*. While threads of connection between chaos theory and Ammons's poetry have been suggested previously, Tobin's essay is the first sustained treatment of the topic. By drawing upon the work of such chaos theorists as Edward Lorenz, Mitchell Feigenbaum, and Benoit Mandelbrot, Tobin finds that Ammons's work reveals a profound sympathy with this new science. His article complements nicely Perloff's essay, in that both see fractal geometry as a key to understanding Ammons's preoccupation with relationships of scale in nature and poetry.

My essay "The Long Poem as A Geological Force" is concerned with the ways in which recent discoveries in geology have influenced the form and content of three of Ammons's long poems, *Tape for the Turn of the Year*, "Extremes and Moderations," and *Sphere*. Ammons's "poetics of geology" roots his poetry in the language and theories of the earth. In addition, this essay explores the ways in which we might read Ammons's work as "environmentally oriented."

Robert Harrison's lyrical and idiosyncratic response to Ammons's poem "Tombstones" concludes this section of the book. Harrison's essay is in the Midrashic tradition, providing commentary by way of writing along side as well as "inside" and "outside" the original text of the poem. Harrison's piece provides the most provocatively original response to Ammons's long poems. While he draws upon history, Harrison cites a number of passages from *Tombstones* that are especially interested in the question of duration and scale, and for this reason the piece works nicely as a fitting conclusion to this section on scientific elements in the long poems.

The third section of this book assembles a wide array of critical responses to individual long poems written over the course of four decades. In a very real sense, this section of the book rewinds the tapes, beginning with a look at Ammons's most recent long poem, *Glare,* and working backward to *Tape for the Turn of the Year,* Ammons's first long poem. By presenting them in this order, I hope first of all to capture the excitement and immediacy of Roger Gilbert's critical response to Ammons's newest long poem and also to suggest how a look backwards may reveal unexpected discoveries. It is particularly interesting to consider *Glare* as the most mature of all Ammons's long poems, incorporating techniques and devices that the poet has mastered over the course of four decades.

While this book attempts to address the complete range of Ammons's long poems, not every long poem in his canon is treated in this volume. There simply is not room for essays on all of them. However, the poems that are treated in this third section of the book represent every stage in the development of Ammons's long poems, including the early, middle, and later period of his career. Several other long poems, such as *Sphere* and *The Snow Poems,* are examined in different contexts elsewhere in the book.

The first of the essays in section three was written prior to the publication of *Glare.* Roger Gilbert, who has the good fortune of being a colleague of Ammons at Cornell University, knew of this long poem long before it went to press and suggested an essay on it for this volume. We both agreed that this would be an exciting prospect, fully aware that such an essay might very well be the first critically sustained piece on *Glare.* Gilbert has produced a stunning essay, illuminating both the unusual structure of the poem and its jazzy improvisational qualities. He notes that what is most striking about the poem is its profound doubleness, manifested simultaneously on many different levels.

In the next essay Frederick Buell links two of Ammons's tape poems, *Tape for the Turn of The Year* and *Garbage,* in an extended analysis of their relationship to the American tradition of the democratic epic. Buell's piece is especially helpful in understanding the complex relationship between Ammons's long poems and larger historical and literary developments. It is the first of two essays in this section of the book that considers Ammons's work in relationship to postmodern theory, the other being that of Stephen Cushman.

Between these two essays is Miriam Marty Clark's compelling piece on Ammons's moral landscape in "The Ridge Farm." She argues that "dwell" and "dwelling" appear often in Ammons's long poems. Drawing upon the work of Kenneth Burke, Clark suggests that in "The Ridge Farm," "dwelling defines the encounter of symbolic action—human agency and institutions from property to poetry—with the non-symbolic realm of sheer matter and inarticulate nature." Clark's essay contributes significantly to our understanding of the tension in Ammons's work between the natural world and human nature.

Stephen B. Cushman reads Ammons's poem "Pray Without Ceasing" through the lens of postmodernist self-descriptions, and also examines postmodernist self-descriptions through the lens of "Pray Without Ceasing." In doing so, he suggests that some critics and anthologizers have underestimated a significant aspect of Ammons's work and that literary-historical accounts of postmodernism need reexamination. James S. Hans looks carefully at one of Ammons's most self-conscious versions of the life of the word: "Essay on Poetics." Hans argues that the longer form of this poem—combined with its deliberate attempt to create a poem that is also essayistic in nature—allows Ammons to develop the flow of his ideas at length, to demonstrate the ways in which his conventions are capable of laying bare the most fundamental patterns of existence.

The final essay in *Complexities of Motion* rightfully belongs to William Harmon, a long-time friend of Archie Ammons. His essay "'How Does One Come Home': A. R. Ammons's *Tape for the Turn of the Year*" was originally published in *The Southern Literary Journal* (volume 7, no. 2, spring 1975). More than twenty years later, Harmon's article, one of the first to devote itself to *Tape*, still illuminates this elusive poem. In this updated version of his essay, Harmon develops a fascinating historical theory to explain the composition of *Tape* and then analyzes the journey motif as it appears throughout the poem. A long-time resident of Ammons's native North Carolina, Harmon is an astute observer of the cadences of Ammons's speech.

In section four, I include an interview with A. R. Ammons conducted at his home in Ithaca, New York in the spring of 1996. We met over the course of three days, talking mostly about his longer poems. This interview is a record of that conversation and provides insight into the poet's thinking about the composing of these poems and a range of other topics relevant to them.

A. R. Ammons, at the age of seventy, continues to write and publish long poems, to startle and amaze us with his consummate skill. Critics in the future may have new (yet unwritten) long poems by Ammons to interrogate and ponder, despite his exclamation in *Glare* that "when I use up / this tape, I'm not buying another." With the recent publication of *Glare,* however, it is fortunate that we have this collection of essays to celebrate his work of four decades—the tapes that have been threaded through Ammons's typewriter and coiled into the wastebasket beneath his desk, lifted from there and sent out into the world.

Notes

1. Roger Gilbert, "A. R. Ammons," *Dictionary of Literary Biography 165: American Poets since World War II,* fourth series, ed. Joseph Conte (Detroit: Gale Research, 1996). I am grateful to Roger Gilbert for providing me with valuable information about Ammons's (in)formal procedures in composing his long poems.
2. Gilbert, "A. R. Ammons."

Abbreviations

Quotations from A. R. Ammons's works are cited in the text using the following abbreviations. When lines are sufficiently located by sections of longer poems, no citation appears.

T   *Tape for the Turn of the Year.* Ithaca: Cornell University Press, 1965. New York: W.W. Norton. First Norton Edition, 1993.

B   *Briefings: Poems Small and Easy.* New York: W.W. Norton, 1971.

CP   *Collected Poems 1951–1971.* New York: W.W. Norton, 1972.

S   *Sphere: The Form of A Motion.* New York: W.W. Norton, 1974.

D   *Diversifications: Poems.* New York: W.W. Norton, 1975.

SP   *The Snow Poems.* New York: W.W. Norton, 1977.

SLP *Selected Longer Poems.* New York: W.W. Norton, 1980.

SV   *Sumerian Vistas.* New York: W.W. Norton, 1987.

G   *Garbage.* New York: W.W. Norton, 1993.

SM   *Set in Motion: Essays, Interviews, & Dialogues.* Edited by Zofia Burr. Ann Arbor: University of Michigan Press, 1996.

Complexities of Motion

Part I
The Shapes that Motion Makes:
Poetics of the Long Poem

The Snow Poems and Garbage: Episodes in an Evolving Poetics

HELEN VENDLER

Ammons's *Garbage* (1993), that great *memento mori,* seems to demand of me a return to *The Snow Poems* (1977), which I wrote about long ago. Imperfectly though I understood *The Snow Poems* at the time, I knew that I liked what I saw. With the advantage of hindsight, I hope to say more about this extraordinary document in the history of American poetry, and about its foretaste of, and differences from, *Garbage.*[1]

The Ammons of *The Snow Poems* has literary antecedents, yes—in Williams's experiments in disjunction, in Stein's experiments with childish aspects of language, in Thoreau's wood-watching, in Whitman's broad democratic vistas, in Frost's shapeliness of form, even in the Beats. Yet none of these poets, except occasionally Whitman, rises and falls from the geophysical sublime to the ignobly ridiculous in Ammons's daring way. Williams—most notably in *Paterson*—arranges his poem so that it rises, repeatedly, from the basso ostinato of the communal to the flute of solo lyric: he usually distinguishes melodic personal lyric from the *continuo* of the social. Ammons, however, insists in both *The Snow Poems* and *Garbage* that there is a *continuo* of the personal—the "noise" of the everyday mind—from which the lyric rises and into which it subsides. (Ashbery later suggested something cognate in *Flow Chart*). This contextualizing of the lyric moment within its non-lyric "surround" is the fundamental device of the modern lyric long poem, from *The Waste Land* on; we distinguish among poets using this genre by their description of that surround as well as by the nature of their embodied lyrics. Ammons's context is an extraordinarily broad one, in one respect (he does not shrink from showing himself on the toilet, or telling dirty jokes, or experiencing severe, if sometimes comic, anxiety); yet in another respect, the surround of the Ammons lyric moment is narrow. Though amply extended into the natural world, and occasionally into the domestic

23

one, it is rarely political, social, or commercial in the ordinary
meanings of those words. It is even rarely literary in an overt sense
(though covert literary allusions occur profusely as a form of in-
joke). In short, Ammons's definition of the human person is differ-
ent both internally and contextually from the one we meet in the
long poems of his fellow poets. And since that definition is made
through poetic language, the language also defines what it is, for
Ammons, to be human in this moment, in this country.

I want first to take inventory of many items in *The Snow Poems*
that suggest principles in a poetics, and draw from each (hoping
not to misrepresent the author) a poetic "commandment" that it is
obeying. I then want to suggest how many of these principles have
survived in the later poem *Garbage,* but also to point out what has
been modified in the recent work. *Garbage* is a masterpiece of a
different sort, I think, from *The Snow Poems*—less whimsical
(though by no means entirely grave), less linguistically arrogant
(though not linguistically humble), less taunting (though not with-
out mockery), less disjunctive (though not without its own leaps
and gaps). Yet *Garbage* is recognizably a descendant of *The Snow
Poems,* and I want to show what Ammons has kept as well as what
he has (perhaps only provisionally) discarded. I should begin by
saying that all of Ammons's poems, long and short, descend from
his first book, *Ommateum with Doxology* (Philadelphia: Dorrance,
1955), and from its initial manifesto, which reads, in part:

> These poems are, for the most part, dramatic presentations of thought
> and emotion, as in themes of the fear of the loss of identity, the appre-
> ciation of transient natural beauty, the conflict between the individual
> and the group, the chaotic particle in the classical field, the creation of
> false gods to serve real human needs. While maintaining a perspective
> from the hub, the poet ventures out in each poem to explore one of
> the numberless radii of experience. The poems suggest a many-sided
> view of reality; an adoption of tentative, provisional attitudes, replacing
> the partial, unified, prejudicial, and rigid.[2]

The modern long poem, as has been frequently remarked, is the
lyric poet's cast for epic breadth. In the nineteenth century, the
novel so dominated utterance that Browning competed with it by
writing his lyrically perspectival long poem, *The Ring and the
Book.* Other lyric poets (from Wordsworth to Eliot to Frost) turned
to the drama as a possible arena for breadth, but experienced a
notable lack of success. The lyric temperament, with its commit-
ment to inward-reflective form, is in most cases the enemy of the
social temperament, which is committed to forms and themes that

permit interactions among agents (agon, dialogue, marriage, social mobility, war). It is not that lyric dialogue-poems do not exist, but they enact the inner dialogue of the mind with itself, as Arnold (to his own wincing disapproval) saw. The tensions in *The Waste Land* (no matter what social metaphors they may borrow) project upon a screen not so much the social interactions of the twentieth century as the patterns of the ravaged Eliotic nerves.

By what strategy, then, can the long lyric poem, confined to the inwardly reflective as its material, achieve both breadth and depth? Each original poet answers the challenge differently. Eliot chose a far-ranging mental discontinuity—of scenes, of voices, of cultures, and of epochs; Williams chose to identify a man and a city as his version of the one and the many; Stevens (in *Notes toward a Supreme Fiction*) invented a series of allegorical personae (Nanzia Nunzio, Canon Aspirin) projecting different aspects of his own personality; Crane flung a single continental symbol (the Bridge) of his own Shelleyan aspiration over American times and places; Lowell dissected (in *Life Studies*) the typology of his own declining class of Boston Brahmins by means of sketches of his family *mis à nu,* or (in *History*) wrote a chronicle of his personal "takes" on famous people from Adam to Stalin; Berryman sang the Freudian self in Dream Songs that extended from his own Henry-Id to his whole generation of *poètes maudits.*

But these are thematic choices, and do not cover another, more exigent, requirement of the long lyric poem: that it represent contemporary language, both in depth and in breadth. Eliot's idea of depth in language was a class-stratified one (from the demotic to classical Greek, from the music-hall to Wagner) and his idea of breadth in language was historical citation (from Jerusalem to London via Athens and Alexandria). To mention only one very different instance, Stevens's idea of depth (or height) in language was a philosophical one (from instantiation to abstraction); his idea of breadth in linguistic reference was a geographic one (Europe to the United States, North to South, Rome to "the more merciful Rome beyond").

And even theme and language-range do not exhaust lyric strategy. A field of resemblance (metaphor, simile, analogy, allegory) tends to characterize any original poet, and can serve (as, for a lyric writer, narrative or agon cannot) as an organizing matrix on which the long poem can be plotted. I have mentioned how Williams "plots" the man Paterson on the matrix of the city: this is Williams's fundamental micro-macro field of resemblance, and, as he hovers over it, he makes the cataract of language equal the falls, the realm of innocent pleasure equal the park, the site of individual guilty violence the slums, and so on. Eliot's matrix of resemblance is the Dantesque one of Heaven, Purgatory, and Hell, and almost any incident in *The Waste Land* can be plotted against those three allegorical places. Stevens re-plots reality as resemblance: "Things seen are things as seen" (*Adagia*). Resemblance itself therefore becomes the originating ground of being, while "reality" (in all of Stevens's long poems) becomes a secondary derivation from an initiating resemblance perceived (or posited) by the poet.

And—to conclude this brief set of conditions of creation—the fourth consideration of strategy must be external form: What does the long poem look like on the page? The distracted forms summoned by the ruined mind in *The Waste Land* extend from the song to the heroic couplet, from free verse to metered verse, and from the continuous (the episode of the typist) to the discontinuous (scraps of language blown past the hearer). Nothing could be further from *The Waste Land,* in this respect, than Stevens's imperturbable blank-verse tercets—the emblem of his long-breathed speculative mind—unrolling down the page. And these do not resemble Lowell's phalanxes of sonnets—which by their form assert, for a considerable period, that the Procrustean bed of verse can control the mess of reality.

When we turn to *The Snow Poems,* what do we find to be Ammons's choice of unifying theme, linguistic depth and breadth, matrix of resemblance, and external forms? The volume, which covers a period from fall to spring, is thematically unified on the "outside" by its series of weather reports on "snow" (the word includes all hideous and beautiful Ithacan varieties of frozen water—icy rain, hail, sleet, slush, icicles, crystal, flake). Ammons's emphasis on his region of the United States explains the dedication of the volume: "for my country." The book is thematically unified on the "inside" by the author's turning fifty and by his father's death. For linguistic depth we are given a "social" scale from the rustic to the philosophic, a literary scale from the obscene to the sublime, and an emotional scale from terror to joy. For linguistic breadth we find a scientific scale extending from electrons through bacteria to galaxies (from quantum physics through biochemistry to astronomy), and a natural scale that runs from chipmunks to mountains. For a field of resemblance, we have the (mostly) visual scenes in the vicinity of Ammons's house, landscapes (from earth to sky) that are drawn on for metaphors of physical and mental dynamisms. And for external form, we have a free-verse ground (comprising 119 short-lined lyric poems, entitled by their own incipits) on which

various entertainments are superimposed: small inserted lyrics,
bearing their own titles; word-lists linked by sound; little doodles
on the typewriter while the writer waits for his compositional impe-
tus to cohere; double and even triple-columns; words running ver-
tically instead of horizontally; and idiosyncratic punctuation (no
periods, just colons and exclamation points, with the odd asterisk
thrown in). The book immediately says to the reader "variability,"
"oddity," "competing impulses," while yet showing these corralled
into 119 distinct units. Ammons intends—as he remarked in 1963—
a prosody in which "the movement is not across the page but
actually, centrally down the page" (SM, 7). More recently, in 1994,
Ammons said that *The Snow Poems* remains his favorite among
his long poems:

> It seems to me in that poem I had a more ready availability to the
> names of things and to images of them than in any of the other long
> poems. The other long poems were more nearly juggling by some pro-
> gram. (SM, 101)

Before I turn to *The Snow Poems* in more detail, I want to sketch
a thematic and stylistic inventory for *Garbage*. Its unifying "out-
side" theme (what Ammons would call its "program") is named in
its title: everything in the universe eventually loses function and
is discarded as trash. The "inside" theme of the poem is the mean-
ing (or meaninglessness) to the poet himself of his life and his art,
given the certainty of personal death and the equal certainty of the
eventual unintelligibility of all cultural production. The linguistic
range of *Garbage* is narrower than that of *The Snow Poems:* there
is less obscenity and less sublimity, and a less high-pitched (though
no less moving) emotional expression: exclamation points are very
rare. (In *Garbage,* as in most of Ammons's long poems, the usual
terminal punctuation is the colon, the symbol of his commitment to
provisionality of thought.) To the panorama of the natural world—
Ammons's perennial matrix of resemblance—*Garbage* adds the
terrifying vision of the landfill to which everything is eventually
consigned for burning. Stevens's version of this was "the trashcan
at the end of the world" ("Owl's Clover"), manifested also as a
dump ("The Man on the Dump"); but those were cool approachable
places on which one can even perch. Ammons's landfill is an unap-
proachable Florida pit where the silhouetted bulldozer, manned by
its new Charon, heaves everything over the edge into a fire. In the
fire, everything is cremated into smoke that rises and disperses in
the air. Gulls wheel and scream over the site. In terms of external

form, *Garbage* (a 121-page poem) is comprised of eighteen "cantos": though these are of irregular length, they are all written (except for an occasional tercet or single line) in loose-pentameter blank-verse couplets, which are separated by stanza-breaks that aerate the page. The impression given by the page is one of neatness, but the line-breaks are sufficiently unexpected to keep the couplets from seeming conclusive. Though a steady ongoingness (rather than *The Snow Poems'* lyric fits and starts) is felt in *Garbage,* Ammons escapes, by his waywardness of development, a Lucretian finality.

The aim of any long piece in lyric form (as of any extensive art-piece—drama, novel, opera, a painting-sequence like that of the Sistine Chapel) is to equal the world, to be a "take" on the whole world. To this end, a long poem should be (in Ammons's thinking) as unmanageable as the world. His long poems are all strictly incomprehensible (though entirely understandable): one cannot get one's (mental) arms to encompass them. Yeats wanted to pull "the balloon of the mind" into the "narrow shed" of organized metrical form: Ammons wants the balloon to stay a balloon, to remain buoyant, to hover and float and rise, alluring and evading sight. Thus the uncontainable form of the long poem represents the poet's putting out tentative feelers toward understanding a world not yet delineated:

> The work of art is undertaken by the practitioner as a means of finding out and defining (if just tonally) something he doesn't already know. The elaboration of known or imaginable positions in morality, epistemology, politics, feminism needs no forms not already available to rationality and produces no surprise. In art, the form enables a self-becoming that brings up in its arising materials not previously touched on or, possibly, suspected. This confers the edge of advancement we call creativity. (SM, 28)

Readers have succeeded in memorizing Shakespeare's *Sonnets* and even *Paradise Lost:* but only a person with an eidetic memory could learn one of Ammons's long poems by heart; even then, the digressive form of the poem would militate against his comprehending it as a unity. Ammons's way of having his poems "resist the intelligence almost successfully" (Stevens) is to have them become all-inclusive, defeating not only the mind's will-to-consequence (its dependence on cause and effect, priority, hierarchy, and so on), and the eye's will-to-mapping (its dependence on a consistency of scene and focus), but also the heart's will-to-resolution (its dependence on a stable organization of feeling on which it can repose). In this respect, he makes his long poems emblems of a world that has become so full of information that it is no longer fully graspable (unlike, say, Milton's world as Milton portrays it, mastered by himself and by God).

To come to the particulars of *The Snow Poems:* the first thing to be said is how shocking a book it was in diction and tone and self-presentation (at least to this habitual reader of lyric) when it appeared. It was not that I was unacquainted with surrealism or futurism or the Poundian experiment of the *Cantos,* but those versions of shock were predominantly high-tech and high-culture (Pound's occasional Uncle Ez passages being the exception proving the rule). And I had read Ginsberg's *Howl,* which permitted an urban vulgarity (and even obscenity) in serious writing. But Ammons consistently offered something quite different—a rural poetry in which the delicate lay cheek by jowl with the vulgar, the commercial next to the lyric, the momentarily unclear next to the clear:

<pre>
Dawn clear
by sunrise
hazes riffles   you want to be
furrows and floats   bullfucked when
of fluff   mine is no longer
appear   than a penguin
so the sun
has too much   quilt raffle
to come through   antiques
to come through   handcrafted gifts
                     live country music
                     whimsies, furbelows, and
                     sundries
</pre>

                                                        (SP, 71)

If I hadn't lived in Ithaca between 1960 and 1963, I might not have so joyously recognized the components of *The Snow Poems,* but the volume so completely transferred not only the weather and the scenery but the "handcrafted gifts" of that (then rural) town to the page that I was a hypnotized reader, ready to forgive (and at first I felt the need to forgive) any disturbances to my sense of the aesthetic from a poet so marvellously gifted at summoning up a known environment.

The language of *The Snow Poems* represents a new amalgam in American poetry. Ammons has a tendency to both the allusive and the parodic, so that some anterior form of expression is often playing hide-and-seek throughout his poems. Rustic diction, in his hands, is perhaps more shapely than it would be on the farm: but the "poetic" use of dialect (which has a long history in our poetry) has rarely descended to Ammons's glee in the "said-song" of the vernacular:

> I declare the crows have
> come right in to hanging
> around in the maple tree
> and I jest bet you five
> dollars since it's over
> thirty today they got the
> scent of that suet and
> they jest a waitin' that's
> what they doin' they jest
> a waitin' sooner or later
> they gonna plunk right
> there on the porch and
> start a grabbin' and a
> tearin'

(SP, 136)

This laconic rustic repetition being one of Ammons's mother-tongues (from his childhood in North Carolina), he insists on its occasional presence in his writing, but he reorders it into a slightly parodic form of itself.

The coarse, extending to the obscene, is another of Ammons's mother-tongues (as it is of all men, and now increasingly of women). Ammons knows, I think, that it sits uneasily in the margins of his lexicon, but he will not fence it out entirely. It is often disturbing. In the poem I want to use as representative of the procedures of *The Snow Poems,* a piece called "Poetry Is the Smallest," coarseness (in a double-columned marital form representing a married couple) closes the lyric: at the end, by punning on the word "relief" to mean "urination" and "bas-relief," Ammons turns a man huddled in a urinal into a Parthenon metope:

> poet friend of mine's
> dick's so short
> he can't pull it long enough   still his fat wife's
> to pee straight with: radiant every morning
> not to pee on   he humps well, probably,
> anybody by surprise   stringing her out far and
> sideways, he hunkers   loose on the frail hook:
> into the urinal so far   and, too, I notice she
> he looks like, to achieve,   follows his words
> relief: closely like one who
>   knows what a tongue can do

(SP, 82)

The burden of this poem, as its title "Poetry Is the Smallest" implies, and as its earlier metaphors convey, is the apparent paltriness of lyric breath compared to the grand motions of the universal wind, the poet's insignificance in the landscape when he is placed against a mountain. The analogy of the surprising power of frail poetry to the surprising sexual success of the fellow-poet's insignificant penis (aided by his tongue) makes the closing coarseness another manner of asserting what has been said twice before in the poem, first by didactic statement, secondly by allegorical dialogue. A twenty-line didactic statement had begun the poem, saying three times, "poetry is":

Poetry is the smallest
trickle trinket
bauble burst
   the lightest   f
windseed leaftip   r
snowdown   e
poetry is the breaks   e
the least loop   d
from   o
   the general curvature   m
into delight
poetry is
the slightest   f
hue, hint, hurt   r
   its dance too light   e
not to be the wind's: e
yet nothing   d
becomes itself   o
without the overspill   m
of this small abundance

(SP, 81)

This opening portion of "Poetry is the Smallest" is a conventionally shapely four-stanza free-verse lyric (with the stanza breaks suppressed into invisibility); yet it is "disturbed" by the presence on the page of the word "freedom" twice inscribed vertically next to it. Still, we recognize the poem's kinship with earlier lyrics through its Dickinsonian definition-mode, its use of conventional praise-hyperbole, its alliteration, its "refrains" ("poetry is" and "freedom"), and its occasional rhymes ("lightest" and "slightest"; the Herbertian "light" and "delight"; "dance" and its portmanteau appearance in "abundance"). As our eye strays to the right, we notice that the first vertical "freedom" begins at the line "the lightest," while the second begins at the matching line, "the slightest."

The hosanna implicit in "freedom freedom" suggests the nature of
our delight when we arrive at a personal characterization of real-
ity—an idiosyncratic delight as available to those whom Words-
worth called "silent poets" as to the speaking poets, whose
perceptions are given permanence in language.

If I could, as an early reader of *The Snow Poems,* assent to this
exquisite hymn to the lightness and yet consequentiality of the
lyric breeze, I could equally well assent to the allegorical Her-
bertian dialogue that follows it in "Poetry Is the Smallest." This
faux-naïf dialogue takes place between the poet, on his way to an
apparently minor height, and the mountain on whose terrain the
poet asks permission to intrude:

> you don't mind, do you, I
> said to the mountain, if
> I use this ledge or, like,
> inspiration pavilion to say
>
> a few things out over the
> various woods, streams, and
> so on: by all means, said
> the mountain: I was a little

concerned, I said, because	
the speech is, like, about	only
the individual vs. the major	where
structures and, like, I	we
	are
was thinking of siding with	to
the individual: but, of	lose
course, said the mountain:	all
well, but, I said, it	are
	we
doesn't make any difference	to
what I say if it doesn't	have
make any difference: please,	here
said the mountain, be my guest	and

(SP, 81–82)

Though the dialogue is self-contained in its five shy and apologetic
quatrains (incorporating into poetry, in one of Ammons's charac-
teristic forays into the colloquial, the now-universal adolescent
marker "like"), it is not allowed to achieve equanimity because a
new poem—consisting of one-word, mostly monosyllabic, lines—
has "started up" within reach of our right eye.

The bicameral mind, earlier introduced into the poem by the
single-word obbligato "freedom freedom" running alongside the

initial praise-lyric, has now started up a second vertical effort, this time as a rival to the mountain-lyric. This second vertical poem, thirty lines long, reads (if conventionally punctuated and written out horizontally) as follows:

[Only where we are to lose all, are we to have, here and there, a trifle; only where we are to lose all, are we to be here beholding everything.]
(SP, 81–82)

We are forced, by the way Ammons runs this aphoristic mini-poem down the right column, word by unpunctuated word, to read it as quasi-nonsense, as it reiterates its weak, almost meaningless, phrases: "we are to" and "all are we to" and "lose all are we." Though a second reading parses it into sense, our first impression is that of bits and pieces of language offered as a flotsam-and-jetsam do-it-yourself-kit of verse. Its tentatively-accreting vertical form stands, we can say, for the poet's gradual admission of the truth that its horizontally-written version too summarily and too neatly announces.

Before the right-brain aphorism has concluded—in fact more or less at its halfway point down the right-hand margin—the left brain, having taken a three-line rest after its dialogue with the mountain, starts up its next lyric, a narrative on the transiency of any reality-effect in nature, and on the consequent brevity of its lyric represen-tation—a narrative, in short, that enacts the truth of the already-in-process right-brain aphorism accompanying it in the vertical column:

```
                                        there
                                        a
                                        trifle
a slice of clearing                     only
widened over the ridge at               where
sundown and the sun                     we
stood in it a minute,                    are
full glow flapping up against           to
the garage and trees                     lose
and through the windows against          all
the walls and it was very nice           are
say around four twenty,                  we
gold effluvia gone                       to
by four twentyseven                      be
                                         here
                                         beholding
                                         everything
                                                    (SP, 82)
```

Ammons's commitment to intensely patterned speech can be seen
in the descending aphorism, at the same time that his commitment
to inert quotidian expression ("and it was very nice / say around
four twenty") can be seen in the landscape lyric—which pointedly
throws in the word "effluvia" just so that we know the "very nice /
say" is as deliberate as any other portion of the author's diction.

It is only at this stage—after we have seen the four-part quasi-
Elizabethan fanciful praise-lyric "poetry is" (and its vertical "free-
dom" refrain); the five-stanza plain-style Herbertian allegorical
mountain-dialogue; and the brief sunset-lyric (with its shared verti-
cal aphorism on losing and beholding)—that we come to the
already-cited poet-friend's questionable dick (and *its* right-hand
counterpart, his fat wife's apparent sexual satisfaction). Much
could be said about this affronting closure of "Poetry Is the Small-
est" as an index of Ammons's poetics in *The Snow Poems;* but
since I am instancing this closure as an example of the coarse in
Ammons's diction, let me say that in addition to paralleling the
bicameral nature of the mind (lyric and philosophical) through the
double columns of the marital verse, Ammons affirms (through his
descent from the sublimity of language belonging to the mountain's
inspiration pavilion—"gold effluvia"—to the comic relish of the
urinary and the sexual) that the mind is stratified horizontally, too,
and that lyric omits at its peril the material that is usually repressed
in "polite" discourse. Ammons's poetry wishes to be both tragic
and comic, high and low, concentrated and dispersive, and in *The
Snow Poems* he resorts to scores of strategies (of which only a few
are present in any one poem) to insist on the breadth of lyric as
he conceives it. Yet Ammons's language for the sexual is not uni-
formly coarse: the cunnilingus hinted at in the ending of "Poetry
is the Smallest" turns up again, for example, in "You Can't Get It
Right," in a diction mixing the romantic with the clinical:

> the tongue, powerful,
> moving organ, will in the
> dark find bliss's button,
> describe its contours,
> buffet gently and swirl it,
> and then swarm warmth (and
> grease) into other areas
> equally touchy and astonishing
> suffusingly

                                                              (SP,132)

I find the diction in this passage not entirely satisfactory, but I admire Ammons's attempt to describe a common sexual act that until recently has been (as we say these days) "underrepresented" in poetry.

I want to give an example of a lyric in *The Snow Poems* where Ammons's experimentation seems unsuccessful—a short poem called "Teeth Out." It rages against the deformities of age—lost teeth and ingrown toenails and whatever else makes one feel ugly and odd and old (reading down on the right yields "old guy ugly"):

Teeth Out

Teeth out	og	u
toenails in	lu	gl
	dy	y

when you're
up you're
out of this   le mismo
world and when   difference
you're down   chickweedo
you're out   gone
                          to
                     goodness

poetry is the life of criticism

(SP, 128)

We can see Ammons insisting here, as always in *The Snow Poems*, on:

a) the writer's workshop, which contains rearrangeable bits and pieces of language (here, the letters of three words—spelling "old" and "guy" and "ugly"—plus the stray word from Spanish);
b) the witty rearrangement of colloquial idiom (here "down and out") into lyric aphorism;
c) reference to anterior literary tradition (here, Arnold's dictum that poetry is a criticism of life);
d) the ethics of compensation (here, in the chickweed gone to goodness, just as the loss of teeth helps the necessary perpetual conversion, through decay, of matter into energy);
e) the bicameral and tristratified (sublime, colloquial, coarse) mind.

The allusion to Arnold is not fully enough worked out in reference
to the earlier parts of the poem to provide a coherent closure, nor
is it clear why the Spanish is done wrong ("le mismo" instead of
"el mismo"), nor why the chickweed is Hispanified into "chick-
weedo." But the occasional failure in *The Snow Poems* is part of
its grand and outrageous raid on language and form.

It would be impossible to characterize every kind of experiment
in the volume. Let me cite just one more, which occurs in a poem
written on the first of March. Ammons is experimenting with the
difference between a monocameral version of a lyric and its bicam-
eral version. Here is lyric #1:

> march one and
> in the clear
> thicket highchoired
> grackles grate squeak,
> dissonant as
> a music school

(SP, 189)

So far so good: the human analogue (a music school, where in one
room someone is playing the piano, in another someone is singing)
will do for the conjoined dissonance of grackles, who have landed
on high perches in the as-yet-unleafed thicket of early March. (The
covert literary allusions are, of course, to Shakespeare's "choirs"
of birds in Sonnet 73 and to Stevens's grackles in both "Snow
and Stars"—"The grackles sing avant the spring"—and "Autumn
Refrain"—"The skreak and skritter of evening gone / And grackles
gone . . . / Some . . . residuum . . . grates.")

Now here is another version of the same poem, in which Am-
mons has rewritten the monocameral lyric #1 into a split lyric,
which I will call #2. Nothing has changed, except that a curving—
not straight—vertical gutter has been established within the poem,
slowing it down:

> march   one and
> in the   clear
> thicket   highchoired
> grackles   grate squeak,
> dissonant   as
> a music   school

(SP, 189)

Though this looks "bicameral," it isn't, since the right-hand column does not have a justified left margin. But the new format emphasizes the activity of the mind, since it shows the hesitations implicit in composition. Shall I begin the poem with the month? Saying "march?" Well, why not be more precise and begin it "march one?" Shall I say "in the thicket?" Well, but that sounds like a leafy place, and the trees are still bare. Shall I say "bare thicket?"; no, too Shakespearean, since I'm planning to say "highchoired" about the grackles. Let's make it visual and say "clear thicket." Grackles do what? Ah, Stevens tells me, "grate squeak"; and they are dissonant as—as what? a music school.

Well, that's interesting, to reveal that the poem that in lyric #1 seemed a single burst of observation, was also—now that we have seen it via lyric #2 in its workshop form, fraught with the hesitations of the mind as it considers word-choice. The poet is considering both of these potential printings of the lyric; and to let us inhabit this fact, Ammons establishes on the page the vertical gutter of true bicameral opposition, showing us the two alternative lyrics, #1 and #2, competing formally for his attention. This arrangement I will call lyric #3, and this is what actually appears on the page as one portion of the poem called "It's Half an Hour Later before":

march one and	march	one and
in the clear	in the	clear
thicket highchoired	thicket	highchoired
grackles grate squeak,	grackles	grate squeak,
dissonant as	dissonant	as
a music school	a music	school

(SP, 189)

If the poet presented the tight lyric #1 and the hesitant "revisionary" lyric #2 sequentially, one following the other, we would still see his considering mind, but we would not perceive it as split in two while he ponders his apparently imminent print-choice between the two versions. The normal result of being split in two is that the poet acts to preserve one alternative by suppressing the other; it is a mark of the "reveal all" workshop-poetics of *The Snow Poems* that the mind says, "I am divided *and* I choose both, so here they are, both kept in print, exhibiting a right-left stand-off."

Of course, all these techniques—separating words into letters and phonemes, spelling words vertically, inscribing one-word-per-line poems vertically down the unpunctuated page, paralleling one version of a poem with its alternative version and letting them both stand—are (like Ammons's many other tricks of allusion, punning, sound-string lists, and rewritten clichés) devices that prevent us from reading the poems as transparent "statements." At all costs, the Ammons of *The Snow Poems* wants us to know that the appearance of "spontaneity" in poetry arises from innumerable tinkerings and decisions that take place in the presence of historically anterior literary and colloquial expression. The tinkerings are one way of showing the reader that the poem, as Ammons always insists, is not merely a tissue of statements but a congeries of actions:

> Verbal actions imitate human actions or the actions of wind or river or rain. Poems are actions, of which one action is the making of statements. . . . Value is represented in poems. Poems exemplify ways to behave . . . . The poem can be accessible or distraught, harsh or melodic, abstract or graphic, and from these traits we can form our own models and traits. . . . Poetry's actions are like other actions. They are at once actions themselves and symbolic actions, representative models of behavior. (SM, 32–33)

All the ostentatious workshoppery of *The Snow Poems,* all its grasshopper-jumping among levels of diction, all its sly literariness, all its determination on the coarse and the colloquial mixed with the intellectual and the sublime, do not interfere with Ammons's commitment to a sustained, if abstract and stylized, revelation of human emotional life, both its highs and its lows. Nor do the tricks prevent the appearance of beautiful and shapely inner lyrics within the welter of language-forms. I want to close my look at *The Snow Poems* by citing one of its classic lyrics, a Keatsian elegy written in couplets that anticipate the form of *Garbage:*

> *One Must Recall As One Mourns the Dead*
>
> One must recall as one mourns the dead
> to mourn the dead and so not mourn too much
>
> thinking how deprived away the dead lie
> from the gold and red of our rapt wishes
>
> and not mourn the dead too much who having
> broken at the lip the nonesuch
>
> bubble oblivion, the cold grape of ease at
> last in whose range no further

ravages afflict the bones, no more
fires flash through the flarings of dreams

do not mourn the dead too much who bear no
knowledge, have no need or fear of pain,

and who never again must see death
come upon what does not wish to die.

(SP, 3)

Ammons remains a strong poet because he is always torn between his desire for shapeliness and his awareness of the ragged dispersions that are repressed in the tracing of any contour. Thought, emotion, and composition are congruent in Ammons, in that each must respect the world's Heraclitean strife: thought must acknowledge both creation and entropy; emotion must be torn between joy at love and rage at deprivation; poetic composition must respect both the truth of dynamic coherence into (temporary) form and the truth of chaotic dispersal into meaninglessness and death. In *Garbage*, the latter terms are no longer represented by the sprinkling of linguistic detritus over the page or by competing poem-forms, as they were in *The Snow Poems*. Ammons's creation is no longer intent on revealing its doodling workshop-methods. In that sense, *Garbage* appears to be a more conventional poem than *The Snow Poems*. Yet it too offers great resistance to the mind seeking an assimilable form of the long lyric.

To begin with the first difficulty in writing about *Garbage:* it is almost impossible to quote briefly from it, since its mind-loops are long pensive arcs. Like *The Snow Poems* (and Ammons's other long pieces), *Garbage* can't be kept in the memory all at once, even if (like *The Bridge*) *Garbage* is unified by a powerful central symbol to which it consistently returns. Since the very subject of the poem is destruction, Ammons does not dedicate it to a single entity (such as "my country" in the case of *The Snow Poems*). *Garbage* is dedicated to multiple Shelleyan destroyers and preservers: "to the bacteria, tumblebugs, scavengers, wordsmiths—the transfigurers, restorers." Because Ammons has—somewhat pragmatically—decided for optimism (though conscious of all the reasons for pessimism) the dedication concludes with the creative side of the law of the conservation of energy. Yet readers of *Garbage* may conclude that in this late poem Ammons's imagination is more actively committed to destruction than to transfiguration and restoration. In any case, its internal dynamic of perpetual change

means that its cantos do not proceed in any easily foreseeable (and
therefore graspable) form.

The poem begins, however, with a meditation that is Shelleyan
in effect, if not in language. "Be through my lips to unawakened
earth / The trumpet of a prophecy!" Shelley cried to the West
Wind, asserting the social use of poetry in establishing new loci of
value when the old values are in ruins. Ammons's version crosses
Williams with Shelley in a self-mocking contemporary version of
the Muse's summoning the poet to his vocation:

> Creepy little creepers are insinuatingly
> curling up my spine (bringing the message)
>
> saying, Boy!, are you writing that great poem
> the world's waiting for: don't you know you
>
> have an unaccomplished mission unaccomplished;
> someone somewhere may be at this very moment
>
> dying for the lack of what W. C. Williams says
> you could (or somebody could) be giving: yeah?
>
> so, these little messengers say, what do you
> mean teaching school (teaching *poetry* and
>
> *poetry writing* and wasting your time painting
> sober little organic, meaningful pictures)
>
> when values thought lost (but only scrambled into
> disengagement) lie around demolished
>
> and centerless because you (that's me, boy)
> haven't elaborated everything in everybody's
>
> face, yet: on the other hand (I say to myself,
> receiving the messengers and cutting them down)
>
> who has done anything or am I likely to do
> anything the world won't twirl without:
>
> (G, 13)

To such a pass has the poet come that he questions not only his
own authority but that of the Muse, debasing her messengers into
"creepy little creepers." Yet this self-excoriation is followed by a
long meditation on "elegance and simplicity," the qualities (one

aesthetic, one primarily ethical) that Ammons names as central to the poetics of his poem, a poetics that eschews both organized religion (from Sinai or Zeus's thunderbolts) and the history of philosophy:

> . . . elegance and simplicity: I wonder
> if we need those celestial guidance systems
>
> striking mountaintops or if we need fuzzy
> philosophy's abstruse failed reasonings: isn't
>
> it simple and elegant enough to believe in
> qualities, simplicity and elegance . . .
>
> (G, 15)

Such a poetics of simplicity and elegance must rule out the fancy footwork of *The Snow Poems.* The couplets of *Garbage* stand for its simplicity, while its generic complexity and its manifold resources of diction and syntax stand for its elegance.

"My hope" (said Ammons of *Garbage)* "was to see the resemblances between the high and low of the secular and the sacred":

> The garbage heap of used-up language is thrown at the feet of poets, and it is their job to make or revamp a language that will fly again. We are brought low through sin and death and hope that religion can make us new. I used garbage as the material submitted to such possible transformations, and I wanted to play out the interrelationships of the high and the low. (SM, 102)

Both high and low participate in Ammons's characteristic turns of mind. In almost any canto of *Garbage,* no matter what the specific subject, the following generic ingredients appear, sometimes in overlapping form:

a) An emotional meditation in the first person, either singular or plural;
b) A narrative;
c) A scene;
d) One or more aphorisms;
e) Something ugly or frightening (destruction, death);
f) Something beautiful or reassuring (an aspect of nature, love);
g) Remarks about poetry.

This is all so cunningly managed that only someone studying the poem closely would see its recursive forms. A first-time (or even second-time) reader merely has the impression of a storytelling, meditating, far-seeing, celebratory, grieving voice unspooling its seductive language. Here are brief samples of the poem's seven recurrent genres:

First-person emotional meditation: here, a reflection on the disappearance of Ammons's past, both in its remote North Carolina form and in its proximate Cornell form:

> I can't believe
> I'm merely an old person: whose mother is dead,
>
> whose father is gone and many of whose
> friends and associates have wended away to the
>
> ground, which is only heavy wind, or to ashes,
> a lighter breeze: but it was all quite frankly
>
> to be expected and not looked forward to: even
> old trees, I remember some of them, where they
>
> used to stand: pictures taken by some of them:
> and old dogs, specially one imperial black one,
>
> quad dogs with their hier*archies* (another *archie*)
> one succeeding another, the barking and romping
>
> sliding away like slides from a projector: what
> were they then that are what they are now:

(G, 22–23)

Narrative: here, a short anecdote from Ammons' life as a teacher in the Cornell English Department (housed in Goldwin Smith Hall):

> I
> was coming out of Goldwin Smith Hall after mail
>
> call on a nova-bright late May day, the blues
> and greens outdoing each other, when a dear friend
>
> said, come and see, it's Ralph, he's in the car, and
> thinking, I've never been asked to come see
>
> Ralph before, I said, is anything the
> matter, and she said, terminal cancer of the brain,

and I said, terminal cancer of the brain, and
she said, I found out a week ago, but don't say

anything to him: so, in the glaring light, his
window rolled down, I was talking with an old friend

as if the past twenty-five years of all three of us
as colleagues had shifted out of reach:

(G, 41)

Scene: here, one from Ammons's return to his birthplace, the town of Whiteville in North Carolina:

I saw in Carolina morning flies

midair like floating stones: the dew, heavy;
the sun, blood red: a road dipping round a

pine grove down a hill to a pond, the spillway
clogged with cattails bent with breezes and with

redwings awilding day: a crippled old farmer
up early with his dog, noon likely to melt tar,

a benchlong of old blacks at the crossroads
gas station, dogfennel high on the woods' edge,

some scraggly roastnear corn used up, tomato
plants sprawled out, become vines: morning,

gentlemen, how you all doing: these bitty
events, near pangs commonplace on this planet

so strangely turned out, we mustn't take on so. . . .

(G, 95)

Aphorism: here, one addressed to the reader, describing a Levinas-like relation with the ethically-constituting other:

In your end is my beginning, I repeat; also,
my end; my end is, in fact, your end, in a way:

are we not bound together by our ends: and when,
end to end, our ends meet, then we begin to

see the end of disturbing endlessness:

(G, 63)

The ugly or frightening: here, old people's knowledge of oncoming death:

> sometimes old people snap back into life for a
> streak and start making plans, ridiculous, you know,
>
> when they will suddenly think of death again
> and they will see their coffins plunge upward
>
> like whales out of the refused depths of their
> minds and the change will feel so shockingly
>
> different—from the warm movement of a possibility
> to a cold acknowledgment—they will seem not
>
> to understand for a minute: at other times
> with the expiration of plans and friends and
>
> dreams and with the assaults on all sides of
> relapses and pains, they will feel a
>
> smallish ambition to creep into their boxes
> at last and lid the light out and be gone,
>
> nevermore, nevermore to see again, let alone
> see trouble come on anyone again: oh yes, there
>
> are these moods and transitions, these bolt
> recollections and these foolish temptations . . . .

(G, 53)

The beautiful: here, the adaptive beauty of a web-worm, introduced, because of its motion, with an allusion to Gertrude's lament on the death of Ophelia ("There is a willow grows aslant a brook") and dismissed with an allusive nod to Whitman's dung-beetle:

> there is a web-worm falls
> sometimes aslant the honeysuckle hedge in spring
>
> breeze or other dislocation and finds itself
> asquirm dangerously dangled in the open air (I've
>
> seen hornets trim those babies right out of the
> air): this one I paused to view was wrestling

up the single thread of web, nipping and tucking,
reaching up for a hold on the tight and bringing

itself up till the bit length could be added
to the tiny cotton ball gathered at its

head: but this is mere mechanics: down its
back was a purplish streak exactly the color

of honeysucklebushlimbstems, the top part (buds)
of the stems: his feet, his laterals, were

exactly the color of the lateralhoneysucklebush
limbstems: while this waits explanation, I

hold it a sufficient miracle. . . .

                                              (G, 71–72)

Poetry: here, as a defense after looking into the pit of death: "I /
looked into the pit of death and it was there, // the pit was, and the
death" (G, 81), but with consequent guilt as to the time spent on
poetry instead of on primary sensation:

                    so I derived the nature
of each thing from itself and made each derivation

speak, the mountains quietly resounding and very
authoritative, their exalted air perfect grain

of the spiritual, the sense of looking down so
scary half-love for height held: I made tongues

for adder's-tongue, periwinkle, and jimminycricket;
they wagged, and these tongues rang in my head

as in a chanson delicate of essence and point:
an assemblage, a concourse of intercourse, a

recourse: what is it, that you would turn down
a prairie for it, the prairie said as I went

on, my eyes set longsighted, and the turtle
eased needlepoint airholes up from swampwater,

his eyes quizzical in a downturn, and said,
where else does the shadow of the logknots fall

more sharply dark on the water, but I didn't
have time to take time: I spent every coin I

had into the good business of my own burning:

(G, 81–82)

While each of these excerpts is perfectly clear in itself, Am-
mons's interweaving of his generic set-pieces makes any canto
seem a farrago of cross-cuts and jump-starts, especially since the
genre-pieces can themselves be voiced in any one of Ammons's
manners—the rustic, the scientific, the faux-naïf, the philosophical,
the descriptive, the religious. Since the whole of *Garbage* is a
hymn to the necessary principle of extinction (as life is "consumed
with that which it was nourished by," the enlivening and extin-
guishing flame of the *calor vitae*), it is of the essence that the poem
be engaged in constant change of both genre and diction. Ammons
risks a great deal, since he asks from his reader more alertness
than many readers can provide. Accustomed as we are to a narra-
tive thread, or a temporal progression, or a hierarchical scheme,
or a philosophical proposal ("It Must Be Abstract") as the clue to
a long poem's labyrinth, we are surprised to find no such auxiliary
pointers in Ammons. Indeed, we find ourselves in the midden-heap
of language and literature, comparable to the Florida pit with its
life-detritus:

a priestly plume rises, a signal, smoke

like flies intermediating between orange peel
and buzzing blur: is a poem about garbage garbage

or will this abstract, hollow junk seem beautiful
and necessary as just another offering to the

high assimilations (that means up on top where
the smoke is; the incinerations of sin,

corruption, misconstruction pass through the
purification of flame:) old deck chairs,

crippled aluminum lawn chairs, lemon crates
with busted slats or hinges, strollers with

whacking or spinningly idle wheels: stub ends
of hotdogs:

(G, 30–31)

The point of all Ammons's unsettling changes (thematic, generic, lexical) is to mimic a universe constituted of continual creations and destructions, to ratify a metaphysics acceding to the necessity of change, and to announce an ethics of protest, urgent (if helplessly so) against the human waste entailed by the universal principles of destruction—genetic, metabolic, political, catastrophic:

> how about the
> one who finds alcohol at eleven, drugs at seventeen
>
> death at thirty-two: how about the little
> boy on the street who with puffy-smooth face and
>
> slit eyes reaches up to you for a handshake:
> supposing politics swings back like a breeze and
>
> sails tanks through a young crowd: what about the
> hopes withered up in screams like crops in
>
> sandy winds: how about the letting out of streams
> of blood where rain might have sprinkled into
>
> roadpools:
>
> (G, 90)

Ammons may have in mind a particular dead youth, an individual Down's syndrome child, the events in Tiananmen Square, his own mother's tears at the death of his little brother, massacres in Europe: but he abstracts from the particular in his catalogue of horror, so as to make his indictment of human waste broadly applicable. He will not take refuge with the fortunate "who can in safety call evil essential to the / differentiations of good" (G, 90), but neither can he explain (or hope to eliminate) evil. He can merely ask, "After the balances are toted up, is there // a streak of light defining the cutting edge as celebration[?]" (G, 91) But he cannot hold firmly even to this hope. At the threshold of death we may, he speculates, decide that life, through the treasuring force of love, has had value; but it is equally probable that we end by admitting that the troubles caused by love have merely exhausted us:

> but, then, for the trouble of love, we may be
>
> so tired that indifference will join ours to the
> hills' indifference and the broad currents of

the deep and the high windings of the sky, and
we may indeed see the ease beyond our

understanding because, till now, always beyond

(G, 96)

It is Ammons's willingness to suspect, and say, and show, in
Garbage, that at our end we are subsumed into the vast indifferent
dynamics of the universe, that makes him a poet for our non-
anthropocentric consciousness. The attempt to protect what is be-
loved, knowing the certainty of its destruction, is beneath all of
Ammons's poetry. He has said that "the most powerful image of
my emotional life is something I had repressed and one of my
sisters lately reminded me of":

> It was when my little brother, who was two and a half years younger
> than I, died at eighteen months. My mother some days later found his
> footprint in the yard and tried to build something over it to keep the
> wind from blowing it away. That's the most powerful image I've ever
> known. (SM, 71)

And yet Ammons does not adopt the "inhuman" perspective of
Robinson Jeffers: he is acutely conscious of the place and worth
of human attachment, human investment in others, human grief at
the loss of love. It is his consciousness of damage and grief (suf-
fered first in his own life, and subsequently known in historical
and external ways) that makes for the tenderness that suffuses his
poetry. It is a tenderness held in check—as indeed, all his passions
are held in check—by an aesthetic responsibility to the law of
form. Among Ammons's harshest passages in *Garbage* is a long
excoriation of "hackers," those contemporary writers who, wish-
ing to proclaim themselves *engagés,* exaggerate their rhetoric for
audience-effect:

> the hackers, having none,
> hack away at intensity: they want to move,
>
> disturb, shock: they show the idleness of
> pretended feeling: feeling moves by moving
>
> into considerations of moving away: real
> feeling assigns its weight gently to others,
>
> helps them meet, deal with the harsh, brutal,
> the ineluctable, eases the burdens of unclouded

facts: the strident hackers miss no chance to
dramatize, hurt, fairly or unfairly, for they

fear their emptiness: the gentlest, the most
refined language, so little engaged it is hardly

engaging, deserves to tell the deepest wishes,
roundabout fears: loud boys, the declaimers,

the deaf listen to them: to the whisperers,
even the silent, their moody abundance: the

poem that goes dumb holds tears: the line,
the fire line, where passion and control waver

for the field, that is a line so difficult to
keep in the right degree, one side not raiding

the other:

                                        (G, 120–121)

 This is Ammons's most didactic expression of his recent poetic
of "elegance and simplicity." As we read the late Ammons of *Garbage*, we can see that he has kept, from *The Snow Poems*, the
technique of broad musing flow gathering into an eddy of lyric; the
rapid changes of lexicon; the turn to abstraction; the aphoristic
summation; the rewriting of clichéd idiom; the preferred matrix of
resemblance offered by the natural world; even the metaphysics
of compensation of material loss by gain in energy. But he has
restrained both his coarseness and his fancifulness; he is less con-
cerned to toy with the concept of a bicameral mind; he has added
more narrative and a greater proportion of personal anecdote; and
he has adopted a regular ongoing scheme of long numbered cantos
rather than *The Snow Poems*' more volatile scheme of individually-
titled short lyrics.
 As the successive weather-reports (emblematic of the ongoing
and changing life of nature) connected the parts of *The Snow
Poems*, so the symbol of the Florida funeral pyre (emblematic of
the conversion of matter into energy) unifies *Garbage*. *Garbage* is
a sadder poem than *The Snow Poems*, and a less showy one: if the
exuberance of creation lies behind the earlier sequence, the cer-
tainty of destruction lies behind the later one. *Garbage* belongs,
in the history of literature, to the category of restrained later
works: among the monuments of poetry in English, *Paradise Re-
gained, Four Quartets,* and *The Rock* have been customarily

thought of in this way. In poems such as these, authors of great early display-poems decide that their subsequent sense of the world requires a less ostentatious style. Not everyone prefers the later moment; and I continue to vary between my old attachment to the nervy, splashy, spontaneous, willing-to-be-silly *Snow Poems* and my current admiration for the grave canto-summations of *Garbage*. What is really remarkable is that the same poet should have written both these compelling poems.

Notes

1. A. R. Ammons, *The Snow Poems* (New York: Norton, 1977). Quotations from this collection will be parenthetically identified in my text by the abbreviation SP. A. R. Ammons, *Garbage* (New York: Norton, 1993). Quotations from this collection will be parenthetically identified in my text by the abbreviation G.

2. "Foreword to *Ommateum*," in A. R. Ammons, *Set in Motion: Essays, Interviews, Dialogues*, ed. Zofia Burr (Ann Arbor: University of Michigan Press, 1996).

Building Up and Breaking Down: The Poetics of Composting

WILLARD SPIEGELMAN

> . . . trash is what
> you make of it
>
> —"The Ridge Farm" (*Sumerian Vistas*)

It may be time to reconsider and re-evaluate organicism. This staple of an older literary vocabulary and critical theory germinated in the work of the German romantics, was transplanted into English soil under the cultivation of Coleridge, and flowered most recently on the American literary scene in the techniques of the New Critics and then in the criticism of such neo-romantic scholars as M. H. Abrams. Poststructuralist theories of language and New Historicist analyses of romanticism, however, have tended to bury the idea of "Nature" of which Wordsworth and his earliest critics made much, and to replace it with a poetics in which "History" is the major force, always visible, even in its apparent absence, repressed but ever-returning.

But speaking of the eternal return: let us assume that Rip Van Winkle had fallen asleep shortly after Matthew Arnold wrote that "Wordsworth's poetry is great because of the extraordinary power with which Wordsworth feels the joy offered to us in nature. . . . It might seem that Nature not only gave him the matter for his poem, but wrote his poem for him" (1869). And that he awoke only yesterday. He would have missed the apocalyptic Wordsworth, fearful of consciousness, whom Geoffrey Hartman masterfully presented in *Wordsworth's Poetry* (1964), as well as the history-haunted Wordsworth of Alan Liu (*Wordsworth: The Sense of History*, 1989), two versions of Wordsworth that not only influenced scores of readings of a single poet but also inspired general revaluations of English romanticism. He would have awakened to learn, from Jonathan Bate and Nicholas Roe *inter alia*, that Wordsworth is the authentic fountainhead of a new "green" criticism. The wheel

51

has turned. Mutatis mutandis, Wordsworth is once again a nature poet.[1] And in an era when even the *New York Times* features a piece on eco-criticism, it looks as though nature has returned to the classroom, profiting from the attention of a new brand of literary scholar.[2]

The case of A. R. Ammons makes it clear that a Wordsworthian interest in the natural world has never died, and that the nature derided by poststructuralists as a human construct instead of an external given retains its power to inspire original, powerful, sometimes somber and sometimes whimsical poetic observations. His case also returns us to the twin analogies of organicism: the relationship between a work of literature and a natural creation, and that between human consciousness and the external, nonhuman but living world.[3]

The most unabashedly Coleridgean of twentieth-century American poets, Ammons never hewed to the dictates of the New Critics; never worshipped unreflectingly at the altars of Irony, Paradox, and Tension. He has produced during almost a half century a *body* of poetry (the organic phrase is unavoidable) notable for its measure of the natural world, the data within the terrain and the climate that the poet has assiduously collected, and for the often explicit theorizing within the poems about the kind of poem he wishes to write, about the relationship between the shape of his poem and the shapes available to the discerning eye within the natural world. In poems "small and easy" and others expansive and even book-length, Ammons has shown how human consciousness, indeed the entire human self, is always connected to the larger cosmos—call it nature, call it the universe—whose movements and weather it records, reflects, and repeats. He is the poet as ecologist: his most unlikely but powerful analogue in American poetry may well be James Merrill (in so many obvious ways his opposite), born in 1926, the year of Ammons's birth, who tested in his own smaller lyrics as well as the epic *Changing Light at Sandover* the fundamental law of conservation of matter and energy that exists both on a cosmic level and within the human mind's economy:

> . . . nothing's lost. Or else: all is translation
> And every bit of us is lost in it
> . . . .
> And in that loss a self-effacing tree,
> Color of context, imperceptibly
> Rustling with its angel, turns the waste
> To shade and fiber, milk and memory.
>
> ("Lost in Translation")[4]

Merrill's lyric mingles narrative, autobiography, philosophy, and landscape. He asks us to puzzle over the convoluted connections between his own poem and the translation by Rilke of Valéry's "Palme" that he fears he has lost. Such fancifulness might not appeal to Ammons's temperament. In *Tape For the Turn of the Year* he remarks point-blank: "I've hated at times the / self-conscious poem."[5] But he has made his stock-in-trade, especially in such long poems as *Tape,* out of his own elaborate self-consciousness, and he would no doubt applaud (because he himself has obsessively employed) the trope of that which is eternally present, however transformed. Indeed, it comes as a delightful frisson to see, in one of his most recent renderings of this trope, a key term that allies him with his more nacreous contemporary. Here is Ammons describing the pinnacle of a giant garbage heap:

> where the disposal
> flows out of form, where the last *translations*
>
> cast away their immutable bits and scraps,
> flits of steel, shivers of bottle and tumbler,
>
> here is the gateway to beginning, here the portal
> of renewing change, the birdshit, even, melding
>
> enrichingly in with debris, a loam for the roots
> of placenta . . . [my emphasis][6]

It is with this heap, and the translations, transformations, and other changes it permits, denies, or otherwise inspires in the poem piled around it, that this essay concerns itself. Such troping on change goes back, of course, to Ovid, at whom recent eco-critics might take a new look. The *terminus a quo* is Book 15 of the *Metamorphoses,* in which the lengthy address of Pythagoras serves as philosophical summation and justification of the whole. In the book's end comes its beginning:

> Nec species sua cuique manet, rerumque novatrix
> ex aliis alias reparat natura figuras:
> nec perit in toto quicquam, mihi credite, mundo,
> sed variat faciemque novat, nascique vocatur
> incipere esse aliud, quam quod fuit ante, morique
> desinere illud idem. Cum sint huc forsitan illa,
> haec translata illuc, summa tamen omnia constant.

[No species stays the same, but Nature the renewer always creates new forms from other ones: Believe me, nothing ever dies in the world;

it rather changes and renews its form. What we call birth is simply a new beginning from something else, and death is a stop to a former state. Although things may shift from this to that, their totality always remains the same.]

(Book 15, ll. 252–58)[7]

Ammons himself improves upon my prosaic translation, rendering the spirit, and even a good deal of the letter, of the Ovidian commonplaces this way:

> . . . forms are never
>
> permanent form, change the permanence, so
> that one thing one day is something else another
>
> day, and the energy that informs all forms just
> breezes right through filth as clean as a whistle:

(G, 115)

Ammons is Ovid *redivivus*. The original readers of the first five sections of *Garbage,* which appeared in *American Poetry Review* in March/April 1992, confronted something peculiar if not unique: a towering image possessing a heft not usually present in the work of this poet of the peripheries, of spheres, saliences, and meteorology. I am referring to the enormous landfill, dumping site, mountain of refuse, "portal / of renewing change," on Route I–95 near Boca Raton that apparently provided the poet with an inspiring starting-point to what became his 1993 National Book Award–winning volume. The landfill, including its cast of characters—scavenging birds, garbage trucks, the garbage spreader who "stands in the presence / of the momentarily everlasting," the "Commissioner of Sanitation" creeping in his chauffeur-driven Cadillac up the ziggurat, and the bulldozer operator's fat wife Minnie Furher—takes on, for the hopeful Ammons reader, the generative force of the adding machine tape in *Tape for the Turn of the Year* or the titular shape in *Sphere:* it virtually establishes itself as a symbolic icon around which we legitimately expect the rest of the poem to revolve.

Ammons announces in his opening salvo what will become his great theme during the remainder of his deliberations: "garbage has to be the poem of our time because / garbage is spiritual, believable enough // to get our attention" (18). The poem proceeds, in fact, from the earthly to the spiritual, as Ammons pursues a pilgrimage of almost Dantean proportions, moving from the warm, burning garbage of the earth to speculations about the heavens and eternity itself. The surprise—or one of them in this poem of many turns and many layers—is that the looming garbage mound turns out to be both more and less than a *memento mori*, selected in lieu of the more conventional skull or gravesite, and the beginning of the poet's contemplations in old age of mortality, death, disappearance, metamorphosis, and the laws of conservation of matter and energy. The garbage mountain is, indeed, an originary point, but origins deceive. Far from sitting squarely at the poem's core, the dumpsite, immortal gigantic compost pile, towering symbolic presence vanishes, after section 5, from the rest of the poem, which, true to Ammons's preference for discursive, meandering, rambling maneuvers, leaves it far behind. And I wonder why. Seldom does a poem begin so auspiciously and then light out for the territory. Since Ammons has always—like Frost and Howard Nemerov—played with clichés, giving them new spins whenever possible, I might start by suggesting two that his long poem explores: what goes up must come down, or out; and now you see it, now you don't.

The garbage in *Garbage* encourages an analysis of the poem's imagery and theme, its structure, its new turns on old-fashioned Coleridgean organicism, and finally its place in American poetry. It also allows us to take the measure of the difference between Ammons's poetics and those of an earlier generation of romantics, precisely because he creates a powerful image and then, instead of relying on it to give ballast, weight, or a symbolic center to the alternative universe of his poem, he merely and cavalierly tosses it aside. If for a New Critic or a poet schooled in the tenets of New Criticism, balance is the key force in poetic unity, for a postmodern, neo-romantic like Ammons a magic wave of the hand undoes all efforts at structural integrity and symmetry. The poet builds, and the poet removes. Entropy has complemented closure or threatened to undo it as a structural principle, especially in Ammons's longer poems.

As he always has done in his even-tempered but insistent way, Ammons creates a triad consisting of nature (the world of garbage), man (the observing self) and art (his own poem). Garbage is the poem of our time, and we are it: "we're trash, plenty wondrous" (46). Is a poem about garbage garbage? (30) Ammons wonders, and he also regards the insubstantiality of even the surrounding piles of matter as equivalent to the emptiness (42–43) or vacuum that the mind repairs—by filling—in the act of writing a poem. Vacuums and the filling of them (109–10) become a primary obsession: he realizes that all of us disappear, like the very mound that vanishes

from the poem but not from the landscape. *Garbage* not only cele-
brates what remains behind; it also is a dark grieving, or a series
of them, for our common destiny. The poem includes poignant,
delicate, pseudo-Renaissance laments, elegiac moments ("what /
were they then that are what they are now," [23]), amid Ammons's
more capacious or inclusive gestures to read us into the landscape,
and to construct a poem ample enough for everything—the dis-
tasteful, the toxic, the tossed off, the indissolvable.

As "a scientific poem" *Garbage* inductively reports a reality,
"asserting that nature models values, that we / have invented little
(copied)" (20). But as a romantic poem organized, at least in part,
along the lines of Coleridgean organicism it tries to imitate as well
as describe the reality of which it constitutes a part. A poem may
be shapely, like a life. And life, the poet says portentously and
with tongue-also-in-cheek, is like a poem (66) and anything is po-
etry (103). What is built up counters what is reduced. Poetry con-
verts trash to aesthetic artifact (108). The analogy continues: the
parts of a life are like the parts of a poem, an Ammons poem that
is: the "minor forms within larger constructs" (66) are equivalent
to "pure local lyrics" that coexist, sometimes uneasily, within a
gigantic shambles. It all comes down, as it always has in Ammons,
to unity and multeity, the whole and the parts of which it is
composed:

> . . . the shambles questioning the lyric
>
> out of easy shape, and the lyric providing
> intervals of symmetry in the jumbled enlargement,
>
> but it is subservient when art imitates life:
> art makes life, just as it makes itself, an
>
> imitation: art makes shape, order, meaning,
> purpose where there was none, or none discernible
>
> (G, 67)

But such wandering by the way, raising the old questions of art,
life, imitation, priority, and shapes, always provokes in Ammons a
final ho-hum. "Argument," he confesses with a sigh at the end of
this chapter, "is like dining: / mess with a nice dinner long enough,
it's garbage" (68). So much for heavy-going with aesthetic ques-
tions: they all turn into leftovers.

Still, Ammons encourages us to find the poem's form imitative
of, or parallel to, its themes of building, destroying, filling and

evaporating, as he careens among his subjects of scientific exploration, organic breakdown in the food chain, hazardous wastes and undisposables, account-keeping, elegies for friends and wondering about his own demise, and generalized contemplations about the nature of nature. *Garbage* ends, like the *Metamorphoses,* with a philosophical inquiry into the ecology of mind and feeling, by which point nature has evaporated from the poem as a subject. On the one hand, "everything [is] holy" (115), on the other, "all this stuff here is illusory" (115); Ammons moves toward wondering about "celestial garbage" (116), and, at last, about the kind of poetry best suited to "deal with the harsh, brutal, / the ineluctable" (121). It is no surprise that he gives his nod of approbation not to the hackers, the gougers, and the loudmouths, but to the whisperers, those who can keep a balance, in poems that—like Ammons's own best work—stand poised between "passion and control." Reaching outer space poses its own dilemmas: "If I reap the peripheries will I / get hardweed seed and dried roughage, roughage // like teasel and cattail and brush above snow in / winter, pure design lifeless in a painted hold" (121). Whereas the beginning of the poem confronted us with a seething, inchoate mass of material in the tropics, at the end all is insubstantial form, the bare outline of a wintry silhouette, what Shakespeare (Sonnet 5) memorably calls "beauty o'ersnowed and bareness everywhere."

Trash is what you make of it. Garbage has disappeared from a poem which is, like all of Ammons's long poems, a compost heap of matter, useful for building through decomposing. Organic matter undergoes changes in form; inorganic matter, the stuff that does not decompose in the landfill, remains as an ironic testimony to human civilization, Ammons's equivalent of the fragments and waste in Shelley's "Ozymandias" that testify to human ambition and energy. Since it is the point of compost to disappear—or at least to change—we may regard the use of the initial garbage mound as a brilliant, if fortuitous, device to attract our attention and then to let it go amid the widening paths Ammons follows toward disappearance along the peripheries.

As a compost heap itself, *Garbage* pays more than incidental homage to at least two major precursors, the Whitman of "This Compost," and the Stevens of "The Man on the Dump," poems that might be said to have inspired a subgenre within American poetry (Frost's "The Wood-Pile" may be added to the group). Whitman claimed that he bequeathed his "poems and essays as nutriment and influences to help truly assimilate and harden" a national identity.[8] His speaker stops dead in his tracks before the potentially murderous but equally nutritive compost heap he comes upon, through which life comes out of death. Whether by instinct, scientific ignorance, or poetic choice, Whitman initially examines "this compost" with fear of exposure and disease. The poem opens by recoiling from pestilence:

> Something startles me where I thought I was safest,
> I withdraw from the still woods I loved,
> I will not go now on the pastures to walk,
> I will not strip the clothes from my body to meet my lover the sea,
> I will not touch my flesh to the earth as to other flesh to renew me.[9]

Whitman arranges his poetics of beholding into a neat symmetry so that he can command us and himself at the start of the second part: "Behold this compost! behold it well! / Perhaps every mite has once form'd part of a sick person—yet behold!" The "yet" readies us for the poem's turn and subsequent revelations in its conclusion. The watching poet notices and lists the beauties of the surround, and he then transforms despair into acceptance and celebration, with the realization that biology and chemistry have produced winds that "are really not infectious . . . That all is clean forever and forever." The calm, patient Earth "grows such sweet things out of such corruptions. . . . It gives such divine materials to men, and accepts such leavings from them at last." "This Compost" displays an organizing symmetry rare in Whitman. Perhaps too neatly, it takes disease and corruption, turns them inside out, and moves from horror to acceptance to grateful wonder.

As one recent critic, Ed Folsom, has reminded us, for Whitman composting and composition share more than an incidental phonic and etymological resemblance. Like composting, composing demands attention to what we place or set together, and how. Whitman thought of dictionaries as the compost-heap of all English-language literature, and literature always exists over, and emerges out of, layers of other, dead languages.[10] Sublimation is the great theme, but the intrigue of deception and struggle which Whitman works through in this poem is a *via negativa* for Ammons, who looks around, wondering, but without Whitman's distrust of nature's pathology, threat, and poisonous effluvia.

Ammons differs from Whitman in his open, comedic expansiveness; he seldom suffers from discomposure. All garbage, even when it partakes of the noxious, the gothic, the indestructible, becomes for him an occasion for celebration. Decay, miasma, and putrefaction give way to artistic inspection and cyclic renewal, as they do at the end of Ammons's poem. (Or even earlier: in the poet's mind dead language is hauled to a mound and burned down [20].)[11]

From the initially off-putting and then celebratory tones of "This Compost," we can move through Stevens's great poem of the Depression, with its own refraction of the earlier Stevens of *Harmonium*, where "dew," according to Harold Bloom, represented everything in nature that promises pure attraction and refreshment.[12] The "dump is full / Of images," and by the second stanza, Stevens's second take on the dew, he goes so wild with punning that delicate dew has turned, aurally, into something else:

> The green smacks in the eye, the dew in the green
> Smacks like fresh water in a can, like the sea
> On a cocoanut—how many men have copied dew
> For buttons, how many women have covered themselves
> With dew, dew dresses, stories and chains of dew, beads
> Of the floweriest flowers dewed with the dewiest dew.
> One grows to hate these things except on the dump.[13]

From early to mid-Stevens to Ammons, the course is clear: dew becomes doo-doo. Ammons extends the linguistic metamorphosis begun by his predecessor in the process of transforming an early candor into its late plural. Having been struck (literally and figuratively) by various detritus, Ammons wonders:

> do migrating geese not do do as they, sprinkling, go,
> or are they so high their droppings achieve
>
> vaporizing accelerations, like rocket launchers and
> reentry cones, often part solid: or are there
>
> not diarrhetic exceptions to control one might
> have seen splat or been shloshed by: so many
>
> specialties in our little knowledge: undone by
> do, I forged on . . .
>
> (G, 97)

It all comes out, one way or another. Ammons asks about shit what he has also asked, using analogous terms, about poetry and its own shapes:

> . . . is there intermediacy
>
> between hallucinatory flux and pure form's rigid
> thought and count: between diarrhea and constipation,
>
> how about chunky intermediacy, some motion with
> minor forms clear, clusters or bindings, with the
>
> concomitant gaps, tie-offs and recommencements
> expected . . .
>
> (G, 98)

The length of *Garbage* forbids the easy schematizing that both
Whitman and Stevens use as an organizing tool in a short lyric.
For Whitman, miasma and poison turn into beneficent fertilizer;
for Stevens, dew becomes garbage. Both poems rest on elegant
dichotomies. In his more capacious gestures, Ammons has the ad-
vantage of returning to his subject, moving from it to other topics
and then slyly coming back.

His search for a middle way between diarrhea and constipation
helps to explain Ammons's use of a favorite rhetorical device he
shares with Coleridge: chiasmus.[14] The figure becomes, in Am-
mons as in Coleridge, a trope, standing for a deep truth about the
universe itself—namely, the interrelationship of parts within an
ecological or psychological whole, or the importance of boundaries
and centers. Thus, in an early depiction of the transmutations of
energy, Ammons can offhandedly refer to the "returns from the
light downward // to the staid gross: stone to wind, wind to / stone"
(25), everything contained within one system that eliminates our
fear of something beyond or "outside." A less formal chiastic figure
appears a bit later to balance the earlier hopefulness with a sterner
view of the universe: scientists "plunge into matter looking for the /
matter but the matter lessens and, looked too // far into, expands
away: it was insubstantial all / along" (30). The synergistic relation-
ship of all organic matter elicits a formulation at once chiastic and
parallel: "if you've derived from life / a going thing called life, life
has a right to // derive life from you" (98–99). And finally, to make
clear his equation between nature and poetry Ammons calls the
effortlessness of poetry "a plentiful waste and / waste of plenty"
(103). As the trope of containment, chiasmus ideally images Am-
mons's own aesthetic dilemma, as he puts it succinctly in "The
Ridge Farm": "life: because it is / all one it must be divided / and
because it is / divided it must be all one" (*Sumerian Vistas*, 28).[15]

In its multiple tonalities and subjects, *Garbage* represents the triumph of Ammons's own commitment "to the beauty // of gooey language densely managed." Verbiage and garbage have a lot in common (74). A poem dribbles (66). This turn on romantic aesthetics repeats in a different key Ammons's earlier claim (in *Tape for the Turn of the Year*): "only the lively use of / language lives: / can live / on dead words / & falsehood: the / truths poetry creates / die with / their language" (176–77). But like garbage, language never really dies: in a harmonious universe of Lucretian or Pythagorian economy, life comes from death, seeds from shit. Garbage was not garbage to start with, nor was current cliché originally dead language. The processes of poetic composition begin in compost:

> poetry is itself like an installation at Marine
>
> Shale: it reaches down into the dead pit
> and cool oil of stale recognition and words and
>
> brings up hauls of stringy gook which it arrays
> with light and strings with shiny syllables and
>
> gets the mind back into vital relationship with
> communication channels: but, of course, there
>
> is some untransformed material, namely the poem
> itself . . .

(G, 108–9)

Putting it somewhat differently, Ammons relates composition to the composure of draining, filling, and then again emptying the mind. The mind concentrates and eliminates; it goes with the becoming thought, as the poet suggests in "Corsons Inlet." The mind wanders, and it then

> . . . gives way from its triggering, and
> the mechanisms of necessity fall into, grasping the
>
> upheaval, the action of making; the presence
> of pressure appears, forces open a way, the
>
> intensity heightens, groans of anguish and
> satisfaction break from the depths of the
>
> body, and the sweet dream occurs, the work
> payloads, the fall-away slips through, the body

> contracts and returns, ease lengthens throughout
> the byways, and the mind picks up on the
>
> environment again . . .

(G, 43)

Although its maker has been undone by do, he has also done a turn on it. Creation comes as the by-product of (or in an analogy to) excretion, to waste.

Like Ovid, Whitman, and all writers of the Big Book (that *mega biblon* that Callimachus long ago warned against as a *mega kakon*), Ammons normally works by means of a poetics of accretion. Such easy expansiveness has given hostile critics of Whitman, W. C. Williams, Ammons, or Frank O'Hara and John Ashbery plenty to complain about. At their worst, these poets simply ramble, amassing details and observations in the way a walker-in-the-city or by-the-shore takes random notice, or records his doings.

Even a short listing poem, such as Ammons's archetypal "The City Limits" ("When you consider the radiance," *Selected Poems,* (89), develops this way. Its six tercets come as close in their essence to a sonnet as a non-sonnet could, especially since their syntax works within the "When . . . Then" staple of the Shakespearian lyric: "*When* you consider the radiance [line 1]. . . ."

> *then*
> the heart moves roomier, the man stands and looks about
>   . . . and the dark
> work of the deepest cells is of a tune with May bushes
> and fear lit by the breadth of such calmly turns to praise.

(ll. 14–18, my emphasis)

The "city limits" are where, of course, one would find a dump or a recycling station, and where control, tightness, and everything associated with centrality give way to freedom, disorder, and entropy. But the title also makes a neat turn on the trick originally played by Richard Wilbur's "The Beautiful Changes," where what looks like an adjective-noun combination becomes, within the body of the poem, a noun-verb construction ("The beautiful changes as a forest is changed").[16] The "city limits" our effort to cover its grounds. All borders are arbitrary, or, as Emerson's fierce dictum has it, "the only sin is limitation." Ovid may have inspired these grammatical as well as natural transformations in Ammons and Wilbur, since what something looks like may turn out not to be what it actually, or solely, is. Like Ovid, Whitman, and Wilbur,

Ammons calls our attention to the very conditions of peripheries (where limits are porous) and centers (where ore turns out to be shit):

> . . . when you consider
> the abundance of such resource as illuminates the glow-blue
>
> bodies and gold-skeined wings of flies swarming the dumped
> guts of a natural slaughter or the coil of shit and in no
> way winces from its storms of generosity . . .
>
> (ll. 8–12)

Like any poetic form (what Blake called "lineaments"), the city limits with its bounding lines. At the limits as well as the center we find that everything exists in a state of radiant light. Illumination from without fosters and complements the deepest cells within.

Likewise, compost is warmest and most alive underneath, within, at the bottom. The poetics of accretion and development has been supplemented, if not entirely replaced, by a poetics of excretion. Excretion is part of Ammons's theme, from minor asides about laxatives (14) or birdshit (28), or smart-aleckish modesty ("where but in the very asshole of comedown is / redemption" [21]; "drop all this crap about words" [50]), to more serious considerations about landfills:

> . . . guess what's two percent of permanent waste,
>
> yep, disposable diapers, good to last
> five hundred years: cute little babies' shit
>
> (G, 61)

Or even wondering why travelers never report on their bodily functions and where in medieval times early "bannered / / armies" may have "dookied" in the woods (104–5).

Ammons returns in *Garbage* to another of his earliest tropes: dispersal, *sparagmos,* and self-extinction. At the start of the earlier *Selected Poems* he threw away "the pieces of my voice," scattering and grinding them down:

> for I am broken over the earth—
> so little remains
> for the silent offering of my death.
>
> (*Selected Poems,* 3)

Similarly, in "Mansion" (a title that suggests building rather than decomposing) he cedes his body—instead of his voice—to the wind (18); even "Mechanism" (21), with its steady command to "honor a going thing," reminds us that "going" means "disappearing" as well as "operating." And since Ammons everywhere equates external geography and internal selfhood, he can announce with certainty in "Terrain" (25) that "the soul is a region without definite boundaries" (thus proving himself postmodern) but also "a habitat, precise ecology of forms" (thereby proving himself still a romantic). Looseness and steadiness often turn out to exist—like boundaries and centers—in close relationship to one another. Thus, in "Dunes" (*Selected Poems,* 51), where he returns to a characteristic landscape, ever moving, ever changing, the poet uses a characteristic phrasing (his beloved gerunds) to remind us that verbs and nouns exist interchangeably. He depicts a "loose world":

> Mounds from that can rise
>   on held mounds,
> a gesture of building, keeping,
>   a trapping
> into shape.

> Firm ground is not available ground.

(CP, 158)

Not available, presumably, because nonexistent in this, or any other landscape. All things, as Ovid (and even earlier, Lucretius) observed, are on the move. Nothing is thrown away, although it may appear to be, in the poetics of excretion or secretion that complements the aggregative structures by which a long poem is composed. "The odor of shit is like language," Ammons says flatly in "The Ridge Farm." The shifting sands of time overlay the decomposing organic matter of garbage, from which new creations emerge. At the very beginning of his long poem, Ammons's dedication insouciantly proposes a startling, if implicit, metaphor:

> to the bacteria, tumblebugs, scavengers,
>   wordsmiths—the transfigurers, restorers. . . .

Are human poetic wordsmiths merely a culminating item in the list of critters who make up the category of "transfigurers, restorers"? Or is Ammons saying that the bacteria et al. constitute the most genuine, because the most elementary, poetic makers we might know? Both, of course. Like garbage, *Garbage* offers the fact as well as the potential for beauty and poetry at the place where waste becomes the fiber for art. From the organic, fertilizing decay of the original compost heap there has come a rich, heady produce.

NOTES

1. Jonathan Bate, *Romantic Ecology: Wordsworth and the Environmental Tradition* (London and New York: Routledge, 1991); Nicholas Roe, *The Politics of Nature: Wordsworth and Some Contemporaries* (New York: St. Martin's Press, 1992). Neither Bate nor Roe subscribes to a full-fledged return to earlier pieties about romanticism. Both are well-informed in regard to current political readings of their poets. Still, Bate makes the claim that "[t]he time is now right to allow Wordsworth to become once more what he imagined himself to be, what Shelley called him, and what he was to the Victorians: 'Poet of Nature'" (9).

2. See Jay Parini, "The Greening of the Humanities," *New York Times Magazine*, 29 October 1995, 52–53. Parini cites, *inter alia*, Lawrence Buell's recent *The Environmental Imagination: Thoreau, Nature Writing, and the Formation of American Culture* (Cambridge: Belknap Press of Harvard University Press, 1995) as a representative important work that signals the paradigm shift among literary scholars.

3. M. H. Abrams, *The Mirror and the Lamp: Romantic Theory and The Critical Tradition* (New York: Oxford University Press, 1953) remains the locus classicus for discussions of romantic critical theory in England and Germany. Citing an essay by Cleanth Brooks (222), Abrams suggests how romantic organicism filtered into this country via the chief of the New Critics: "One of the critical discoveries of our time—perhaps it is not a discovery but merely a recovery—is that the parts of a poem have an organic relation to each other. . . . The parts of a poem are related as are the parts of a growing plant." Cf. Coleridge, in his *Shakespearian Criticism* (Abrams, 223): ". . . there is a law which all the parts [of a tree] obey. . . . the *rules* of Imagination are . . . the very powers of growth and production." We may now recover Abrams, recovering Brooks, recovering Coleridge. The movement against organicism, and against one aspect of romanticism in particular, is of course due to the tastes of Paul De Man. Borrowing from Abrams himself, De Man points out the problems inherent in one sort of Coleridgean organicism. He quotes Abrams (page 174) on Coleridge's notion of free will, which "runs counter . . . to an inherent tendency of his elected analogue." See "Form and Intent in the American New Criticism," in *Blindness and Insight: Essays in the Rhetoric of Contemporary Criticism* (New York: Oxford University Press, 1971), 20–35. His earlier ground-breaking essay, "The Rhetoric of Temporality," in *Interpretation: Theory and Practice*, ed. Charles S. Singleton (Baltimore: Johns Hopkins University Press, 1969), 173–209, tries to demystify Coleridgean symbolism, preferring to it an allegory that renounces symbolism's nostalgia for wholeness and "establishes its language in the void of this temporal difference." For De Man, the "symbolical style" is, *tout court*, "a veil thrown over a light one no longer wishes to perceive" (191).

4. James Merrill, *From The First Nine: Poems 1946–1976* (New York: Atheneeum, 1982), 352.

5. A. R. Ammons, *Tape for the Turn of the Year* (Ithaca: Cornell University Press, 1965), 144.

6. A. R. Ammons, *Garbage* (New York: W. W. Norton & Co., 1993), 28. All references will be to this edition; pages numbers will be included hereafter in the text. Later in his poem he refers to human evolution in terms that the Merrill of the epic *Changing Light at Sandover* might approve:

> and then along came the frail one, our ancestor,
>
> scavenger, seed finder, nut cracker, fruit
> picker, grubs, bulbs, etc., and here we are at
>
> last, last, probably, behold; we have replaced
> the meadows with oilslick . . .

(G, 75)

7. Ovid, *Metamorphoses*, Loeb Classical Library (Cambridge.: Harvard University Press, 1958), vol. 2, 382. Translation mine.

8. Walt Whitman, *Prose Works 1892*, ed. Floyd Stovall (New York: New York University Press, 1964), 2:469. Kerry C. Larson, *Whitman's Drama of Consciousness* (Chicago: University of Chicago Press, 1988) says of "This Compost" that "art's sublimations cannot hope to rival nature's own" since nature "has mastered the art of sublimation with a deftness that leaves the speaker a dazed, if somewhat distrustful bystander" (179–80).

9. Walt Whitman, *Leaves of Grass*, in *Complete Poetry and Collected Prose* (New York: Library of America, 1982), 495–97.

10. Ed Folsom, *Walt Whitman's Native Representations* (Cambridge: Cambridge University Press, 1994), 15–18. Other useful discussions of the poem are Michael Moon, *Disseminating Whitman: Revision and Corporeality in Leaves of Grass* (Cambridge: Harvard University Press, 1991), 136–38; and Harold Aspiz, *Walt Whitman and the Body Beautiful* (Urbana: University of Illinois Press, 1980), 63–65, whose connection of Whitman's poem to "miasma theory" by which a deadly putrefaction becomes "an affecting metaphor of immortality, artistic inspiration and spiritual renewal" sounds equally appropriate as a summary of Ammons's.

11. In his Whitmanian poem "Laboratory Materials" (*Sumerian Vistas* [New York: W. W. Norton & Co., 1987], 69), Ammons asks: "[the] diseased and afflicted . . . are fields of glory to be reaped / into knowledge . . . [but] what is to be learned of the healthy person[?]"

12. Harold Bloom, *Wallace Stevens: The Poems of Our Climate* (Ithaca: Cornell University Press, 1977), 144, calls Stevens's earlier mutations of dew "a synecdoche for everything in nature that still could be thought of as pure or refreshing, or rather for something that has not yet come into nature."

13. *The Collected Poems of Wallace Stevens* (New York: Alfred A. Knopf, 1957), 202.

14. In *Majestic Indolence: English Romantic Poetry and the Work of Art* (New York: Oxford University Press, 1995), I devote a chapter to examining Coleridge's use of this rhetorical scheme and to inferring some reasons for its recurrence in his poetic style. See "Coleridge and Dejection," 58–82.

15. The most famous example of chiasmus in Ammons is, of course, his lovely poem called "Reflective," which neatly creates a picture of the harmonious balance between perceiver and perceived:

I found a
weed
that had a

mirror in it
and that
mirror

looked in at
a mirror
in

me that
had a
weed in it

See A. R. Ammons, *The Selected Poems, 1951–1977* (New York: W. W. Norton & Co. 1977), 53.

16. *The Poems of Richard Wilbur* (New York: Harcourt, Brace & World, 1963), 226.

"How a thing will / unfold": Fractal Rhythms in A. R. Ammons's *Briefings*

Marjorie Perloff

Briefings: Poems Small and Easy, singled out by Harold Bloom as Ammons's "finest book,"[1] is also, I think, his most enigmatic. To begin with, its eighty-eight poems do not really constitute a "new" book; they were written over a period of twenty years, as their arrangement in the *Collected Poems 1951–1971* testifies. In that volume, the *Briefings* poems are included in four chronological groupings: 1951–1955; 1955–1960; 1961–1965, and 1966–1971. And although the majority (sixty of the eighty-eight) *Briefings* poems come from the fourth of these periods, twenty-two (exactly one quarter) come from 1961–1965, and there are four poems from the early fifties, two from the later. More confusing: why does Ammons include these and not other of the earlier poems, given that the ones chosen are neither, as every critic has remarked, "easy," nor are they especially "small." "Return" (B, 19–21) for example, has forty-five lines; *Collected Poems 1951–1971* has any number of poems much shorter than this one that are omitted from *Briefings*. Why?

But there is a further mystery. The eighty-eight poems, not so small and not so easy, that constitute *Briefings* are arranged alphabetically by first lines. I have not seen a single reference to this decidedly odd phenomenon, but surely the poet knew what he was about when he began with "A bird fills up the," followed by "A clover blossom's a province;" "A clown kite, my," "After yesterday," and "A leaf fallen is" and concluded with "Yes but," "You're sick," and "You would think I'd be a specialist in contemporary." Interestingly, the final poem, the famous "The City Limits" stands outside this alphabetical scheme (It begins with "When"), just as, I shall argue later, it stands outside the particular paradigms that characterize *Briefings*.

Between pages 33 and 56 of this 105-page book, the "I"s have it: from the "I can't decide whether" of "Circles" to the "I wonder

68

what I should do now" of "Looking Over the Acreage," nineteen poems begin with "I," as in "I hope," "I hold," "I look," "I make." This emphasis on the subject may seem peculiar, given Ammons's fabled reticence and modesty. But we should note further that the "I" is actually placed slightly off-center so far as the countdown of poems goes. Then, too, the titles offset these intimate opening lines: "I hold you responsible for" is the first line of "Hymn IV," "I hope I'm / not right," the first line of "The Mark." The abstract, impersonal titles frame those delicate personal observations, as if to say, watch out, you can express emotion but in the larger scheme of things, private feeling may not matter much.

"The flight from form," says Stephen B. Cushman in a consideration of verse form and metrics in Ammons's poetry, "is constant and the refuge in form temporary." And again, "Ammons's stanzas have little or no logical integrity"; they "appear to challenge the Romantic myth of organicism."[2] Etymologically, he suggests, a *stanza* is a stopping place, but for Ammons, there are no full stops, only sites for speeding and slowing down.[3] At the same time, as Cushman notes, the "need for form remains acute"; hence the ubiquitousness of the "left-justified stychic column" of verse,[4] a form whose stability overcomes its many variations.

Cushman is on to something important here. But he does not look closely at the prosodic particulars of Ammons's poems, nor at the larger structures into which those left-justified stychic columns are organized. In this essay I propose to look at those relationships in *Briefings,* reading this volume as one long poem rather than as a miscellany of occasional lyrics or of anthology pieces like "Circles" and "The City Limits." Ammons's curious particularism, I want to suggest, goes hand in hand with a quasi-Oulippean concern for mathematical structure—a structure by no means characteristic of the Emersonian tradition in which Ammons is regularly placed.

Consider the opening poem "Center," whose verse form sets the stage for what is to come, as the following scansion[5] may help to show:

A bird fills up the

streamside bush

with wasteful song,

x   Λx   / x   /
capsizes waterfall,

/   Λ | x   >
mill run, and

/ x /   Λ
superhighway

x   >
to

/   x   / x x   >
song's improvident

/   x
center

/   x   x   /   >
lost in the green

/ | /
bush green

/   x x   /
answering bush:

/   / x
wind varies:

x   /   Λ /   >
the noon sun casts

/ | x /   x
mesh refractions

x   x   /   / x   >
on the stream's amber

/ x
bottom

x   / x   x   /   /
and nothing at all gets,

/   x   /   >
nothing gets

/   x /
caught at all.

                                        (B, 1)

"The given," Harold Bloom comments on this poem, "is mesh that cannot catch because the particulars have been capsized, and so are unavailable for capture. The center is improvident because it stands at the midmost point of mind, not of nature."[6] And Linda Orr adds, "The final sentence has a spare beauty. Clearly at the end no more general correspondence will emerge beside that of bush to bush."[7] My own reading would be more literal: like "Ode to a Nightingale," Ammons's poem tracks the movement of a bird as it gradually flies out of sight. From the initial vantage point of a "streamside bush," the bird's song, like the Solitary Reaper's, generously, indeed "wastefully," dominates and "centers" the scene of waterfall, mill run, and superhighway below, and the green bushes seem to echo its music. But then "wind varies," the bird vanishes, and only the "mesh refractions" of the "noon sun" are reflected "on the stream's amber / bottom." The reflection, of course, changes minute by minute, so that, to the observer looking at the stream and listening for the lost bird song, it appears that "nothing gets / caught at all."

If this is a familiar romantic topos, Ammons succeeds in making it quite new. It is the sound structure rather than any novelty of image or even voicing that makes the poem so distinctive. For here is a twenty-line free verse lyric called "Center," in which the "center" is decentered by being cited in line 9 and, more important, is deconstructed by the poem's refusal of sound repetition. As my scansion shows (and the same holds true even if some of my secondary stresses could be considered primary), there are, within the poem's twenty-line compass, only two lines with the same pro- sodic structure—"center" (line 9) and "bottom" (line 17). Every- thing else is amorphous and jagged: there are no repeated rhythmic groupings, no consistency of enjambment or of caesurae. The logi- cal conclusion would be that the poem is "prosaic"—prose cut up into line lengths—but that would not be accurate either for the discourse is hardly that of prose. For one thing, antecedents are often unclear as in the case of line 10, "lost in the green," where "lost" may modify "center" or "song." In lines 10–12, the lineation creates an echo structure where the bird song creates the illusion of green bush answering green bush. And line 18, "and nothing at all gets," seems transitive (i.e., "the noon sun . . . nothing at all gets") until, in its second appearance, "gets" is completed by "caught."

Lineation, as is generally the case in Ammons's poetry, works to defamiliarize the most ordinary processes. "A bird fills up the," "mill run, and": here article and conjunction are left hanging. But Ammons's is not the suspension system of a William Carlos Wil- liams, despite the many references to Williams in his lyric, of which more below. A Williams poem like "As the cat" moves swiftly and surely, tracking the cat's deliberate movements as it finally steps "into the pit / of the empty / flowerpot." Ammons's bird poem, in contrast, doesn't "go" anywhere; on the contrary, it shifts back and forth somewhat uneasily between the concrete ("streamside bush") and the abstract ("song's improvident / center"), as if the phenomenology of vision were not to be trusted. The stumbling utterance "and nothing at all gets, / nothing gets / caught at all" that concludes the poem testifies to an inability to "make it cohere" that is a kind of Ammons trademark. A poet who longs for the center, who wants to get to the "bottom" of things, to find a cohesion between bird and bush, sun and stream, this "spent seer" is always "caught" short.

In one of his rare statements on verse form, the 1963 "Note on Prosody,"[8] Ammons remarks that his aim is to shift emphasis "from the ends of the lines . . . toward the left-hand margin." In the case of a couplet like

> and the mountain
> pleased

for example, he notes that "*mountain* is played down," because it is followed by the heavy stress that falls on "pleased": "*pleased,* being one sound, has no beginning or end." Accordingly "a slightly stronger than usual emphasis is given to *and.*" By shifting from right to left, the poet contends, "The center of gravity is an imaginary point existing between the two points of beginning and end, so that a downward pull is created that gives a certain downward rush to the movement, something like a waterfall glancing in turn off opposite sides of the canyon, something like the right and left turns of a river."[9] And this "downward swing," Ammons concludes, suggests "that a nonlinear movement is possible," the vertical movement from top to bottom replacing the "normal" left-to-right pull of the individual line.

The emphasis on line beginnings rather than endings accords perfectly with the quirky alphabetizing of first lines in *Briefings*. But the "downward rush" of the verbal "waterfall" is countered, more than Ammons would like us to think, by the broken textures I have described in "Center." "A poem," Ammons declares, "is a linguistic correction of disorder"; "multiplicity is accumulated into symmetry."[10] And Harold Bloom seems to accept this notion when he writes, with reference to the line "the overall endures" in "Saliences," "Overall remains beyond Ammons, but is replaced by "'a round / quiet turning / beyond loss or gain, / beyond concern for the separate reach'," the "assertion of the mind's power over the particulars of being, the universe of death."[11]

But this is not quite what happens, at least not in "Center." The "mind's power over particulars" is asserted by what we might call the alpha game: as the first poem in *Briefings*, "Center" not only begins with "A" but even with "A" plus "b" for "bird," and it ends with two more "a" words: "at all." Alliteration—"bird"/"bush";

"with"/"wasteful"/"waterfall"—is at first reassuring, but by the time we reach that last "all," with its rhyme on "waterfall" sixteen lines earlier, the center has simply not held. Who would have thought, for example, that seemingly identical lines—say, three-syllable lines like "streamside bush" (2) and "mill run, and" (5) could be so distinct? Substitute a conjunction for a monosyllabic noun and you necessarily create a pause with a slight caesura. "Wind varies" (line 13), everything varies, and "nothing gets / caught at all." So much for the poem as "linguistic correction of disorder."

Indeed, Ammons's overt poetics are curiously at odds with his actual poems. He is given to generalizations about the Coleridgean "balance or reconciliation of opposite or discordant qualities," the "accumulation" of "multiplicity . . . into symmetry," and his theory of language is resolutely classical: there is a "reality" out there and "our language [is a] reflection of it."[12] But reflection theory is belied by what we might call Ammons's metrics of difference. The stychic column is a pseudo-column, each line differing from its predecessor, as in

$$x \quad / \quad \wedge \quad / \quad >$$
the noon sun casts

$$/ \quad | \quad x \quad / \quad x$$
mesh refractions

where one four-syllable line is followed by another that couldn't sound more different. The same process occurs in the fifth "A" poem, which bears the colorless title "Event":

$$x \quad / \quad / \quad x \quad / \quad >$$
A leaf fallen is

$$/ \quad x$$
fallen

$$x \quad / \quad x \quad / \quad x \quad /$$
throughout the universe

$$\wedge$$
and

$$x \quad x \quad / \quad x \quad x \quad >$$
from the instant of

$$x \quad / \quad | \quad \wedge \quad >$$
its fall, for

$$/ \quad / \quad /$$
all time gone

$$x \quad x \quad /$$
and to come:

/   /   x ∧ >
worlds jiggle in

/ | / >
webs, drub

x   /   ∧
in leaf lakes,

/   x ∧ >
squiggle in

/   x   /   ∧x
drops of ditchwater:

/   x   /
size and place

/ x   /
begin, end,

/   x x /
time is allowed

x   ∧ /   /   ∧
in event's instant:

x /   x >
away or

x   / | / x /   x   >
at home, universe and

/   ∧ >
leaf try

x /   ‖ x   /
to fall: occur.

Again, the poem is notable for its variability of linear structure, made manifest especially in its "containment" by a seemingly larger order, in this case the stanzaic division into 8–5–8 line units. The "event" in these pseudo-stanzas often takes place at the level of phoneme and morpheme: as I was typing the lines, I wrote line 9 as "words" rather than "worlds jiggle," line 11 as "in leaf flakes," and line 13 as "drops of dishwater," inadvertently naturalizing the words so as to fit into their normal syntactic slots. Paragram is the operative poetic principle: "fall" as in "leaf fallen," repeated three times in the short first stanza and once in the third, contains "all," the "in" in "jiggle in" reappears two lines later in "in leaf lakes," then in the rhyming "squiggle in," and finally twice "in event's instant."

The poem's vocabulary is rigorously restricted, indeed almost aphasic: "is," "and" "its," "for," "to," "is," "or." At first the witness of the "event" seems frozen, tongue-tied: "A leaf fallen is / fallen." A not very interesting tautology. "Fallen / throughout the universe" doesn't help; it sounds at first merely pretentious, a kind of reductive update of Gerard Manley Hopkins's "Spring and Fall" ("Margaret, are you grieving / Over Golden Grove unleaving"). But the last two lines of the stanza, "all time gone / and to come," with their biblical echo, introduce the cycle we thought could not be there: what is "gone" will come back, as we surmise from the sound itself: the substitution of one nasal for another, one voiceless stop (/k/) for another (/g/) produces the desired turn.

But turn to what? The nursery rhyme effect of the "jiggle in"/ 'squiggle in" is offset by line 10, with its two harsh stressed syllables, broken by a caesura: "webs, / drub." What Hopkins referred to as "worlds of wanwood leafmeal" here becomes a kind of compost pile made up of wet leaves ("leaf lakes"), ditchwater, and cobwebs or spiderwebs; a dirt mound that seems to contain a living being, drubbing about inside it. But Ammons does not dwell on the sensuous; the specificity of "webs, drub" quickly gives way to the bleakest of abstractions: "size and place / begin, end"—again, like "A leaf fallen is / fallen" a peculiar truism. "Time," we read, "is allowed / in event's instant." There's a special providence, it seems, in the fall of a leaf, the poet recognizing that "event's instant" is actually a form of motion, that there is no stasis in nature. When the "instant" occurs, the "event" is over; indeed, there is no "event," just a lot of ongoing small changes. In the end we learn that "universe and / leaf try / to fall." Is the leaf's fall then volitional, and if so, how? The poet catches himself up and realizes all that he can say is "to fall: occur": the two iambs on either side of the mid-line caesura match, suggesting that these things do occur, that nothing remains the same, that the "event's instant" destroys the event, the defining moment. And the colon throws the meaning forward: "for / all time gone / and to come" is now understood to be too stagy, too grandiose for a meaningful recognition of the way things are, the ways they "occur."

The concern of "event's instant," exhibited here and elsewhere in Ammons's poetry has, I think, a particular analogue in contemporary chaos theory. "Why," asks Benoit Mandelbrot in the opening of his *Fractal Geometry of Nature*, "is geometry often described as 'cold' and 'dry?' One reason lies in its inability to describe the shape of a cloud, a mountain, a coastline, or a tree. Clouds are not spheres, mountains are not cones, coastlines are not circles, and bark is not smooth, nor does lightning travel in a straight line. . . . Nature exhibits not simply a higher degree but an altogether different level of complexity. . . . The existence of these patterns challenges us to study those forms that Euclid leaves aside as being 'formless,' to investigate the morphology of the

'amorphous.'"[13] Thus the length of a curve—say, the length of the
coastline of Britain, to take Mandelbrot's famous example—will
vary according to what principle of measurement we apply to it.
Far from being the total of individual segments of coast line, length
varies according to the scale of units to be included: the greater
the detail, which is to say, the smaller the measurable sub-bays
and sub-peninsulas, the greater the difficulty in assigning anything
like a "true length" to the coast line's curve.[14]

Ammons's poetry does not contain overt references to fractals;
his "telescopic and microscopic vision," as Steven P. Schneider
calls it in his fine study of the poet as scientist, focuses more imme-
diately on astronomy and biology, especially on the equilibrium
of the ecosystem.[15] But whether directly or indirectly, his poetry
testifies to the fractal geometer's concern for the "morphology of
the amorphous"—the tiny and oddly shaped bay that transforms
a coastline, the minute triangular crystals that make up a snow-
flake—a flake that appears from a distance to be merely a round
blob. And the special fascination of *Briefings* is the way external
"form"—the "alphabetical Ithaca" of the arrangement of the se-
quence, the abstraction and universality of the volume's represen-
tative titles ("Event," "Mechanics," "Increment," "Two
Possibilities," "Attention," "Return," "Civics," "Circles," "Lo-
cus"), the visual shapeliness of the stanzas, and the reassuring
repetition of key words like "center," "circle," "light," "radiance,"
"wind," "leaf," and "green"—is consistently undercut by the ob-
servation of "fractals" that throw the "normal" view of what is
seen and perceived off balance. Ammons's is thus a romantic na-
ture vision with a difference. He is not so much the "spent seer" as
the post–World War II poet-scientist who takes nothing for granted.

We can see this especially clearly when we compare one of Am-
mons's homage-poems to William Carlos Williams ("WCW") to a
precursor like Williams's own "Spring Storm":

The sky has given over

its bitterness.

Out of the dark change

all day long

rain falls and falls

as if it would never end.

   /   x   /   /   >
Still the snow keeps

x   /   ^   x   /
its hold on the ground.

  /   / x   / x
But water, water

  /   x   / x   / x
from a thousand runnels!

x   ^ /   / x
It collects swiftly,

  /   x   ^   /
dappled with black

  /   x   /   x x /
cuts a way for itself

    x   /   / x   x / x
through green ice in the gutters.

  /   x x   /   x /
Drop after drop it falls

x   x   /   x   /   /
from the withered grass-stems

x   x / x   /   x   x   / x
of the overhanging embankment.[16]

Williams's "free verse" poem (1920) is actually written in three-stress lines. Syllables range from three to nine, but the basic three-stress rhythm, the forward thrust from line to line propels us forward to the conclusion of that extra-long cacophonous line, "of the overhanging embankment." Each line in Williams's suspension system is at once independent and anticipatory. The lines are only rarely fully enjambed (as in lines 1 and 2), but the structure of fulfillment operates throughout. Question: what is it that happens "all day long"? Answer: "rain falls and falls." How does it fall? Answer: "as if it would never end." "But water, water" . . . from where? Answer: "from a thousand runnels!" This is a "free verse" still highly structured and characterized by its continuity.

Now compare Ammons's "WCW":

x /   /   >
I turned in

x   x   /   ^
by the bayshore

x   /
and parked,

  x   /   ^   >
the crosswind

 / x   ^   /   >
hitting me hard

                          /   x   /
                        side the head,

                         x   /   /   x
                        the bay scrappy

                        x   /   x
                        and working:

                        /   x >
                        what a

                        /   x   /   >
                        way to read

                        / x ‖ /   >
                        Williams! till

                        x /   x   /
                        a woman came

                        x   /   >
                        and turned

                        x   /   /   /
                        her red dog loose

                        x   /
                        to sniff

                        x   /   >
                        (and piss

                        /
                        on)

                        x   /   /   ∧
                        the dead horseshoe

                        /
                        crabs.

The variability of stress is much greater here, even similar units like "and turned," "(and piss," being differentiated by punctuation and syntax: the opening parenthesis and enjambment of "(and piss / on" changing the tempo ever so slightly. More important: whereas Williams uses a good bit of repetition ("rain falls and falls," "But water, water," "Drop after drop it falls"), Ammons repeats almost nothing, deforms syntax ("hitting me hard / side the head"), and prefers consonance to assonance, as in those guttural final "d's" in "turne*d*" (the only word used twice), "parke*d*," "crosswin*d*," "har*d*," "si*d*e the hea*d*," "rea*d*," "red," and "dea*d*." Ten of the poem's forty-six words (one quarter) end with "d," culminating in the "dead horseshoe / crabs" of the last two lines. So death has been anticipated from the first "turned." And the discordant final line, "crabs" stands out in bold relief against the internal chiming of "Wi*lli*ams ! t*ill*" and "*sniff* / (and *piss*."

Again, then, a poem without center that tries to capture the particular mood of loneliness, ugliness, the instinctive anticipation of death. *Briefings* contains many such, with enigmatic titles like "Making," "Countering," and "Square," the latter eleven-line lyric as "unsquare" as possible (see B, 80). But what about the poem that concludes *Briefings,* "The City Limits" (B, 105)? As I remarked earlier, this is the only of the eighty-eight poems outside the alphabet system, its first line, beginning with a "W" ("When you consider the radiance"), whereas the three preceding poems are "Y" lyrics. And not only is "The City Limits" thus a kind of epilogue rather than a part of the sequence; it is much more orderly than Ammons's other poems "small and easy," consisting of one long sentence broken into six open tercets, with a great deal of repetition (especially of "when you consider"), and a slow stately rhythm (six or seven stresses per line), culminating in the final iambic heptameter:

$$\overset{x}{\text{and}}\ \overset{/}{\text{fear}}\ \overset{/}{\text{lit}}\ \overset{x}{\text{by}}\ \overset{x}{\text{the}}\ \overset{/}{\text{breadth}}\ \overset{x}{\text{of}}\ \overset{/}{\text{such}}\ \overset{/}{\text{calmly}}\ \overset{x}{\text{turns}}\ \overset{/}{\text{to}}\ \overset{x}{\text{praise.}}$$

Most of Ammons's critics concur that this "majestic" poem, as Bloom calls it,[17] is one of Ammons's finest. Richard Howard typically calls it "the greatest poem in this latest book" [*Briefings*], and comments that it "ends with the acknowledgement that each thing is merely what it is, and all that can be transcended is our desire for each thing to be more than what it is, so that for such a consideration of the losses of being, the very being of loss, 'fear lit by the breadth of such calmly turns to praise'."[18] And David Kalstone praises the poem's "wonderfully sustained rhetorical structure almost like that of the most controlled and contemplative of Shakespeare's sonnets."[19]

This is an odd sort of compliment, for Ammons's poetics, after all, are wholly at odds with the "sustained rhetorical structure" of a Shakespeare sonnet. "If fear ever turns 'calmly' to anything," remarks Robert Pinsky in one of the few dissenting views of "The City Limits," "being 'of a tune with May bushes' is a lamely rhetorical motive for such turning, especially given the sinister cancerous implications of 'the dark work of the deepest cells'."[20] And one might add that the very rhythm and neat tercet structure, along with the five-fold repetition of "When you consider," gives "The City Limits" a willed air, as if to say, yes, I *am* an Emersonian poet and should therefore talk of the mysterious "radiance, that . . . does not withhold itself," although it cannot penetrate the "overhung or hidden." I should present the epiphany that makes "the heart move roomier," and "fear" somehow (I agree with Pinsky that it's not at all clear how) "calmly turn to praise."

What role, then, does "The City Limits" play in *Briefings*? My own hunch is that Ammons feared his poems "small and easy" might be perceived as too slight, too trivial. After all, poems like "Center" and "Event" don't have "great themes," they don't challenge the reader to "Consider" the truths of the natural and transcendent world. I would guess that the poet had already arranged all the other lyrics in order, culminating in the two "You" poems, "The Run-Through" and "The Put Down Come On." The latter poem has the long lines and stanzaic structure of "City Limits" but takes a gingerly approach to transcendence, recognizing that "Only a little of that kind of thinking flashes through" (B, 104). At this point, evidently, Ammons lost his nerve and wanted a wrap-up poem, replete with pun (as in the title), symbol, and metaphor. And so enthusiastic was the response of the poet's leading critics and supporters, that as time went on, Roethke-esque poems like "Hibernaculum" sometimes crowd out their more modest but more satisfying neighbors. Consider the twenty-line "Locus," which begins:

> Here
> it is
> the middle of April
> (and a day or so more)

(B, 32)

The seasonal cycle is measured by arithmetic progression: 1, 2, 4, 6 (the word count) combines multiples of 2 with Fibbonaci numbers (2 + 4 = 6). These multipliers matter because the poet is terrified by the time gap, as represented by the "small oak / down in / the / hollow," which "is / lit up (winter-burned, ice-gold / leaves on) / at sundown, / ruin transfigured to / stillest shining."

But those moments of "stillest shining" (the "radiance" of "City Limits") have to be given up. "Locus" concludes:

> I let it as center
> go
> and
> can't believe
> our peripheral
> speed.

"Peripheral speed" must be accepted. And when one stops "consider[ing] the radiance" of what is pointed to, *words* become themselves radiant. "L*et*" / "*center*" / "*can't*" form a triad; "and" / "*can't*" a column of near-rhymes. So small are the words that "peripheral," with its four syllables stands out. But what is most striking in this little stanza is that isolated word "go" after "center," suggesting that the "form of a motion" never comes to rest. *Go:* it is the "*locus*" (again, a rhyme) of what Ammons called his "nonlinear movement," the recognition that, as the poet puts it in "Two Possibilities":

> Coming out of the earth and going
> into the earth compose
> an interval or arc where
> what to do's
>
> difficult to fix

                                      (B, 11)

Notes

1. Harold Bloom," When You Consider the Radiance," *The Ringers in the Tower* (Chicago: University of Chicago Press, 1971), 286. This essay is reprinted as the introduction to *A. R. Ammons: Modern Critical Views* (New York: Chelsea House, 1986), 1–31.

2. Stephen B. Cushman, "Stanzas, Organic Myth, and the Metaformalism of A. R. Ammons," *American Literature* 59, no. 4 (December 1987): 514–15.

3. Cushman, "Stanzas, Organic Myth, and the Metaformalism of A. R. Ammons," 521.

4. Cushman, "Stanzas, Organic Myth, and the Metaformalism of A. R. Ammons," 513.

5. In what follows, I use the following scansion marks, adapted from George Trager and Henry Le Smith Jr., in *An Outline of English Structure* (Washington, D.C.: American Council of Learned Societies, 1957):

/	syllable with primary stress
∧	syllable with secondary stress, as in a compound noun like "blackbird"
x	unstressed syllable
|	pause
||	caesura or heavy pause
>	enjambed line

6. Bloom, "When You Consider the Radiance," 29.

7. Linda Orr, "The Cosmic Backyard of A. R. Ammons," *Diacritics* 3 (Winter 1973); rpt. in Bloom, *A. R. Ammons: Modern Critical Views*, p. 135.

8. A. R. Ammons, "A Note on Prosody," *Poetry* 203, no. 3 (June 1963): 202–3; rpt. in Ammons, *Set in Motion: Essays, Interviews, & Dialogues,* ed. Zofia Burr (Ann Arbor: University of Michigan Press, 1996), 6–7.

9. Ammons, "A Note on Prosody," 7.

10. Ammons, "A Note on Incongruence," *Epoch* 15 (Winter 1966): 192; rpt. *Set in Motion,* 8–9.

11. Bloom, "When You Consider the Radiance," 20.

12. See Ammons, *Set in Motion,* 13, 8–9.

13. Benoit B. Mandelbrot, *The Fractal Geometry of Nature* (New York: W. H. Freeman & Co, 1983), 1.

14. Mandelbrot, *The Fractal Geometry of Nature,* 25–26.

15. Steven P. Schneider, *A. R. Ammons and the Poetics of Widening Scope* (Rutherford, N.J.: Fairleigh Dickinson University Press, 1994); see esp. chapter 4.

16. William Carlos Williams, "Spring Storm," *The Collected Poems of William Carlos Williams. Volume I, 1909–1939,* ed. A. Walton Litz & Christopher MacGowan (New York: New Directions, 1986), 54–55.

17. Harold Bloom, "When You Consider the Radiance" in Bloom, *A. R. Ammons: Modern Critical Views,* p. 31.

18. Richard Howard, "'The Spent Seer Consigns Order to the Vehicle of Change,'" *Alone with America* (New York: Atheneum, 1980), rpt. in Bloom, *A. R. Ammons,* 33–56; see p. 53.

19. David Kalstone, "Ammons' Radiant Toys," *Diacritics* 3 (Winter 1973); rpt. in Bloom, *A. R. Ammons,* 99–116; see p. 116.

20. Robert Pinsky, "Ammons," *The Situation of Poetry* (Princeton: Princeton University Press, 1976); rpt. in Bloom, *A. R. Ammons,* 185–94, see p. 191.

Ammons, Kerouac, and Their New Romantic Scrolls

Alex Albright

A. R. Ammons and Jack Kerouac share much beyond the coincidence that both typed some of their best work on scrolls. Both Ammons's *Tape for the Turn of the Year* (1965) and Kerouac's *On the Road* (1957)[1] sought an immediacy in their composition that would transcend traditional approaches to their genres—taking them and their readers into "the seething poetry of the incarnate Now." Both used the scrolls on which they typed to help force into being the seamless compositional style they hoped would free them from the poetry of "perfected bygone moments" and of the "glimmering futurity,"[2] a style that would arise out of the moment but that could flow like time itself. Yet, even as Ammons and Kerouac try in their spontaneous composition to tap into an eternally flowing *now*, their heroes try valiantly to stop time and to understand it in its many implications, to "accept Time absolutely."[3]

Tape and *Road* are more conservative versions of experiments Ammons and Kerouac conducted with composition on scrolls. *Tape* is a tighter, more controlled version of Ammons's critically maligned volume, *The Snow Poems* (1977); both seek to depict the commingling flows of tape, time, and thought, product, process and poem, and both use the moment's atmospheric conditions, its weather *right now*, as metaphor fraught with a multiplicity of meanings. *Visions of Cody* (1972) was the book Kerouac felt came closest to fulfilling the promise of the compositional method he first called "sketching" and, later, "spontaneous prose," a method Ammons freely admits having employed in most of his long poems and many of his shorter ones, but with much more critical success, generally, than Kerouac has yet to attain.

Ammons himself is the hero of *Tape*, the poem he composed on an adding-machine roll between 6 December 1963 and 10 January 1974, using each day's date as the poem's dividers. As others have noted, his is a mock-epic journey that leads him to an acceptance

of his limitations, his mortality, despite his desire that things be
different: "I wish I had a great / story to tell," he writes, but then,
as if to set out the true Sisyphean nature of his quest, he says why
he wishes this: "the / words then / could be quiet, as I'm / trying
to make them now—/ immersed in the play / of events" (T, 8).
Impossibly, the hero wishes to "get / right up next to the / break
between / what-is-to-be and / what-has-been and / dance like a
bubble / held underwater by water's / pouring in" (T, 19). He won-
ders why "can't we break loose / and live" (T, 8), and he implores
us, like Whitman, to remember our bodies: "let's touch, patiently, /
thoroughly" (T, 202); "To touch my person to some one else's is
about as much as I can stand."[4] Although Kerouac's persona, Sal
Paradise, narrates *Road,* the Neal Cassady–based character Dean
Moriarity is its hero, the one who talks "about every detail of
every moment that passed," and who knows that the only thing to
do is *go* with the energy of a jazzman's solo: that's the only way to
know time (OTR, 114, 121–22, 184–85, 194–96).[5] Cassady/Moriarty
becomes, for Kerouac, the perfect physical embodiment of what
he and Ammons sought: release "from mental / prisons into the
actual / fact, the mere / occurrence—the touched, / tasted, heard,
seen" (T, 99).

Both *Tape* and *Road* are revolts in compositional mode and in
theme against the currency of their days. "Poetry & prose had for
long time fallen into the false hands of the false," Kerouac writes;[6]
Ammons demands to "let a new / order occur / from the random
& / nondescript" (T, 17). Both play off the notions of their central
metaphors to demonstrate that, while we like to think the road
goes on forever and the tape of our days will keep uncoiling indefi-
nitely, both will end; all we really have to treasure is in front of us
right now, for we cannot know what lies in our future, if, even, we
will have a future. Thus the heightened interest on intensely feeling
what Lawrence called that "quivering momentaneity,"[7] with blow-
ing the moment up like a bubble so that we can luxuriate in its
fullness, allowing our imagination full and free range into a timeless
and eternal-seeming now, where we have *time* to touch "patiently,
thoroughly."

Ammons and Kerouac, like Whitman and Emerson, Lawrence
and Charles Olson, seek original thought, "the essence of genius,
of virtue, and of life, which we call Spontaneity or Instinct."[8] In
their respective approaches to a spontaneous poetics, Ammons
and Kerouac flaunt the traditionally held notion that true literary
art is created through carefully considered revision; and they both
glory in the celebration of the quotidian as the essential key to

understanding the sacred, or mystic. In their quest to bring to their new romanticism a heightened realism, one that rides a "moment-/to-moment crest" (T, 31) "running from one falling star to another till I drop" (OTR, 8) both Ammons and Kerouac explore their similar aesthetics, expressed by Kerouac as "the essentials of spontaneous prose."

* * *

Despite Kerouac's blustery claims to the contrary, spontaneous writing did not originate with him. Robert Hipkiss points out that Blake claimed that his "Milton" was written effortlessly, the transcription of a voice speaking to the poet, and that André Breton and the surrealists had experimented with automatic writing and free association.[9] John Tytell notes the automatic writing experiments of William James and Gertrude Stein at Harvard.[10] But such questions—did the author revise or otherwise *think* about word choice?—detract from the texts at hand, from what, ultimately, we are left to deal with: the printed words on the page, in the order that an author has placed them. Tim Hunt has demonstrated that Kerouac—despite the legend—was a careful revisionist with much of his work; *On the Road,* in fact, is but one of five very different versions of what Kerouac came to call his Road manuscript.[11] Donald Reimann notes that Ammons, in *Tape,* did not always go with whatever flow of words he found himself in, but instead made a number of aesthetic choices that "produced a work of art rather than a collage of random jottings."[12] Still, both authors used their scrolls to shape and to pace their respective manuscripts, forcing on their writing a rush of motion that delineates over and over again the infinite range of moments that comprise the continuums of our lives. Kerouac's legendary teletype roll afforded him the nonstop pacing and long rambling "sentences" that he sought as the format for plunging headlong into the spontaneous composition of his narrative; Ammons's roll of adding machine tape gave him the seamlessness he sought for his narrative, and in its boundaries prescribed for him the slim lines of his song. Ultimately, it is their unique commingling of form, format, and subject to emphasize theme that best unifies them.

Reimann also traces the history of using physical materials to shape a poem back to Homer and up through Gertrude Stein; he suggests that in *Tape* Ammons uses "form and content to echo the poem's theme: humanity must be content to go with the flow and to renounce—or downplay—systems and structures, rational constructs, in favor of untutored reality."[13] To perceive an untutored

reality, what Emerson distinguished as intuition as opposed to tui-
tion, gets us back to experiencing life beyond language and inter-
pretation, to the immediacy of vision. "[R]elease us from mental /
prisons into the actual / fact, the mere / occurrence," Ammons
writes in *Tape*. "[L]et's not make up / categories to toss ourselves /
around with" (99).

Kerouac claims to have invented the idea of a spontaneous bop
prosody in order to rewrite the first draft of *On the Road*, which
was composed in April 1951 on a very long teletype roll. He told
Allen Ginsberg that the idea, which he originally called "sketch-
ing," came to him on 25 October 1951;[14] but letters recently pub-
lished indicate he was developing his "finally-at-last-found style &
hope" earlier in the month.[15] Charters also credits Neal Cassady,
both in a famous lost letter and in his rough attempts at beginning
his own autobiography, as helping Kerouac solidify his poetics.[16]
Robert Hipkiss believes that Kerouac, in *Vanity of Duluoz* (1967),
claims a 1944 origin point for this new style. He suggests, as others
do, that precedences for spontaneous prose are to be found in
Charlie Parker's bop, Jackson Pollock's action painting, and Dylan
Thomas's organic verse.[17] Regina Weinreich credits John Clellon
Holmes with suggesting to Kerouac that he fill his "head (and page)
with everything you can think of, in its natural order."[18] Gerald
Nicosia cites Kerouac's explanation that his new "notion of writing
as Reichian release" was also an attempt to combine "Dostoyev-
sky's confessional method in *Notes from the Underground*" with
William Carlos Williams's "measured pauses of speech."[19] Wher-
ever its origin, the first draft of Kerouac's "Essentials of Spontane-
ous Prose" was composed at the request of Allen Ginsberg and
William Burroughs just after Kerouac had written *The Subterrane-
ans* on a teletype roll in three nights in 1953.[20]

Philosophically, the idea of getting outside one's consciousness
and into a stream of time, or life, that is beyond interpretation
and language, had intrigued Kerouac since his first introduction to
Buddhism, at least as early as 1950, although his readings several
years earlier of Whitman and Emerson had acquainted him with
ideas on spontaneity. He sees its aesthetic origins expressed by
Buddha, "2,500 years ago as 'The Seven Streams of Swiftness': 'If
you are desirous of more perfectly understanding Supreme Enlight-
enment, you must learn to answer questions spontaneously." He
also sees precedent in Mark 13:11: "Take no thought beforehand
what ye shall speak, neither do ye premeditate: but whatsoever
shall be given you in that hour, that speak ye: for it is not ye that
speak, but the Holy Ghost." And he notes that both Mozart and

Blake often felt "twas the 'Muse' singing and pushing."[21] Ammons's *Tape*, of course, is addressed to his muse, and the poem itself can easily be read as one long, continuous attempt by the poet to re-connect with that muse, to get back in "the river of going" (T, 191).

Kerouac also was intrigued by Lao-Tse, whose notion that "Nothing that can be said in words is worth saying" is central to Ammons's philosophy. (Ammons uses Lao-Tse's words as the epigram of his essay, "A Poem Is a Walk.") But before we can so easily dismiss the work, then, of one who has labored some fifty years with words as being "not worth saying," we should know too that Ammons sees poetry as "maybe one way of / coming home" to "silence, / restfulness from words" (T, 87). For Ammons, "non-verbal assimilations" are the "things that really draw us" to poems (SM, 47). He has acknowledged being influenced by Whitman and Emerson but has also pointed out that "my source is the same as theirs."[22] And Kerouac shares all of these influences—Lao-Tse, Blake, Whitman, Emerson, the Eastern notions of transcendence. And like Ammons, he never had much interest or trust in the American academy. Ammons wonders, for example, "what it is about critics that enables them to know so much about poetry when they obviously don't have the faintest idea how it comes about" (SM, 31); Kerouac writes: "I hadn't learned anything in college that was going to help me to be a writer anyway and the only place to learn was in my own mind. . . ."[23] Kerouac's dissatisfaction with Columbia University and its formalized traditions—coupled with his introduction into the hipster scene in New York in the late 1940s—led him to explore the notion of a spontaneous poetics that could reflect individual, untutored genius. As published in the last issue of the *Black Mountain Review* (1957), "Essentials of Spontaneous Prose" offers a way of explicating the compositional method Ammons has used in *Tape* and other poems, which helps place Ammons firmly in the company of the Beats and of those who are sometimes identified as the Black Mountain College poets, as both Alan Holder and Donald Reimann have suggested but not fully explored.[24]

Although loosely defined, the Black Mountain College poets are generally seen to have worked under Charles Olson's influence, and his 1950 essay "Projective Verse" is this group's aesthetic pronouncement.[25] Whether Olson influenced Kerouac or vice versa is not clear; most likely, they were influenced in like ways through mutual friends and ideas that were gaining currency after World War II. Hipkiss says Kerouac obviously used some of the ideas being discussed by Olson, Robert Duncan, and Robert Creeley, a core of the writers who dominated Black Mountain College in the early 1950s.[26]

In "Projective Verse," Olson makes three main points preceded by his assertion that "composition by field" is a new method of writing poems, contrasted with the "old" base of "inherited line, stanza, over-all form." He asserts that (1) "a poem is energy transferred from the poet who got it, by way of the poem itself to . . . the reader"; (2) "form is never more than an extension of content"—an idea he credits to Creeley; and (3) "[The poet should] "USE USE USE the process at all points. . . . Move, instanter, on to another." Olson also argues that the syllable (born from the "union of the mind and the ear"), not "rime and meter" or "sense and sound" should be allowed "to lead the harmony [of the poem] on." He credits Edward Dahlberg with having first instructed him that "One perception must immediately and directly lead to a further perception," which, he says, "means exactly what it says . . . keep it moving as fast as you can, citizen" (PV, 148–49). D. H. Lawrence, Holder has pointed out, was anxious for "another kind of poetry: the poetry of that which is at hand: the immediate present. . . . ," to find the "inexhaustible, forever-unfolding creative spark."[27] Duncan adds: "We begin to imagine a cosmos in which the poet and the poem are one in a moving process." He thanks projective verse for showing him that one could "derive melody and story from impulse not from plan," and he quotes Whitehead, "The present contains all that there is."[28]

The reliance of Black Mountain poets on an objectivist aesthetic has led to the occasional charge that they in general and Olson in particular are too cold and removed from nature. Yet Olson begins the conclusion of "Projective Verse" with a description that fits Ammons and his poetry perfectly:

> It comes to this: the use of a man, by himself and thus by others, lies in how he conceives his relation to nature, that force to which he owes his somewhat small existence. . . . [I]f he is contained within his nature as he is participant in the larger force, he will be able to listen, and his hearing through himself will give him secrets objects share. (PV, 156)

Ammons listens keenly—no American poet has so persistently sought to deduce the mystery in mundane objects of nature—and his poems reveal that "nature's message is, for / the special reader, / though clear, sometimes written / as on a tablet underwater" (SP, 241). That message, when things are clear, bright, sunny, and their edges distinct, might be that "nature goes so far to make us / one of a kind / and treat us all alike" (SP, 170); it might be a simple reminder that "the flawless evidence favoring / death leaves us / unconvinced / and we're ready / on no evidence / to believe we live forever" (SP, 249); or it might be an extended lesson on how to "absorb the margins: / enlarge the range: / give life room" so that we might "widen / the band / of acceptance (T, 191).

Olson is most important to understanding Ammons in his discussions of man himself as an object in a poem, and of objectivism as the "getting rid of the lyrical interference of the individual as ego, of the 'subject' and his soul, that peculiar presumption by which western man has interposed himself between what he is as a creature of nature . . . and those other creations of nature which we may . . . call objects," himself included. (PV, 156)[29] Projective verse, or composition by field, yields a relationship between poet, object, and poem that cannot be delineated; Duncan adds: "We begin to imagine a cosmos in which the poet and the poem are one in a moving process. . . ."[30] Boundaries blur, as Ammons suggests repeatedly in the natural imagery of *Tape,* much like Steven Schneider has suggested in reminding us that what we once thought of as "solid" and fixed in science, even in space-time, is both permeable and fluid. No longer does science so much recognize discrete particles as it does levels of excitation of abstract underlying fields.[31] And, to borrow from Ammons's metaphorical warehouse, from a distance, the edges of these fields blur—in seeing the one, we lose sight of the many, although they are still there—and we think, then, that what we're seeing is solid, in much the same way we think of ourselves as solid and fixed, though we know that we are not.

Ammons writes of "the circles of reach," how they expand in our lives to a certain point in a "widening circle," then begin contracting, "the gradual / shrinking" (T, 92–93). In *The Snow Poems,* he watches from his distance the action of objects in the "field" of his neighbor's lawn, where a chained dog tests the limits of his range. Ammons compares the worn ground the dog can reach with the "unworn . . . untouchable / other" (SP, 26), a boundary as real as that separating life from death, or an object from the words that describe it. But in other cases, what we believe to be peripheries are in fact the "moment-to-moment edge of growth"; given enough distance, these peripheries will blur "into nothingness" (T, 113, 104).

Kerouac, too, is intrigued with peripheries—the point where things "disappear"—in *Road,* although in his field nature rarely stands as predominately as man will, and he will usually stand for loss. Leaving New Orleans, for example, Paradise wonders, "What is that feeling when you're driving away from people and they recede on the plain till you see their specks dispersing?—it's the too-huge world vaulting us, and it's good-bye" (OTR, 148). Leaving a friend in Tucson, Paradise says, "It was sad to see his tall figure receding in the dark just like the other figures [we've left] in New York and New Orleans: they stand uncertainly underneath immense skies, and everything about them is drowned. Where go? what do? what for?" (158). As they leave Montana, Paradise and Moriarty watch a friend "recede . . . till there was nothing but a growing absence in space . . . that led all the way back to my home" in the East (252). Like Ammons, he sees how the "periphery / vanishes into nothingness / the stabilizer" (T, 104).

But where Olson is helpful for contemplating a philosophy behind Ammons's imagery (and for explaining, too, what Vendler has noted as his lack of adjectives), Kerouac's spontaneous poetics is better suited for exploring Ammons's actual method of composition, not just in *Tape for the Turn of the Year,* but in much of his poetry. Ammons has said, "I was in South Jersey at the time [1963] of *T[ape] for the T[urn] of the Year,* and I don't know if I was aware of the automatic-extemporaneous writing of Kerouac. I guess I was beat, but not Beat."[32] Yet, consider how closely the two writers explain what Kerouac called the first of his nine essential steps, "the set up." Kerouac says that the poet must first have an "image-object . . . set before the mind either in reality . . . or in memory" (ESP, 69). Ammons ascribes such a beginning to his long poems, including *Tape:* "When I found a single image that could sustain multiplicity, I usually could begin to write" (SM, 102). Over his career, the most powerfully realized of these images have been the adding machine tape, the earth as seen from outer space, snow, and a garbage dump.

But the image that most dominates Ammons's poetry goes back to his experience in the navy, at age nineteen, of looking from the bow of a ship to a distant horizon at

the line inscribed across the variable land mass, determining where people would or would not live, where palm trees would or could not grow. . . . The whole world changed as a result of an interior illumination: the water level was not what it was because of a single command by a higher power but because of an average result of a host of actions—runoffs, wind currents, melting glaciers. I began to apprehend things in the dynamics of themselves. . . . (SM, 95)[33]

That line of water's level, of course, is the dominant image of the title poem of Ammons's second collection, *Expressions of Sea Level;* it and its variations will inform much of the rest of his poetry, including *Tape, The Snow Poems, Garbage* (1993), *Brink Road* (1996), and many of the individual poems he's published along the way: "into the salt marshes the water comes fast with rising tide: / an inch of rise spreads by yards / through tidal creeks, round fingerway of land: . . . is there a point of rest where / the tide turns: is there one / infinitely tiny higher touch / on the legs of egrets . . ." (ESL, 31).

In addition to giving him an image to contemplate for a lifetime, the question of where and when the sea levels neatly wraps up for Ammons two interrelated themes that permeate his work: (1) our natural boundaries are not truly fixed once we see the edges of their growth (or decay, a sort of "growth" towards nothingness), which we cannot see if we distance ourselves too far away—distance, we might say, makes the edge seem solid; and (2) we should seek the appropriate "zones" where each of us "do best in" (T, 53). These leave us with the notion that nature, especially its weather, affords us a limitless supply of metaphors with which to explore "centers & peripheries / in motion, / organic, interrelations" (T, 112). In *Tape,* Ammons considers these questions in "the slow accretion of hard rock"; sunshine and shade alternating; the line between surf and shore; and the transformation of water into ice, to name but a few (T, 14, 24, 175, 149, 171).

Olson says in "Projective Verse" that "objects which occur in every given moment of composition (of recognition, we can call it)" must be treated as they occur in the poem, and not by ideas outside the poem. They "must be handled as a series of objects in field in such a way that a series of tensions (which they also are) are made to hold, and to hold exactly inside the content and the context of the poem which has forced itself, through the poet and them, into being" (152). Ammons is playing directly in Olson's field when he begins the third day of *Tape* with this declaration of fact derived from a *negative* field: "the way I could tell / today / that yesterday is dead / is that / the little gray bird / that sat in the empty / tree / yesterday is gone" (T, 11). *Tape,* throughout, is a series of "tensions" observed by the poet in the moments he witnesses passing: "can a lip quiver with / more need / . . . than now?" (T, 87). Ammons continues to combine the weighted object with fluid moments captured, frozen and examined, on December 28, noting parenthetically "(just now, the / thorns / are black / against the wall)" (T, 117). And, over and over, we are made to wait, tensely, to see what happens next: Will the water turn to ice? Will the leaf turn over? Will the sun drop behind a cloud, obliterating thorn's shadow—the object itself? In Ammons's tape, we see levels of tensions, too, in the pull of tape through typewriter, "the centers & peipheries / in motion, / organic" (T, 112).

Kerouac's "procedure," the second essential, recommends writing with the "undisturbed flow from the mind of personal secret idea-words, blowing (as per jazz musician) on subject of image" (ESP, 69). *Tape* is, essentially, one long jazz blowing on the search for idea-words that will get the poet back in touch with his Muse, where "only the lively use of language lives" (176). Each day's notations contain undisturbed flow, although on some days the flow gets disturbed, as all flows ultimately must—too many intervals break up the road, Ammons writes in *The Snow Poems* (19)—but "all this is just coming / out of my head" (T, 47).

Ammons told an interviewer in 1984 that "my first drafts would indicate that my best poems . . . come almost as they are" (SM, 42). He explains that he attempts to write a complete poem at a first sitting—"I try to let that happen spontaneously"—and adds:

> [I]n the long essay poems and in *The Snow Poems,* and earlier in the *Tape for the Turn of the Year* . . . I tested my ability to say it right the first time in a long poem. . . . [T]hat is an exaggerated test to place on oneself but if it does come right somehow it has a . . . necessary quality to it that seems inevitable; it seems that there was something taking place in the mind and there was no difference between that and what happened on the page and so it just became itself. (SM, 43)

Realistically, the simultaneous describing of imagery or thought as it flashes by in a flickering moment is, of course, impossible. The lightning Ammons observes in *Tape* on December 8 flashes and is gone ("just flashed") before the poet can finish typing the word (15). Still, Ammons finds himself "running to catch up: to / be at the / crest's break, the / running crest, / event becoming word" (T, 37). To help indicate that flow in the artifice of story-on-paper, Kerouac's "method" suggests "no periods separating sentence-structures" but offers dashes as alternative. He composed his first Road scroll with dashes only; he remarks in *Vanity of Dulouz,* "Insofar as nobody loves my dashes anyway, I'll use regular punctuation for the new illiterate generation."[34] Ammons has been luckier with his colons: nobody changes them to periods for him, and critics can talk about how democratic they are, how they fit—like Kerouac's dashes—with the flow of his poems, indicating for us the "measured pauses which are the essentials of our speech" and "divisions of the sounds we hear" (ESP, 69). Olson, however, goes after more than mere punctuation marks: "Do not tenses, must they not also be kicked around anew, in order that time, that other governing absolute may be kept, as must the space-tensions of a poem, immediate, contemporary to the acting-on-you of the poem?" (PV, 152). Ammons doesn't so much kick verb tenses around as kick them *out* on occasion, allowing particular phrases special emphasis without verbs, separated on either side by colons: "a spinning of diameter into / nothingness: exclusions: lepers on their islands . . ." or "raining: / at the borderline & / promise / of snow" (T, 59, 150), for example.

Ammons has also been much luckier with critical reception to his spontaneous poems. Weinreich and others have noted how the main controversy over the quality of Kerouac's prose has "always been centered around the basic tenets of his writing philosophy, especially those that preclude the writer's essential control: revision."[35] Truman Capote's oft-repeated charge—that's not writing, that's typing—could easily be leveled against *Tape* and other Ammons poems, by the poet's own admission; but although occasional critics have commented negatively on Ammons's "doodling," most have agreed that *Tape* is an important poem. Kerouac suffers, perhaps, from his insistence on thumbing his nose at the literary establishment; Ammons, on the other hand, has operated for much of his career from within the academy, so his taunts are not as threatening. Ammons, like Kerouac, seems to have "gotten sick and tired of the conventional English sentence which seemed to me so ironbound in its rules." Kerouac came to detest what he saw as the "shameful" process of revision; to revise meant that the writer was ashamed of what had just been written. He saw craft and revision as antithetical to art, as "laborious and dreary lying," the "sheer blockage" of the spontaneous mental process that might allow the writer to "finally say something we never heard before." He made these proclamations over and over in the last years of his desperate career, and they are what he is remembered for, not his recognition of the "delicate balancing point between bombast and babble."[36] Ammons, on the other hand, has written his lyrics as well as his long poems in his own doggedly individualistic fashion; he's made few statements on poetics, the most prominent of which are collected in *Set in Motion*. He has opted for the spontaneous and original but has done so quietly, all the while garnering increasing critical acclaim.

As if to emphasize that his lessons in technique are really variations on the same notion, three of Kerouac's essentials, "Scoping,"

"Lag in Procedure," and "Timing," reiterate the importance of "following free deviation (association) of mind into limitless blow-on-subject seas of thought with no pause to think of proper word," and "no revisions" (ESP, 70). Both *Tape* and especially *The Snow Poems* (as well as *Road* and much else of Kerouac's work) have been assailed by critics for their inclusion of material deemed, by the critics, as being extraneous. *Tape* includes "verbal doodling . . . from time to time to feed the empty page";[37] *The Snow Poems* contains "mental garbage . . . graffiti."[38] Vendler, although generally impressed, complains that in *Tape* "there is also a trust that everything you do, like everything the weather does, has its part in the configuration of the whole."[39] These complaints basically attack Ammons for his lack of revision; yet, for him, these "doodlings" are an integral part of the whole, and an essential part of spontaneous poetics. Of *Tape,* he has admitted, "The material itself seemed secondary; it fulfilled its function whether it was good or bad material just by occupying space. In many ways the arbitrary was indistinguishable from the functional" (SM, 102). Both *Tape* and *The Snow Poems,* then, are exercises in a "free association of mind" as Ammons explores the myriad ways of figuring out "time and how to note it down" (OTR, 69); both are riddled throughout with time indicators and expressions of what is happening *right now* in front of the poet; that event-object is the (sometimes floating) center of each poetic sequence and the start of another experiment in spontaneous poetics of free-associational responses.

Using a tape to compose *Tape* was, of course, intended to allow Ammons as close an access as possible to "the going tension / that holds us, / suspends, rises, & falls, / the going on" (T, 177). In that suspension, we can meditate, go back in memory, forward in dream, or we can watch wide-eyed as "a drop forms at the / icicle-tip, tapers, pulls / free, rounds-up . . . / breaks free . . . / the precise event . . . / when it hits the ground" (T, 171). That Ammons, too, could not have been working toward the moment when his tape ends unless it had been for his typewriter seems on the surface, perhaps, pointless to mention; but in 1950 Olson believed that the typewriter had advantages that had not been used "sufficiently." He found it ironic that this machine would lead "directly on toward projective verse and its consequences"; but he saw that, "due to its rigidity and its space precisions, it can, for a poet, indicate exactly the breath, the pauses, the suspensions of syllables, the juxtapositions even of parts of phrases, which he intends. For the first time the poet has the stave and the bar a musician has had" (PV, 154).

One of the most evocative examples of Ammons's movement in
Tape, through streams of consciousness triggered by poetic images
associating freely in his mind, is December 17th's entry. It begins
with the retelling of Sisyphus's story. In Ammons's version, he
quits his task, throws down his rock, and lets "out a / cry of joy
that / rang through the / valley / mixing with stone-thunder" (77).
Using "rang" to suggest perhaps a cash register, he segues, with a
couple of cents marks as an indicator of a break in the text, into
an extended rumination on Christmas trees that shifts from an
indictment of commercialized holiday customs ("everything differ-
ent / now & sort of loused up"), into a poignant recollection of
childhood Christmases: "we had no electricity but / we had pine-
cones & / colored paper & / some tinsel: it / was beautiful enough: /
it was very lovely: / and it's lost." Out of the reverie comes a
crashing reality: "now, a tree from / somewhere—maybe Ver-
mont—/ got by handing over / two or three green / pcs of paper."
A line of dollar signs follows, breaking the text before the poet
asks, "do you hear me, Sisyphus, / durn you? do you hear me /
groan: / like: / wow." (T, 79–81) "Wow!" Kerouac echoes in *Road*,
over and over again: "the only Word I had was Wow!" (38).

Kerouac's "Center of Interest," the seventh of his essentials,
suggests that the poet "begin not from preconceived idea of what
to say . . . but from jewel center of interest in subject of image at
moment of writing" (ESP, 70). As noted, Ammons has needed that
"jewel center of interest," one that can "sustain multiplicity," in
order to begin his long poems especially. Although the roll of tape
is one literal center of interest for Ammons, *Tape* is more about
the subject of poetry, so much and so intensely that at one point,
on December 15, he writes of the poem as subject having become
object: "My poem went for a ride / today: I / backgutted it all /
the way out / of the typewriter, / rewinding the roll, / stuck it in a
paper / bag, then in the / glove compartment: / we all went to York,
Pa. / to visit relatives." By the time he's then writing, 10 p.m., he's
returned to Ithaca and "reinserted & rewound: / I'm beat" (T,
70–71) Ammons's physical tape also has, as a center of interest,
its own center, "organic, in motion," with peripheries constantly—
at least when the poet writes—in flux. "look! / there's the red ink
rising from the / floor," Ammons writes as his tape nears its end;
and we see then that the poem arises out of—is created from—the
consumption of the tape, which rises like a Phoenix, only to be
relegated once again into "trash," into the "unity of its / conflicts"
(T, 10).

Ammons most differs from the literalness of both Kerouac's and Olson's poetics in one key way. They both insist on a poetic "line" as related to the natural motions of speech and pauses; Ammons, in *Tape* and *The Snow Poems,* uses the vertical linearity of his medium to go beyond *suggesting* a flow to *becoming* flow itself. He is, then, using "line" in a an even newer way, one that suggests *time's* flow and pauses, not speech's.

Ammons is fond of using the numerical stating of time's present as though he is taunting his readers with the duality inherent in a Western mind trying to think in Eastern concepts. He told one interviewer, "I have tried to get rid of the Western tradition as much as possible" (SM, 105); but time's marking is one tradition he cannot escape. Helga Nowotny notes that "[s]ince the 1880s, psychologists had been in search of the duration of the present," and that William James's formulation of 1890—that time is 'a stream of thought'—showed the present to be more like a 'saddle-back' than a knife's edge, having as each moment has 'a certain breadth of its own . . . from which we look in two directions." Time is more than just a fleeting moment, because it is "dense enough to perceive more than just one event, to hear more than just one melody" simultaneously. She also discusses how Western culture developed its systems of uniform time measurement, culminating in 1884 with the international time conference that established the world's twenty-four time zones.[40] Herbert Rappaport believes that the Western mind sees time as a line, with a past, present, and future, so that we can be led forward into "progress." He sees in our insistence that time is linear and not circular "inherent anxieties" that account "for much of the stress of modern Western society." Non-Westerners, he asserts, are able to experience time as circular, in waves that do not "lose" time to the past but simply move events "to another point in the cycle."[41]

Ammons discusses how he started *Tape* in a 1996 interview: "I had been thinking of having the primary motion of the poem down the page rather than across. . . . Soon after I started . . . I noticed resemblances between it and a novel. The point, like and unlike a novel, was to get to the other end; an arbitrary end would also be an 'organic' end" (SM, 101–2). Ammons calls the "tape itself" the "hero" in his novelistic poem (SM, 192). The unrolling poem itself—its "endless unfolding of words," as Whitman said—is also a dominant image of the text, which continually addresses variations on "the circles of reach / . . . always / the widening circle" as well as "the gradual[ly] shrinking" one (T, 92–93). But circles for Ammons are also containers, barriers that he wants to transcend into a wholeness: "Absorb the margins," he urges (T, 91); observe "the moment-to-moment edge / of growth" and "let centers / proliferate / from / self-justifying motions!" (T, 113, 116).

If, as Ammons suggests, the tape itself is the hero of *Tape*, then the story's climax, say, would occur simultaneously to the tape as hero, the tape as object-subject, and the poet; throw in "reader," who's *there* at the same time as the rest of them, and that's potentially one heck of a simultaneous orgasm. But Ammons teases us with climaxes: at the mid-point, he says "I admit / I've shot my load" and pleads for a second chance: "give / me a second wind: / it's there, I'm sure / of it, somewhere in the / mind—another valve to / open: / let it open & / fill this tape / plentifully up" (T, 101).

The last of Kerouac's nine elements of spontaneous poetics, "Mental State," urges, "write excitedly, swiftly . . . in accordance (as from center to periphery) with laws of orgasm . . . Come from within, out" to the "relaxed, said" (ESP, 70). Much of *Tape* is addressed directly to the poet's seductive Muse; on December 11, he asks her, "who are you / anyhow? some kind of a / prickteaser?" But things work out well for them: a couple of weeks later he urges her to "come again / and make your will in me. . . ." After the mid-point "climax," Ammons proclaims, "the volcano shoots & / rests, gathering" (101). Later, on the last day of *Tape*, he notes that "somehow in taking / pleasure / from yr body, / I have given you / my heart: / I care now / more for you than for / the pleasure you give / me: you, your total / self, my anchorage: / the universe shifts its / center: / it turns about you" (T, 198).

Climaxes, of course, are pivots, and in his eighth essential Kerouac suggests in addressing the "structure of your work" that in your "mindflow" you arrive at the "pivot, where what was dim formed beginning becomes sharp-necessitating ending and language shortens in race to wire of time-race of work" (ESP, 70). Ammons, from a "dim-formed beginning," sees his tape as an "epic" task, the tape moving almost imperceptibly at its beginning. By New Year's eve, nearly a month into it, he finds the empty tape is still imposing, frightening: "the unconscious will / have to act out / several more shows / before the marginal red / ink / warns it's time / for a new tape" (T, 145). But the pivot arrives; the red ink rises from the floor. Ammons searches for pivotal points, too, in much of his imagery; he especially likes getting inside the bubble of the pivotal moment and watching it equivocate, *not* change: On December 10, he awaits the turn to winter, which "seems about to, but hasn't / quite decided how to / happen" (T, 24); on January 1, it's "raining: / at the borderline & / promise / of snow" (T, 150);

and he spends a couple of pages anticipating the moment that a leaf might finally turn over (T, 170–72). We never find out if the leaf turns; it's left flapping in time, pinned *there* to a rock in the poet's back yard, in a tension that's lasted long past leaf's decomposition.

Kerouac's last stage—"mental state"—also defines this idea of writing as one that uses a new language, one that conscious art would censor. Ammons, too, is "looking for a level / of language / that could take in all / kinds of matter" (T, 142–43), because "only the lively use of / language lives" (T, 176). Olson, like Kerouac and Ammons, is also intrigued by the untapped potentials of language. He says that "*all* parts of speech suddenly, in composition by field, are fresh for both sound and percussive use, spring up like unknown, unnamed vegetables in the patch, when you work it, come spring" (PV, 153). Ammons has already been generally credited with adding scientific language to contemporary poetic language, yielding in the process Steven Schneider's book, which discusses Ammons's use of anatomy, archaeology, astronomy, behavioral optometry, biology, botany, chemistry, ecology, geology, relativity, quantum physics, statistics, and zoology, not just in terms of language but also Ammons's use of scientific metaphors. Schneider also discusses "rheomode" (from the Greek meaning "to flow"), a new language proposed by Larry Dossey, "to be consistent with physics' understanding of reality."[42] Such a language might approximate the flow that Ammons and Kerouac sought to re-create in their scrolls, although Kerouac's, with its traditional paragraphing and punctuation imposed by editorial dictum, loses some of its intended flow and much of its experimental nature. Ammons's use of language, especially his sentence and phrase constructions, is a much closer approximation of how poetry in "rheomode" might be composed, in a truly new language that operates at associational levels that break down the subject/verb and subject/object dualities inherent in how we learn to use our existing language.

What Ammons achieves in *Tape for the Turn of the Year* is what Kerouac sought, as the ideal, in his spontaneous poetics, which are, for Kerouac, best demonstrated in the highly experimental *Visions of Cody*. For *Road*, despite its compositional method, is still a retelling of a very linear narrative, out of the narrator's past. *Cody*, on the other hand, employs verbatim tape recordings and lots of sketching to "restructure time and space beyond" the "fiction" of traditional narrative form.[43] The result is a circular, rather than linear design, which approximates how we actually experience time as it flows: moments are blown up into larger significances, time sometimes slows down in them and at other times speeds up. In each moment's "saddle," we are sometimes able to "dwell in the ongoing, onbreaking wave" in a "symmetry of actions" that gets us into the "effortless harmony of things" (SM, 21). Ammons captures a multiplicity of such moments in both *Tape* and *The Snow Poems.*

*   *   *

"There's no news like snow news."
                                                    —A.R. Ammons
"Hast thou entered into the treasures of the snow?"
                                                    —Job 38:22

The Snow Poems, as Steven Schneider points out, met with "almost unanimous disapproval" when it was published in 1977.[44] Today, it is long since out of print and virtually impossible to discuss for other reasons as well. Helen Vendler and Michael McFee have offered its most sympathetic readings, Vendler suggesting that it "needs to be lived in for days, reread after the first reading has sorted out its preoccupations and methods, and used as a *livre de chevet* if its leisurely paths are to be followed in their waywardness." Vendler recognizes, it seems, how *The Snow Poems* echoes Ammons's essay "A Poem Is a Walk." And she hears the poet's "voice reasonable in loss" evidence of an "eviscerated Ammons, doggedly writing down the weather day after day . . . Beckett-like, hard on himself as ice." Yet, Vendler still chides him for his excesses, finding parts of the book "annoying," evidence of the poet's "distracting habit of doodling on the typewriter."[45]

Both McFee and Vendler have, like others, remarked on the compositional, prosaic, and thematic similarities between *The Snow Poems* and *Tape,* which was much more generally praised (and remains in print). McFee refers to *The Snow Poems'* "testy reception" as being evidence of readers' general inability to appreciate "being spilled on their fine-fannies." He calls it "antiformalist," but it is also anti-*poetry* and he goes on to make an excellent case for the rereading of *The Snow Poems* that Vendler recommends, referring to it along the way as audacious, contentious, garrulous, moody, unpredictable, and "even more radical" than *Tape.* McFee uses Ammons's descriptions of *The Snow Poems,* taken from its early pages (17–18), to refer back to it as a puzzler, sleeper, a tiresome business that nobody can make any sense of, a shindig, fracas, uproar, high shimmy uncompletable.

McFee also sees, like Vendler, how *The Snow Poems* "shows us the dark side of Ammons's radiant sublimity."[46]

Yet, despite the near polar critical responses to *Tape* and *The Snow Poems*—*Tape* seems generally well-liked despite its doodling, while complaints about the doodling seem to dominate critical views of *The Snow Poems*—they are simply different versions of the same notion, as Ammons so frequently has tried to establish in his poems' images, and they are these different versions in a multiplicity of ways. When seen together, they show that looking at the one, or the few, loses the perspective of the larger view, the many, and the larger view, conversely, loses the focus of the closer one. And they must be looked at together, for *The Snow Poems* is a *Tape* from a larger perspective than *Tape*'s clearly delineated plot—I'm going to type this poem till the tape runs out—and time markers: *Tape*, of course, is divided into thirty-three sections according to the consecutive days of its composition, from 6 December 1963 to 10 January 1964, and it talks often of one year's ending, another's beginning. *The Snow Poems*, however, is the larger chronicle of *season's* change, as well as of one man's change at middle-age. These are the larger contexts, then, of *Tape*'s specific one: not just one calendar year changing (and not just one book coming out, either, for *The Snow Poems* presages in both theme and imagery *Garbage*, "Ridge Farm," and *Glare*, Ammons's most recent book-length poem), but one man's epochal, pivotal move cast against the larger backdrop of the march through the ending and beginning of yet another cycle of life. These are the ways Ammons's images work best: in multiplicities, impossible to pin down precisely, one wheel within another, centers moving about and peripheries crossing into planes that surprise us. It's a wearisome move, annually, the agony of waking up seeds' dormant forces, the release of nature's flows, both in life-giving energy and life-giving water turned loose from frozen snows, moment by moment, drop by drop; and it's wearying to suddenly find one's self old, and to realize that the "crest due . . . to arrive" has already "arrived or isn't coming, not / ever coming" (SP, 2).

Tape has dates to signify its neat and orderly march through linear time, a notion as comfortable to Western minds as stanzas. But what does snow, the weather, care for such time? It holds time—at least linear time, as we know it, in abeyance. And in *The Snow Poems*, the poet holds us, too, in the tense circle of becoming that doesn't always become either snow, or poem, but sometimes dissipates into thin air, or doodling.

Ammons has said: "[Poems] are not written to be studied or discussed, but to be encountered, and to become standing points that we can come to and try to feel out, impressionistically, what this poem is recommending" (SM, 58). Yet, we continue to study and discuss them. But with *The Snow Poems*, Ammons has finally accomplished writing a poem we can't easily discuss without, it seems, first dismissing it. (He's also said, of course, that he'd prefer silence to poems, yet he's continued to write them, because "I can't do anything else" [T, 58]; critics, it might be said, operate under the same imperative.) Few critics thus far have been very forgiving of Ammons's excesses in *The Snow Poems*, which will grow increasingly offensive to policers of correct speech—what to do, say, with poems titled "Things Change, the Shit Shifts," images of "hairpie dinners," wishes of "better laid than never or up," aphorisms such as "sores run / scabs / stay put" (SP, 4, 73, 154, 182). What can we make of a poet who says, elegaically, that a poem is a walk, but then turns around and says that "on the walk a fart worked its / way loose" (SP, 177)? He would be a hard poet to talk about in classrooms, especially if other passages make those above look rather tame—wildness in language that gets, as Whitman said of himself, "hankering, mystical, gross, and nude." Which, of course, is the point: Ammons is putting up, in *The Snow Poems*, to back up all his poetics-talk: "Our experience of poetry is least injured when we accept it as useless, meaningless, and nonrational" (SM, 19), and "Nothing that can be said about it in words is worth saying" (SM, 20).

The Snow Poems is a flaunting of critical intrusion—verbal intrusion—into the experience of encountering a poem. Ammons's general disdain for critics is plain from both his prose and poems, especially *Tape* and *The Snow Poems*, which contains a truly violent attack on contemporary criticism in the form of the quotidian narrative arranged, at its beginning, in six regular stanzas of tercets. "I cut the quince down the other day into so / many stalks it all made a big bundle / upon the lawn high as my head I'd say" it begins (9), in an ironic deconstruction of "The Quince Bush." While cleaning his yard, he's cleaning up the landscape of his poems, taking away the symbol we've wanted to play with: "quince" suggestive of Stevens, quince as leafless but thorny as it blossoms. The experience of dismantling his quince leads him to "whiff . . . eighty times, / the universal smell of rotten meat" that a dead blue jay has brought to the scene of the poet's walk in "Here I Sit, Fifty in the." Here, significantly, as the poet sits in the bubble of turning that critical age, that pivot, the regular stanzas cease, and the poet will not go back to them for the remainder of the book. Immediately after we've been hit with the smell of death, the stanzaic structure of the narrative disintegrates: "I do not, can not, will not / care for plain simple things / with straightforward fences round them" (9).

The act of the poet cutting down—literally deconstructing—the predominant image of several of his poems is one of protest; but over the stench of death, and after he has gotten out of the straightforward fences of stanzas, he finds "a live jay lit on the pearlimb (pearl imb) / over the dead jay / . . . shrieked . . . / a scolding for dying / or grief trying to make itself heard" (SP, 10). We might wonder if the "jay" of "Sight Seed" might be the same jay of "Winter Scene," the one that can turn a winter's bare branches blue. But we can be sure that the dead, stinking jay is equivalent to what Ammons thinks of theory. This version of Ammons's attack on theory and interpretation is much harsher than *Tape*'s playful observation: "look: it's snowing . . . / without theory / and beyond help . . . / I see black & / white . . . / if I were / looking with the snow, / I'd see all white" (T, 100). But it remains consistent with other notions: "Writing about the stone cannot replace the stone" (SM, 32), and "the only representation / of the sea's floor / is the sea's floor itself" (T, 184).

So it would seem natural that critics might not like the larger view of things, the harsher one that *The Snow Poems* represents, but one that's needed to understand *Tape*'s larger contexts more forcefully, beyond the intellectualizing *Tape* allows us. *The Snow Poems* pushes us into a much more brutal confrontation with the ideas we are more comfortable with in *Tape*'s niceties. Still, both poems recommend—insist—that we pay attention to the weather. *Tape* does it in its controlled fashion, but *The Snow Poems* explores it in its intensity in ways organically different from *Tape*'s successful use of the adding machine tape to "grow" itself. Where *Tape* seeks to become "a long / thin / poem / employing certain / classical considerations" (1) on an adding machine tape the poet has purchased at a hardware store, *The Snow Poems,* in its first poem, "Words of Comfort," announces that it will be "a drone, narrative, longer than mourning." (SP, 1). We don't know how long this dirge is going to go on, and we're thrust uneasily into a world that's "misty drizzling" (SP, 1). Sometimes, it will seem, we'll find ourselves in a sort of perverse Hallmark-Cards writers' workshop, where aphorisms might sound churchy but just as likely will be as earthy as the "whiff of earthworm" (22)

But whereas the task of *Tape* proves do-able, not Sysiphean after all, the original task of *The Snow Poems* proved impossible:

I had meant to write a book of a thousand pages. . . . I wanted to say here is a thousand pages of trash that nevertheless indicates that every image and every event on the planet and everywhere else is significant and could be great poetry, sometimes is in passages and lines. But I stopped at 300. I had worn myself and everybody else out. But I went on long enough to give the idea that we really are in a poetically inexhaustible world, inside and out. (SM, 66)

Both *The Snow Poems* and *Tape* reiterate Ammons's dominant metaphors taken directly from the atmosphere that we live in (though *The Snow Poems* has a lot more time, and thus weather, to play with, for the poet to watch): the settling into levels, or zones, that belies the illusion of distinctness, of fixity, and proves flux and flow, growth and decay. Weather itself becomes—as the poet wishes it to become—a perfect metaphor for proving the inexhaustible source of poetry about us. It controls not only the elements that we take for our symbols, the objects in the world about us, obscuring, rearranging, sculpting what we see, but also us, when we're not too removed from it. Schneider quotes one critic of *The Snow Poems*, who said, "We talk about the weather when we are self-conscious or embarrassed, when we are looking for distractions, and when we want to break the awkward silence of having nothing at all to say."[47] She was probably not a farmer, and self-depracatingly Ammons might say to her, in his courtly fashion, should they meet, "people who have a life / to live don't notice weather" (SP, 93). But under his breath, he'd just as likely say, "when we / have nothing / significant / to say / spelling it / right matters" (SP, 65).

This is the kind of critical attitude that no doubt troubles poets such as Ammons, whose experience is so radically different from that of most academics. He has said plainly, "I had wanted to stay a farmer. . . . I love the land and the terrible dependency on the weather. . . . [M]y life and my family and people around me depended on weather and seasons and farming and seeds and things like that" (SM, 60, 105). Yet, the assertion of the individual critic's view—in this case the bold cliché quoted above, assuming that "we" talk of weather only when "we" have nothing to say—as a universal one denies the individual experience that Ammons seeks in his poetry. For him, clearly, weather has lots of meaning, import, and whether we learn to appreciate it or not, we should, it seems, at least give him credit for being passionate in his weather obsessions and, perhaps, look a second time at what he *does* with weather, which sometimes, for *some* people, might be the *only* thing worth talking about, despite what the occasional critic might believe.

Still, good intentions don't necessarily make good poetry, as *The Snow Poems'* critics should all be quick to agree, though clearly they'd not be of one accord in defining "good." But that, for Ammons, would seem to be how he'd prefer things to be, for *The Snow Poems* was written as an affront to critical dissecting of poetry. McFee calls it "anti-formalist," but it's really more anti-poetry, at least in the sense of how poetry is taught and discussed in universities. Olson, the Black Mountain poets, and the Beats—Kerouac and William Burroughs especially—fall outside the realm of *how* we learned to think about literature. In their push for the spontaneous and the new, they have dug new critical furrows yet to be fully explored. Ammons is clearly playing in their collective "fields."

As if giving example of Kerouac's insistence that we not pause to think of "proper" words, Ammons at one point in *The Snow Poems* writes "whiff of earthworm / (I almost said earthroom)" (22–23). Critics have generally disregarded *The Snow Poems* because of such "doodling," which Ammons took to a new level by including "his second thoughts in the margin" of some poems.[48] What he has also done in these instances, where lines run in parallel columns, is create a tension within the physical body of his poem that is constant, what Olson had sought in the use of objects in his. Ammons also suggests in his special arrangement of text blocks on the physical page the cut-up methods and permutated sentence experiments of William S. Burroughs and Brion Gysin, both of which employ "the principle of randomness" and seek creation of art through "the success of its own accident."[49] Like Ammons, Burroughs is intrigued by "how word and image get around on very . . . complex association lines." Burroughs calls "The Waste Land" the first "great cut-up collage," notes that Tristan Tzara did similar work, and that Dos Passos uses the same idea of incorporating the artist's collage method into writing to produce "The Camera Eye" sections of *U.S.A.* "Cut-ups," he explains, "establish new connections between images, and one's range of vision consequently expands."[50]

Ammons also goes beyond the literal, linear reading we yearn to give to words on a page when he employs in the physical arrangement of text-blocks a kind of concrete poetry that represents, in its visual display on the page, the flow of rivers, the play of tides, and the breakup of geological forces. Schneider notices a similar technique in "Ridge Farm," with its text blocks "resembling the irregularities of topology on a ridge."[51] But when we've been trained to seek in writing coherence and flow of logic, not image and association, it's difficult to maintain the distance required to "look" anew at a printed page, to drop back for a moment and study how Ammons, for example, displays "Hard Fist" in *The Snow Poems* (44–47), a section representative of both the collage, or cut-up, technique and the topographic display.

Ammons's *The Snow Poems* is a rugged version of *Tape,* more graphic and mournful and tragic. In *Tape,* the poet recognizes, finally, that "it's as brave to accept / boundaries, / . . . & do the best you can" (T, 201); its ending is final, with the curl of its tape: "so long" (T, 205). *The Snow Poems,* on the other hand, ends enigmatically, on-goingly, an obvious fragment and thus, again, more difficult to discuss. Given the extent and range of the poet's word play throughout, its last line, the single word "we(l)come" might translate as "we'll come," "well, come," "we/I come," or "welcome," as an ironic response to the critical "thank you" the poet knows he will not receive.

Given past criticisms of *The Snow Poems,* it may not return to print anytime soon. Both it and *Tape* are important poems to consider together because they provide a core for seeing virtually all of Ammons's work as one vast poem about his own personal poetic sense of wonder and exploration. Willard Spiegelman has already noted that the differences in Ammons's long poems and his lyrics are quantitative only, that otherwise his poems, "from the very beginning" have not changed or developed, "formally or technically, in any significant ways.[52] Although both books have been discussed as diaries, Ammons has not yet been looked at as an autobiographical poet, perhaps because the poetry of his autobiography is not of days of momentous import; future biographers will find little of significance to report, based on the facts of the poet's life, as revealed in his poems. Kerouac, on the other hand, is most easily dismissed, when he's dismissed, by charges that he writes autobiography, not literature, that he has no aesthetic at work beyond the spewing of words on a page. Kerouac's are certainly bigger stories, his characters grander than a store clerk chanced to meet, their narratives more pressing and frantic than a casual walk to a brook, or the gentle play of sunshine and shade on a wall. Ammons, who employs the same aesthetic but doesn't talk about it nearly as much, remains firmly ensconced—at least with his shorter lyrics—in those arbiters of American lit, the college textbooks, as he has for the last twenty-five years.

Still, Kerouac's *On the Road* is an important book for what it says about the boundaries of America; critics have yet to notice, for example, how the main characters find the "wilderness" of modern America to be in its roads, which—like jazz—afford for them the same access to an eternal now that Emerson found in the woods. They bounce off the "walls" of America like Melville's Bartleby looking for a place to be, some thing to do. Nor have they caught yet what seems an essential part of Kerouac's story, the home his narrator always returns to when things collapse into sadness, as they always do at their ends. Ammons, in *Tape*, might be writing that alternate version, "*Off* the Road." He says, for example, that his "story is how / a man comes home / from haunted / lands and transformations" (T, 9). He doesn't need the "going" of Kerouac's road, because he has already felt "the bitterness of fate: / what it means to / drive away from the / house" (60).

Both Kerouac and Ammons are working with variations of what M. M. Bakhtin referred to as the road chronotope, which "permits everyday life to be realized" within its narrative. Bakhtin's idea of "chronotope" comes, as he explains it, from science, indicating for us the temporal and spatial relationships that are artistically expressed in literature. Like Einstein's theory of relativity—and rheomode—it indicates for us that space and time are inseparable, that time is the fourth dimension of space. Bakhtin's discussion is clearly directed to classical forms of literature, but his definition of "adventure-time" in novels (whose traits he also sees in drama and epic poems) seems perfectly suited as descriptive of both Ammons's and Kerouac's work: Moments of adventure time occur when the normal course of events is interrupted, providing an opening for the intrusion of nonhuman forces, which then take the initiative. The temporal marker, for Bakhtin, is inseparable from the spatial marker. In using the chronotope of the road, the writer permits everyday life to be realized within his narrative; choice controls the path he will take. However, once on the path, chance encounters predominate. The *Tape for the Turn of the Year* and *The Snow Poems*, like *Visions of Cody*, combine elements of what Bakhtin, using Dante's *Inferno* as example, calls a "vertical chronotope," which is a world outside of time's flow, with one where spatial and temporal coordinates define human fates. Bakhtin's "road" is formed when time fuses with space and flows in it; it is "both a point of new departures and a place for events to find their denouement."[53] Both Kerouac and Ammons sometimes take that new departure into a bubble of time that holds itself, for a while, outside the flow, in vertical time.

Ammons in his poems and Kerouac, in *Vision of Cody* especially, demonstrate that the notion of a "denouement" might not so easily apply to life as it does to literature. Ammons suggests, in the process, that if we can break our conditioning to expect in literature the neat containers and resolute endings we never get in life, *Tape* and *The Snow Poems* will reveal to us, if we read openly and freely enough and translate the "lessons" of our reading into the daily "walks" of our lives, how to be less rigid in our thinking, more considerate of differing points of view, less likely to see things from the hierarchical and polar views of Western philosophy. We might, along the way, even learn how to water bees. Ammons might be talking to the critic in us all when, after giving us an elaborate lesson in this arcane procedure, he writes near the end of *The Snow Poems:*

> if people who can think of
> nothing to do would
> water bees
> they would find themselves
> working with the principles
> of the universe . . . (260)

NOTES

1. Ammons, *Tape for the Turn of the Year* (Ithaca, N.Y.: Cornell University Press, 1965), referred to in the text as T; Kerouac, *On the Road* (New York, N.Y.: Viking, 1965), referred to in the text as OTR.

2. D. H. Lawrence, "Preface to the American Edition of *New Poems*" [1919], in *Poetics of the New American Poetry,* ed. Allen and Tallman (New York: Grove, 1973), 71, 70.

3. Walt Whitman, "Song of Myself," in *Leaves of Grass* (New York: New York University Press, 1965), 910.

4. Ibid., 915.

5. Moriarty says over and over, "God exists, we know time" (115); Ammons, for example, recommends throwing "yourself / into the river / of going" (T, 119).

6. Kerouac, "The Origins of Joy in Poetry" [1958], in *Good Blonde & Others* (San Francisco: Grey Fox, 1993), 74.

7. Lawrence, "Preface," 71.

8. Ralph Waldo Emerson, "Self-Reliance" [1841], in *The Complete Essays and Other Writings* (New York: Modern Library, 1950), 637.

9. Robert A. Hipkiss, *Jack Kerouac: Prophet of the New Romanticism* (Lawrence: Regents Press of Kansas, 1976). 80.

10. John Tytell, *Naked Angels: The Lives and Literature of the Beat Generation* (New York: McGraw-Hill, 1976), 17.

11. Tim Hunt, *Kerouac's Crooked Road: Development of a Fiction* (Storrs Conn.: Archon, 1981), 106–21.

12. Donald Reimann, "A. R. Ammons: Ecological Naturalism and the Romantic Tradition," *Twentieth Century Literature* 31, no. 1 (Spring 1985): 35.

13. Ibid.

14. Ann Charters, *Kerouac* (New York: Warner, 1974), 139, 124.

15. Kerouac, *Selected Letters: 1940–56* (New York: Viking, 1995), 325.

16. Charters, *Kerouac,* 147; Hunt offers the most thorough narrative of the scroll draft of *On the Road.* Kerouac himself over the next years enjoyed rewriting the circumstances of its composition, and combined with others' claims, time's passing, and memories' reconstructions, the exact circumstances are probably impossible to reconstruct—even the scroll's length is debated. Ginsberg first used the term "spontaneous bop prosody" to describe Kerouac's method, which Kerouac first described as "sketching" in 1951 as he tried to transform his first Road manuscript from a traditional narrative into a "thickly layered multidimensional conscious and unconscious invocation" of Cassady's character. His friend, the painter Ed White, said to him, "Why don't you just sketch in the streets like a painter but with words?" (Tytell, *Naked Angels,* 143), a description that would seem to fit perfectly what Ammons does in *Tape,* except that he sits in his study instead of the street. After Sputnik in 1957 (and the resultant coinage by the media of the term "beatnik"), Kerouac sometimes used the term "Space Age Prose," because "when the astronauts are flowing through space and time they too have no chance to stop and reconsider and go back" (Kerouac, "The First Word" [1967], in *Good Blonde & Others,* 190).

Cassady's 23,000-word letter, sometimes known as the "Joan Anderson letter," was shared by Kerouac with several of his friends and ultimately lost. Kerouac received the letter on 30 December 1950 and immediately proclaimed it "the greatest story" every written by an American, the beginning of an "American Renaissance." He compared it favorably in the process to Dostoyevsky, Joyce, Céline, Proust, Dreiser, Wolfe, Melville, Hemingway, and Fitzgerald. (See also Gerald Nicosia, *Memory Babe: A Critical Biography of Jack Kerouac* (Carbondale: Southern Illinois University Press), 336–38.) The portion of Cassady's autobiography published as *The First Third* (San Francisco: City Lights, 1971) includes a few letters and fragments.

17. Hipkiss, *Jack Kerouac,* 86, 78.

18. Regina Weinreich, *The Spontaneous Poetics of Jack Kerouac* (Carbondale: Southern Illinois University Press), 112

19. Nicosia, *Memory Babe,* 453.

20. Jack Kerouac, "Essentials of Spontaneous Prose," hereafter cited in-text as ESP. Charters, *Kerouac,* 189. *Good Blonde & Others* collects Kerouac's various statements on poetics, which also were published in the *Evergreen Review* (1956), the *Chicago Review* (1958) Grove Press's *The New American Poetry* (1960), *Writers Digest* (1962), and *Escapade,* the men's magazine (1959–60, 1967).

21. Kerouac, "The First Word," 189–90.

22. Reimann, "A. R. Ammons," 24.

23. Kerouac, *Vanity of Duluoz* [1967] (London: Quartet, 1974), 130.

24. Holder, *A. R. Ammons* (Boston, Twayne, 1978), 161; Reimann, "A. R. Ammons," 35.

25. Charles Olson, "Projective Verse," in Allen and Tallman. *Poetics of the New American Poetry.* New York: Grove, 1973. Hereafter cited in text as PV.

26. Hipkiss, *Jack Kerouac,* 80. Other writers at Black Mountain College in the early 1950s were Fielding Dawson, Michael Rumaker, and Jonathan Williams. Donald Allen's anthology *The New American Poetry: 1945–60* defines the Black

Mountain writers as those who had published in Creeley's *Black Mountain Review* and the journal *Origin,* begun by Cid Corman in 1951. Mary Emma Harris points out: "Although there is often a common point of view shared by Black Mountain artists, writers, dancers, and musicians, there is not a Black Mountain style" (*The Arts at Black Mountain* [Cambridge: MIT Press, 1987], 245). As a result, many writers who studied or taught at BMC are not generally included in the group known as "Black Mountain writers": Russell Edson, Elaine Gottlieb, Francine du Plessix Gray, James Leo Herlihy, Jane Mayhall, Hilda Morley, M. C. Richards, and José Yglesias, among others.

27. Lawrence, "Preface," 70.

28. Robert Duncan, "Towards an Open Universe," in *Poetics of the New American Poetry,* ed. Allen and Tallman, 217, 224.

29. Kerouac, it could be argued, sees his narrator, Sal Paradise, and Moriarty/Cassady primarily as subjects who act on objects such as cars, women, drugs. Occasionally, the objects seem to be doing the acting, but always in conjunction with one or the other of the main characters, never alone, "in a field." Action in *Road* is, in a sense, the object, and the narrator of this action delights in "lyrical interference" of the individual who witnesses and records.

30. Duncan, "Towards an Open Universe," 28.

31. Schneider, *A. R. Ammons and the Poetics of Widening Scope* (Madison, N.J.: Fairleigh Dickinson University Press, 1994), 194, 201.

32. A. R. Ammons, Letter to author, 30 Oct. 95.

33. Waggoner has successfully reclaimed "visionary," attaching it to its roots in "vision," and he includes Ammons in his catalog of contemporary poets who write visionary poems and whose "[i]maginative, interpretive perception, both subjective and objective," shape and dominate their point of view (*American Visionary Poetry* [Baton Rouge: Louisiana State University Press, 1982], 3, 12). Schneider also uses "visionary" as a way of describing one who sees "better or farther, deeper or more truly, than we," and adds that the "visionary poet is not 'mystical'" (71–72). Yet, I would suggest that Ammons is "visionary" in both senses of the term. Ammons uses his acute physical vision to see, in multiplicities, a unity that seems to apply, for discussion's sake, to what R. M. Bucke called "cosmic consciousness," a term no longer discussed in literary studies. But Ammons's description of this singular experience—both in prose and in its repeated employment as image in his subsequent poetry—fits neatly with how Bucke defined the "intellectual illumination" and "transfiguration" that cosmic consciousness affords. (*Cosmic Consciousness* [New York: Dutton, 1901]. See page 79, especially, for the eleven common traits.) Ammons's "vision" might well have been highlighted by a "subjective light" that allowed him to see more clearly—or deeply—what he had looked at before; the experience afforded him both moral and intellectual illumination; his poems have often indicated his sense of immortality, and the loss of his fear of death and sense of sin. The experience of his awakening was sudden, and it came upon a man of impressive intellectual, moral, and physical maturity. Many of his poems can be read as examples of what Schneider calls "vision therapy," allowing us "to see better and understand more" (72).

34. Kerouac, *Vanity of Duluoz,* 1.

35. Weinreich, *Spontaneous Poetics,* 3.

36. Kerouac, "The First Word," 188–89, 191.

37. Holder, *A. R. Ammons,* 110.

38. Schneider, *A. R. Ammons,* 157. Schneider, who is quoting DeRosa, does an excellent job of summarizing the critical reception to *The Snow Poems* (155–66).

39. Vendler, *Part of Nature, Part of Us: Modern American Poets* (Cambridge: Harvard University Press, 1980), 331.

40. Nowotny. *Time, The Modern and Postmodern Experience* (Cambridge: Polity, 1994), 21, 24–27.

41. Herbert Rappaport, *Marking Time* (New York: Simon and Schuster, 1990), 173. The point of Rappaport's book, interestingly, is to demonstrate how to use, in the treatment of psychological disorders, his RTL (Rappaport Time Line), which is constructed by patients in therapy on a 24″ piece of adding machine tape.

42. Schneider, *A. R. Ammons,* 192.

43. Weinreich, *Spontaneous Poetics,* 58–61.

44. Schneider, *A. R. Ammons,* 166

45. Vendler, *Part of Nature,* 369.

46. Michael McFee, "A. R. Ammons and The Snow Poems Reconsidered," *Chicago Review* 33, no. 1 (Summer 1981): 33, 36–37.

47. Schneider, *A. R. Ammons,* 190.

48. Waggoner, *American Visionary Poetry,* 172.

49. Charles Olson, *The Special View of History* (Berkeley, Calif.: Oyez, 1970), 48. Olson spoke of the importance of accidents to the "creation" of art as well as life in a series of lectures delivered in the last days of Black Mountain College and collected in 1970. The best explanation of the Burroughs/Gysin experiments with word collages is in *The Third Mind* (New York: Viking, 1978).

50. Burroughs, *The Third Mind,* 3–4.

51. Schneider, *A. R. Ammons,* 190.

52. Willard Spiegelman, *The Didactic Muse* (Princeton: Princeton University Press, 1989), 112.

53. M. M. Bakhtin, *The Dialogic Imagination* (Austin: University of Texas Press, 1981), 84, 94, 120, 157, 243–44. Dante's world is "vertical," not horizontal, because there is no past or future, only an eternal now, a single time where all is simultaneous.

Part II
Chaos, Earth, and Stones: "Elements" of Science in the Long Poems

A. R. Ammons and the Poetics of Chaos

Daniel Tobin

A great disorder is an order.
—Wallace Stevens, "Connoisseur of Chaos"

"A butterfly stirring the air today in Peking can transform storm systems next month in New York."[1] James Gleick's pithy description of what has come to be known in chaos studies as *The Butterfly Effect*, the notion that the most insignificant phenomenon can effect drastic changes in even the most apparently ordered system, exemplifies the kind of natural occasion that would attract the eccentric gaze of A. R. Ammons, whose work reveals at every turn its profound sympathy with the new science. Ammons finds his most precise and stirringly imaginative insights through his meditation on "dynamical systems." In such systems the poet not only discerns the seemingly random, "nonlinear" deviations from the expected pattern of order, but uncovers new orders arising spontaneously. Ammons's poetry thus embodies in its substance and style what Gleick might call a vision of "chaos and order together,"[2] and so his work is deeply mimetic of chaos's fundamental vision. It is at once imaginatively eccentric and, often, stylistically "nonlinear," as in such poems as "Corsons Inlet," where Ammons himself declares "I have drawn no lines" in his quest for "narrow orders" (CP, 149).

Therefore, as in physicist Stephen Smale's "topographies,"[3] Ammons's poems may be understood as "systems" that are at once "robust" and "strange"—robust because they hold together chaos and stability, order and disorder, and strange because they incorporate the unexpected, the unpredictable. Throughout Ammons's career his poetry manifests these essential properties, enabling his work to absorb its remarkable variety of perceptions as well as its stunning array of styles and diction. These properties, as in "global systems," give imaginative shape as well to his longer pieces

113

Sphere and *Garbage*. Yet, as I hope to show by the end of this essay, Ammons's work not only represents an ingenious convergence of scientific perception and artistic composition, it signals a reinvention of romantic sources of imagination. "Nature, the prime genial artist, inexhaustible in diverse powers, is equally inexhaustible in forms," Coleridge declared.[4] His insight is given a new and unexpected meaning in Ammons's "fields of order in disorder" (CP, 151) where, as in the work of Wallace Stevens, we once again find ourselves more truly and more strange.

I

The natural world as portrayed in Ammons's early lyrics anticipates many of the key concepts of chaos theory, and as such the more encompassing visions of *Sphere* and *Garbage*. Without question, the expressly scientific fascination with nature in Ammons's poetry has been evident from the publication in 1955 of his first book, *Ommateum,* which takes its name from the zoological term for an insect's compound eye.[5] Beyond Ammons's adoption of such highly technical scientific knowledge and terminology, his incorporation of science as a mode of perception gestures at a still more fundamental concern with nature's creative potential, as well as his own. In Ammons's vision, particular physical realities always come to intimate cosmic, even metaphysical concerns. In "Poetics," he writes "I look for the way / things will turn out / spiralling from a center, / the shape / things will take to come forth in;" (CP, 199) and, in "Saliences," "here / is this dune fest / releasing / mind feeding out, / gathering clusters, / fields of order in disorder, / where choice / can make beginnings" (CP, 152). As both of these defining early poems suggest, the scanning eye of Ammons's own far-ranging imagination reveals a reality always in process, in which the poet's powers of creation depend on the recognition of their place within the ever-widening scope of the world's unquenchable generation. Both the world and the poet's rendering of it comprise what chaos theorists call a "dynamical system," a system in which apparently sharply defined patterns of order break down to form new unpredictable patterns that, instead of being purely random, actually form new more complex patterns of organization—new provisional "shapes," or "clusters," or "centers" that come forth in what Stevens once called "an always incipient cosmos."

Given his propensity for discerning "order in disorder," perhaps it is no coincidence that Ammons's career takes shape during the same period in which such diverse theorists as Edward Lorenz, Mitchell Feigenbaum, Benoit Mandelbrot, and many others were evolving their ideas about the nature of chaos.[6] Moreover, as Katherine Hayles observes in her fine book *Chaos Bound,* within chaos theory not only is chaos seen "as order's precursor and partner," hidden order is understood to exist "within chaos itself."[7] Yet these attributes of what has come to be called (in part misleadingly) chaos theory, actually define two orientations of study: the "order-behind-chaos" school and the "order-out-of-chaos" school, the latter of which now more often goes by the name of "complexity theory."[8] As the name implies, the theorists of the "order-behind-chaos" school seek to explore the underlying order that may be inferred from apparently chaotic systems. Those associated with the "order-out-of-chaos" school explore complex systems that tend to hover between order and disorder, hoping to discern new orders emerging from seeming disorder. Significantly, we find both approaches present in the work of A. R. Ammons, in whose poems the synchronous insights of poet and scientist strike a remarkably insouciant harmony.

Perhaps this peculiarly fruitful coincidence of poetry and cutting-edge physics in Ammons's work ought to be understood not so much as an eccentric anomaly in contemporary literature but rather as one of the defining examples of literature's embrace of "the field concept." Again, as Katherine Hayles affirms, the field concept—the notion that reality "consists not in discrete objects located in space but rather of an underlying field whose interactions produce both objects and space"[9]—has had a profound influence on twentieth-century literature, through the work of writers as diverse as Henry Adams, Jorge Luis Borges, Doris Lessing, and Thomas Pynchon. For literary theorists like Hayles and writers such as John Barth,[10] the field concept is perhaps the central paradigm of our time, influencing literature and literary theory alike, shaping both the modern and postmodern literary milieus even while it cuts across various academic disciplines and cultural manifestations.[11] It is, as Foucault would define it, an epistime, a system of knowledge that seems to be everywhere present, from popular car commercials to the more innovative trends in contemporary poetry—witness Jorie Graham's *The Dream of the Unified Field,* winner of the 1996 Pulitzer Prize. As Hayles describes, essential to the field concept is the notion that things are interconnected in a kind of "cosmic web" of energy patterns. Reality is a "dance," an all-encompassing motion that ultimately dismisses the notion of a purely objective observer. It is only a short step between conceiving reality as a field and conceiving that field as a system of infinite complexity.

"How can we know the dancer from the dance," Yeats asked and, as Ammons exults, "I will show you / the underlying that takes no image to itself, / cannot be shown or said, / but weaves in and out of moons and bladderweeds, / and is all and / beyond destruction because created fully in no / particular form."[12] This latter conception of nature as "all in all," as harbinger of "something more deeply interfused," is consistent with Ammons's roots in romanticism, as is his emphasis on "the widening scope" of his own imaginative vision, which, as Steven Schneider astutely remarks, also places him in the tradition of Emerson, Whitman, and Thoreau.[13] Ammons's indisputable preoccupation with the discourses of science combined with his interest in romanticism makes his poetry a remarkable contemporary crystallization that at once unites the disparate discourses of science and literature and likewise addresses itself to what is surely the original problem of Western thought: the relationship between order and chaos. Implicated deeply in the western tradition, though perceived of as a formlessness that requires ordering, chaos nevertheless exerts a powerful allure as an idea bound to order's own origin, an idea without which creation itself would be meaningless.

This allure of chaos as something more than merely the antithesis of order and form is a central theme in Ammons's poems. It is, in fact, the primary condition of both natural and imaginative creation. "We are led on," he affirms in "The Misfit," "to the boundaries / where relations loosen into chaos" (CP, 123). The poet, like Thomas Kuhn's scientist whose discoveries result in revolutionary new paradigms,[14] is the misfit whose fascination with peripheries, with the "raw blocks of material," reflects a still profounder conviction that the nature of creation itself is perhaps best discerned in the unformed. It is a notion intimated by the title itself, since to "mis-fit" the form of the poem, to rescue the product of imagination from too strict a closure, is to recognize its place in "an enlarging unity" that eludes total representation. As such, disorder is "ripe," as Ammons observes in "Identity" and "Prodigal," for it discloses "orders moving in and out of orders, collisions/of orders, dispersions" (CP, 77). It is in the dispersed, in the apparently formless, the chaotic, that perhaps a more compelling conception of order reveals itself. This conviction is given mythologized form in *Sphere*, where Ammons pictures chaos as a progenitor of order:

Chaos stirred in himself,
spirals (cellular whirlwinds), upward swoops of bending aspiration,
collisions high with potentials of linkage, dissolvings and

meldings lengthy and free—these "motions" brought particles
into progression often: if the progressions often failed into
tatterdemalions, do-funnies, whatcahmacallits, and thingumbobs,

there was time enough in the slow motions of landforms, oceans,
of moon and sun for Chaos to undo and recommence: certain
weaves caught on to random hooks and came into separations and

identity.

(S, 33)

These lines from *Sphere* offer a typically tongue-in-cheek vision
of the role of disorder in the creation of order. It is a vision that
foreshadows Ammons's celebration of waste in *Garbage* as yet
another avatar of order in the wake of degeneration. Like the gar-
den web of the early poem "Identity," poetry paradoxically "keeps
order at the center where space is freest" (CP, 115–16). From the
outset of his work, the order of poetry is conceived of by Ammons
as being bound inextricably to the kind of radical freedom and
elusive progression that might best be understood as "nonlinear."
    In nature, the radical freedom of nonlinear systems reflects a
propensity for small causes to compound into effects well out of
proportion to the original scale. In technical terms, they exhibit
acute sensitivity to initial conditions.[15] An example may be drawn
from a recent television commercial where, safe in their new Range
Rover, newlyweds pore frantically over their rumpled map on a
deserted mountain road. "Nothing to worry about," the husband
assures his wife. Altogether elsewhere, in a swamp miles away, a
hawk grips a turtle in its claws and carries it off. High over the
receding landscape it slips free, bouncing shell-first onto a huge
boulder at the top of a mountain, then landing on its feet below.
The turtle, unharmed, hunkers off. But the slightest tap of the
turtle's shell has jarred loose the boulder from its precarious ridge.
"We're not lost," the husband, still fumbling with the map, again
assures his wife as the ground begins to tremble underneath them,
louder and louder, the boulder now rolling directly at them down
the road, now cresting in the windshield. Madison Avenue notwith-
standing, for the order-behind-chaos school even such radical in-
stances of disorder, if examined with the appropriate instrument,
often reveal "little spikes of order." Still more startlingly, fine
structures and indeed remarkably complex patterns like the infinite
variety of snowflakes born "of imbalance in the flow of energy from
one piece of nature to another,"[16] often reveal themselves. As Alan
Holder points out, in a similar way "order and disorder in Ammons

do not typically occur in . . . purity or isolation," but "tend to be found together."[17] More emphatically than Holder suggests, however, the co-presence of order and disorder in Ammons's poetry suggests that the weather of his imagination naturally acclimates itself to such apparently chaotic richness, the very diversity of which occasions the poet's participation in the visionary field:

> I will show you
> the underlying that takes no image to itself,
>   cannot be shown or said,
> but weaves in and out of moons or bladderweeds,
>   is all and
>   beyond destruction
>   because created fully in no
> particular form:

                                                                        (CP, 115)

Certainly, of all Ammons's early work, "Corsons Inlet" articulates most acutely his preoccupation with nature's "disorderly orders," as well as with what is so deeply yet elusively interfused in the whole widening scope of the field: the Overall. Walking among dunes along an inlet shore the poet finds liberation in a "release from forms / from the perpendiculars, / straight lines, blocks, boxes, binds / of thought" (CP, 148). The zig-zag motion of the poem's lines down the page are intended to mirror both the motions of the poet's mind as it moves through its "eddies of meaning" and the elusive scope of the seashore itself in all the shifting amplitude of its flux. Here, the poet is not so much released from forms as from fixed forms of thought and being. Instead, through "the overall wandering of mirroring mind" in which he traces the clarified ephemera of the shore, all the while "erecting no boundaries," he discerns "an order held / in constant change" (CP, 150). Unwilling, however, to indulge in the kind of speculation that would affirm an abstraction at the expense of living particulars, he declares "Overall is beyond me" (CP, 148). Clearly Ammons's "Overall" is not the same as Emerson's "Oversoul," an abstraction that prizes transcendence over an immanence teeming with generation and decay.[18] What does get affirmed through the whole motion of the poem, however, is the process itself, what Alfred North Whitehead would have called the living "nexus of actual occasions" that compose reality.[19] The ultimate reality of "Corsons Inlet" is, as the poem itself suggests, "a congregation / rich with entropy: nevertheless, separable, noticeable / as one event, / not chaos . . . a 'field' of action / with moving, incalculable center" (CP, 150). Quoting these lines, Roger Gilbert goes on to make explicit Ammons's affinity to chaos theory: "complexity is not chaos."[20] In short, the "ultimate reality" for Ammons is not an order defined from above and entirely knowable, but something at most "noticeable" amidst the shifting flow or reality—a field unified paradoxically by grace of its very diversity.

From the widest scope of the macrocosm to the most intimate glimpse of the microcosm, "Corsons Inlet" revels in a system at once seemingly infinite in diversity and continuous in its integrity. Nevertheless, for Ammons, there is no "finality of vision," for the creative process, like the ecological process of his dune-swept shore, depends likewise on "the wider forces," the "enlarging grasps of disorder," out of which order itself is momentarily fastened. In short, in a manner consistent with Coleridge's insight on the nature of imagination, though far more radical in his organicism, Ammons would recapture in his poetry the living dynamic of nature. He would reveal through the *naturata* of its forms the *naturans* of the whole system, an aspiration whose very impossibility bears witness to the inexhaustible flow of reality itself.

Not surprisingly, then, in the early poem "Choice" Ammons invokes "the god / that rolls up circles of our linear / sight" (CP, 35). On the one hand, Ammons implicitly refers here to our genetically programmed ability to see only within a very circumscribed band of lightwaves. On the other hand, his claim metaphorically implies a moral inadequacy—our tendency as humans to limit the scope of imagination, to circumscribe it within a limited valency. Linear sight would conceive a world of strict proportionality in which causes and their effects are congruent. In the scientific realm this is precisely the kind of Newtonian world that chaos theory has shown to be so limiting in its representation of reality. Chaos theory, as I have already remarked, demonstrates that such linearity is the exception, and that nonlinearity—a world of startlingly disproportionate relations between causes and effects—is in fact the norm.[21] That is why, as James Gleick points out, so many chaos theorists are fascinated by flow, which he defines as "shape plus change, motion plus form." What "dynamical shapes like flames and organic shapes like leaves" reveal, according to Gleick, is "some not yet understood weaving of forces" and, perhaps ultimately, "a connection between motion and universal form."[22] Flow is the dynamic conjoining of form and motion.

The problem Ammons sets for himself in the long poems *Sphere* (tellingly subtitled "the form of a motion") and *Garbage* is to sustain just such dynamic flow or, as he himself declares, "a rugged variety of the formless formed" (S, 16). Characteristically, what fascinates him in both these capacious works are "the shapes nearest shapelessness," for it is such shapes that he says "awe us most" and "suggest the god" (S, 16). The god of *Sphere* is, of course, the same "nonlinear" god of "Choice" who inspires the poet, now in both these longer poems, to subvert the tight proportions of apparent form by allowing the fixed sections of each poem to flow into those that follow. Similarly, the three-line stanzas of *Sphere*, like the unrhymed couplets of *Garbage*, merely allude to traditional fixed forms. One might say that in the flow of both poems, linearity breaks free into nonlinearity to form more elaborate patterns of sense and organization. This is most evident in *Sphere* and *Garbage*, where the ongoing motion of the poet's meditations breaks free of each poem's delineated sections. It is as if the sections themselves were there to announce their provisional nature, rather than to indicate to the reader any real sense of closure. They are like rocks in a stream whose currents flow back on themselves and each other even as the stream itself flows forward. Apparent order and apparent disorder mingle to form, in each poem, a seemingly self-generating flow that composes the poet's diverse observations of nature, shards of memory and history, news items, his own proprioperceptive musings, swimmingly elaborated refluxes of philosophy, theology, science, as well as a range of diction from street slang to high romantic rhetoric, into "narratives of motion" that he would simultaneously shape into the sustained whole of the poem. "These are the motions," Ammons affirms in *Garbage*, "this is the dance," suggesting that the art of the poem itself derives from the poet's organization of his material into intensely complex patterns across assumed boundaries.

II

In *Sphere*, Ammons's penchant for creating complex patterns becomes evident at the poem's outset. *Sphere* begins with a meditation on the "sexual basis of all things rare," which in succeeding sections quickly modulates to contemplations on thought itself, or the relationship between "knowledge and carnal knowledge," and finally on death as dramatized by "the vultures' pull and gulp," as well as the work of "the lessening transformers" (S, 11). These opening sections establish what is the poem's central recurrent theme: the necessary coexistence of creation and destruction and its meaning for human consciousness. The mutual processes of birth and death—the godlike forces now divorced from myth, though periodically mythologized throughout the poem—are the omnipresent muses of physical reality. Not surprisingly, near the poem's end, Ammons reiterates his initial meditation by claiming that male and female are the two principles that give birth to the mind and presumably to the poem. Throughout the poem's 155 twelve-line sections, Ammons plays riffs on this encompassing theme through a series of meditations, speculations, and vignettes that range from musings on the misguided ideas of New York City writers, to the launch of Apollo 16, to the Most High, to a catbird perched on the jungle gym nearby his vegetable garden. For Ammons, these discrete occasions, seemingly unconnected, are bound to each other as pervasively as is the physical universe to itself, the universe that holds in dynamic relation the totality of single things. Again, the key word here is "dynamic," for what Ammons abhors above all else is a static unity. As always, it is the relationship between the one and the many, the center and the periphery, that forms the primary axis of Ammons's poetic, with its seemingly infinite vectors of knowledge and experience. From this perspective, *Sphere* is the embodiment of the poem as complex system.

Indeed, it is the wondrous complexity of material reality that Ammons would seek to mirror in the poem, a complexity so stirring to his imagination that *Sphere* would create a bridge between the scientific world and the world of religion. From one perspective, "the scope of oneness under which / the proud ephemerals play discretely their energizing / laws and play out" (S, 38) bears witness to the splendor of the universe's physical cosmogenesis, as well as its ongoing transformations within the infinitely complex and variable field of space-time. From another perspective— though really *through* this primary perspective—matter itself is "a mere seed afloat in radiance" (S, 39). Ammons's claim here echoes the vision of scientist and mystic Teilhard de Chardin, who saw the universe as a "divine milieu" in which matter and spirit exist in a mysterious and transfiguring communion. Ammons is not so very far from that vision when he writes "in the comprehensiveness and focus of the Most High is the obliteration / total that contains all and in that we rest" (S, 39). Both the scientist-mystic and the scientist-poet apprehend in material existence the lineaments of the spirit. Ammons, of course, has no interest in aligning his vision with Christian doctrine, and in particular the spiritualization of matter implied by the doctrine of the incarnation. The materials *are* materials for Ammons, and not grounds for religious confirmation. The cosmic forces are cosmic forces, and science is

the symbolic system in which Ammons has his primary imagina-
tive life.

Nevertheless, in *Sphere* (and elsewhere) he shows himself to be
profoundly conversant with the symbols of faith. What is born of
this remarkable union of science and religion is a kind of hybrid
consciousness in which the supernatural eternity of religion is dis-
placed by what Ammons repeatedly calls "the ongoing," and "the
ongoing mind," which is at once immanent in material reality and
yet transcends our full comprehension: "the highest god / we never
meet, essence out of essence, motion without motion" (S, 17). Not
unlike the contemplative's steady prayer, the poem's job is to instill
in the reader a kind of equipoise or focus, the singular repetition
of the highest god's fusion of stillness and movement:

> the purpose of the motion of a poem is to bring the focused,
> awakened mind to no-motion, to a still contemplation of the
> whole motion, all the motions, of the poem. . . .
>
> (S, 40)

I use the word "repetition" above as a purposeful echo of Cole-
ridge's definition of the imagination: "a repetition in the finite mind
of the eternal act of creation in the infinite I Am."[23] What we find
in Ammons's declaration of a poem's purpose is the same kind of
understanding of the relationship between macrocosm and micro-
cosm that predicates Coleridge's conception of the imagination.
Likewise, both poets are concerned to align what Ammons calls
in *Garbage* the poet's "action of making" with the wider reality of
an "eternal" creation. The key difference is that whereas Cole-
ridge's view of imagination finds its model in biblical sources, Am-
mons looks toward the revelations of modern physics, as well as
his own intuited understanding of the nature of reality, for his con-
ception of poetry's place in the cosmic scheme. As such, while it
would be wrong to read into *Sphere* evidence of a new "natural
supernaturalism," it nevertheless seems obvious that Ammons's
enterprise in the poem is, in part, to synthesize this key aspect of
the romantic tradition and to adapt it both to our turbulent time
and to his own poetic needs.

Ammons's cross-fertilization of modern physics with his own
version of the romantic imagination is perhaps most clearly evident
in *Sphere* when he claims "There is a faculty or knack, smallish,
in the mind that can turn / as with tooling irons immediacy into
bends of concision, shapes / struck with airs to keep. . ." (S, 42).
Coleridge called the imagination an "esemplastic" or shaping

power. Yet, again there are differences. Ammons calls this faculty "smallish," a reconfiguration that tempers any pretense toward the "glorious faculty" of Wordsworth's revelation on Mount Snowdon at the end of *The Prelude.* Nevertheless, *Sphere* can ring with the old Wordsworthian grandeur: "the real force of the gods return to its heights / where it dwells, its everlasting home" (S, 48). Similarly, when Ammons surveys the cheated, maimed, afflicted, the castaways of society, he declares "I know them: I love them: I am theirs," a proclamation that resounds with Whitman's uncanny powers of identification. To be sure, identity is another central theme of *Sphere,* as is the poet's ability to negotiate between the claims of identity and the claims of a reality that exists in constant flow both below and above the solid appearances of the world. The poet's exploration of this theme brings him to a recognition of the fundamental pathos of conscious life: "We want to change without changing." Every line of *Sphere* ultimately resonates with this paradox, for on the one hand Ammons sings the identification of the one and the many ("crush a bug and the universe goes hollow / with hereafter"), while on the other he prizes the radically individual nature of existence: "you have your identity when / you find out not what you can keep your mind on but what / you can't keep your mind off" (S, 57–58).

Likewise, then, *Sphere* at once "insists on differences" yet these "contours of staying" must finally commune in a harmony that "can be recognized in the highest / ambience of diversity" (S, 57–58). At its most insistent, what *Sphere* awakens us to is that each of us, and not just the poet, "stands in the peak and center / of perception," at once a discrete and yet an intimate part of the whole. Ultimately, for the Ammons of *Sphere,* we are all called to "make a home of motion" in actions that would to our best abilities accomplish the ideal equipoise between identification and difference. As such, the ferris wheel Ammons introduces at the end of the poem stands at once as an intact, discernible form and a figure that is not only in motion but *is* its motion. It is at once the orb of the earth and of its inhabitants. We are at once "ourselves," discrete individuals, and we are "sailing," a part of the ongoing; and so, in the best sense, the vision that ends *Sphere* is Ammons's mundane version of Dante's whirling heavenly kaleidoscope at the end of his *Divine Comedy,* a figure that unites the transcendent and immanent worlds. Achieved through Ammons's understanding of the deep structure of reality, and not through the supernatural, the wheel is the symbolic answer to the question he voices earlier in the poem: "How do you fare and how may we fare to Thee?"

If, as its title suggests, *Sphere* means to quicken the reader's reverence for the dynamic order that both underlies and at times seems to emerge from the flux of reality, it does so without negating the forces of limitation and, in particular, death. Indeed, the ongoing process of loss is integral to that vital, underlying order, an essential aspect of what Ammons calls "the mystery." The work of the poet's imagination must therefore engage the fact that there is no birth without death, that sooner or later everything becomes part of an immense waste. In *Sphere,* Ammons embraces this essential aspect of the nature of things when he writes "I want to be the shambles, / the dump, the hills of gook the bulldozer shoves, so gulls / in carrion-gatherings can fan my smouldering" (S, 68). Written nearly twenty years after *Sphere, Garbage* is the elaborate creation of Ammons's glancing wish. Where *Sphere* announces a vision of the whole and begins with a meditation on the sources of life in sexual union, *Garbage* announces a vision of decay and begins with a march of "creepy little creepers," harbingers of death, who in a brilliant transformation become the poet's insinuating muses. Decomposition is the true, unheralded source of composition that Ammons will now celebrate. "If you've derived from life, a going thing called life," Ammons concludes near the poem's end, "life has a right to derive life from you" (G, 98–99). From this ethical standpoint, the key conception of life as a complex web of mutuality so central to *Sphere* reappears in *Garbage,* only now Ammons's vantage is even more stridently from the ground up rather than from the pinnacle of the whole.

Consistent with Ammons's Heraclitian desire to make the way down the way up, *Garbage* moves through its eighteen sections by extending further his approach of organizing *Sphere* as a sequence of brilliantly rambling meditations and vignettes. Fat Minnie Fuhrer, a colleague dying of cancer, Ole Liza who used to work in the fields of Ammons's childhood, all become woven into the poem's flow which would, as in *Sphere,* assimilate itself into "the ongoing." One of the most moving of these vignettes is Ammons's vivid description of his own father, slumped and strapped in his wheelchair shortly before his death from diabetes. Here we find the inverse of the Ferris Wheel, that final vision of motion and stillness upon which *Sphere* itself turns. Mulling over the wheels with the other men dying in the ward, Ammons's father appears an image of stasis, of life's final heartbreaking waste. Again, the poet is driven to reconcile the particular with the inexorable motion of the whole. What we find in *Garbage,* then, is not merely an elaboration of themes already explored earlier in *Sphere* and in his short lyrics, but a new and necessary confrontation with "the gap" between Ammons's vision of dynamic unity—the whole motion intimated in its discrete forms—and the integrity of those forms in themselves. The spirit, as Ammons observes, may be forever, "the residual and informing energy," but what about "this manifestation, this man, this incredible flavoring and / building up of character and eclat, gone . . . a local / event, infinitely unrepeatable?" (G, 38) Thus, while *Garbage* would bear witness to "the spindle of energy" that runs through all things from high to low, from "boulders to dead stars," the poem positively requires the messiness of its many tangents.

Of course, Ammons cannot fill in the gap the poem implicitly opens throughout his ruminations on everything from galaxies, to language, to the poem itself regarded reflexively as though in mid-composition; and so it is the gap between whole and part itself that, in effect, generates surpluses of meaning both in the poem and, as Ammons would have it, in reality. The infinitely complex system of the universe is in essence a garbage dump that recycles itself in an everlasting communion among its diverse parts. As such, the conflict between the "order-behind-chaos" school and the "order-out-of-chaos" school is simply a moot point for Ammons. From the poet's perspective, in "the crux of matter" both are true. Faced with our own dissolution, the poet calls us to "an ease beyond our understanding" because it is the very nature of the universe to call us out of our egocentrism into a plenitude that eludes any totalizing conception:

> forms are never
>
> permanent form, change the permanence, so
> that one thing one day is something else another
>
> day, and the energy that informs all forms just
> breezes right through filth as clean as a whistle:
>
> all this stuff here is illusory, you know, and
> while it gives you bad dreams and wilding desires
>
> and sometimes makes you spit up at night, it is
> the very efflorescence of the fountain of shapes. . . .
>
> (G, 115)

Ammons's "ease that passes understanding" is a reconsideration of Eliot's promised peace, though in Ammons's version the wasteland is anything but arid. Instead, the decomposition of individual forms carries within itself the potential for positive rebirth. Samsara, our world of illusion, as some Buddhists say, becomes Nirvana, the condition of enlightened being, in the moment of transformed vision that supervenes our old paradigms of thought.

It is a similar belief in the mind's capacity to attain transforming vision that shapes the wider aim of *Garbage*. For this reason, one of Ammons's most prominent objects of concern in the poem is poetry itself, as well as the poet's action of making. "Art," as Ammons reminds us, "makes shape, order, meaning, / purpose where there was none, or none discernible, / none derivable" (G, 67), and this meaning-making function is the very stuff of life; and the stuff of life, as Ammons continually takes pains to remind us, is garbage. When he recounts the beginnings of a poem developing in the mind in section six, the process culminates in "a brutal burning—a rich, raw urgency" that mimics both the body's own production of "waste" and the laws of necessity that form volcanoes. Ammons here is neither being ironic nor indulging in hyperbole. Governed by the poem's overarching conceit, everything is both waste and generation. Poetry itself is "like an installation at Marine / Shale: it reaches down into the dead pit / and cool oil of recognition and words" into the "stringy gook" of what lies below our conscious minds (G, 108). The purpose of that descent is to remind the mind of its vital relationship to "communication channels" that lead well out beyond its own inner workings into the wider universe of which it is a part. In the fullest sense, *Garbage* is an epic of the mind's quest for what Wordsworth called the love that "subsists all lasting grandeur," though in Ammons's version that grandeur includes the least likely elements of the sublime—trash and birdshit as well as "our cold / killing brothers the stars"—all of which must be held in our "right regard." To attain as much is to recall the ideal Ammons articulated twenty years earlier in *Sphere*. It is to embrace a hope for each of us poised at the peak and center of perception:

> have
> you stopped to think what existence is, to be here
>
> now where so much has been or is yet to come and
> where isness itself is just the name of a segment
>
> of flow: stop, think: millennia jiggle in your eyes
> at night, the twinklers, eye and star. . . .

(G, 48)

III

"Pattern born amid formlessness: that is biology's basic beauty and its basic mystery," so James Gleick summarizes the role of chaos in the formation of life.[24] The same words could adequately describe Ammons's radically organic aesthetic in *Sphere* and *Garbage*. In a profound sense, Ammons's use of such scientific insights likewise represents the fullest application of organicism's ideal of internally realized form. Here again is Coleridge on the difference between mechanic and organic form:

> The form is mechanic when on any given material we impress a predetermined form, not necessarily arising out of the properties of the material, as when to a mass of red clay we give it whatever shape we wish it to retain when hardened. The organic form, on the other hand, is innate; it shapes as it develops itself from within, and the fullness of its development is one and the same with the perfection of its outward form. Such is the life, such is the form. Nature, the prime genial artist, inexhaustible in diverse powers, is equally inexhaustible in forms.[25]

Ammons might have had this famous passage in mind when in *Sphere* he explicitly eschews the poem conceived of as "the painted gourd on the mantelpiece" for the poem conceived of as a dynamic flow, the purpose of which as stated earlier is "is to bring the focused, / awakened mind to no-motion, to a still contemplation of the / whole motion, all the motions, of the poem" (S, 40). To read the poem in this manner is to accept the poem as a "self-referential system," or "field" in which "the sense of moving along, coming closer to an end point, is revealed not exactly as an illusion but as a half-truth as the seeker merges with the sought, the periphery with the center, the journey with its end."[26] This complex interpenetration of self, world, and language in the dynamic field of the poem precludes atomization because to enter the poem at all is to enter an evolving motion, a field that would compose its own ever-widening hermeneutical circle of the seeker and the sought, of reader and poem. Typically for Ammons, the blueprint for this expansive relationship is found in nature, as this passage from *Sphere* suggests:

> though the surface is crisp with pattern still we know
> that there are generalized underlyings, planes of substratum
> lessening from differentiation: under all life, fly and

dandelion, protozoan, bushmaster, and ladybird, tendon
and tendril (excluding protocellular organelles) is the same
cell: and under the cell is water, a widely generalized

condition, and under that energy and under that perhaps the
spirit of the place . . .

                                         our selves float here. . . .
                                                      (S, 14–15)

What *Sphere* affirms above all are "the mirrorments" that bind
together discrete existence with the whole field of becoming that
at once underlies and overlies our human condition: each of us
stands at the peak and center of perception. Human beings exist
in the liminal space where microcosm and macrocosm meet. In a
radical way, *Sphere* and *Garbage* deny the absolute distinction
between the poem as a mirror of nature and the poem as lamp, the
pure product of the poet's imagination. The mirror is the lamp, the
lamp is the mirror, for what both poems finally embody in their
whole motion is "the recursive power of flows within flows," the
multifarious unity of "similarities across scales," of "patterns in-
side patterns."[27] To be sure, Ammons appears to echo such ideas
directly in the poem when he writes "though the surface is crisp
with pattern still we know / that there are generalized underlyings,
planes of substratum / lessening from differentiation" (S, 14). Here,
again, Ammons sounds remarkably like an "order-behind-chaos"
theorist, proclaiming "the one cell" underlying all things. Yet, when
later in the poem he observes: "keep jiggling the innumerable ele-
ments and / even integrations can fall out of disintegrations," he
appears to echo the "order-out-of-chaos" school. Again, for Am-
mons, there is no contradiction since in his reality, though chaos
is "the ampler twin" of order, always "the visible, coherent, dis-
crete dwell / in flotation which faces out on the illimitable" (S, 71).
    Similarly, Ammons's preoccupation with relationships of scale
in both nature and poetry is evident in the grand shifts of percep-
tion, from microscopic and subatomic to galactic and universal,
that characterize both poems as well as the whole of his work.
Indeed, his range of poetic production, from the shortest lyrics to
his book-length works, embodies this concern as a matter of form
as well as theme. What we find in Ammons's poetry, then, and
particularly in *Sphere* and *Garbage,* is his embrace of complex
forms; to be sure, the kind of complex forms that are characteristic
of chaotic systems as found in nature.[28] The measurement of regu-
lar forms such as circles and rectangles remains unaffected by the

scale of the instrument used to measure them. If the diameter of a particular circle is one inch, it will be so whether you measure it with a yardstick or a ruler. As Katherine Hayles points out, this is not the case with irregular forms like coastlines or the human vascular system.[29] In such complex forms, measurements increase as the scales decrease so that, as Benoit Mandelbrot the founder of fractal geometry realized, in such forms infinite space exists within a finite space.[30] As such, the more you measure a coastline, like Corsons Inlet for example, by "breaking" it into discrete segments, the more it reveals self-similar details that project into infinity. The idea recalls Zeno's paradox, where an arrow fired at its target theoretically never reaches its mark since the path of its flight may be divided an infinite number of times. In a sense, fractal geometry confirms the "widening scope" Ammons affirms not only in "Corsons Inlet" but in *Sphere* and *Garbage* as well. Though "Overall" is ultimately beyond him—"the mind cannot visualize the whole self-embedding of complexity"[31]—he nevertheless glimpses a partial infinity implied by recursive symmetries between scales. In fact, his poems are predicated upon such symmetries.

On a still grander scale, *Garbage* organizes its patterns of recurrent images and themes according to a similar embrace of complex form. The mound of garbage that looms like a ziggurat at the opening of the poem, churning new orders on a microscopic scale out of our human waste, finds a self-similar mound of "celestial garbage" at the poem's end, both of which reiterate the further self-reflexive fact that "there is a mound, / too, in the poet's mind dead language is hauled / off to and burned down on, / the energy held and / shaped into new turns and clusters, / the mind / strengthened by what it strengthens" (G, 20). In these lines, what might be called the "fractal organization" of the poem—its tendency to arrive at its shape organically through the poet's hypersensitive attraction to the partial, the particular, and the marginal, as well as his willingness to delay the reader as a way of inferring the whole—becomes specifically implicated in the poet's creation of new orders out of an apparent chaos. In any case, the complexity of the interconnections among the poem's strands of theme or imagery harken back to the still more perfect symmetry discovered in nature:

> we are natural: nature, not
>
> we, gave rise to us: we are not, though, though
> natural, divorced from higher, finer configurations:

        tissues and holograms of energy circulate in
        us and seek and find representations of themselves

        outside us, so that we can participate in
        celebrations high and know reaches of feeling

        and sight and thought that penetrate (really
        penetrate) far, far beyond these our wet cells,

        right on up past our stories, the planets, moons,
        and other bodies locally to the other end of

        the pole where matter's forms diffuse and
        energy loses all means to express itself except

        as spirit. . . .

                                                    (G, 21)

As Steven Schneider observes, these lines reveal Ammons's over-
whelming desire to place even personal grief and suffering—what
Teilhard de Chardin called in another context "the passivities of
our diminishments"—within the context of a wider cosmic vision.[32]
Or, as Ammons observed in *Sphere,* "we are not half-in and / half-
out of the universe but unmendably integral" (S, 43).

    Ammons's vision of a universe that forms an integral whole, not
in spite of, but precisely through its infinite diversity, has remained
consistent throughout his career. A conception of unity without
diversity, as he takes pains to remind us in the early poem "One:
Many," is debilitating to the imagination. The "abstract one," the
false "unity unavailable to change," leads to destruction. "Not
unity by the winnowing out of difference, / not unity thin and sub-
stanceless as abstraction" (G, 38), he reiterates. Similarly, in
Sphere, Ammons's concern with "the one: many problem" as he
calls it, leads him to declare that "if there are / no boundaries that
hold firm, everything can be ground into / everything else" (S,
61). Here, Ammons sounds as if he might be drawing the kind of
conclusion consistent with someone who has thought long and hard
about the kind of chaotic turbulence that emerges from the slight
alteration of the most determined system—"for want of a nail the
shoe was lost" and so, by increments, is the entire battle. At the
same time he can ask the question "when does water seeping into
the roothairs / pass the boundary after which it is a tree?" (S, 21)
On the one hand, from slight alterations order may devolve into
chaos; on the other, from the "chaos" of minute particulars an

encompassing order emerges. What Ammons seeks to maintain in such apparently contradictory statements is not simply a balance between unity and diversity but the embodiment of a paradox: how can one be many, how can many be one? Rather than run to any "easy victory," as he says in "Corsons Inlet," he would keep his readers alive in the paradox—the very same paradox that, like Blake in the palm of a hand, or Mandelbrot in a coastline, can hold infinity in a finite space. As James Gleick writes of the chaos theorists, "they had an eye for pattern, especially for pattern that appeared on different scales at the same time . . . they are looking for the whole."[33] The same ought to be said of Ammons, whose sense of the whole is inextricable from his sense of the many.

Moreover, as I suggested earlier, the relationship of one to many is of moral significance to Ammons. As he wryly observes in *Sphere,* "they ask why I'm so big on the / one:many problem, they never saw one: my readers what do they / expect from a man born and raised in a country whose motto is *E / pluribus unum?*" (S, 65) The problem attracts not only Ammons's thoughts on the nature of reality and poetry, it reflects intimately the nature of our society. In *Garbage,* Ammons pushes his preoccupation with the relationship between one and many still further:

> if there is to be any regard for
>
> human life, it will have to be ours, right regard
> for human life including all other forms of life,
>
> including plant life: when we eat the body of
> another animal, we must undergo the sacrifice
>
> of noticing that life has been spent into our
> life, and we must care, then, for the life we
>
> have and for the life our life has cost, and we
> must make proper acknowledgements and sway some
>
> with reverence for the cruel and splendid tissue
> biospheric. . . .

(G, 117–118)

These lines do more than restate the ecological vision articulated by Ammons in "Extremes and Moderations"; they recast the one:many problem within a still wider moral framework, a framework that similarly encompasses the celebration of human diversity. Once again, what we find in *Sphere* and *Garbage,* as throughout Ammons's work, is a poetry of elaborated and constantly reconfiguring patterns across multiple scales of experience. In a sense, these poems are constructed like huge attractors that perform the tensive union of the one and the many in a manner that would imitate, as far as language is able, the deep structure of physical reality.

An attractor, as Katherine Hayles explains, "is any point within an orbit that seems to attract the system to it."[34] In nature, the dynamics of such systems as a swinging pendulum or one's heartbeat are determined by such points. In the case of the pendulum, all motion tends to rest at the midpoint; in the case of one's heartbeat, any limited disturbance (with the exception of a massive heart attack) returns to its characteristic rhythm. In the case of what chaos theorists call a "strange attractor"—an attractor whose pattern of organization appears to lack any discernable idea of order—the apparently random cycles of systems as varied as fluid turbulence, viral outbreaks, schizophrenic eye movements, stock market prices, and a dripping faucet in fact reveal a deep structure in which disorder "is mixed with clear remnants of order."[35] It is as if, paradoxically, randomness generated order, as if the peripheral through its very marginality gave rise to a shifting though nevertheless definable center. Chaos thus may be conceived as a dynamic motion that binds together the pure freedom of the apparently random and the organizational necessity of the seemingly intended. In *Sphere* and *Garbage,* it is as if the deep structure of both poems were modeled on such a conception of order emerging out of disorder, widely swinging arcs of thought, discursive patternings of ideas and images, vignettes, excursions that nonetheless cohere— "minor forms," as Ammons himself states, "within larger constructs" (G, 66). Here, again, Ammons betrays an inclination toward a vision of order-out-of-chaos. Perhaps not surprisingly, then, the figure of "the center" recurs in both poems, not as a conceit that would rush the poem to an abstract closure, but as a kind of "strange attractor" that allows the poem to range over wide expanses of experience, while retaining its coherent, albeit complex organic form. "Touch the universe anywhere you touch it / everywhere," Ammons declares (S, 72). In other words, as if to answer the common postmodern claim that the desire for "the center" is merely nostalgic, the poem bears witness to the idea that any part may become "a living center" that would connect you to the ongoing motion of the whole.

Yet even while Ammons appears attracted to creating such complex unities in *Sphere* and *Garbage,* he nevertheless continually confronts processes that would seem to disturb the symmetry of the whole. These are the fearful symmetries of entropy and death. "How can and how long can an identity / hold to the skin of the earth?" (S, 23) Ammons asks in *Sphere.* In one of that poem's most moving passages, the poet's reflection on the universe's "long, empty freezing gulfs" caught in the grip of entropy segues into the time "when the younger brother sickened and then moved no more." This interfusion of the most impersonal of deaths with the death of the poet's own brother would make death itself perhaps the strangest of strange attractors, drawing the cosmic and the particular alike into the orbit of its dark center. Without diminishing such "terrible transformations," Ammons would make death itself an occasion for exploring the positive implications of our natures as perishable beings. "In your end is my beginning," Ammons repeats over again in *Garbage.* The play on Eliot's refrain in *Four Quartets*—"in my beginning is my end, in my end is my beginning"—clearly intends to dislodge the self's quest for wholeness and even holiness from its reliance on self alone, the egocentric "my" giving way to an acknowledgement of the other, the "you" without whom there is no connection. Instead, Ammons would underscore that "we are bound together by our ends" and knowing as much, "we begin to / see the end of disturbing endlessness" (G, 63). Ultimately, the fact of death, both cosmic and personal, clarifies Ammons's implied network of mutuality. To this extent we are "trash," perishable, subject to dissolution and decay, though nonetheless, "plenty wondrous." Toward the end of *Garbage,* Ammons pushes this insight even further:

> it's a wonder natural
> selection hasn't thinned out anything not perfectly
>
> beautiful: but nature, if I may speak for it,
> likes a broad spectrum approaching disorder so
>
> as to maintain the potential of change with
> variety and environment: the true shape of
>
> perfect beauty, hard to find, somehow floats
> implicit and stable there. . . .
>
> (G, 101)

Just as in the final pages of *The Origin of Species* Darwin celebrates the grandeur of life that brings forth "endless forms most beautiful,"[36] so here Ammons links an almost Platonic idea of the beautiful to the diversity of life cast as it is against the relief of particular deaths. In both cases, observations of physical processes obtained through science converge with revelations normally considered within the province of the spiritual.

Indeed, Ammons directly addresses the metaphysical implications of his poetic forays into physical reality when in *Sphere* he asks the following question: "How to / devise a means that assimilates small inspirations into a / large space, network, reticulation complex . . . but moved forward by a controlling motion, design symmetry, / suasion, so that harmony can be recognized in the highest / ambience of diversity?" (S, 58) The question Ammons poses in *Sphere* is essentially answered by the complex form of the poem itself, with its requirement that the reader discern the poem's wider symmetry precisely through its ambience of diversity. Still more significantly, it could be the question asked by chaos theorists trying to catch a glimpse of the universal across multiple scales of existence. Should we push the implications further, it would be the question the universe asks itself in elaborating its own immense design, were it somehow conscious of its own ends and beginnings. And, if one were to assume a theological perspective, it is the question that predicates the origin of creation itself. Ultimately, Ammons's exploration of this question from the latter standpoint is precisely what distinguishes *Garbage* from *Sphere*. To be sure, *Sphere* conjures images of cosmogony in ways that pique the religious imagination, but not so boldly as does *Garbage* where, from the outset, the waste mound that serves as the work's recurring center and conceit is pictured as a sacred pyramid up which garbage trucks circle as they "intone the morning," their garglings become unlikely prayers.

Such figurations harken back to Ammons's first poems, with their appeal to the mythic sources of Sumer, a source revisited in the poems of *Sumerian Vistas*.[37] At the same time, Ammons's concern in *Garbage* with the relationship between energy and form, and of both to spirit, brings to full expression his work's remarkable convergence of the imaginative resources of science and religion:

> this is just a poem with a job to do: and that
>
> is to declare, however roundabout, sideways,
> or meanderingly (or in those ways) the perfect

> scientific and materialistic notion of the
> spindle of energy: when energy is gross,
>
> rocklike, it resembles the gross, and when
> fine it mists away into mystical refinements,
>
> sometimes passes right out of material
> recognizability and becomes, what?, motion,
>
> spirit, all forms translated into energy, as at
> the bottom of Dante's hell all motion is
>
> translated into form. . . .
>
> (G, 24–25)

For Ammons, the reciprocity that exists between matter and spirit—spirit itself being, so it seems, a more rarified form of energy—so inheres in his sacred mound that he can portray his truck driver crying "holy, holy, / holy," as he flicks his cigarette in a "spiritual swoop" to where "the consummations gather." Yet Ammons is not content merely to assert this intimate connection between matter and spirit. Rather, throughout the poem he further speculates on its nature:

> oh, yes, yes, the matter goes on,
>
> turning into this and that, never the same thing
> twice: but what about the spirit, does it die
>
> in an instant, being nothing in an instant out of
> matter, or does it hold on to some measure of
>
> time, not just the eternity in which it is not,
> but does death go on being death for a billion
>
> years—to infinity:
>
> (G, 37–38)

"The spirit was forever / and is forever, the residual and informing / energy," he goes on to declare, as though once again to echo Teilhard de Chardin: "In each of us, through matter, the whole history of the world is in part reflected . . . by the totality of the energies of the earth."[38]

Even so, despite so harmonious a vision, in *Garbage* Ammons would once again step back from the easy victory of claiming to have attained "Overall." The human world inevitably "trims the spirit too sharply back," and even the poet's words, "which attach to edges, cannot / represent wholeness, so if all is all, the it / just is" (G, 114). Finally, for Ammons, to capture the sacredness of everything in words is an impossibility, just as for the chaos theorist, the conception of universality across scales will always remain limited by the human mind's finitude. Nevertheless, as the poet observes, though we may "kick the *l* out of world and cuddle / up with the avenues and byways of the word," we are still "not alone in language" though "we may be alone in words" (G, 50). Such an expanded notion of language as an integral aspect of the motions of reality and not merely a province of human creation at once chastens the presumption of those who would, in Ammons's words, make it "fashionable to mean nothing" and at the same time enables us to affirm that "there is truly *only* meaning, / only meaning, meanings, so many meanings, / meaninglessness becomes what to make of so many / meanings" (G, 86). To assume as much enables us to widen the scope of our own vision, to see the poet's words as helping us to fend for ourselves and each other, and for the world—and finally, to paraphrase Wallace Stevens, to see in our own chaotic time the ghostlier demarcations of a keener idea of order.

NOTES

1. James Gleick, *Chaos: The Making of a New Science* (New York: Viking, 1987), 8.
2. Ibid.
3. See Gleick, *Chaos*, 45–53.
4. S. T. Coleridge, *Selected Poetry and Prose* (New York: New American Library, 1951), 433.
5. Steven P. Schneider, *A. R. Ammons and the Poetics of Widening Scope* (Madison, N.J.: Fairleigh Dickinson University Press, 1994), 21.
6. See Gleick, *Chaos*, 35.
7. N. Katherine Hayles, *Chaos Bound: Orderly Disorder in Contemporary Literature and Science*(Ithaca: Cornell University Press, 1990), 9.
8. See Steven Johnson, "Strange Attraction," *Lingua Franca* (March/April 1996): 42–50; John Barth, "Chaos Theory: PostMod Science, Literary Model," in *Further Fridays: Essays, Levtures and Other Non-Fiction, 1984–1994* (Boston: Little, Brown, 1995), 328–42.
9. Hayles, *Chaos Bound*, xi.
10. See N. Katherine Hayles, *The Cosmic Web: Scientific Field Strategies and Literary Strategies in the 20th Century* (Ithaca: Cornell University Press, 1984); John Barth, *Further Fridays*, 328–42.
11. See Hayles, *Chaos Bound*, 3–5; *Cosmic Web*, 9.
12. Ammons, *Selected Poems* (New York: Norton, 1986), 28.

13. See Schneider, *A. R. Ammons*, 15.
14. See Thomas Kuhn, *The Structure of Scientific Revolutions*, 2nd ed. (Chicago: University of Chicago Press, 1970).
15. See Hayles, *Chaos Bound*, 11.
16. Gleick, *Chaos*, 314.
17. Alan Holder, *A. R. Ammons* (New York: Twayne, 1978), 48.
18. See Schneider, *A. R. Ammons*, 84.
19. Alfred North Whitehead, *Adventures in Ideas* (New York: MacMillian, 1933), 258.
20. Roger Gilbert, "A. R. Ammons," *Dictionary of Literary Biography 165: American Poets since World War II*, fourth series, ed. Joseph Conte (Detroit: Gale Research, 1996), 23.
21. Hayles, *Chaos Bound*, 11.
22. Gleick, *Chaos*, 195–96.
23. Coleridge, *Selected Poetry and Prose*, 263.
24. Gleick, *Chaos*, 299.
25. Coleridge, *Selected Poetry and Prose*, 432–33.
26. Hayles, *Cosmic Web*, 150–51.
27. Gleick, *Chaos*, 195, 103.
28. Hayles, *Chaos Bound*, 12–13.
29. Ibid., 12.
30. See Gleick, *Chaos*, 100.
31. Ibid.
32. Schneider, *A. R. Ammons*, 223–24.
33. Gleick, *Chaos*, 5.
34. Hayles, *Chaos Bound*, 147.
35. Gleick, *Chaos*, 147.
36. Charles Darwin, *The Origin of Species* (New York: New American Library, 1958), 460.
37. A. R. Ammons, *Sumerian Vistas* (New York: Norton, 1987).
38. Teilhard de Chardin, *Divine Milieu*, 59.

The Long Poem as a Geological Force

Steven P. Schneider

Geology—the study of the origin, history, and structure of the earth—is one of the branches of science central to Ammons's poetry. From his earliest lyrics collected in *Ommateum*, up through many of the widely anthologized poems from *Collected Poems 1951–1971*, and interspersed throughout his major long poems, Ammons has been fascinated with the earth itself, both as a poetic trope and as the form of many motions that pull at and under and through the currents of his poetry. Central to his art, then, is what we might call the "poetics of geology"—the inscribing of the language, concepts, and discoveries of geological science within the body of a long poem.

This essay is concerned with three of Ammons's longer poems in which the poetics of geology plays a significant role, helping us to understand his conception of the long poem as a geological force. These three poems, *Tape for The Turn of The Year*, "Extremes and Moderations," and *Sphere: The Form of A Motion*, were published within a nine-year time frame, the first appearing in 1965, toward the middle of a decade marked by cataclysmic shifts both social and political, and the last appearing in 1974, at a time when the aftershocks of this decade of upheaval were still being felt. It is more than mere coincidence that Ammons's poetics of the earth, with its remarkable concern for motion and seismic upheaval as evidenced in these three poems, coincides with a period of great social change in the United States.

What are the consequences of Ammons's interest in geology? First, it provides both him and his readers with a metaphor for conceptualizing poetic practice, process, and form in the longer poems. Second, geology provides Ammons with the the facts, language, and concepts that become essential to the development of central images and ideas in his longer poems. Finally, Ammons draws upon geological knowledge to inform his ecological vision of the natural world.

The literal root meaning of "geology" is *geo-logos,* or "earth-word," which is quite different from "geography," or "earth-writing," the human activity of mapping and controlling the earth by writing human language onto it. "Geo-logos," on the other hand, posits an earth that speaks its own language, a word *of* the earth, not a writing *on* the earth. Perhaps this is what Walt Whitman meant when he wrote in "A Song of the Rolling Earth": "Delve! mould! pile the words of the earth!"[1] Ammons, in his poem "Poetics," declares his intention to look "for the way / things will turn / out spiralling from a center" (CP, 199). One of those centers is the earth, and in *Sphere: The Form of A Motion* Ammons is determined to let the earth speak, to find a form and an angle of vision through which his poetry becomes "earth-words."

More than any other poet writing today, Ammons can be linked to the Whitman who wrote in the 1855 Preface to *Leaves of Grass:*

> Exact science and its practical movements are no checks on the greatest poet but always his encouragement and support. The outset and remembrance are there . . there the arms that lifted him first and brace him best . . . . there he returns after all his goings and comings. The sailor and traveler . . the anatomist, chemist, astronomer, geologist, phrenologist, spiritualist, mathematician, historian and lexicographer are not poets, but they are the lawgivers of poets and their construction underlies the structure of every perfect poem. *(LOG, 720)*

Ammons has always been fascinated by science, and although he claims to have no more than a casual knowledge of it, garnered through his browsing in journals such as *Scientific American,* there is much evidence to suggest that his knowledge is quite sophisticated and well-informed. In Ammons's poetry, the poet's mind and "longing" is persistently influenced by natural facts.[2] No less an authority than Nobel Prize–winning chemist and poet Roald Hoffmann, a close friend and colleague of Ammons at Cornell University, is quoted in a 1996 *Audubon* magazine article as saying that Ammons "really does hear nature singing, and it's at some deep philosophical, scientific, poetic level. I think he could be a great biologist in another existence."[3] A. R. Ammons did, after all, major in science at Wake Forest University. His poetry has from its very beginnings drawn upon scientific terminology. He has demonstrated in both his long poems and his shorter lyrics a firm grasp of such complex scientific phenomena as the "light cone" in astronomy and mechanisms of perception and digestion in human physiology. Moreover, Ammons's vision of the world has been shaped largely by developments in twentieth century physics, which have undermined subject/object dualities and evoked a fluid view of the universe in which subatomic particles swirl about in an interconnected "field" of activity.

Like modern astronomy and physics, geological science provides Ammons with a widened perspective, with what he has referred to in "Corsons Inlet" as "widening scope."[4] Geology is the science in which human time and perspectives are viewed in the context of much larger time frames and forces. One consequence of this widening of scope is a reexamination of human time and action, and more specifically the development of an ecological consciousness in which one's individual actions have far-reaching consequences.

By using geology, as well as astronomy, biology, and physics to develop a more "ecocentric way of being," Ammons can and has been read as a poet whose work is "environmentally oriented." In *The Environmental Imagination,* Lawrence Buell suggests several criteria by which we can determine if a text is so oriented: "the nonhuman environment is present not merely as a framing device but as a presence that begins to suggest that human history is implicated in natural history"; "the human interest is not understood to be the only legitimate interest"; "human accountability to the environment is part of the text's ethical orientation"; "some sense of the environment as a process rather than as a constant or a given is at least implicit in the text."[5] Long before "eco-criticism" entered the lexicon of contemporary critical theory, A. R. Ammons—most especially in his long poems—exhibited these features.

Ammons's first major long poem, *Tape for the Turn of the Year,* was composed during the winter of 1963 and in early 1964. The journal entries that form the text of the poem begin on 6 December 1963 and end on 10 January 1964. The individual dates of each entry in and of themselves are significant only in that they provide Ammons with a way to register and mark the news of the universe etched into each entry—characterized as they are by references to weather, observations of birds, and speculations on digestion. Ammons writes on December 18th:

> I hold these days aloft,
> empty boxes
> you can exist in: but
> when you live in them
> you hurry out of your own
> life:[6]

While the speaker downplays the significance of any one of these days, and of the entire period of time when he coaxed the roll ("scrolling") of adding machine tape through his typewriter, William Harmon in his essay "How Does One Come Home" has speculated that Ammons's first major long poem was triggered by a very specific historical event, the assassination of President John F. Kennedy. Harmon suggests that Ammons felt compelled to invent a project that would "help stave off confusion" during a time of national mourning. Harmon's theory provides a fascinating context for reading *Tape,* but I would like to propose another context, another type of "upheaval" in the early 1960s that would more significantly influence Ammons's poetry throughout the rest of the decade and indeed for the duration of his poetic career.

I am referring to discoveries in the field of geology that altered our conception of the earth. No aspect of geologic research remains unaffected by the plate tectonic theory advanced in the early 1960s. According to Peter Westbroek, author of *Life as a Geological Force,* "volcanism, earthquakes, the relief of the ocean floors and continents are all now revealed as part of an all-embracing master theme."[7] The plate tectonic theory displaced the previous understanding of the earth as a continuous global sheet and suggested rather that the earth's surface "is made up of huge crustal plates that move and shift."[8] This scientific discovery, like many others in the twentieth century, substituted the conception of material creation as something solid and fixed with a more dynamic conception of matter that adopted flux and uncertainty as the norm.

The plate tectonic theory explains that shifts in the lithosphere, which includes not only the earth's crust of oceans and continents, but also the top rigid layer of the earth's mantle, result from a process of creation and destruction. According to Westbroek, "if fresh lithospheric material is created in one place it must be destroyed in another, or the globe would be an ever-expanding balloon."[9] In considering the long poem as a geological force, we need to consider how for Ammons the plate tectonic theory illuminates his sense of poetic form and process.

As John Elder points out in his chapter on Ammons in *The Imagined Earth,* the poem itself is a kind of "terrain into which the reader may step."[10] It is, however, a shifting terrain. Although the boxlike stanzaic structures of "Extremes and Moderations" and *Sphere* and the arbitrary narrowness of *Tape for the Turn of the Year* (restricted by the width of adding machine tape on which the poem is composed) suggest rigidity and stability, in fact each of these long poems draws the reader into a far more shifting and open-ended "terrain" of experience than one might anticipate.

Ammons is cognizant as early as *Tape for the Turn of the Year* of the plate tectonic theory, and uses it to inform his sense of "surface" and "depth" that are the poles of his thinking in this and other long poems.

> I mean to stay on the
> crusty
> hard-clear surface: tho
>   congealed
> it reflects the deep,
> the fluid, hot motions
> and intermotions where,
>   after all, we
>   do not live:
>
> (T, 6)

Throughout his major long poems, in which "surface" and "depth" are central, Ammons compares the process of composing them to geological forces associated with the motion of the earth's plates. According to Westbroek, "the motion of the plates is driven by heat released by radioactive decay deep inside the earth."[11] Sometimes during the process, rock slabs are heated, melted, and absorbed into the earth's mantle. Those heated rocks that escape upwards to the land surface "form a stream of rising magmas and lavas that are associated with mountain building and extensive volcanism."[12] In his December 8th entry of *Tape for the Turn of the Year*, Ammons likens the writing of his poem to the eruption of a volcano:

> the crust keeps us: the
> volcano-mind
> emits
> this ribbon of speech,
> smoke & heat
> that held
> would bust the cone off,
> inundate the house
> with direct melt:
> but let off, there's
> easing, mind cool, the
> slow accretion of hard
> rock:
> doesn't matter how much

the core shifts
long as we have these
islands to live on:

(T, 13–14)

The heat, combustion, and the blowing off of steam from the "volcano-mind" indicate the forces the poet feels within himself that cannot be contained ("bust the cone off") and which manifest themselves in the daily journal entries of *Tape*. Ammons, throughout his career, has characterized poetry as a kind of *release*. When asked by David Lehman in a *Paris Review* interview whether inspiration originates in nature or in the self, Ammons responds:

> I think it comes from anxiety. That is to say, either the mind or the body is already rather highly charged and in need of some kind of expression, some way to crystallize and relieve the pressure. And it seems to me that if you're in that condition and an idea, an insight, an association occurs to you, then that energy is released through the expression of that insight or idea, and after the poem is written, you feel a certain resolution and calmness.[13]

The volcano, then, is an apt metaphor for the poet's sense of his own creative processes and compulsions to write. The buildup of internal pressure must find a release. The use of the volcano as a trope for artistic "release" is a common one. It was a favorite of Emily Dickinson, who in such poems as "Volcanoes be in Sicily" and "A Still—Volcano—Life" uses volcanoes to represent the way poetic inspiration works—vast, dangerous eruptions occurring unpredictably in an otherwise dormant and placid life. The metaphor as used by Ammons retains this conventional meaning, but becomes something more. His desire seems to be to construct a trope that moves poetry from a personal source to a geological source, to tie the flow of his lines and thoughts in *Tape* to some geothermal origin—"the fluid, hot motions / and intermotions." Unlike Dickinson, Ammons is also interested in the detailed physical dynamics of volcanic eruption and works elements of the phenomenon into his poem.

Certainly imaginative "heat" and "combustion" are needed to sustain the impetus and energy of *Tape for the Turn of the Year* and many other of Ammons's long poems. The "volcano-mind" then may provide readers with an apt metaphor to explain the many "eruptions" of long poems in Ammons's illustrious career. Those who have followed the development of his work are not surprised to discover that, just when the volcano seems to have calmed down, it will erupt again. For Ammons, never one to sit still for very long, has distinguished his poetic journey by a series of abrupt shifts, seeming periods of quiescence only to be followed by such outbursts as *Sphere* and *Garbage,* and more recently *Glare,* book-length poems dizzying in their effluvium of thought.

In the heat of composition, the poet suggests in the above passage from *Tape,* the house in which he writes is liable to experience "direct melt." But the poet of extremes and moderations understands that such creative burning is to be followed by a period of "easing," or "mind cool." So too are geological processes composed of periods of extreme pressure (heat) and phases of cooling down, the "slow accretion of hard rock." In geological terms, the islands Ammons refers to may be the "detritus" of volcanism, seeming oases of repose in an ever-shifting sea of geological activity. In the context of the poem, the "islands" we have to live on are the individual journal entries that compose *Tape for the Turn of the Year,* or the stanzaic "islands" of "Extremes and Moderations" or the numbered sections of *Sphere.* They provide places to *dwell in* and *dwell upon,* both for Ammons as poet and for his readers.

In developing a poetics of geology, Ammons has followed Whitman's lead in "A Song of the Rolling Earth." Whitman's 1856 poem was influenced by Emerson's theory of language, in which "words are signs of natural facts." Thus, as Whitman writes, "the substantial words are in the / ground and sea" (LOG, 219). One could say the same for Ammons, who has identified the earth (*Sphere: The Form of A Motion*) and water ("Expressions of Sea Level," "Corsons Inlet") as two key natural elements in the development of his poetry. For Whitman, the earth itself not only provides a rich mine of language but also is a source of great power: "I swear there is no greatness or power that does not emulate / those of the earth" (LOG, 223). *Those* powers Whitman alludes to are the natural forces working *beneath* and *upon* the earth's surface to form mountains, volcanoes, and glaciers. Ammons, too, will "emulate" those powers of the earth, informed however, by a more sophisticated understanding of the earth's dynamics, which in *Sphere* will provide him with an analogy for his own sense of poetic process in that poem.

As early as *Tape for the Turn of the Year,* Ammons is cognizant of the poetic potential inherent in the earth and in the work of the geologist. Like his contemporaries Charles Olson and Gary Snyder and their forebear Walt Whitman, Ammons seizes upon the language, discoveries, and theories of geology in reflecting upon the significance of vast geological time frames and forces. Often, Ammons does so in order to suggest the ways in which (to quote Buell again) "human interest is not understood to be the only legitimate interest" and Ammons's view of "the environment as a process rather than as a constant." He writes in his December 7th entry of *Tape:*

> last
> night I
> read
> about the
> geologic times
> of the Northwest, the
> periodic eruptions into
> lava plateaus,
> forests grown, stabilized,
> and drowned
> between eruptions:
> in the
> last
> 10,000 years (a bit of
>   time) the
> glaciers have been
> melting, some now unfed,
> disconnected, lying dead
> and dissolving in
> high
> valleys: how strange
> we are here,
> raw, new, how ephemeral our
>   lives and cultures,
>   how unrelated
>   to the honing out of
>   caves and canyons:

(T, 5–6)

One consequence of geological time is to see "how ephemeral our / lives and cultures" are in contrast to the durations of geological time and force. The speaker's reflection on geological activity in the Northwest, with its volcanoes, forests, and glaciers, enables the reader to see how that region has been a scene of cosmic activity that predates much human drama and narrative. Ten thousand years ago, Ammons writes, the Sumerians had not yet "compiled / their / holy bundle of / the elements of civil / ization" (T, 7). Ammons, distrustful of human nature, is often ready to cast a wry commentary upon our lives and (Western) cultures, which he calls "ephemeral" in contrast to the more enduring powers of geological force. He does not exclude himself or his own work from such consideration and uses self-deprecating humor to deflate whatever pretensions his long poems may aspire to. In *Garbage,* for example, he refers to his composition as "a straw bag full of fleas."

Ammons expresses what Lawrence Buell describes as an "eco-centric literary vision," offering "a critique of the centrality and even the legitimacy of human assertion."[14] As the poet reminds us, geological time dwarfs human time and its accomplishments. Many human cultures and empires have arisen and disappeared from the face of the earth in the last ten thousand years—"Troy / burned since then" (6). Yet the workings of glaciers upon the earth's surface, the honing out of canyons and caves remain as testimony to some larger, more elemental, and more enduring forces. Ammons also registers his criticism here of the distance he feels between human culture and geological activity, a gap ("how unrelated") he laments. He is not only calling attention to the *transient* nature of human culture, but also its *apartness* from the processes of natural force.

Two major conclusions can be derived from Ammons's use of geological references in the above passage from *Tape for the Turn of The Year.* First, geology, which includes the study of glaciers, forests, and volcanoes, is a tool in the poet's mind for questioning the significance of much human action and the inflated meaning we attach to it. The weight of the word "ephemeral" is enormous, emphasizing that "the human interest is not understood to be the only legitimate interest" because it is of short duration ("raw," "new," "ephemeral") in comparison to other equally legitimate and more enduring interests. At the same time, Ammons also recognizes in this same section of the poem, that although human life is but a "blip" on a radar screen, "in the blip is all / imperishable possibility." He is willing to acknowledge human life is the manifestation of a unique frequency of energy in the long history of the universe. This recognition, however, is tempered by the steely knowledge that geological time and perspective dwarf human time and perspective. Indeed, the humbling of Western "civilization" is one of the essential consequences of Ammons's interest in geology, the science which provides knowledge of a prehuman earth, a vast time when life existed without our interference.

It is not surprising, then, to discover that Ammons has distanced himself from the poetry of confessionalism, with its excessive emphasis on personality, and favored a more detached poetics of earth and space. In a 1984 interview with Jim Stahl, Ammons criticizes poets Robert Lowell and John Berryman for "hacking" away at their lives so "as to get the greatest conflict and density and brutality and energy and tension and whatever else concentrated and focused in the poem." He goes on to suggest an alternative way of composing a poem:

> There is, apart from this poet who is constantly trying to intensify, there is the poet who is himself in such an anxious state that he turns to the poem not to create an even more intense verbal environment, but to do just the contrary; to ease that pressure. And this poet is I think potentially the greatest poet. *But,* he must in the very dissolution or effort to ease that pressure, he must not lose it; the reader must know that it's there, that that pressure is there. (SM, 45)

Here the poet understands that there is "already enough energy in the world to write out of without having to hack his way into some kind of artificial violence" (SM, 45). Ammons is intent on discovering the event in the natural world that destabilizes a narrow fixation upon the self and restricted mental definitions. In "Corsons Inlet," for example, the speaker celebrates the fact that a new walk is a new walk, that each turn around the inlet promises relief from the "blocks, boxes, binds / of thought." In lyrics such as "Clarity" and "Eyesight," the speaker encourages readers to be alert to subtle changes ("events") in the natural world that have the power to freshen the sources of our being. In addressing the purpose of poetry in a 1973 interview, Ammons says: "To rehearse, to alert, to freshen, to awaken the energies, not to lunacy and meaningless motion, but to concentration and focus. That is the desirable state to which art should bring you, and to the extent that the poem becomes an image of this, and a generator of it, it is a desirable thing."[15]

Throughout *Tape for the Turn of the Year,* Ammons seeks out the energy of nature, both for the material of his long poem and as the source of psychic release he values. One major source for this release can be found in the poet's contemplation of geological epochs; another, of course, is in his direct engagement with the weather and his immediate environment. Such engagement for Ammons provides renewal, what he refers to as "starting over." For this reason, Ammons's long poems have far fewer allusions to *human* history and culture than the long poems of his modernist predecessors, T. S. Eliot and Ezra Pound. In commenting upon his deliberate choice to minimize such allusions in his work, Ammons explains:

> See, I start over with stumps and birds and streams and brooks and the sky. I may be seeking the purity that was there first, but I don't think that's it. I take some kind of comfort in the inexhaustibility of the devisings of nature, that it can keep coming up with new things.[16]

Ammons's interest in the "devisings of nature" feeds his interest in the sciences and, in particular, geology. While the confessional poets in the 1960s continued to pursue what today Lawrence Buell might call an "egocentric" aesthetics, Ammons, after the publication of *Tape* in 1963, would vigorously counter this with an "eco-centric" approach to the composition of his long poems, informed by the natural sciences and an abiding fascination with the earth.

The decade of social upheaval, the sixties, saw a renewed interest in things "earthy." For the first time in human history we were provided with pictures of our planet from a perspective in outer space. This, in turn, led to a heightened interest in ecology, a word that Ammons in *Tape for the Turn of the Year* admits that he can be "tagged with."

> *ecology* is my word: tag
> me with that: come
> in there:
> you will find yourself
> in a firmless country:
> centers & peripheries
> in motion,
> organic,
>   interrelations!
>
> (T, 112)

Seen from a distance, the earth suddenly seemed vulnerable, strangely beautiful, interrelated, and for many a cause worthy of support. While the 1960s began with advances in plate tectonic theory, the 1970s began with the celebration of Earth Day (April 1970) and the publication of a series of editions of the *Whole Earth Catalog,* and by the mid-1970s Earth shoes would have swarms of devotees.

Ammons's long poems of this period reflect a keen interest in the earth, in geology, and in an environmental vision that decries the despoliation of the planet. His long poem "Extremes and Moderations," published in the *Collected Poems 1951–1971,* more than any other of his longer poems, including *Garbage,* takes on the polluters and considers the consequences of a too limited scope.

In "Extremes and Moderations," Ammons evokes a precariously balanced world, one whose cosmic forces are self-regulating but susceptible to artificial disturbance. He is especially concerned with the ways in which nature achieves balance through circulations that the poet fears may become trapped.

> circulations are moderations, currents triggered by extremes:
> we must at all costs keep the circulations free and clear,
> open and unimpeded: otherwise, extremes will become trapped,
> local, locked in themselves, incapable of transaction:
>
> (CP, 333)

Ammons's sense of the earth and its living matter—air, ocean, and land surfaces—as a complex interconnected system anticipates the idea of the Gaia theory advanced by James Lovelock in the mid-1970s and published in 1979 in his landmark book, *Gaia: A New Look at Life on Earth.* Ammons's poem shares much with Lovelock's theory of Gaia in acknowledging the tendency toward balance and constancy in the currents of natural systems. Both the human body and larger bodies of water, oceans, for example, are regulated by "extremes and moderations" :

> go to look for the ocean currents and
> though they are always flowing there they are, right in place, if
> with seasonal leans and sways: the human body
> staying in change, time rushing through, ingestion,
>
> elimination: if change stopped, the mechanisms of
> holding would lose their tune: current informs us,
> is the means of our temporary stay:
>
> (CP, 334–35)

In these lines the poet invokes the underlying hypothesis of Gaia, that many of the variables in nature and human physiology are maintained automatically. Stability, in fact, is a consequence of change, as Ammons suggests throughout "Extremes and Moderations." In biology and medicine, the stable condition of healthy organisms is called *homeostasis.* According to Peter Westbroek, "Lovelock maintains that homeostasis is also an essential concept for understanding the earth. A network of Gaian regulatory mechanisms, operating at a global scale, keeps the earth in this remarkable state."[17] Although the Gaia theory has its critics, Westbroek reports that "Lovelock has drawn the notice of the worldwide scientific community" and "bits of data are accumulating that, although they don't prove Lovelock's hypothesis, tend to support its overall conclusions."[18]

Ammons anticipates Lovelock's theory in several ways. The conceptualization of large entities such as ecosystems—in which the air, the oceans, and the rocks all combine in one system as Gaia—is predicated on the understanding that human, plant, and animal life are composed from a myriad of smaller building blocks, ultimately a vast set of ultramicroscopic parts. Westbroek cautions that Lovelock's interest is in "the operation of the Gaia system— all organisms and their environment together."[19] Ammons too has long been interested in the ways in which the parts of biological life contribute to larger wholes. In this sense, he has also anticipated recent attempts to integrate the sciences of biology and geology.

Ammons would have derived such a view of the natural world from such sources as *The Science of Botany,* by Paul B. Weisz and Melvin S. Fuller. In another of his long poems from this period, "Essay on Poetics," he inserts an entire paragraph from *The Science of Botany* to make a point about poetic organization, one of the subjects of "Essay on Poetics."

"We may sum up. Carbohydrates, fats, proteins, nucleic acids, and their various derivatives, together with water and other inorganic materials, plus numerous additional compounds found specifically in particular types of living matter—these are the molecular bricks out of which living matter is made. To be sure, a mere random pile of such bricks does not make a living structure, any more than a mere pile of real bricks makes a house. First and foremost, if the whole is to be living, the molecular components must be organized into a specific variety of larger microscopic bodies; and these in turn, into actual, appropriately structured cells."

(CP, 314–15)

Such organization reflects one of the key principles in nature that Ammons celebrates in his work, involving the inner mechanisms of intelligence whereby a system organizes itself, whether that system be the human body, a goldfinch, the oceans on the surface of the earth, or a long poem. The problem, he laments in "Extremes and Moderations," is that human beings are constantly fouling up the works: "we apparently cannot let well enough / alone" (CP, 337). "Just think," he writes, "the best cure / would arise by subtle influence of itself if only we would / disappear" (CP, 337).

Because we won't simply disappear, however, one of the best things we can do is to expose ourselves to poems. Always one to explore the possibilities inherent in parallel universes, Ammons suggests that poems are like natural systems in their ability to balance oneness and diversity. The above citation from *The Science of Botany* is followed by this crucial insight:

> poems are verbal
> symbols for these organizations: they imprint upon the mind
> examples of integration in which the energy flows with maximum
>
> effect and economy between the high levels of oneness and the
> numerous subordinations and divisions of diversity: it is simply
> good to have the mind exposed to and reflected by such examples:
>
> (CP, 314–15)

This delicate balance between one and many has long been a major preoccupation for him. Its many iterations are imprinted in both the shorter lyrics ("One:Many," "Corsons Inlet," "Lines") and the longer poems ("Extremes and Moderations," "Essay on Poetics") in his *Collected Poems, 1951–1971*. Moreover, in what seems almost like a second career in the vast body of work that followed the publication of *Collected Poems 1951–1971*, Ammons has continued his obsession with "centers" and "peripheries."

If geology, biology, and botany take as one of their concerns the balancing of discrete parts with larger wholes, then Ammons must register alarm over the impact of pollution on the environment. Early in "Extremes and Moderations," he declares:

> I feel this is the last poem to the world: every
> poet probably feels he is writing the last poem to the world:
> man, in motion how avaricious, has by the exaggeration of his
>
> refinement shown what intelligence can commit in the universe:
> bleak scald of lakes, underground poisonous tides, air litter
> like a dusk, clouds not like the clouds . . .
>
> (CP, 330–31)

This litany of environmental abuses, the poisoning of the air and water, echoes back, of course, to the pioneering work of Rachel Carson and her 1962 book, *Silent Spring*. Ammons, who was working on "Extremes and Moderations" in the mid to late 1960s, would have known of Carson's work. He would have also been familiar with such environmental degradation from any number of sources, including *Scientific American*. In reflecting upon such matters as acid rain, polluted oceans and lakes, Ammons told an interviewer for *Audubon* magazine: "When I first learned that the rain was not clean, it was a dramatic shift for me. It was a very *painful* thing to accept."[20] Like so many other prominent poets in the 1960s, most notably W. S. Merwin and Gary Snyder, he registered his concern that the consequences of large-scale environmental despoliation could lead to the end of the human species. Although this is an anthropocentric concern, Ammons spares no vitriol in his condemnation of the adverse ways in which "human history is implicated in natural history."

The irony in these lines lies in Ammons's use of the word *intelligence*. For it is by the "exaggeration of his refinement" that man has shown what "intelligence can commit in the universe." Although Ammons in "Extremes and Moderations" pays homage to the natural intelligence at work in human and nonhuman systems, he vilifies human intelligence, *man's* intelligence, for what it has done to the planet. In eschewing a gender neutral term for the term "man," he clearly seems to attribute blame here to a patriarchal system that has asserted its will upon the natural world. Geological science, which had given him an ironic perspective on human activity in *Tape for the Turn of the Year,* provides the poet with a rich context for expressing his "ethical orientation" in "Extremes and Moderations," an orientation that condemns the excesses of "human intelligence" that have directly contributed to the poisoning of the water and air.

Ammons has always sided with natural forces over human ones. In "Extremes and Moderations" he opposes the city to the currents of nature.

> O city, I cry at
> the gate, the glacier is your
> mother, the currents of the deep father you, you sleep
>
> in the ministry of trees, the boulders are your brothers sustaining
> you: come out, I cry, into the lofty assimilations: women, let
> down your hair under the dark leaves of the night grove, enter
> the currents with a sage whining, rising into the circular
>
> dance:

> (CP, 335)

Here the poet identifies the city with constraint and stasis in contrast to the processes and currents of the natural world. His vision demands a greater latitude. In these lines, the poet urges movement beyond the limited parameters of the city. He invites the reader into the mystery of nature and its power to transform. While it is true that Ammons is particularly interested in natural systems as dynamic models for ethical human interaction, here we see him inviting the reader to participate in the "circular dance," freely enjoying the energy of nature rather than simply contemplating it.

To "enter the currents" is also an invitation to participate in the many different "currents" of his long poems. These include, of course, the natural currents he alludes to in "Extremes and Moderations," those found in rivers and oceans, in the biosphere, and in the farthest reaches of the galaxy. Such "currents," however, would encompass the range, or *currents,* of his thinking, which in "Extremes and Moderations" and Ammons's other long poems fuse with his descriptions of nature and his references to science. Ammons, as John Elder has astutely pointed out, knows that "poetry is the medium . . . within which mind and nature interfuse."[21]

The natural world is never very far removed from this poet's own consciousness of it, a consciousness that is cognizant of the many "currents" of discourse (scientific and poetic) employed in his long poems. While the above passage is indicative of a highly romantic strain in Ammons, he can just as easily slip into the discourse of a geologist in describing the drift of coastal land with sea currents.

> coastal land, say, drifts with sea currents
>
> north a couple of inches a year, setting up a strain along a
> line with the land's end: at some point, tension gives in
> a wrack and wrecks stability, restoring lassitude:
>
> (CP, 337–38)

The slow drift of coastal land is the type of phenomenon that interests Ammons, for inherent in it is the kind of "slowed motion" that fascinates him. He is an astute observer of the processes whereby seemingly fixed phenomena "drift," wrecking stability. Indeed, this has been one of his consistent preoccupations. Even rocks in Ammons's poetry are unstable, as evidenced in the lyric "Motion's Holdings" in the volume *Sumerian Vistas.*

> boulders, their green and white
> moss-molds, high-held in moist
> hill woods, stir, hum with

stall and spill, take in and give
off heat, adjust nearby to
geomagnetic fields, tip liquid with

change should a trunk or rock loosen
to let rollers roll, or they loll
inwardly with earth's lie

in space, oxidize at their surfaces
exchanges with fungal thread and rain:

(SV, 113)

The science of geology provides Ammons with a lens for observing such phenomena and the language to describe them. Apparently stationary objects such as boulders, become in Ammons's poem, sites of much activity, and the exchanges of energy that occur between them and the atmosphere are evidence of a dynamic natural process. The poet's incorporation of the language of science ("geomagnetic fields," "oxidize") with the language of more colloquial speech ("stir," "hum") is one of the ways that his discourse mirrors the interpenetration of natural events that he so meticulously records. In Ammons's poetics of geology, however, *interpenetration* is more than just an apt description of the collision of different types of language. *Interpenetration* is also suggestive of the degree to which mind and nature are integrated in his poetry. *Interpenetrate* was a key word for Whitman too, who sought out a self that realizes its own geological connections and origins. In "A Song of the Rolling Earth" he writes: "Air, soil, water, fire—those are words, / I myself am a word with them—my qualities interpenetrate with / theirs" (LOG, 220).

Like the geologist, Ammons possesses a passion for the stories that rocks tell, for the events that glaciers signal, for the identity that can be discovered in a valley. He writes toward the middle of "Extremes and Moderations":

there is
memory enough in the rock, unscriptured history in
the wind, sufficient identity in the curve
of the valley:

(CP, 335)

Ammons has never abandoned his allegiance to natural history for that of human history. Perhaps this is why he has not been a terribly fashionable poet. In a time dominated by historicist approaches both in criticism and in the writing of poetry, Ammons has eschewed human history for the histories of earth and space. Like the geologist, Ammons knows that rocks contain memories, histories of land formations, and global shifts in weather that can be read and interpreted. The qualifying adjectives in these lines— "enough", "sufficient"—are chosen carefully to suggest the poet's sense of satisfaction that can be derived from entering and observing the natural "currents." In commenting on these lines to D. I. Grossvogel in a 1973 issue of *diacritics*, Ammons says: "And what I mean is that if you see the shape of the valley, it's there, immediate in this moment. But in that shape is the entire history of its coming there."[22]

He also relishes the unrehearsed, non-dogmatic, unsanctioned, and yes, unprivileged quality of "unscriptured history" found in the wind. Cut loose from all fetters, the wind circulates freely. Ammons has been listening to the wind from his earliest beginnings as a poet: the very first poem, "So I Said I am Ezra," in his *Collected Poems 1951–1971* , asserts: "I listened to the wind / go over my head and up into the night." The wind is a powerful force that bends trees and rips sand from beaches. It is both irreverent ("unscriptured") and unpredictable, qualities that Ammons's long poems manifest.

In these lines on "rock," "wind," and "valley," he presents an alternative, radical view of history, one which emphasizes the immediacy of the present moment, his sense of the environment as a process, and the poet's connection to the forces of natural history that shape the environment. In explaining this concept to Grossvogel, Ammons advocates "another view of history that means more to me" than the one of investing the past with human significance:

> I have written a little poem about it which I have never published, whose last line is "history is a blank." Whatever you see when you look out of the window at any particular moment is history—is the truest history surviving into the immediate moment. The whole history of the planet earth is in your body at this moment, and so on. So that I don't have to structure it into time periods. Perhaps this is another reason why I do not have problems with the anxiety of influence, because I believe that what is here now, at this moment, is the truest version of history that we will ever know. Consequently, I have as much right to enter into it with all the innocence of immediacy as anyone else possibly ever could.[23]

Ammons does have problems ("anxieties") with the artificial forces which threaten this view of history. The "innocence of immediacy" is endangered by industrialists who dump toxic waste into rivers and by factories that pollute the air. He writes towards the conclusion of "Extremes and Moderations":

> extreme and moderation is losing its quality, its effect: the
> artificial has taken on the complication of the natural and where
> to take hold, how to let go, perplexes individual action: ruin
> and gloom are falling off the shoulders of progress: blue-green

> globe, we have tripped your balance and gone into exaggerated
> possession: this seems to me the last poem written to the world
> before its freshness capsizes and sinks into the slush:
>
> (CP, 340)

The poet acknowledges in these stanzas another more common view of history, one in which "exaggerated possession" dominates the arena of human action. Such possession, of course, would include ownership and leads all too often to disregard for the intricate interrelationships on the earth. Ammons pauses to reflect that his poem may be "the last poem written to the world" before it is destroyed. The poet would go on to write many more poems, both long and short, *after* his composition of "Extremes and Moderations." This poem, however, marked a key point in his development, for not only does it register his explicitly ethical concern for the environment, but in it he puts to good use what he refers to as his "ventilator," or "interminable stanza." After reaching what seems to be a nadir of despair over the state of human interference on the planet, the poet acknowledges, at least

>   I have my ventilator
> here, my interminable stanza, my lattice work that lets the world

> breeze unobstructed through: we could use more such harmless
> devices:
>
> (CP, 341)

Thus, the long poem itself, with its lattice-work stanzas that let the world breeze through, becomes the moderating device for the poet's own extremes. It is the means whereby the poet and the poem can stay balanced—maintaining "homeostasis"—in a precarious world. Michael McFee has suggested that "the figure of the stanza as 'lattice work,' screening the flow of the poem into regular units and spaces, is the central metaphor for the form of these middle long poems."[24] It is the mechanism whereby the poet can "ventilate," circulating the currents of his ever-inquisitive mind and probing the mysteries of geology and other sciences that inform both him and his readers.

The four-lined "lattice work" of "Extremes and Moderations" becomes in *Sphere* the three-lined stanzaic "mesh," which "can widen to let everything / breeze through" (S, 28–29). Both the "lattice work" and the "mesh," however, can be envisioned as a weaving, interwoven, not closed, but rather open. The seemingly arbitrary structure of these two mid-career long poems never becomes rigid because the "artifice" Ammons invents is flexible enough to be, what Stephen Cushman has pointed out, "variably invariable."[25] The stanzaic structure in each is not sealed tight because there is sufficient space *between* and *within* each stanza to allow the energy of nature to circulate. This is accomplished within each stanza by the frequent use of colons, which bring to pause but never complete cessation the impetus of the poet's thoughts. And the appearance of open space between each stanza provides a gap sufficient enough to mediate all the extremes and moderations circulating through each poem. In a sense, these predictable spaces between stanzas allow for the stanzaic structures to "breathe;" the gaps then are momentary resting places in the ongoing flux of each poem. In reflecting on the mesh, or latticework structure of the stanzas in these long poems, Ammons explains:

> It's a complex weaving of some kind that has openings. I mean you wouldn't want to build something like a glass tower that obstructs motion. Everything has to go around it. In nature, you have these configurations that are interwoven and yet permit, sometimes I suppose encourage, circulation.[26]

Here Ammons dispels the notion that his stanzaic structure is merely a predetermined and arbitrary "artifice" but is rather modelled upon some kind of natural configuration.

At this juncture you may be lamenting, as Harold Bloom has, the strain in Ammons that Bloom calls "ecological and geological."[27] But in giving oneself up to the experience of reading Ammons's longer poems, and for a reader these are challenging—sometimes daunting—texts, one must acknowledge that the "great lava flows of language," as Helen Vendler has called them, affect readers in ways analogous to geological forces. That is, they require a huge shift—both in our critical awareness and in our approach to reading. As long as we minimize or dismiss the long-range significance of the "geological," as Bloom would have us do, we create a box of thought that the long poems themselves work to unravel, to *deconstruct,* to use a term that seems to have an array of geological associations. For nearly all of Ammons's long poems, despite their differences in form or central metaphors, work by means of improvisation in order to incorporate as much of the world into them as possible. Ammons's effort to delimit the contents of a poem finds its greatest expression in these long poems, which ebb and flow like the tides, congeal and then melt like glaciers, change direction and upset expectation like rock slides. What better way of understanding how they work than by assimilating their geological references, which, after all, provide us with one of the most relevant contexts for experiencing and comprehending them.

Ammons's mid-career long poems—"Extremes and Moderations," "Essay on Poetics," and "Hibernaculum," all of which appeared in *Collected Poems 1951–1971*—served as the "laboratory" of experimentation for later long poems that would garner much greater critical acclaim. Both *Sphere: The Form of A Motion* and *Garbage,* for example, are book-length poems, each of which received notable critical recognition, the former winning the Bollingen Prize (1975), the latter the National Book Award (1993).

In *Sphere,* Ammons returns again and again to the image of the earth itself. He is particularly interested in the polity that might emerge from a re-envisioning of the earth. In a time of increased ethnic clashes both at home and abroad, Ammons looks to the earth as a way of reconciling unity and diversity. The poet of the one and the many finds in the structure of our planet a way of accommodating differences so that the earth itself is not continually turned into a compost heap of human genocide, as it has been too often in the twentieth century. Ammons offers a model for resolving conflict as old as the earth itself. He writes in section 153 of *Sphere:*

> we do have something to
> tune in with and move toward: not homogeneous pudding but
>
> united differences, surface differences expressing the common,
> underlying hope and fate of each person and people, a gathering
> into one place of multiple dissimilarity, each culture to its
>
> own cloth and style and tongue and gait, each culture, like
> the earth itself with commonlode center and variable surface,

. . . .

> still with the sense of the continuous
>
> running through and staying all the discretions, differences
> diminished into the common tide of feelings, so that difference
> cannot harden into aggression or hate fail to move with the
>
> ongoing, the differences not submerged but resting clear at
> the surface, as the surface, and not rising above the surface
> so as to become more visible and edgy than the continuum
>
> (S, 78–79)

The poet converts the earth into a symbol of unity and diversity, "with commonlode center and variable surface." He pursues the analogy vigorously, linking the earth's surface variations with the uniqueness of individual human languages and cultures, yet reminding the reader of a common core. The coexistence of unity and variety, then, in the very structure of the earth should serve as a model to its inhabitants, too often forgetful, with dire consequences, of the unity that Ammons finds underlying diversity. It's interesting to note that in these lines Ammons anticipates much of the current debate concerning multiculturalism. His poetics of geology has enabled him to discover a mediating position between the extremes of minimizing difference—what Ammons refers to in the poem as "homogeneous pudding"—and accentuating *only* difference, which Ammons fears can "harden into aggression." Ammons has discovered a moral truth in the facts of geology, using them, as Emerson did, to inspire an inward revolution, a rotation of the mind toward the celebration of differences with the underlying principle of unity.

The earth, with its variable surface and common-lode center is, of course, yet another manifestation of the one:many paradox that has attracted Ammons's interest throughout his career. *Sphere,* of all his long poems, is most obsessed with the implications of the one:many problem, the splintering of unity into diversity. The poet himself has acknowledged *Sphere* to be his most elaborate and satisfactory working out of this problem. In an interview with William Walsh, he notes:

> *Sphere,* finally, was the place where I was able to deal with the problem of the One and the Many to my own satisfaction. It was a time when we were first beginning to see an image of the earth from outer space on the television screen, at a time when it was inevitable to think about that as the central image of our lives—that sphere. (SM, 65)

The one:many problem Ammons alludes to is addressed by many philosophical and religious traditions, including Indian and Chinese philosophy. Ammons, in a 1973 *diacritics* interview, acknowledges Lao-Tsu as his "philosophical source in its most complete version."[28] Both Indian and Chinese philosophical texts, such as the *Bhagavad-Gita* and the *Tao Te Ching,* present extensive narrative, dramatic, and philosophical accounts of the one:many problem, the relationship between the unseen Source of creation (Tao, Brahman) and its various manifestations. Indeed, the central theme of these works focuses on the reconciliation of unity with diversity. In Ammons's poetry, this is reflected in a variety of ways, in his quest for self-transcendence, his fascination with the concept of Maya, or illusion, and in his use of science to explore natural systems and the ways in which they balance "centers" and "peripheries," all of which are major concerns in *Sphere.*

Although the *Tao Te Ching* may have been one of the earliest influences on Ammons's thinking about the one and the many, it's clear that his continued interest in this "problem" as expressed and worked out in *Sphere* is equally influenced by a far different source, the photographic images of the earth from outer space. In the 1996 *Paris Review* interview he once again attributes these photographs as the catalyst for his contemplation of the one:many question in *Sphere.* Although he has claimed to have distanced himself from Western culture and knowledge, he cannot ultimately do so. In fact, it is the advanced technology of outer space photography that informs his extensive philosophical meditations in *Sphere.* This reliance upon Western technology and science to inform his work even as he disavows Western tradition may seem paradoxical. However, Ammons views the photographs as another confirmation of his unique and non-Western view of history. For these photographs are, after all, what one sees through the lens of a camera situated in outer space. The images in the photographs are, according to Ammons, the truest version of history at the moment they were taken.

He chooses to interpret such pictures not as evidence of Western hegemony, or the will to dominate the planet, but rather as testimony to the precarious balance of natural forces suggested by such images. Peter Westbroek, in *Life as a Geological Force,* comments on the irony of those first photographs of the earth taken from outer space.

Ironically, those pictures, which symbolized human triumph over nature, also marked the end of the general sense of promise and progress.

The sixties were winding down, and in those snapshots we now read a message of global vulnerability and human impotence. What were we doing to our planet? In the years that followed we grew increasingly aware of pollution, acid rain, desertification, the rise of greenhouse gasses, and the disintegration of the ozone shield.[29]

These are the very environmental concerns Ammons expresses in "Extremes and Moderations." Moreover, in transcending the limitations of being culturally situated, the view from outer space as presented by such images enables Ammons to imagine the earth from a more cosmic perspective. In such pictures his interest in astronomy and geology merge and provide him with a metaphor in *Sphere* for exploring the philosophical questions most important to him. He notes:

Sphere had the image of the whole earth, then for the first time seen on television, at its center. I guess it was about 1972. There was the orb. And it seemed to me the perfect image to put at the center of a reconciliation of One-Many forces. (SM, 103)

In his effort to reconcile unity with diversity, Ammons explores in *Sphere* a vast array of natural "events" and "structures" wherein he discovers similarities underlying discrete boundaries. In *Sphere,* section 9, he invokes once again surface difference and underlying unities:

though the surface is crisp with pattern still we know
that there are generalized underlyings, planes of substratum
lessening from differentiation: under all life, fly and

dandelion, protozoan, bushmaster, and ladybird, tendon
and tendril (excluding protocellular organelles) is the same
cell:

(S, 14)

The poet is cognizant of the layered or textured nature of reality, corroborated by his understanding of biology and geology. These lines anticipate and are parallel in insight to the lines in *Sphere* about "the earth itself with commonlode center and variable surface." Both groupings of lines provide metaphors for understanding Ammons's own consciousness as it operates within *Sphere*. The poet's mind constantly explores the surfaces of the natural world, yet simultaneously discovers at its depths a common core.

He would have us believe that each of us is "unmendably integral" with the universe, "attached" to the earth by the force of

gravity yet floating free on this star that is held in orbit in the solar
system. Ammons's ecological vision is affirmed in many instances,
but perhaps no more powerfully than in sections 74 and 75:

> you and I cannot walk the street
> or rise to the occasion except via the sum total of effect
> and possibility of the universe: we are not half-in and

> half-out of the universe but unmendably integral: when we
> move, something yields to us and accepts our steps: our
> tensions play against, find rightness in, other tensions not

> our own:

(S, 43–44)

Here he acknowledges the principle of reciprocity, a fundamental
of natural and human behavior described in great detail by both
Asian wisdom texts and Western science. Put simply, this principle
affirms that we can never be completely apart from the world but
in some essential way are integral with it. As a result, our actions
have consequences that ripple out into the universe. Elsewhere in
Sphere, Ammons writes: "touch the universe anywhere / you touch
it everywhere."

To recognize that we are "unmendably integral" is the first step
in developing an ecological vision, in recognizing that our actions
have far-reaching consequences for the planet and for the people
who inhabit it. Although Ammons has been characterized as a
reclusive figure, aloof from the politics of the world, it's clear from
these lines that his vision has important consequences for the con-
cept of "human community" and the world that we share.

Ammons's use of the term "unmendably" in this context also
provides a key to understanding his conceptualization of form in
Sphere. Although the poem has an abundance of colons, it never
comes to complete cessation because there are no end-stops until
the final period. It is essentially one long sentence, and this is
consistent with their being one earth. For Ammons, in *Sphere,* the
earth is "the contour that resolves all the action. Everything hap-
pens on this circle, in this sphere."[30]

The thinking that is the crux of so much of the "action" in this
poem is also another important consequence of its poetics of geol-
ogy. Ammons sees a parallel between the way the mind works
and the plate tectonics theory. When asked about this parallel, he
explains: "You can't just have something happen on the earth with-
out something else having to give way."[31] And it is this awareness

of the "law of compensation," as Emerson referred to it, that influ-
ences the poet's sense of cognitive and poetic process in *Sphere*.
In reflecting on this analogy between the dynamics of the earth
and the mind, Ammons says:

> Our minds have identified, have grown into dynamics that are similar
> to the ones on earth itself. So then our minds, when we make allowance
> for one thing, we make allowance for the other. We take into considera-
> tion both sides of something, or if something that goes forward, some-
> thing is displaced in front of it and will have to find another place
> to go.[32]

While "building-up" forms of thought in one section of *Sphere*, he
is aware that something must give way somewhere else within the
poem. What some critics have identified as "entropy" in this and
his other long poems may in fact be the necessary tension between
creation and destruction that such poems depend upon for their
force.

Another consequence of Ammons's "unmendably integral" vi-
sion is the interdependence of human history and natural history.
In finding "rightness" between our tensions and "other tensions
not our own," we enter into the flow, dynamics, and balance of life
that Taoism would have us experience daily. For Ammons this is
not a conventionally prescribed Christian religious experience, but
rather a discovery of individual consciousness. He first gained in-
sight into the dynamics of things in what he describes as an "inte-
rior illumination" while serving as a young man (age nineteen) in
the Navy on board a ship in the South Pacific. Describing this
to David Lehman, who inquired about Ammons's employment of
"scientific means to reach a kind of religious end," the poet says:

> One day when I was nineteen, I was sitting on the bow of the ship
> anchored in a bay in the South Pacific. As I looked at the land, heard
> the roosters crowing, saw the thatched huts etc., I thought down to the
> water level and then to the immediately changed and strange world
> below the waterline. But it was the line inscribed across the variable
> land mass, determining where people would or would not live, where
> palm trees would or could not grow, that hypnotized me. The whole
> world changed as a result of an interior illumination: the water level
> was not what it was because of a single command by a higher power
> but because of an average result of a host of actions—runoff, wind
> currents, melting glaciers. I began to apprehend things in the dynamics
> of themselves—motions and bodies—the full account of how we came
> to be still a mystery with still plenty of room for religion, though, in

164 STEVEN P. SCHNEIDER

my case, a religion of what we don't yet know rather than what we are certain of. I was de-denominated. (SM, 95)

Ammons's fall from grace has proven to be a lucky tumble. For in his capacity to "apprehend things in the dynamics of them-selves"—runoffs, wind currents, melting glaciers—he has un-locked a tremendous resource for his poetry. In *Sphere: The Form of a Motion,* he incorporates as much of these dynamics as he possibly can, including the dynamics of the earth, the forms of its motions and the motions of the forms that inhabit it. This is a poem in which Ammons brings to fruition the poetics of geology by incorporating the earth itself as the central image and symbol in the poem.

In the concluding section of *Sphere,* Ammons celebrates both attachment and freedom, gravity and weightlessness.

to float the orb or suggest the orb is floating: and, with the
mind thereto attached, to float free: the orb floats, a bluegreen
wonder: so to touch the structures as to free them into rafts

that reveal the tide: many rafts to ride and the tides make a
place to go: let's go and regard the structures, the six-starred
easter lily, the beans feeling up the stakes: we're gliding, we

are gliding: ask the astronomer, if you don't believe it: but
motion as a summary of time and space is gliding us: for a while,
we may ride such forces: then, we must get off: but now this

beats any amusement park by the shore: our Ferris wheel, what a
wheel: our roller coaster, what mathematics of stoop and climb: sew
my name on my cap: we're clear: we're ourselves: we're sailing.

(S, 79)

The earth's movement, both its rotation along its axis, and its floating as an orb in the solar system, fascinates the poet. The mind attached suggests just how "unmendably integral" world and mind are. The earth is the "anchor" for the mind, among its easter lilies and vines growing upward in spirals around stakes. To regard the structures is, of course, one of Ammons's preoccupations in his role as poet-scientist. This can be accomplished through direct visual perception, through the lenses of science, or through the mathematics of the mind. However, as any reader of the long poems quickly discovers, *to regard* in Ammons's universe of motion is not merely to look, but rather to assimilate, to envision, to seek and uncover rays of relation between self and cosmos, between the geologic forces at play in our world and the motions a long poem will make.

NOTES

1. Walt Whitman, *Leaves of Grass,* ed. Harold W. Blodgett and Sculley Bradley (New York: New York University Press, 1965), 224. Additional references in this text to works from this volume will be indicated by the abbreviation LOG.

2. For interesting discussions of the relationship between mind and nature in Ammons's poetry, see John Elder, *Imagining the Earth: Poetry and the Vision of Nature* (Urbana and Chicago: University of Illinois Press, 1985). Also Robert Harrison, *Forests: The Shadow of Civilization* (Chicago: University of Chicago Press, 1992).

3. Jon Gertner, "A Walk With A. R. Ammons," *Audubon* 98, no. 5 (September-October, 1996) 80.

4. For an extensive treatment of Ammons's "poetics of widening scope," see Steven P. Schneider, *A. R. Ammons and the Poetics of Widening Scope* (Madison, N. J.: Fairleigh Dickinson University Press, 1994).

5. Lawrence Buell, *The Environmental Imagination* (Cambridge: Harvard University Press, 1995), 7–8. Although Buell sees Ammons as "cooly cognitive" in his approach to nature, he does acknowledge that Ammons to some degree is a practitioner of what Buell calls "The Aesthetics of Relinquishment." As this essay shows, Ammons's "poetics of geology" enable his work to meet Buell's criteria of an "environmentally oriented" text.

6. A. R. Ammons, *Tape for the Turn of the Year* (New York: W.W. Norton, 1993), 88. All future references to this poem are from this edition and indicated by the abbreviation T.

7. Peter Westbroek, *Life as a Geological Source* (New York, W.W. Norton, 1991), 48.

8. Westbroek, *Life as a Geological Force,* 48.

9. Ibid., 50.

10. Elder, *Imagining the Earth,* 140.

11. Westbroek, *Life as a Geological Force,* 50.

12. Ibid.

13. "The *Paris Review* Interview" with David Lehman in A. R. Ammons, *Set in Motion: Essays, Interviews, Dialogues,* ed. Zofia Burr (Ann Arbor: University of Michigan Press, 1996) 89. Other quotations from this collection will be parenthetically identified in my essay by the abbreviation SM.

14. Lawrence Buell, *The Environmental Imagination,* 143.

15. David I. Grossvogel, "Interview / A. R. Ammons," *Diacritics* 32 (Winter 1973): 48.

16. Gertner, "A Walk With Ammons," 80.

17. Westbroek, *Life as a Geological Force,* 206.

18. Ibid.

19. Ibid., 205.

20. Gertner, "A Walk With Ammons," 80.

21. Elder, *Imagining The Earth,* 138.

22. Grossvogel, "Interview / A. R. Ammons," 52.

23. Ibid.

24. Michael McFee, *"Lattice Work": Essay on Poetics, Extremes and Moderations, Hibernaculum, Sphere,* (M.A. thesis, University of North Carolina-Chapel Hill), 44.

25. Stephen B. Cushman, "Stanzas, Organic Myth, and the Metaformalism of A. R. Ammons," *American Literature* 59, no. 4 (December 1987): 520.

26. "From the Wind to the Earth: An Interview with Steven Schneider." *Complexities of Motion: Essays on the Long Poems of A. R. Ammons* (Madison, N. J.: Fairleigh Dickinson University Press, 1998), 347.

27. Harold Bloom, "A. R. Ammons: When You Consider the Radiance," in *The Ringers in the Tower: Studies in the Romantic Tradition* (Chicago: University of Chicago Press, 1971), 257–89.

28. Grossvogel, "Interview / A. R. Ammons," 51.

29. Westbroek, *Life as a Geological Force,* 20.

30. Schneider, "From the Wind to the Earth," 343.

31. Schneider, "From the Wind to the Earth," 337.

32. Schneider, "From the Wind to the Earth," 343.

Tombstones

ROBERT P. HARRISON

The poem "Tombstones" in *Sumerian Vistas* (1987) contains twenty-nine sections, the first of which reads:

> the chisel, chipping in,
> finds names the
> wind can't blow away

(SV, 45)

If you happened to have been "a young English poet," though, falling mortally ill in Rome, the chisel never found your name in the tombstone. Here lies one whose name was writ in water. What did Keats have against water? That like the wind it is too soft. That it doesn't stay put enough to write in. Only the hard, or *le dur,* endures. Rome has a way of reminding you of that, having entrusted its laws and legacies to stone and consigned the greater part of its memory to marble. Compared to the lapidary memorials that surrounded Keats in his last months of life, his curly English rimes were but a bit of dust swirling in the air. Memory mothered the Muses, they say, but most poets honor the Gorgon head. Petrification is their highest ambition. Maybe Memory and Medusa are finally the same enchantress. Certainly stone is common to them both:

> dust's shape in air
> could be a momentary
> memorial, an instant signifying its interval,
>
> that what is gone is
> going on with other
> going things,
>
> a stability of motion
> in time
> accompanying its own time:

167

```
instead, a stone's
block
halts ongoing,

a blockage that says,
timelessness hereby measures
time going on as usual
```
(SV, 47)

What would the history of civilizations amount to without stone to outlast this human time of ours, which moves too rapidly for us? Most of what the makers of history have done—horrible or sublime—has been done for the sake of a stone's memorial. We measure our destinies by a mineral standard. We commit to stone what we ourselves can't inhabit, for the stone's block can block only our names. Yet what are our names? They are who we are, minus the content. Most of what we call civilization is its discontents:

```
it breaks the heart
that stone holds
what time let go

but the stones are
the time left
that the names can be in
```
(SV, 45)

Our hearts are not nearly as hard as the stone that breaks them. On the other hand, stone is not nearly as hard as the heart that letters it, since we do, after all, break into its block with a chisel, so that it may receive the impression of our broken hearts. Only the perishable can be chiseled, chipped, and grooved into letters. There is no writing in eternity, no diamond hard enough to inscribe its element. In sum, a stone is not really a slab of timelessness in the midst of time going on as usual. It too has its time, albeit a wondrously unhurried time:

```
the wind roars, sweeps, whirls,
nearly free even in its calms,
and the wind carries leaves, sand,
seed, whatever: rain pours,
puddles, flows: the ground
yields to this or that pull, break,
flush: among the swirling
```

> motions, the stone's slow swirl
> keeps the name

(SV, 49)

The stone swirls slowly enough to affect stability, *e pure si move*. There is always a time left for Rome to be in, as long as its stones withstand the chipping, scarring, wearing, and tearing of the tempestuous winters and burning summers that sooner or later will get the better of them. Again, stones are "in" time as much as everything else is "in" time, although they are not "in" time the way names are "in" the stones. They *are* their time, or slow swirl. Time is not a simple matter of duration but a complex of matter that enfolds a great many durations—as many as the measures of motion of whatever moves. The good thing about stones, though, apart from the fact that they hold our names, is that they hold their ground:

> the ground flat or,
> rolling from a hill rise, slightly
> shedding,
> no downpour can
>
> organize flows to displace
> the stones,
> identifications tumbling
> from one mound to another

(SV, 46)

His name may be writ in water, but the poet's gravestone in Rome's Protestant cemetery still says "here lies one. . . ." That "here" is a shifter that doesn't shift. No storm, at least for a while, will wash away its indication that something here has passed away and yet endures. As long as tombstones hold in the ground they hold the place of what is no longer there, marking and preserving a "here" distinct from all the "theres" in relation to which it is situated. Space itself may be infinite, but place is created by a bounding or localization of space. Where the dead are not memorialized there are no places. The grave marker is the first place marker. Only death in its abysmal finality has power and authority enough to bound and localize space in its memorial:

> set on the line between
> time and abyss,
> at the intersection

> of usual time ongoing
> and a time stopped within
> other times,
> the time of protons and electrons
> going on as usual—a stone—
> levels of existence
> in existence, times
> in time, one organization
> gone still; otherwise
> nothing appears lost
>
> (SV, 46)

Where time has stopped, or where a motion has lost its form, there is the abyss. Death is a form or organization gone still. Where time meets the abyss—that's a meeting you want to mark, and say "here" is where they came together for such and such a person. The tombstone does not stop or freeze time in its durable element any more than Rome freezes its past in its cobblestones. The stone's name, as well as its date, call the abyss into time. It calls the stillness of what has gone still into the world of things going on as usual. That is what makes a place: a "here" that doesn't move while everything else in and around it does. But in order to call the dead into time and create a place for history to happen in, the stone must bring an absence to presence and keep it there:

> as if the name were not
> already nothing,
> stone, chipped away,
>
> leaves the name nothingly
> present,
> grooves of absence
>
> a further sign of a sign
> that lightens
> the anchorage of its carriage
>
> (SV, 48)

A tombstone with a name in it signifies that, within the multitude of times that complicate time's complexity, a moving form has become nothing, even if we don't know what nothing is. It was not for nothing, in any case, that the Greeks called the gravepost the *sema,* or sign. A sign by its very nature traces an absence. But the grave-marking *sema* is not a sign among signs: it's the sign that signifies the abysmal source of signification, since it "stands for" what it "stands in"—the ground of burial as such, on which history, placehood, memory, and all that has legacy in the longevities of culture are grounded. In its pointing to a "here" the *sema* points first and foremost to itself—its recall of something that is there in name only:

> what does it matter if
> a stone falls or slides and
> misidentifies a mound:
> the stone's outward
> reference given up it
> calls to itself
>
> (SV, 50)

Again, only as long as the stone holds in the ground does it keep the place its "here" refers to. Once uprooted its "here" is nowhere. Yet even after its outward reference has been given up and its "here" displaced, the wind still can't blow away the names, which now refer to their own pure sign of what is no longer there. Is this a victory of *écriture* over *référence,* of stone over wind? Hardly. What the tombstone's call-to-itself refers to is the loss of wind that kept a lifetime going. The wind, we say, is nothing compared to the massive lasting power (and signifying power) of stone, but take away this windy nothing and you take away that without which we are mostly nothing:

> the spirit, though, invisible,
> weightless is lost: its
> winding kept the winding
> going: but only
> winding when winding stops
> disappears:
> when one loses nothing one
> loses everything
>
> (SV, 46)

We are all, in that respect, losers, set on the line between everything and nothing. We come into the world gasping, and before we can catch our breath the breath is gone. It is hard to speak of that which lets us speak, this breath of nothing that winds the universe and keeps it going, and of which poems are made. No wonder the wind can't blow the name away: the name names what the wind has blown away. The spirit is "in" whatever moves—in the prophet's breath as well as the stone's slow swirl—and not only in what moves across the face of the water. In the elusive life of the spirit the stones of Rome are dust's memorial in air:

> stones, as if forms of intelligence,
> stir: concentrate light
> still and you have them:
>
> still, other durances exceed stones'—
> a pulse in one of earth's orbits
> beats once in four hundred thousand years:
>
> in certain orders of time
> stones blow by like the wind:
> starlight pricks them like bubbles

(SV, 50)

It is not merely the juxtaposition of temporal scales that marries the nature of stone to that of the wind. An aboriginal kinship speaks of their common nature, the nature of which is motion. (The poem born of such nature is anything but "nature poetry.") Nothing that comes to be has any other nature than that by which it comes to be. Heraclitus spoke of the "loving strife" between the elements that lets them to relate to one another, affect one another, vie with one another, combine with one another. He called the nature of nature "fire," an elemental essence that is neither an essence nor an element but an endless agglutination of transformations. We are finally starting to get the hint:

> the things of earth are not objects,
> there is no nature,
> no nature of stones and brooks, stumps, and ditches,
>
> for these are pools of energy cooled into place,
> or they are starlight pressed
> to store,
>
> or they are speeding light held still:
> the woods are a fire green-slow
> and the pathway of solid earthwork
>
> is just light concentrated blind

(SV, 50–51)

Michelangelo knew a thing or two about the divinity of fire. Chipping away into stone to discover a form in the block's brute mass,

his chisel every now and then would send out sparks—evidence
enough to the artist that fire is the element, the very medium, of
creation. Augustine spoke of the "weight of love"—the *pondus
amoris*—and described his innermost desire as a spiritual fire that
rises ever upwards toward God, through the superfine ether of the
universe. Those elements that are the lightest rise the highest and
attain to the most enduring nature of the universe:

> not coarse, hard
> things last
> longest, perhaps,
>
> but fine, the very fine:
> if only the wind
> could take letters:
>
> if only light
> spelled names:
> when love brushes
>
> through our nerves
> and sends
> a summary to our brains,
>
> perhaps the summary
> is sent by
> vibrations
>
> really the universe's—
> the universe, something as old as that
> and with as much future
>
> (SV, 51–52)

History would not be nearly so mortiferous if the wind could take
letters and light spell our names. Instead of commiting our love to
the wind we engrave our dread in stone. Our loathing of death
causes us to court its petrifications to death. If we believed our
nerves instead of our spleen, we would take our finitude in stride
as only one of the manifold times that enfold us. (History has
taught me that all is not well under the sun, said Camus, while the
sun taught me that history is not everything.) At the hard heart of
finitude (the heart that breaks at the thought of finitude) swirls the
fine, superfine dust of a cosmic fire that brushes through our nerves
and, for a moment at least, makes us as old and young as the
universe. Call it what you will—spirit, light, élan, *l'amor che move*

il sol e le altre stelle—the love it ignites in us is unbounded in nature, although (and here's the rub), being finite, we have only so much love to dispose of:

> if love is fine
> and stones are harsh evanescences,
> how we may dishonor
> love to letter down its name,
> wasting the love
> on the hard waters of inscription

(SV, 52)

Socrates, for one, did not waste his on the hard waters. Neither did Jesus. Nor did Saint Francis. Such lovers as had no need for letters had this much in common: the certitude that death has no substantial hold on us, that our dread is simply a deficiency of love. Perhaps there is something rather than nothing because the nothing, abundant in nature, has love enough to squander on its living memorial. (We who think on such matters are part of the memorial.) The universe is a surplus of nothingness that love condenses, compresses, or compounds until it succeeds in drawing a line between time and abyss, or forming a perimeter at whose edges an event can take place: a spark of light, an inside turning into an outside, a pull or a push in this or that direction. It is not for us to understand such events but to fulfill our implication in them:

> the universe is itself
> love's memorial,
> every cliff-face,
> rocky loft having
> spent
> itself through love's light,
> here held
> till love again burn it free:
> ninety percent
> of the universe is dead stars,
> but look how the light still
> plays flumes down
> millenial ranges

(SV, 53)

If it takes nine dead stars to let one blaze, or to give motion something to circle around, so be it. The surplus that makes something out of nothing is ninety percent wasted, yes, but look at how the remainder burns! *Nihil est sine ratione:* nothing is without reason. Nothing *is,* and it *is* without reason:

> if the tombstones were
> thrown together in one pile
> that would be some gathering,
> a record higher than
> Everest:
> but if time crumbled the stones,
> washed out the grit,
> melted down the shapes,
> all the names distilled would
> spell nothing

(SV, 53–54)

If they were to spell anything else we would be in heaps of trouble, caught in a stony universe with no nothingness for spirit to catch its breath in, before winding up a life again. The cliff-face could not stand there as love's memorial until love burns it free again. Stone could not hold the name long enough for the grooves to fill with moss and for the cold to burn the green into winter's black writing. And love could not brush through our nerves and send a summary to our brains with vibrations as old as the time that's always left over. That which amounts to nothing when it crumbles and washes away is the sum of what the wind can't blow away, not because its name is writ in stone but because the hard waters of inscription can't mark the place of its invagination:

> nothing, though, not stone
> nor light lasts
> like the place I keep
> the love of you in and this
>
> though nothing can write it down
> and nothing keep it:
> nothingness
> lasts long enough to keep it

(SV, 53)

Compared to the one who wrote that down, other modern poets are like blind men battering blind men in a ditch over the dead letters of love. What would a civilization look like if, instead of opting for the Medusa stone, it built its foundations in a place nothing can keep? There is such a place in each of us, which is not a place at all but which, precisely for that reason, we can keep such a love in. Something as old as the universe and with as much future you can't keep in any demarcated place. It takes a no-place in us for it to vibrate and last forever in. The *sema* can't hold it, for the *sema* says "here." Its *hic jacet* marks the very placehood of place. But in that other place, which has no placehood, the tombstone's place marker is but the glint of an eye:

> a flock of
> gulls flew
> by I thought but
>
> it was a
> hillside of stones

(SV, 54)

Let's not mistake the "I thought" for a mistake, say of perception or impression. At most it was an oversight, an event taking place in another order of time than the one in which a hillside is one thing, a flock of gulls another. Or maybe it was vision of stones from light years away. Only thought can travel faster than the speed of light. At such speeds everything burns. Thank God for hills and stones and other heavy things that, in their own tenacious way, keep thought honest—in and out of tune with the local harmonies. Thought is free, somewhat. It can overreach a hillside, a planet, a galaxy, but only when it returns from its millenial ranges to usual time ongoing does it justify its true vocation: the re-estrangement of the ordinary. If we could not wander far and wide without displacing ourselves, we could hardly be aware of things. But thanks to the intrinsic vagrancy of thought we can see things around us for what they are: more or less densely articulated phenomena adrift in a nothingness utterly divine and utterly terrible in nature. It is because thought is not bound to the here that it can constantly return to the here and attest to its marvel. As soon as the world in its familiar guises ceases to amaze us we may as well be dead, for it means that something in us has stopped moving. That is bad news for the tombstones:

> the stone-name signifies
> what it can find to mean
> in some living head:
> when the heads
> are empty,
> the stone's name names emptiness,
> not the one

> neither a thing that is nor was
>
> (SV, 48)

Fine enough to move between what is present and what is not, thinking enters into the "space" of what a name names and so (thinking) keeps open the relations between the dead and the living, the quick and the still. There is something living in what is dead, and, whatever it be, thought can commune with it. Maybe that's because what's living in what is dead is the thought (or love, or spirit, or fire) that never died in it. Even trees, in their own green or browning ways, think. The mind of the universe is not in our heads only, although it would seem that what's in our heads is somewhat special in its own right. When these heads are empty, the tombstone is just a stone. When they're not, there is just enough difference between a stone and a stone with a name in it to make all the difference in the world:

> stones, names in them, are
> just stones: when the stone
> brushes mind, memory
> changes the stone clear through
>
> (SV, 50)

Stone brushes mind the way love brushes our nerves, sending a summary to our brains. A thought that saints and philosophers have been at pains to articulate is that thought and love share a common nature, that they are modes of the same self-overreaching impulse. The notion of "spirit" has been frequently invoked here, but all in all fire is not a bad word for this commonality either, if by fire we understand the event of element or change that thought brings about when it "changes the stone clear through." Thought may "interpret" and even "change" the world, but such are its derivative activities. First and foremost thought is the world become aware of its own circulations. It is the (no)place the universe keeps its love in ("that Rome where Christ is a Roman," Dante puts it). Hence the transfiguration of stone, when it brushes mind, has a future as old as the universe itself. Once the stone has been changed clear through by mind, memory, love or thought, there is no telling where its names may end up:

> the letters,
> holding what they can, hold
> in the stone
>
> but holding flakes or

mists away—a
grainweight of memory

or a rememberer goes:
in so many hundred years,
the names

will be light enough
and as if balloons
will rise out of stone

(SV, 54–55)

What the stone could never hold in the first place is finally surren-
dered to the wind when the stone breaks up and mists away. The
names that were once nothingly present are on their own now, with
nothing but thought to register their claims. When Rome will have
finally relinquished the hard evidence of its having-been to the
erosion of the elements, it may rise to its true eternity at last.
What is left over once history is over is what never made it into
the annals of history. Between the name lettered in stone and what
the name names there is a distance that history takes place in. But
once that distance is traversed, anything can happen:

rivulets of scattering,
corruption's way
of getting on with things,
rememberers unremembered,
still the name
will call together in the last
time, the new time, in the new morning,
all the bits of information and,
the name said,
the form will come again—the distance
between named and name run

(SV, 47)

These are heady words from a poet who knows that even if we
could ascertain their meaning we could not grasp their import. All
we know for sure is that the distance has not yet run, or, if it has,
it has run countless times before—every time love brushes our
nerves and sends a summary to our brains. Meanwhile the clock
ticks, the earth revolves, and space makes room for itself as it goes
along. We cannot prophecize our way out of time. Love must hold
to what is here, even if the here cannot hold on to it:

the stone makes
its longest, hardest
"effort"
to hold on to, memorialize
the glint
or glow
once
in someone's eye

(SV, 51)

POSTSCRIPT

Ten years have passed since the author of "Tombstones" lettered those words about the "last" and "new" time in which the name will call together whatever time has scattered. Today, revisiting their inscription, he confesses: "I haven't the faintest idea what #7 means. Could it mean the resurrection, the time out of time which is eternity? Of course, there's no such place—except now, in time, while we think on what is finally all together and forever. Love—Archie." Such was the response I received from A. R. Ammons when I queried him about that stanza (#7), which I still find "problematic," as they say. I tend not to believe poets when they say of something they have written that they don't understand it themselves, but in this case it may well be true. In the context of a poem that scrambles the line of time, frees it from the straightforward, uniform drive toward a final end or outcome, section #7 of "Tombstones" remains a teasing contradiction, in the most literal sense of the word. Ammons's response to me confirms as much. As I ponder that response, it strikes me that what it says and doesn't say about what section #7 means and doesn't mean are summarized by the closing words: "Love—Archie." When Ammons declares that "there's no such place" as "the time out of time which is eternity," I can't help but think of the place we keep our universal love in, which nothing can keep. This place is "now," in time, and it takes place whenever we think on what is finally all together and forever. The poetry of Ammons is a sustained, sublime, and inexhaustible thinking on the nature of this "now." I know of nothing like it in poetry. I love Ammons, it's true, but it's not for that reason alone that I said that, compared to him, other modern poets are blind men battering blind men in a ditch over the dead letters of love—a reckless thing to affirm perhaps, especially since the image comes from Yeats, but one that nevertheless registers my conviction Ammons is the only poet (known to me) who thinks the nature of motion (time) in its unthinkable complexity. His poetry is not simply the medium for such thinking, it is the thinking and the motion become one in the poem. This poetry, written in the wind, moves with the love that moves the sun and the other stars, and the place I keep the love of him in moves with it, now and forever.

Part III
Rewinding the Tape: The Texts from *Glare* (1997) to *Tape for the Turn of the Year* (1965)

Möbius Meets Satchmo: Mixed Metaphor As Form and Vision in *Glare*

Roger Gilbert

More than any other American poet, A. R. Ammons has treated the long poem as an occasional genre. From Virgil to James Merrill, long poems traditionally stand as summa, crowning achievements within their authors' corpuses. But in shaping his oeuvre over the past four decades, Ammons has adopted the wisdom of "Corsons Inlet," with its famous declaration that "tomorrow a new walk is a new walk." For Ammons the long poem is as much a product and reflection of its experiential surroundings as the short poem, as open to random impingements and passing moods. Because new occasions keep arriving, moreover, new stretches of life to transcribe, no long poem can ever be final or definitive. It's hardly surprising, then, that Ammons has been so prolific in the genre, producing five full-length and seven "longer" or mid-length poems since 1965. The most recent of these, *Glare,* is in many respects his most audaciously original to date, both in structure and vision. What's most striking about the poem is its profound doubleness, a quality manifested on several levels. Founded on that cardinal literary sin, the mixed metaphor, *Glare* is really two poems in one, with each half obeying its own peculiar logic. Part One, "Strip," marks a conscious return to the mode of Ammons's first long poem, *Tape for the Turn of the Year:* typed on a narrow roll of adding machine tape, the poem intermittently reflects on the difficulties of its composition and the cosmic implications of its form, which is that of a Möbius strip. The governing trope of the second part, "Scat Scan," is jazz-like improvisation; written on a fatter tape, this part recasts the themes of Part One in a less oppressive light, discovering within the bounded space of mortality a wider margin for imaginative play and redemptive vision.

What does it mean to construct a single long poem around two essentially heterogenous formal tropes? Either of the poem's two parts could easily have stood alone; indeed Ammons originally planned to publish "Strip" as a complete work, but then after writing "Scat Scan" chose to combine the two tapes into a single poem. While publishing two long poems in close succession would doubtless have seemed excessive even for so prolific a poet as Ammons, his decision to couple them needs to be understood as more than simply pragmatic. Read together, "Strip" and "Scat Scan" gain a degree of resonance and pathos neither possesses purely in itself. A Möbius strip and a jazz solo may seem an unlikely pairing, but the very incongruity of their conjunction powerfully embodies the contradictory energies and insights that fuel Ammons's poetry. It's perhaps a measure of the growing complexity and humanity of the poet's vision that single tropes, however richly elaborated, can no longer suffice him as vehicles for its expression. One might say that *Glare*'s dual structure produces a kind of parallax effect; like the twinned images of a stereopticon, the poem's two tropes combine to create a deeper, rounder picture of mortal existence than either could alone. By allowing difference itself to occupy the center of his poem, Ammons acknowledges the partial and provisional nature of his art more forthrightly than ever.

The poem's double metaphors of Möbius strip and jazz function in the first instance as two distinct ways of interpreting the scroll or tape form, the one stressing its spatial, the other its temporal dimension, or in more Ammonsian terms, its shape and its flow. This bifurcation of space and time in turn generates contrasted graphic and vocal models for the act of poetic creation itself: where "Strip" repeatedly conflates the poetic act with the mechanical process of typing, poetry in "Scat Scan" is more traditionally figured as singing. The two models suggest very different understandings of the nature and function of poetry, with "Strip" offering a more skeptical, diminished view of the poem and its efficacy, "Scat Scan" a more expansively Whitmanian view. These divisions point to still more basic contrasts in tone and meaning. With its obsessive emphasis on the limitations of its medium and the closed circle it describes, "Strip" voices an almost claustrophobic sense of human frailty and futility. The greater improvisational freedom of "Scat Scan" by contrast seems to allow for a fuller sense of possibility, a larger faith in the power of imagination to relieve if not remove the burdens of existence.

All these generalizations need qualifying; there is both more variety within each part and more continuity between them than my quick sketch can suggest. Some of the continuity is implied by the complete work's title, *Glare,* which like the titles of its two parts is richly overdetermined. If the title serves chiefly to unite the poem's two parts under a common banner, it also subtly reinforces the double vision at its core. The word "glare" appears only twice in the poem, and neither instance seems especially significant; Ammons doesn't trope on it as he does on the subtitles "Strip" and "Scat Scan," instead leaving it to gather resonance of its own accord. All the word's several meanings are relevant, including that of a hostile or baleful gaze—the poem abounds in passages that could be said to "glare" in this sense—but its primary association with light is certainly uppermost. Even here a crucial doubleness emerges: on the one hand "glare" can designate a harsh, merciless illumination like that cast by floodlights, imposing a total lucidity of vision in which every blemish and imperfection shows up in stark relief; on the other it can denote an excess of reflected light, a kind of nimbus or aura that dazzles the eye and clothes the objects of sight in radiance. These contradictory meanings beautifully capture the poem's ongoing struggle between reductive and expansive modes of vision, or more simply put between truth and beauty, a struggle enacted both in its broad division of parts and tropes and more minutely in the oscillations of its language.

The kinds of unity conferred by the poem's various tropes and titles remain fragile at best, however. More perhaps than any of Ammons's long poems to date, *Glare* is an omnium-gatherum, a work that sweeps up and assimilates everything in its path. In a passage that implicitly contrasts the poem with its immediate predecessor, Ammons wryly suggests that an apposite image for his present undertaking is not garbage but litter:

> litter, litter is without centrality
> it is not budgeted, it flies in the
>
> face of organization, it can be, and
> is, dropped anywhere, item unrelated
>
> to item, caught up into the wind or
> down into ditch trenches: the central
>
> image of this poem is that it has no
> mound gathering stuff up but strews
>
> itself across a random plain randomly:[1]

The smoldering ziggurat of trash that served as the organizing emblem of *Garbage* implied at least a minimal ordering of chaos, a centripetal drift of words and images. In replacing garbage with

litter as his paradigm, Ammons renounces even so modest a degree
of shaping control over his materials. Scattered and strewn rather
than gathered and heaped, the "items" that make up *Glare* mark
not a site but a path, a wandering itinerary across a darkling plain.

The absence of a central mound or cynosure means that *Glare*
is able to accommodate an exceptionally diverse range of topics
and styles. The sixty-five sections of "Strip" and fifty-two sections
of "Scat Scan" contain many passages that could easily stand as
separate poems. These include autobiographical reminiscences of
an impoverished tenant on Ammons's father's farm and a genial
fishing captain named Uncle John, along with other childhood vi-
gnettes; accounts of various errands and excursions, particularly
to open-air markets and roadside stands, for which Ammons ex-
hibits a special fondness; miniature verse essays on such topics
as the ties between money and language, the role of etiquette in
contemporary society, and the nature of truth; and lyrical inter-
ludes, including a brief section entitled "Love Poem," the spare
lines of which seem wholly out of key with the chatty discur-
siveness that pervades most of *Glare:*

> You come on
> like a comber
> foaming
>
> at the crest:
> stir me
> only
>
> please as a
> pond lap
> slips

(229–230)

A passage like this one is clearly an anomaly in *Glare,* if only
prosodically—the poem consists mainly of two-line strophes that
occupy the full width of the tape—yet the work is so open and
varied that it's impossible to designate any single mode as norma-
tive. With its aesthetic of inclusion, *Glare* makes room for such
local coherences within a broader continuum of restless motion.

Certain tones and gestures recur, to be sure, functioning as leit-
motifs or ongoing threads in the tapestry. Prominent among these
is a strain of sardonic laughter familiar to us from ironic seers like
Yeats and Nietzsche. Indeed the poem opens on this note, lending
it a kind of generative force:

wdn't it be silly to be serious, now;
I mean, the hardheads and the eggheads

are agreed that we are an absurd
irrelevance on this slice of curvature

and that a boulder from the blue
could confirm it: imagine, mathematics

wiped out by a wandering stone, or
grecian urns not forever fair when

the sun expands: can you imagine
cracking the story off we've built

up so long—the simian ancestries,
the lapses and leaps, the discovery

of life in the burial of grains:
the scratch of pictorial and syllabic

script, millennia of evenings around
the fires: nothing: meaninglessness

our only meaning: our deepest concerns
such as death or love or child-pain

arousing a belly laugh or a witty
dismissal: a bunch of baloney: it's

already starting to feel funny: I
think I may laugh:

(3)

This mode of dark hilarity at the prospect of destruction returns
periodically in the course of the poem, eventually swelling into a
chorus of cosmic mockery: "I / hear giggles along the outer limbs
of the / galaxies and belly laughs in the cores:" (275). But alongside
this nihilistic laughter the poem sounds another, equally prominent
note of religious longing tempered by intellectual uncertainty that
issues in a series of playful prayers to a reticent God:

Lord, here I am old, and

my life of service has drained me,
and I have worked to earn the respect

of those I no longer respect: have mercy
on me: you cannot, I suppose, give

me another chance: right? well, I
never expected it:

(21–22)

The sardonic and the devotional mark two tonal extremes in *Glare,*
and Ammons moves between them with the ease readers have
come to expect from a poet who refuses to strike any fixed posture
for long.

Another tonal division in the poem falls between the many pas-
sages that address lofty philosophical issues of morality and episte-
mology—what is truth? what is justice? etc.—and those passages,
also numerous, that graphically dwell on bodily parts and func-
tions, especially those of a sexual or excretory nature. To my
knowledge no previous long poem in English has succeeded in
using the word "smegma" even once, let alone four or five times,
as Ammons does. (While it may be coincidental, I can't resist not-
ing that in at least two American dictionaries the word "glare" is
immediately preceded by "glans penis," which also shows up in
the poem.) Less clinical terms abound as well: "peckers," "pricks,"
"tits," "clits," "asshole," to mention a few. Here are some repre-
sentative lines:

. . . there really is a

pecking order of peckers: measly
peckered guys feel like covering up

in showers, and swingers clunk about
like metronomes, a rhythm noted and

fiercely despised even by the moderate:

(19)

Ammons's work has always shown a marked propensity for the
bawdy and the lowdown, but in *Glare* he gives those impulses fuller
rein than ever before. To take this kind of writing as mere self-
indulgence risks missing the ultimate seriousness of Ammons's
purpose, which is to articulate the full range of human concerns
from the most abstract to the most intimate. Relations of high and
low fascinate him, and he's learned to move between such ex-
tremes with astonishing speed; no other poet is capable of such

dizzying ascensions or vertiginous drops. In *Glare* these vertical movements sometimes occur purely at the level of diction and idiom, as pseudo-Shakespearean phrases give way to down-home Southernisms:

> I was not thought
> likely, never likable: look you now who
>
> stuffs bucks and smiles: I say, we are blind
> to what we do will do: I say, responsible for
>
> what we intend, what did we intend: help us
> out there: do us a little good: I say to
>
> people twisting in their minds, come on over
> here to me, honey, I've been twisted fo-fi
>
> times:
>
> (204)

What's perhaps most remarkable about Ammons's incessant shifting of voice, accent, and manner is that we always know who's talking. The garrulous, quizzical personality of the poet, or his invented self, remains a felt presence beneath the local fluctuations of his style. For all its rhetorical mobility and variety, *Glare* is recognizably the product of one typewriter, one larynx.

"STRIP"

As is the case with the collective title *Glare,* the titles of the poem's individual parts are laden with thematic and formal implications; each title points to the section's organizing trope while also hinting at something of its dominant tone and style. Part One, "Strip," plays on its title in several ways, some more peripheral than others. "Airstrip," "strip mining," and "stripping down" are some of the associations unpacked from the title at various points in the poem, while others remain latent, like "comic strip," "film strip," "strip mall," "strip tease." Ammons doesn't encyclopedically work through every variant, since doing so would inhibit the kind of free, exploratory movement he wants to maintain, but he clearly relishes the word's multiple valences and exploits them at will. Although its primary status is that of a noun, the verb "to strip" hovers over the poem as well, which is undoubtedly the most confessional and self-revealing of Ammons's career, full of candid details about his past, his health, his fears and guilts, his appetites and ambitions. In one section Ammons rings comic variations on the phrase "but enough about me," as though to acknowledge an unseemly degree of self-absorption, and Part One as a whole ends on a similarly rueful note: "enough about me: I sure wish I could / think about something else." Stripping in "Strip" entails not only a stripping or denuding of the self, however, but of the world and its possibilities as well. Vision itself is laid bare in the poem, divested of the aesthetic and sacramental glow it has so often possessed for Ammons.

The stripped down or reduced quality of "Strip"'s seeing is in large measure a function of its form, which is of course the title's primary reference. Ammons's prosody in his tape poems is based not on feet or syllables but typewritten characters, of which the tape he uses for "Strip" allows a maximum of thirty-six per line. This constraint proves a recurrent source of aggravation to the poet; "Strip" is regularly punctuated by complaints about the narrowness of its format:

> . . . the tape is too narrow:
>
> the lines turn in on themselves:
> they can't get loose, they break
>
> back, they can't lope into loops!
>
> (26)

> I struggle on in this pointless war:
> I can't get the rhythms across the
>
> page: I'm narrowed, cramped, sliced
> up, pinched between the shoulder blades,
>
> the words spilling off the edge:
>
> (42)

> . . . what a
>
> narrow strip this walled road is:
> shave a micron or two and you're
>
> off-roading: try to get a whole
> stretch out, and you get cut back:

see what it will do and before you
can your speed is broken: I declare

I don't know what to do with this
thing, these cramps, this breaking

back:

(63)

            . . . this strip is so narrow:
a rhythm cannot unwind across it:

it cracks my shoulder blades with
pressing confinement: the next time

I take up prosody, I'm not going to
take up this

(97)

            . . . my typewriter's my only
outlet into this cramped-up strip:

I don't get any easing away before a
margin cracks me stilted or forces me

back in on myself: when I use up
this tape, I'm not buying another:

(120)

            . . . this tape is so skinny: I
have to crack off the lines and roll

the trimmings back into the next line:
there is never enough room: the

lines have to digest something, pack
it down, shove stuff together:

(135)

        . . . oh, this tight strip breaks my

rhythms, loosens my stable tables,
pours everything toward the middle

where it runs off, a streak: there
isn't room enough to lay something

down flat:

(140)

I was thinking how this tape cramps
my style: it breaks down my extended

gestures: it doesn't give your
asshole time to reconfigure after a

dump: everything happens before its
time, interrupted, turned back, cracked

up:

(175)

The sense of confinement so plangently expressed in these pas-
sages is of course more than prosodic (though the limiting of metri-
cal possibility Ammons complains of is real—his use of the tape
to set fixed parameters for his lines doesn't mean he has no interest
in creating local rhythms and cadences). *Glare* is quite consciously
a poem of incipient old age. Ammons turned seventy while writing
it; several years earlier he almost died after suffering a major heart
attack, an event he alludes to more than once in the poem. The
spatial narrowing his medium imposes in "Strip" can thus be taken
to figure a narrowing of the poet's own temporal horizon, as the
poem's frequent meditations on death and mortality seem to con-
firm. The strongly somatic language Ammons uses to describe the
tape's effects—cramps, cracked shoulder blades, etc.—likewise
suggests that his textual and corporeal bodies have become inti-
mately connected, and that the limitations of the former reflect the
attrition of the latter.

On a more practical level the tape's narrowness introduces cer-
tain procedural problems, as the poet finds his text spilling off both
ends of the paper:

. . . I am brittlized,

run like a cow through a cow dip, my
flourishes stripped down, my feathers

deflowered: so cramped, my words
lose letters on the right-hand edge or

I start typing too early on the left-
hand side and slice words up: I

keep thinking, oh, I'll remember what
that word was supposed to be, but

I've already told you about my memory
but I figure when I xerox the strip

onto regular paper, I'll fill out the
words in pencil, so a typist can get

it right: what, though, is right:
wouldn't it be better to let the words

come out of and go into breakage in
the usual way we, too, come and go:

wouldn't it be truer: wouldn't
accidence be bodied forth into

revelation:

(175–76)

The question of whether to restore the pieces of words accidentally
lopped off during the poem's composition, or to preserve such
elisions as evidence of the disfiguring forces we all face, is a serious
one for Ammons, who generally prefers not to revise away traces
of process from his poems. In this case he wisely opts for legibility
over fidelity, while letting his readers peek behind the curtain
where the smoothing is accomplished.

The thinness of the tape has broader epistemological implica-
tions as well, enforcing a stark mode of knowledge that reduces all
objects and issues to their barest form: " . . . there isn't a bit of /
room on this tape for a little / expansion or elaboration:" (167–68).
At one point Ammons explicitly links narrowness with a kind of
brutally reductive definition that kills what it seeks to understand:

                    . . . Socrates destroyed
        worlds looking for definition: he

        found none: by the time such narrowing
        locates a carcass, the carcass has

> no stomach for meaning: by the time
> anything gets that narrow, little
>
> is in it:

(40)

As an epistemologist Ammons has always favored expansion and elaboration over narrowing and definition, but in "Strip" he forces himself to accept a set of severe limits on both language and knowledge, limits closely bound up with age and death. Frost's elegiac question "what to make of a diminished thing" gets literalized by Ammons's form, which becomes a powerful emblem of necessity overruling desire.

If the narrowness of the tape evokes the harsh powers of breakage and disruption, however, its length fosters a comforting sense of continuity and sustained motion, free from the arbitrary divisions of pages:

> . . . I'm
> more miserable than most anybody I
> know, so don't take after me: I'm
>
> okay when I'm typing like this, tho:
> I'm in motion and the worm I am
>
> extruding has a long wiggle:

(51)

"Strip" repeatedly reflects not only on its physical medium, the tape itself, but on the mechanical means of its production. Like virtually all Ammons's poems, *Glare* was composed on a manual typewriter, thus joining a distinguished line of typewritten poetry that includes the work of Cummings and Olson, and whose true progenitor may be Don Marquis's voluble poet-cockroach Archy, who painfully turns out *vers libre* by hurling himself at each key in turn. A method that early in the century had seemed the epitome of technological sophistication has by the nineties come to appear quaintly anachronistic, which of course explains much of its appeal for Ammons: "as with a quill (or stylus) I / plink upon my machine outmoded as / hell (I hope hell's outmoded)" (90). Indeed its archaicism seems to lend the typewriter an almost magical aura in Ammons's eyes, as though it were the postmodern equivalent of an Orphic lyre:

one types to please and appease, to
belay the furies, to charm the real

and unreal threats into a kind of
growling submission: typing is this

ancient skill, now so rare it is as
if priestcraft, intoned knowledge in

the legend of words: this idle skill
is an offering, symbolic in kind,

a tribute to the makers of fear:
oh, we say, look at this typing:

note the actual ink, the pressure of
the keys against paper: isn't that

we say, curious: don't you find it
distracting: doesn't it recall to

you old rich worlds you'll be all
day recovering: meanwhile, we

typists will be eased enough to have
dinner, maybe take a nap:

                                              (100)

With its cumbersome physicality typing takes on a nearly hieratic
mystique, in sharp contrast to the disembodied efficiencies of the
computer:

              . . . oh, yes, typing is not easy
        these days, especially for those

        already accustomed to computers:
        they can't go back—what? and erase

        things or do whole pages over or
        type the whole poem over to station

        it differently on the page: they
        won't do: their backs are sped: of

        course, sometimes they push the wrong
        button and the hard stuff dissolves

> or vandals tear off with a
> computer in a hard drive to fly: I
>
> have nothing to say I can't take all
> day at, because fifty years of yapping,
>
> what have I finalized, not that one
> can't be diffident about finalization:
>
> computers cannot give me back what
> I want, which is what neither I nor
>
> the computer ever heard of before:
> the happening of something that never
>
> happened, laying it out not so much
> that nature can be abrogated as that
>
> its becoming is unencompassed: I'm
> sorry, I don't care about information:
>
> I can make up all I need:
>
> (63–64)

Ammons's rejection of the computer as a medium for poetry may seem surprising insofar as word-processing readily allows the kind of scrolling continuity that can only be achieved on the typewriter through the expedient of the tape. But of course it's precisely the tape's stubborn materiality, the way its oddness draws attention to the poem's status as physical artifact rather than mere "information," that commends it to Ammons, who dwells on the sheer mechanics of typing with something like an artisan's affection for the tools of his craft:

> . . . you can't type
> without dealing with the roller, the
>
> return carriage, the space bar, the
> margins, the ribbon, the paper, the
>
> keys—not to mention thoughts and
> feelings:
>
> (102)

Playfully demoting content to the status of afterthought, Ammons repeatedly ascribes a tonic power to the mere process of typing as a means of engaging mind and body in motion:

how wonderful to be able to write:
it's something you can't do, like

playing the piano, without thinking:
it's not important thinking, but the

strip has to wind, the right keys
have to be hit, you have to look to

see if you're spelling the words
right:
. . . .

                        . . . since I started this, 15
fairly pleasant minutes have passed:

my gratitude for that is, like,
boundless:

                                                    (77, 79)

Truman Capote is said to have sneered about Jack Kerouac's prose
"That's not writing, it's typing," but Ammons welcomes that me-
tonymy in "Strip." In a section of a poem that shows an almost
masochistic impulse to strip away and curtail, art here retains its
minimal yet saving power as *occupation*, in the most basic sense
of the word.

In addition to its horizontal and vertical dimensions, "Strip"
possesses a hidden formal property as well, a kind of third dimen-
sion hinted at but never fully disclosed in the text itself. As I've
noted already, Ammons's governing trope in Part One of *Glare* is
not just any strip but specifically a Möbius strip, that topological
anomaly in which a twisted loop's two surfaces fuse into one. How
can a poem assume so radically nonlinear a shape? Though only
an approximation, Ammons's solution is quite ingenious. Having
filled his strip with text and dismembered it into sixty-six sections,
he proceeded to reorder it according to a chiastic scheme whereby
sections from opposite ends of the tape are interleaved. In mathe-
matical terms this leads to the following pattern, where the first
number marks the section's place in the finished poem, the
bracketed number its place in the order of composition: 1 [66], 2
[1], 3 [65], 4 [2], 5 [64], 6 [3], etc. The sequence ends with a
convergence from both directions on the middle: 62 [32], 63 [35],
64 [33], 65 [34] (Ammons evidently dropped one section from the
final poem). The text thus forms a kind of loop without distinct

beginning or end points, in which forward and retrograde motions are intricately woven together.

Ammons does not advertise his use of this scheme in "Strip," and it's therefore worth asking what impact it can have on the poem's readers, who might be hard-pressed to recognize its presence without the help of outside sources like this essay. Of course if one holds, as the Black Mountain and Beat writers do, that the process of composition has an inherent integrity that always shows itself in the resulting text, then any manipulation of the text's initial form must perforce be felt, if only subliminally, as a violation of that organic process. Perhaps this notion mystifies the poetic process unduly, but it clearly informs Ammons's own practice, especially in his long poems; asked about his habits of revision, he told one interviewer that he had "tested the possibility of writing spontaneously—getting it- 'right' the first time—in the long essay poems and in *The Snow Poems*, and earlier in the *Tape for the Turn of the Year*."[2] Ammons's previous long poems, with the exception of "The Ridge Farm," had all been presented in the order of initial composition, in some cases with dates or other markers incorporated to confirm the poem's relation to lived time. The act of rearranging the individual sections of "Strip" is thus a genuinely radical one for Ammons, and gives the poem a shape and movement palpably different from those of his earlier long poems, whether or not readers are able to detect the schematic source of that difference. (The more alert among them, to be sure, may pick up on certain telltale discontinuities; sections 38–42, for example, alternate in their seasonal references between winter and summer.)

If the poem's structural simulation of a Möbius strip remains something of a secret, however, its adoption of the Möbius strip as an informing trope does not. Ammons alludes several times to the looping itinerary of his strip-poem, as in these lines:

> . . . stripping is
> what I do, keeling to this band of
>
> paper, a fleet rig on a round-the-world
> and back-around-again:

(113)

Note that this poetic voyage entails not one but two complete circuits, presumably because it requires two trips around the loop to revisit any point on a Möbius strip. An even more explicit allusion links the form with the traditional emblem of infinity:

> . . . though we see
> ourselves too short to bend, look
>
> how our figure 8 contains infinity:
> our figure 8 Möbius keeps two sides
>
> on a single side:
>
> (128)

By conflating figure 8 and Möbius strip Ammons suggests that for all its narrowness and constraint his medium can, with the right kinds of twists and bends, be opened to the infinite. At once a claim about aesthetic form and about temporal existence, this assertion of contained limitlessness helps to counteract the claustrophobic sense of limitation that dominates much of "Strip."

What really draws Ammons to the Möbius strip as a model for his work, though, is its power to dissolve antinomies: "our figure 8 Möbius keeps two sides / on a single side." Both reliant on and distrustful of binary thinking, Ammons finds in the Möbius strip an ideal vehicle for exploring the way apparent opposites flow into one another. Throughout "Strip" he ponders the question "is there no side / but one side or the other:" (9), resisting the impulse to draw categorical distinctions and seeking out instead the place where boundaries blur and contraries merge. Through aphoristic pronouncements, part Zen and part Henny Youngman, Ammons playfully inverts established dichotomies and demonstrates the kind of paradoxical logic he favors: "I keep proving I'm not god's gift to / the world by trying to prove I am:" (11); "the straight is crooked and the / crooked, straight: go, boy" (49). He reveals his preference for a syntax of convergence rather than antithesis in these lines:

> heads or tails: ups or
> downs: tops or bottoms: heads and
>
> tails: ups and downs: tops and
> bottoms:
>
> (76)

Ammons expounds on this preference for "and" over "or" more fully in the penultimate lines of "Strip," taking a Whitmanian touchstone as his starting point:

> . . . do I contradict myself, you
>
> say: well, I get interested in both
> sides of the argument: I am unhappily
>
> not an either/or person but a
> both/and: I have more sides than
>
> two: I have so many they round off
> like a glazed stob or bead of water:
>
> (178)

A Möbius strip has only one side while Ammons claims to have many, but as his metaphor of roundness implies, one and many are themselves opposites that melt imperceptibly together. As a figure of knowledge the Möbius strip represents a significant departure from the wedding of topology and epistemology in Ammons's earlier long poem *Sphere,* which based itself on distinctions between center and periphery, surface and core. A single continuous surface that confounds all dichotomies of inside and outside, the Möbius strip represents knowledge as endless, circular, and to venture an oxymoron, profoundly superficial. But if Ammons has moved away from his earlier faith in the cognitive accessibilty of centers and depths, he has developed a corresponding faith in the inexhaustibility of surfaces and peripheries. *Glare* is a poem that refuses to posit a center for its wanderings, instead lavishing itself on all the available surfaces of experience: language, memory, perception, feeling.

This doesn't mean that *Glare* is devoid of thematic content. In the midst of its various disquisitions, anecdotes, and confessions, the poem unfolds a difficult vision of the interconnected comings and goings of earthly things that subtly harmonizes with the closed loop of the Möbius strip. Countering the Christian postulate of the immortality of spirit, Ammons proposes instead the immortality of matter:

> oh, the spirit dies, but the body
> lives forever, run out of its limits
>
> though and caught up into others,
> the housing spirits of others,
>
> mold feed, ant freight, the mouth
> parts and anuses of riddling larvae:

>   alas, not as ourselves do we come
>   again or go anywhere else, after we
>
>   go: oh, we go, we go, we go, so
>   long—forever: though, when we go,
>
>   it is only for an instant and then
>   we are gone, and staying gone, we
>
>   are gone timelessly and once and for
>   all:
>
>   (7–8)

Matter and spirit are one dichotomy Ammons seems reluctant to dissolve, but he keeps the two terms in motion. The Newtonian principle of the conservation of matter ensures that our atoms will outlive our souls:

>   actually, the spirit which was never
>   anything goes: the rest stays here
>
>   (68)

Later Ammons reformulates this bleak dualism:

>   . . . material
>
>   tries to make it to eternity but
>   recycles, and spirit that forever
>
>   was forever is: forever, possibly,
>   because it isn't anything; that is,
>
>   it's nothing, or else it's something
>   time doesn't fool with:
>
>   (110)

Now the persistence of spirit is granted, but only as a corollary to its possible nothingness. The qualifying "or else" clause helps to maintain a delicate balance between nihilism and Platonism, but the burden of "Strip" is darkness, with only occasional flickerings of the old faiths showing themselves.

Armed with his varied knowledge of modern science, Ammons sets forth a kind of cosmic economy in which all debts and credits eventually cancel out:

        . . . funny balances pop up:

    one thing certain is the overall
    effect: all balances end in perfect

    zeros: well, with the exception that
    some zeros are bigger than others:

                                                    (32)

The strip's loop itself forms a kind of zero, and figures the circular
or cycling movement that makes all economies work. Ammons
halfheartedly protests against this harshly economic view of being,
but is quickly brought to acknowledge its force:

        I don't think things go round and
        round and come out zero (0), do

        you: unless that 0 is a planet:
        seems like there's been no material

        advantage to the swirl so far: we
        pick up sky detritus, and sometimes

        it isn't detritus, if you get my
        drift: take that mile-wide hole in

        Arizona, and take the blurp when by
        the addition of something large, we

        lost the moon: let's not get excited:
        I do think, though, we've hit on the

        reason for a lot of stuff: on the
        planet, if anything moves it moves

        something else, often backwards:
        that scrambles directions so when you

        go out to do good, you may get your
        boots crusty with evil:

                                                    (47)

For every action an equal and opposite reaction: the causality
limned in these lines is so pervasive that it invades even the moral
realm and undermines our futile efforts to come out ahead. The
recycling swirl of matter adds nothing, subtracts nothing, merely

keeps things restlessly moving, looping forward and backward at
once. We are the tragic exceptions to the rule that everything stays
here, but only because we were never really here at all:

> we'll just be here while we're here
> and then we'll just be gone: things
>
> will appear uninterrupted either way:
> while we're here the figure we cut
>
> will be as if vacant, and when we go
> the cutout we left will cave in on
>
> itself:

(160)

We devise forlorn schemes to pull ourselves out of the economy
of matter, but as Ammons grimly puts it, "stuff happens":

> a meditation like this is somewhat
> melancholy: hopes of setting a bit
>
> of stuff aside out of the round are
> founded like other hopes on hope: we
>
> pour in the formaldehyde and brick
> bodies up tight from rain and stuff
>
> and more stuff but stuff happens and
> earthquakes and volcanoes and cutting
>
> floods grab stuff back into the swim
> and motion cannot be prevented from
>
> getting back whatever stalled in it
> a "moment":

(161)

In the end all imbalances are, cruelly, made right:

> . . . how
> can leftover things keep building
>
> up and not deprive the circulations
> of their soup: alas, it is all made

          right: I'm terribly sorry: it is
          made right

                                              (161–162)

In "Scat Scan" Ammons offers a final statement of this eco-
nomic theme:

                              . . . pound to
          pound, quid to quo—evenness, evenness, oh,
          it's all even: it comes out as much of this

          as that, life having been some sort of
          imbalance in our favor:

                                              (243–244)

In these passages Ammons sets forth a powerfully synthesizing
vision in which biological life figures only as a fleeting episode in
the larger life of matter, a brief surplus quickly swallowed up by
the levelling motion of a vast economy. Ammons's equable, ironic
tone belies the despair behind these recognitions, which neverthe-
less make up only a fraction of the poem's content. Neither central
nor peripheral to *Glare,* these melancholy meditations mark one
of many threads woven into its variegated surface.

"Scat Scan"

In its second part, *Glare* revisits a number of themes and topics
taken up in "Strip," but with a difference. If "Strip" explores and
laments the conditions of constraint, enclosure and materiality im-
posed by its formal medium, "Scat Scan" seems to free itself from
that constricting awareness of form, entering a looser, less bounded
space in which imaginative possibilities expand. The most immedi-
ate source of this difference is purely quantitative; where the tape
"Strip" was composed on allows a maximum of thirty-six charac-
ters per line, the tape used for "Scat Scan" permits forty-five. A
difference of nine characters may not seem significant, but in fact
the additional breadth proves enormously liberating to Ammons,
in part because it allows him to approximate a loose pentameter
line, with its easy, speech-like cadence. No longer bumping up
against intractable margins, the poem is able to forget its material
conditions, which had been so stubbornly foregrounded in "Strip."
The fact that *Glare* moves from narrowness to wideness rather
than vice versa is crucial to its broad effect; if the poem seems

thematically to dwell on the diminishments enforced by time and age, its formal and tonal trajectory is paradoxically expansive. "Scat Scan" answers the bleak, circular broodings of "Strip" with a full-throated chorus that keeps the minor notes but mingles them with more ebullient strains.

Another crucial difference between "Strip" and "Scat Scan" is that the latter appears in the order of its composition, without the logarithmic displacements that shape the former. With its freer, more oral and musical idiom, modelled as its title suggests on jazz improvisation, "Scat Scan" presents itself less as an artifact than as a performance. Individual sections of "Strip" feel strongly improvisatory as well, but the act of reordering the sections decisively changes the nature of the whole, cutting the text off from the process that produced it and turning it into a fundamentally different kind of object. No such intervention occurs in "Scat Scan," and it therefore can be taken as a genuinely performative work, in which compositional energy and textual form are one.

The differences between the two parts of *Glare* are reflected in the very sound of their titles. Where the monosyllabic "Strip" seems to reduce the poem's cogitations to a single charged term, "Scat Scan" suggests playful proliferation, an exuberance of the signifier. (Ammons's typescript records the title's emergence from a series of verbal doodles: "Skits or Scans or Scats or Scams or Scuds or Scads.") More openly punning and portmanteau-ish than "Strip," "Scat Scan" exemplifies the kind of purely phonetic variation associated with jazz vocalese, one of the title's primary referents. We're meant to hear many things in the phrase, but the sheer excess or overflow of signification is perhaps its central meaning. If "Strip" obeys and illustrates principles of compaction and economy, "Scat Scan" enacts the contrary principles of fecundity and expansion, of matter and energy run riot.

"Scat Scan" shares "Strip"'s fascination with surfaces, but assumes a more active relation to them. To scan means to skim rapidly over a surface, seeking some point of entry or anchorage; but if the surface is all we have then that search must inevitably fail:

> you scan the surface and not a crevice
> springs light forth and no dark trench
>
> invites you in, so where is the exploratory root to
> fix, where do the stakes that angle up the
>
> spread stand off:

(184)

As a trope the Möbius strip keeps the surface at a distance, inviting us to behold its seamless unity. The trope of scanning implies a more mobile and proximate perspective, though one equally susceptible to frustration:

> . . . just think: if I'd stayed on the farm
>
> I'd be a happy holy roller: instead of this
> smart boy: this shaken isolate, this drained
>
> discard, this dust bit, too disconnected to
> settle, this comical comer touching down
>
> here and there on a surface too hot to stick
> with:
>
> (188–189)

Here scanning is opposed to geographical and metaphysical rootedness, the comforting stabilities of region and religion. By detaching himself from such roots, Ammons (a transplanted Southerner) gains access to an infinite expanse of knowledge and possibility with nowhere to settle. Restless, nomadic movement is the only solution to this dilemma, a movement that pauses "here and there" to sample local particulars, but never stays for long, since the poet evidently needs the coolness of detachment to relieve the heat of involvement. (The fact that Ammons has lived for over thirty years in Ithaca and seldom travels in no way contradicts this self-portrait of what Blake would no doubt call a mental traveller.) A key word in "Scat Scan" is *play,* which describes both its freedom of movement and its flitting engagement with the real:

> . . . language plays
>
> upon what-is the way light plays on water: it
> is without substance (as light nearly is):
>
> moving, glancing, dipping, cresting is its
> veracity:
>
> (182)

Inverting customary usage, Ammons defines language not as the object of scanning but as its instrument. Playing fitfully over surfaces, mapping them with its motion, it shares the poet's mercurial nature, his reluctance to linger in one spot.

"Scat Scan" also rhymes with CAT scan, of course, thereby summoning up the whole sordid sphere of medical technology with which the poet has grown increasingly conversant in recent years. *Glare* is punctuated by dour reflections on minor ailments and the mixed blessings of medicine: "a hip pain, a swollen gum, eyes that stick dry / at night, an ingrown toenail, a skin blemish / precancerous, I tell you, I feel like shoot" (220); "you could wish you were dead before it's too / late; that is, before the devices arrive with / their doctors" (242). The reversal of the expected syntactical relation between devices and doctors shows Ammons's deep kinship with Emerson, who prophetically declaimed "things are in the saddle, and they ride mankind." Though "Scat Scan" seems generally more upbeat than "Strip," the twin tyrannies of flesh and medicine can't be shaken off:

> . . . I am
> finally fatally flawed, I daresay: the pain
>
> in my hipjoint and humerus is—well, not very
> funny: the swelling in the ankles promises
>
> plenty: and a network of other ailments is
> so complicated balancing one ailment
>
> tilts another: medication becomes
> virtually self-diseasing: so many pills you
>
> can't tell the effects from the side effects:
> and who are you, someone before the medications
>
> or during or after: at least, you are being
> kept, but in another place: are your feelings
>
> lofty or zolofty, red or blue, down or double
> downdown: do you, in this condition, have any
>
> right to speak, for who or what is speaking, is
> it milligrams or anagrams, is it tranquility or
>
> tranquilium:

(282–283)

As a trope for the poem, a CAT scan suggests absolute authenticity in mapping the ups and downs, peaks and valleys, and assorted vital signs of its author's inner life. Such authenticity may be threatened by the incursions of medicine upon thought and feeling, but the poem provides its own compelling evidence for Ammons's ability to keep his voice intact despite these alien forces.

The term "Scat" carries its own array of associations. Ammons's fascination with the body and its less glamorous functions leads him in several passages to investigate the "scat" of scatology, a coarse version of the general theme of material remains that runs throughout *Glare* (see in particular "Scat Scan" 110). "Scat" also suggests an exhortation to depart, as in "scram" or "get lost," and there are several places in the poem where the poet seems perversely annoyed with his readers: ". . . I no longer (did I / ever) care what you think: I am so much alone, / you are not here:" (238); "have you developed insufficient faith in my / prior responses (responses verging on answers) / or are you just a miserable little needler who / can't stand anybody else's happiness:" (270). This cranky, belligerent tone (which comports with one sense of *Glare*) is largely an act, but reflects a genuine ambivalence on Ammons's part toward his audience. Both solitary and communal, poetry is an art that requires yet shies away from others and their imagined demands. If Ammons wishes his readers away, however, it's only so as to facilitate the kind of uninhibited utterance he surmises they themselves most want to hear.

The primary meaning of "scat" as it applies to the poem is the mode of improvised jazz singing invented by Louis Armstrong and perfected by Ella Fitzgerald, Sarah Vaughan, and other singers. Based on long strings of syllables chosen mainly for their percussive value, scatting is an art that might seem antithetical to poetry insofar as it rejects semantic content entirely. Yet the delight in sheer sound or phonetic play is never absent from *Glare*, and at times hijacks the poem:

> clamp the c (c-clamp?) of clog on log, it's a
> dog: is too: be beep: bittle de doo doo
>
> daw: de daw daw:

(203)

Northrop Frye identifies two basic kinds of verbal play, "doodle" and "babble," both of which this passage indulges in. These lines are about as close as Ammons comes to scatting in the orthodox sense of the word, and even here he seems as interested in the way words look as in their sound. Jazz poets like Langston Hughes and Sonia Sanchez incorporate scatting in their work much more extensively; yet precisely because Ammons doesn't seem interested in imitating or evoking the particular characteristics of jazz performance, his poem achieves something like a verbal equivalent of jazz, marked by the freshness of continual improvisation. When he finds himself setting down a slightly stale thought, he does so with a sheepish disclaimer:

> oh, I have something
> to tell that I thought of yesterday: I apologize
>
> for the loss of immediacy spontaneity might
> have stirred: and doubly apologize for the
>
> cement of lugubriousness that hardens around
> the reconsidered:
>
> (249)

Yesterday's thought is an embarrassment in a poem that strives to inhabit the moment as fully as possible: "that's what it's all / about, just *now,* that just went by:" (194). What Ammons calls "the / coral-fan immediacy of the present" is the realm where jazz and poem find their common impetus. Several sections of "Scat Scan" end with capitalized phrases that seem to function as deferred titles; by refusing to position them conventionally at the beginning of the text, Ammons illustrates the way his themes emerge out of his process rather than preceding and dictating it.

Even in jazz, of course, improvisation is never pure; the musician needs some preexisting structure to explore, whether song, chord progression, or scale. Ammons's equivalent to the "changes" jazz players solo on is, surprisingly yet plausibly, poetic tradition itself. "Scat Scan" is surely the most playfully allusive of all his works, full of echoes, parodies, and glancing references to canonical touchstones. Among the poets he invokes are Whitman ("When I heard the learned astonisher . . .") and Shakespeare, who along with Mozart serves as *Glare*'s chief representative of human culture at its most sublime. (There's also a running diatribe against Wallace Stevens and what Ammons sees as his stylistic failings.) But the poet who furnishes Ammons with the juiciest texts to blow on is Robert Frost, a close temperamental cousin in the line of Emerson. Several Frost poems briefly appear in the course of "Scat Scan," but it's that hoariest of chestnuts, "The Road Not Taken," that Ammons has most fun with, wailing on it like Charlie Parker on "I Got Rhythm":

> . . . caught up in the woodsy
> wiles, flickers and gleams, of LIFE, Robert,
>
> perceiving he could go either way, went the way
> his imagination less frequently went, which
>
> was, for him, the way most people go, so he had
> a fairly normal life—house, children, wife,
>
> cow, and a side of poems:
>
> (207)

Ammons playfully inverts Frost's claims to nonconformity, suggesting that for an Emersonian maverick domestic normalcy was in fact the road less travelled (though whether Frost's home life could be called normal is debatable). Later in "Scat Scan" Ammons returns to Frost's poem and reads it in a more personal light:

> I don't care what becomes of me now, I'm
> already become of: the end is clear (and
>
> clearly dark) but getting there can be a rugged
> road: so, undifferentiated as the end is, I
>
> suppose I would prefer one road to another,
> though they go to the same place, but way leads
>
> on to way and you can't tell which road you're
> on at first, they look about the same: ages
>
> and ages from now, if there's any story left
> to tell there'll be no telling what the story
>
> is: differences can be important where it's
> hard to make out a difference: this is so
>
> philosophical! but I better look out: I
> might miss the road (if I don't want to): in
>
> any case, whey leads on to whey and pretty
> soon the clabber's all gone: I think I'll take
>
> a stanza break here. . . .
>
> (261)

What begins as a sober meditation on Frost's themes turns to out-right silliness by the end. Ammons is not usually given to this degree of intertextual play, as he acknowledges in a self-deprecating aside: "I hope my literature, / which was mere allusion, has pleased you" (213). If *Glare* consisted entirely of pastiches of Frost and other poets it might justifiably be dismissed in such terms, but passages like these serve to briefly anchor the improvisational energies that play more freely throughout the poem. In this instance, Frost's famous parable about a single all-determining choice gives Ammons the opportunity to display his wider, more diffuse understanding of choice as something that occurs at every moment of consciousness. For Ammons differences are being made all the time, not once and for all; as the last line attests, even stanza breaks, normally dictated by a purely formal scheme, become the product of momentary impulses.

With its lightened sense of limitation and its correspondingly greater sense of improvisational freedom, "Scat Scan" is able to refigure the stultifying economy of matter set forth by "Strip" in more redemptive terms:

> . . . as improvisational melodies
>
> come and go at the piano, so the mind breaks
> against some configuration and makes off into
>
> netlike effusions, or so brooks register at the
> surface a crack in the slate and flow on, the
>
> registration dissolving in the mixed motions:
> so much goes away that saved would fill the
>
> world up with fluff: in fact, so much goes
> away it's a scientific wonder how anything is
>
> still here: I mean, how does so much of it
> find a route back and in what condition does
>
> it arrive and by what appearances and means
> did it effect the transition: I, myself, am
>
> not a scientist: I do not even spend much time
> gathering evidence, so it's unlikely any likely
>
> hypotheses could jump out of my mounds: the
> fact is that so much goes away but hardly

> *anything* really does: that is what gets me:
> how does so much stuff slither in and out or
>
> go round and round, shaping up and shipping
> out: well, it gives me the heebie-jeebies but
>
> doesn't really make any difference to me: if
> things can phony the golden years up out of
>
> rust, why. . . .

PLAYPRETTY

(240–41)

The endless circulation of matter seems less disspiriting in these lines than it had in "Strip," perhaps because they allow more room for variation and surprise, a kind of improvisation on a cosmic scale. Ammons incorporates a couple of sly jazz references in the passage that reinforce its implicit analogy between mutability and melody. When he complains that the flux of form gives him "the heebie-jeebies" he is surely recalling the great 78 rpm recording of that title by Louis Armstrong and his Hot Five—the very record, as it happens, on which Armstrong is reputed to have invented scat singing, after accidentally dropping his lyric sheet on the floor. And the closing tag may echo a phrase Ella Fitzgerald often used when encouraging musicians as they soloed: "play pretty for the people." These allusions suggest that our human efforts to improvise meaning and music out of the randomness around us are ultimately in tune with a wider music of things coming and going and coming round again. Indeed Ammons ends the section by ascribing to mere things the kind of agency normally attributed to art: "if / things can phony the golden years up out of / rust. . . ." The appearance of renewal or revival in the motion of reality may be "phony," inasmuch as time past can never be recaptured intact, but it provides a fragile aesthetic solace for our irreparable losses. And the power of such solace being all we have to protect us from despair, Ammons in "Scat Scan" seems content to call it up and bid it play.

Yet the question of what poetry owes itself and its readers remains open in *Glare*. Solace is, after all, meaningless without an acknowledgment of the terrors that necessitate it:

> should
> poems rehearse the terrors so as to leave us

apprised, and should poems at other times hum
the frantic into a pause: I long for a poem

so high, but not too high, where every agony
can be acknowledged as a quiver in the easy

ongoing of the pacific line:

(285)

In its studied oscillation between agony and ease, *Glare* fails to
achieve the ideal state Ammons envisions of a poem that can ef-
fortlessly absorb every disturbance to its oceanic calm. Relent-
lessly apprising us of the terrors of age and death, the poem also
creates pauses, zones cleared of anxiety and consecrated to the
pleasures of play, yet it cannot finally reconcile these functions.
The structure of the poem reflects this broad division; although
each part blends pain and pleasure to varying degrees, limitation
clearly predominates in "Strip," while "Scat Scan" gives freedom
the upper hand. Like a Möbius strip, *Glare* joins two sides into
one; like a blues harp it plays major and minor notes in turn. If
the poem falls short of a final synthesis, that is because we too are
hopelessly double, torn between the need to know the worst and
to rejoice in the rest. With the wisdom gained from a life of ponder-
ing tropes and emblems, Ammons shows us in *Glare* that the only
true metaphors are mixed metaphors.

NOTES

1. A. R. Ammons, *Glare* (New York: W. W. Norton, 1997), 54. All further page
references to this work will be given parenthetically.
2. A. R. Ammons, *Set in Motion* (Ann Arbor: University of Michigan Press,
1997), 43.

Ammons's Peripheral Vision: *Tape for the Turn of the Year* and *Garbage*

FREDERICK BUELL

If only in its sheer inclusiveness, A. R. Ammons's *Tape for the Turn of the Year* is heir to the American tradition of the democratic epic. If a poem like Whitman's "Song of Myself" is able to range, in style, between the language of the newspapers and that of the sublime, between Yankeeisms and the cadences of *Psalms* or the *Bhagavad Gita*, so Ammons's *Tape* goes from near-slapstick comedy to the heights of philosophic speculation. Similarly, while Whitman's poem contains multitudes, Ammons's *Tape* seeks "a level / of language / that could take in all / kinds of matter / & move easily with / light or heavy burden" (T, 143–4), and the matter referred to in these lines is, in fact, of enormous variety.[1] In the poem's single book-length sentence, the muse is invoked, summoned, and chatted about; classical tales are retold with wit and wisdom; the anxieties, excitements, challenges and ups and downs of writing this particular poem are explored and discussed repeatedly with the reader; a great deal of scientific material—from geology to biology and astronomy—is absorbed and mined for the wealth of correspondences it suggests between nature, society, mind, imagination, and spirit; and elephant jokes alternate with philosophic inquiry into the paradoxes of unity and diversity, plenitude and nothingness. This great variety of subject and rhetoric is, moreover, intermingled with an equally heterogenous array of events from daily life, for the poem is also a diary of the period between December 6 and January 10, a diary into which the reader is familiarly and warmly invited to look even as it is being composed. In a much more domestically intimate tone than Whitman strikes, Ammons includes readers in a host of small daily events, ranging from his trademark commentaries on the various moods of the weather, to such heterogenous material as the news of an aircraft disaster, a list of common nouns and their plurals copied down from Channel 12 (WNET), what the poet has had for lunch, a list of all the varied sounds the poet hears while sitting in a quiet house, the poet's anxieties about a book of poems out for consideration by a publisher, and longer and shorter narratives about a host of bourgeois familial activities, like unpacking his mother-in-law's new dishes, shopping in Wanamaker's, and exchanging unwanted Christmas presents after the holiday at Korvette's.

Tape for the Turn of the Year is also just as reflexively self-conscious about its own innovativeness as Whitman's poetry was. Writing on an adding machine tape purchased in his local House and Garden store, Ammons repeatedly comments, comically and seriously, on the challenges and significances of writing his long, continuous, spontaneously-composed, single-sentence poem. Ammons's particular form of innovation, however, is as different from Whitman's as a cameo is from a large canvas and as plainness and understatement is from operatic rhetoric and gigantism. Even William Carlos Williams, Ammons's more immediate forerunner in the American epic tradition (the *Tape* records a trip Ammons took to New York to attend a Williams memorial) is much more expansive in *Paterson* than Ammons is here. In *Paterson,* Williams writes a complex, modernist epic of many characters and voices, one feistily and polemically bent on making its subject, the provincial New Jersey city, more imaginatively and nationally central than its overshadowing metropolitan neighbor New York and its even more overshadowing and more metropolitan absent antagonist, T. S. Eliot's London. In *Tape,* by contrast, Ammons writes as a pastoralist filiated with Frost as well as an epic poet in the mode of Whitman and Williams. He retells the story of the inner life of one person in a vastly more rural-provincial location in New Jersey than Paterson. The result is a poem that is (at the risk of sounding like Polonius) as pastoral as it is epical, along with being, in its various sections, mystical-comical-elegiacal-philosophical-lyrical to boot.

The poem's filiation to Whitman and the dates of its composition (1963–64) all position it further on the literary historical map of what used to be called contemporary poetry—and perhaps still can be so called, if, in the following decade, what some call the postcontemporary period is inaugurated. In the well-known battle of the anthologies of the early 60s—the battle between Donald Hall and Robert Pack's *New Poets of England and America* (1962) and Donald Allen's *The New American Poetry: 1945–1960* (1960)—Ammons weighed in on the side of the poets who rejected New Critical formalism, "academic" poetry, and emphasis on the poem as a closed, crafted artifact (the poem as a "well-wrought urn" or, as more postcontemporary jargon has it, an "autonomous work of art") in favor of the Whitman tradition, with its evangelicalism, its overt nationalism, its commitment to inclusiveness, experimental open form, spontaneity, and rhetoric. Ammons's commitment to this position is underrecognized, something that is clear when one realizes that, especially after his canonization in the academy by Harold Bloom, very few commentators indeed have followed Ammons's own lead in the preface to *Ommateum* and connected him significantly to poets like Allen Ginsberg, Gary Snyder, Charles Olson, and Frank O'Hara—poets routinely considered avant-garde and experimentalist. In *Tape,* Ammons was and is every bit as much an experimentalist as Kerouac was in *On the Road* and the poets in Donald Allen's anthology, even if Ammons chose to pitch his experimentation in a minor, bourgeois key.

It is equally important, however, to position *Tape* and Ammons's other writing at this time historically in a larger frame. *Tape* helped consolidate Ammons's metamorphosis from the cryptic poet of *Ommateum* (a volume filled with abstract, desert[ed] landscapes, of which some are identified with ancient Sumer) to one who consciously identified himself as an heir to nineteenth-century romanticism. In this, Ammons was influenced by Williams's latter-day poetic nationalism—his second-stage postcolonial cultural nationalism, intent upon wresting modernism away from Europe, even as Emerson and Whitman had preached the arrival of the American scholar and American poet against the mental colonialisms of their day. More interesting, however, is that Ammons was in fact only one of a number of writers in the 1960s who self-consciously aligned themselves with great figures and impulses in the American literary past. Indeed, it seemed almost as if a coordinated process of cloning was going on: if Ammons persistently echoed Whitman and still more completely emerged as the new American Emerson, Allen Ginsberg was establishing himself as Whitman reincarnate and Gary Snyder was crafting himself as a reconfigured Thoreau. Similarly, but much more ambivalently, Robert Lowell was reincarnating himself in his early work as a Melvillean neo-Puritan. An answer to why this updating of the American literary-intellectual past—this recreation of the American renaissance—should have occurred is not far to seek: America's emergence as a (or, rather, the) global power in the wake of World War II had already fueled a widespread return to and reinterpretation of the American cultural past, and the poets of the 1960s represented a specific stage in this process.

Perry Miller's epiphany in Africa between the wars—his "sudden epiphany" on Matadi on the banks of the Congo "of the pressing necessity for expounding my America to the twentieth century"—was a classic case in point. Both the anxiety and the sense of importance created by America's increasing global prominence helped "thrust upon" Miller and others "the mission of expounding what I took to be the innermost propulsion of the United States, while supervising the unloading of drums of case oil flowing out of the inexhaustible wilderness of America."[2] Miller's need to find the source of America's exceptionalism was forerunner to redefinitions of America carried out by national character studies commissioned during wartime, such as Margaret Mead's *And Keep Your Powder Dry* (1942), and the blossoming of the American studies movement in the 1950s.

By the 1970s and 1980s, however, the assumptions behind and claims of such studies had become increasingly sharply contested. For example, in her essay "'Indians': Textualism, Morality, and the Problem of History," Jane Tompkins criticized Miller's recollections and historiography as neo-imperial in character, faulting him for both "his failure to notice *who* was carrying the fuel drums he was supervising the unloading of" and his "failure to see that the land into which European culture had moved was not vacant, but already occupied by a varied and numerous population."[3] Just one of many such recent reappraisals of the work of the "myth and symbol" school of American studies, Tompkins's critique has been repeated in many forms about many aspects of American exceptionalism under the influence of ideology-critique, imperial discourse theory, and postcolonialism. But between the 1950s and the radical/revisionary movements of the last several decades comes, of course, the 1960s. Seen this way, the decade—or at least the first half of it—was neither utopia nor aberration, but an intermediary period, a period in which radical-contrarian voices tried to take over the task of national cultural redefinition, even as the civil rights movement, Vietnam War protests, and the formation of the media-featured counterculture brought such struggles for the heart and mind of the nation into the social arena. In the process, cultural nationalism and political radicalism/cultural avant-gardism overlapped significantly, a conjunction that was strongly reinforced by the upsurge in anticolonial nationalism globally, and Allen's new American poetry was very much a part of this phenomenon. Though Ammons was relatively centrist and apolitical socially compared to figures like Ginsberg and Snyder, he was, as we have seen, like them an aesthetic radical.

Internally, *Tape for the Turn of the Year* not only plays with the signficances of its form and its filiation to Whitman, but elaborates a complex, individualized angle of vision on the world. The poem is crafted according to a double structure, one with narrative and philosophical levels. Most overtly, *Tape* is a comic epic in a narrative mold: Ammons depicts himself as a person on at least several quests. On the one hand, he is trying to pass through a stretch of time at the turn of the year and find, somehow, a "home" in it, an activity that involves locating himself, away from his southern roots, in his familial and domestic life in the north, even as he is attempting to establish himself career-wise as a poet and to obtain a teaching position at Cornell. At the same time, he is on a still more immediate and specific quest, that of taking the reader with him through the voyage of the dauntingly long adding machine tape to the successful completion of the poem. Ammons is, in short, in two ways a contemporary Odysseus, and he makes much fun and some wisdom out of the analogy. When he records the death of eighty passengers in the crash of a plane struck by lightning, he follows that brief memorial with the following lines:

> and he plucked two men
> and broke fast
>
> grieved, we
> rejoice
> as a man rejoices saved
>   from death: we beg
> that men be spared
> calamity & the hard turn:
> we make an offering of our
> praise: we reaccept:
>
>   our choice is
>   gladness:

(T, 16–17)

In these lines Ammons echoes specifically one of Odysseus's adventures (the Cyclops episode); he also attempts more generally to capture Odysseus's marvelous openness to both pathos and joy, his ability to move almost frictionlessly through the worst calamities into moments of sanctuary, from profound grief to auroral gladness, from shipwreck to the enjoyment of delicious food after long hunger, and to do so without constraint on or distraction from either experience. Similarly, at the heart of both Ammons's and

Odysseus's voyages is a deep sense of exile and nostalgia. Longing to get "home," Ammons can equate his present place with Kalypso's island and relate the composition of the poem to his attempt to assuage this fundamental sense of exile:

> (if you were
> sitting on a
> distant strand,
> longing for home,
> you'd have to
> conjure up things to
> occupy the time,
> too)

                                                                    (T, 136)

The vein of nostalgia that this identification suggests is heightened in the poem both by the onset of the Christmas season, with all its burden of mystery and memory, and by a number of actual memories Ammons inscribes in the poem of his lost childhood. But exile has, more importantly, a present, psychological dimension: the poet's story is more immediately how "a man comes home / from haunted / lands and transformations"—how one can manage to reach some kind of home in one's own mind in a world of psychological darknesses and literal, astronomic immensities.

Underneath *Tape's* echoes of the traditional epic drama there is another, less playfully narrative, more philosophically serious plot in *Tape*. For the poem is also on a philosophic quest, the attempt to find "a way of / going along with this / world as it is" (T, 203); Ammons is seeking a "home" in the continuing flow of time, something that, in Ammons's Heraclitan world, always means flux. For Ammons, one is always "standing on loose / ground" (T, 154) and change is a constant that must be lived with and through, not opposed ("nothing permanent is old" [T, 54]). Ammons addresses the difficulties of this challenge philosophically by anticipating complexity theory, and a short version of his thought might go as follows. In nature, there are no fixed centers, only provisional ones, ones constituted by the changing relationships of which they are a part. Such provisional centers "proliferate / from / self-justifying motions" (T, 116) and hold only by accepting and creatively managing surprise, change, and interaction. What they cannot do is try to be impervious to their environment; thus, cell walls get brittle when the cell dies, whereas, in a healthy state, they are permeable and negotiate the exchanges that sustain life. (To return to my historical argument briefly and somewhat facetiously, if one argued that Ammons's emphasis on domestication in a dangerous world in this poem was a sign of his centrism—was part and parcel with the postwar defensive coldwar mentality, its reverence for Frost and the "howling wilderness" school of American exceptionalism—this elaboration of process would be just the opposite, an indication of Ammons's allegiance to the 1960s experimentalists).

The optimum state to be in in such a world is thus what scientists have recently come to call "the edge of chaos," the creative state poised just between order and chaos.[4] Ammons elaborates a psychological version of this state. Imaginatively, we need to release ourselves from "thought jails." At the same time, however, "if we get too free, / all the way / into unrelated, / fractured sensation," we quickly ask that the jails call us back occasionally so "we can get a good / night's sleep" (T, 105). We need, in short, to position ourselves psychologically always on the fertile edge between order and chaos; it is on this fertile edge that one has the best chance of creatively managing surprise and change, the prerequisite for adaptivity and creativity alike.

Chaos theory has, as James Gleick and others have made clear, developed in a dramatically multidisciplinary way: it has been elaborated in a bewildering variety of fields, ranging from mathematics to meteorology, fluid dynamics, computer science, anthropology, biology, evolution, and ecology. Similarly, Ammons's interests have ranged widely across the physical and human sciences, from evolution to astronomy, and his perceptions in *Tape* of the proliferation of provisional centers is an attempt to describe a host of different processes in, for example, nature, social behavior, economics, poetry, and of course the psyche, all of which Ammons depicts as nonlinear dynamical systems. Such systems are systems created by interactions, systems in which the nonlinear interactions of few things can create tremendously divergent behaviors, a kind of "deterministic chaos."[5] As a result, Ammons cultivates, in the structure and style of *Tape*, spontaneity: the poem's many spontaneous jumps in subject and breaks in time and mood, together with its linear rush towards its eventual goal, represents just this sort of "deterministic chaos." Such "deterministic chaos" or ordered spontaneity has been shown, in computer-generated systems of artificial life, to have the greatest potential for evolutionary adaptiveness—for creative response to change. In discussing the work of Christopher Langton, Roger Lewin notes how "as you leave ordered territory and enter the region of chaos you traverse maximum computational capacity, maximum information manipulation."[6] So Ammons, perched on the cusp between routine domestic life with its predictable regularities of weather, dinner, and small family events and a sense of the constant "going in & out / of shape" of all forms of temporal flow, is attempting to write his poem "at the / crest's break, the / running crest, / the event becoming word" (T, 37).

Tape thus embodies a particularly kinetic version of what Steven Schneider has called Ammons's "poetics of widening scope." Schneider follows Harold Bloom in describing a crucial swerve in Ammons's poetic career: though "Corsons Inlet" has been singled out as the pivotal poem in this respect, there are, in fact, a number of poems in which Ammons worked this change through, and *Tape* is one of the most important of them. After the early poems of *Ommateum,* poems animated by a hunger for transcendence that is most often consummated in gestures of loss or a morbid, Poe-esque, conscious experience of physical dissolution and death, Ammons chooses to resist the hunger that previously attracted him. Instead, seeking to uneasily domesticate himself in this world, rather than seek a higher state of Being, he

> opts for the vision of nature because he finds 'direct sight' more liberat-ing than contemplation of the Sublime. In Ammons's universe, the apperception of physical, manifest phenomena and processes yields pleasure and sometimes pain. Despite the lure of the Transcendent, he resists it. Ammons associates the "Overall" with closure, whereas freedom depends on process and visible change.[7]

Henceforth, one of Ammons's chief visionary and poetic strategies couples close observations of spontaneous, disorderly natural processes; these observations, together with detailed scientific knowledge about the processes involved, help Ammons keep his imagination perched on the edge of chaos. Avoiding, on the one hand, what he calls in "Extremes and Moderations" structureless "loose-flowing phantasmagoria" (CP, 339) and resisting, on the other hand, "thought jails," Ammons brings, as John Elder has argued, "the redemption of continual disorder and deflection to the mind's otherwise self-centered round."[8] Staying on the edge, then, represents for Ammons a willed commitment to the processes of life: if Whitman chose happiness at the end of "Song of Myself," Ammons in *Tape* declared that "our choice is / gladness" (T, 17).

Tape's most distinctive mode of operating on the edge of chaos is, perhaps, the *attempt* to ride the crest: indeed, this attempt un-derlies the at times manic, at times depressive fluidity of all of Ammons's long, single-sentence poems, poems given both shape and spontaneity by the use of the colon. Thanks to the colon, small mini-narratives, segments of thought, moments of perception and observation are formed and held loosely together in the forward-directed rush, the ceaseless fluidity that the colon, the same device, also helps create. At times, when Ammons's imagination is strongest and fullest, he is able to ride the crest of time, uniting, in stretches of the poem, form and flow; these moments are, however, neither reliable nor enduring, and he recognizes that the "joy of the crest" (T, 72) is not a place he can stay for all that long. As a result, the *Tape* records periods of dullness, uncertainty, disillusionment, and depression, as well as manic, hectic attempts to get engines going again, when things are not working, attempts that often involve much verbal horseplay. Occasionally, Ammons writes that the only way of coming home in time is in silence; in still more disillusioned moments, he calls his poem an unnatural structure thrown "against the flow / which I cannot stop" (87). At still other times, he advocates acquiescence and acceptance as the necessary paths. But the overall effort of the poem—which includes all of its failures as well as flights, all of the darknesses it touches upon and negotiates a path through, all of its times of muteness and all of its uncomfortable manias—represents Ammons's attempt to live in time in the fullest, most creative way possible: his commitment to the edge of chaos and his attempt to find a way of going with, or some kind of "home" in, flow.

To this goal for the poet in Ammons's poem we must add one for the poet of the poem. In so far as he can involve his reader in the difficulties and enthusiasms of this quest, and in so far as he can create that experience in the tradition of the American epic poem, Ammons is seeking to make his work into a new, albeit still always provisional, center in contemporary American literature. What Ammons says of how natural processes work is meant to be true also, I believe, of how *Tape* invents its own form and engages its reader:

> . . . the center-arising
> form
> [that] adapts, tests the
> peripheries, draws in,
> finds a new factor,
> utilizes a new method,
> gains a new foothold,
> responds to inner & outer
> change:

(T, 116–7)

The result is a poem that, in its innovation, absorbs, changes, and thus renews the very literary tradition (itself a species of nonlinear dynamical system) of which it is a part. Written on an adding machine tape, and dedicated to flux's additive motions, *Tape* has, in comparison to previous works in the Whitman tradition, indeed found a "new factor" and utilized a "new method" in its responses to "inner & outer / change."

One measure of how successfully Ammons created such a provisional center within and out of his poem is the conclusion. In it is expressed, for a moment, the sense of roundness that has been achieved out of the flow, something that hinges on both the epic journey we have taken and the Frostian intimacy that has been created between the reclusive poet and us, his companions for a little over a month and more than two hundred pages. By the end, a sense of a center has been so far established, a world and world-understanding has been sufficiently elaborated, and a comraderie, a shared experience, has been adequately created that Ammons's final "so long" to the reader, a decisive echo of Whitman, has real present resonance to it. It is both an invocation of the tradition Ammons has renewed and a poignant farewell to a reader who has become by now an intimate fellow traveler. It is, in short, the fruit of a companionable text that self-consciously savors and displays its (provisional) narrative closure.

This overall reading of *Tape for the Turn of the Year* should make it clear that one of the "edges of chaos" Ammons inhabits is generic. Equally epic and pastoral, *Tape* combines the aggressive inclusiveness and epic aims of the urban Whitman tradition with the ruralist isolation and intimate personalism of Frost. As pastoral nature poet, Ammons is thus no regionalist, no Wendell Berry, no antimodern cultivator of localist roots. This is the case for two reasons. First, Ammons's nature is not a specific, physical plot of woods, mountains, and streams; it is more abstract than that—it is natural processes—and, as such, it (along with the pleasures and powers it helps liberate) can be found in unconventional, non-rural places—like factories, the subject of another Ammons nature poem. Second, the terrain Ammons writes in is specifically "peripheral"—terrain that is, from the start, no pastoral enclave set apart (or seeking to be set apart) from the metropolis. A periphery is, in fact, defined in part by its metropolis: it is the influence of the urban center that makes the peripheral feel peripheral. Thus, New Jersey is a place without aboriginal connections for Ammons (or most anyone else, for that matter); it is a place of heterogenous mixtures, of heteroglot languages, as Williams has made clear. It is also a place of ordinary democratic-social life, of chats with the guy at the Esso station, of trips to Wanamaker's and Korvettes— a place where commerce, as well as nature, makes the points of reference, a place that Kinney's and the Circle Diner help map. More important, it is a place in which Ammons lives in relationship to outside forces, as we see when he frets over the publication of his book or the fate of his job application and when he travels to New York for the Williams memorial. And it is the place where Ammons buys the commercial artifact he writes on—the adding machine tape, a medium that is a far cry from Whitman's completely naturalized book, his "leaves of grass."

Ammons has continued, in his career as a writer of long poems, to seek maximum inclusiveness while retaining peripherality. Indeed, if anything, Ammons's peripherality has become even more aggressive a position than it was in *Tape,* as the centers against which it measures and deploys itself have changed. As we shall shortly see in examining *Garbage,* Ammons has remained still very much the peripheral iconoclast even as America's cultural and intellectual centers have radically changed. *Garbage* is a poem that is, in many ways, written in an aggressively subversive relationship to that center; to show how this is so, I must focus first on changes to the social and intellectual landscape that occurred in the decades following the 1960s, changes that were, to someone like Ammons, ones both to be drawn to and to resist.

Socially, the changes were immense. Starting in the 1970s, national frames of reference began, both in the United States and abroad, to give way to awareness of the constitutive importance of global interrelationships. More importantly, the United States commenced its economic and cultural postmodernization. Intellectually, Ammons's academy (Cornell), like many American universities, entered the era of the theory revolution. Both of these developments mean that, in many different ways, the experimentalist poetry of the 1960s—the time I have characterized as a neo-American renaissance—is no longer so radical or experimentalist as it once seemed to be, as the cutting-edge of the avant-garde has moved on. Against the theoretical and stylistic innovations of, for example, language poetry, many of the landmark experiments of the "contemporary" period, from the Blakean visions of *Howl* to Snyder's Thoreauvian poetic diaries, seem hopelessly neo-romantic and pre-deconstructionist, even as they anticipate "postcontemporary" poetry. Space will limit me to discussing only one of a number of aspects of these social changes and intellectual developments that were, arguably, very important to Ammons's later work:

I want to focus on Ammons's relationship to what has emerged as
the most important category for avant-garde poetry in the present,
namely postmodernism, a coinage that, as Fredric Jameson has
written, has had "all the reality impact of a corporate merger."[9] In
the following, I will argue, more specifically, that the globalization
and postmodernization of the United States constitutes a new, and
vastly more arrogant and encompassing kind of metropolitan cen-
teredness than American postwar neo-imperial nationalism did.
And I shall maintain that, in his book-length poem, *Garbage,* Am-
mons has tried aesthetically to stake out as aggressively peripheral
a position vis à vis the cultural features of this new metropolitanism
as, in *Tape,* he did toward older official centers, when he resisted
(by resituating it) "international" European modernism in the man-
ner of Williams and took part in a contrarian attempt to recraft
American cultural identity at the height of what was then called
"the American century."

Focusing on postmodernism brings up, of course, a whole set of
vexed questions: just what it is (its defining characteristics;
whether one can speak of it as a singular form, or whether one must
speak only of postmodernisms, each determined by the particular
aesthetic discourse it arises from); whether it constitutes a break
with modernism or is an extension of it; whether it is a progressive
or reactionary cultural movement; and whether, as Jameson has
written, it expresses or represses some deeper historical reality,
be it a new stage of capitalism or a new, media-created regime of
information and representation.[10] While a serious discussion of all
of these questions is not possible (or relevant) here, it would be
helpful to do some mapping of the term before proceeding to use
it. As I have discussed elsewhere, one can isolate several large-
scale tendencies within the various discourses of postmodernism.[11]
On the one hand, one can focus on postmodernism as a response
to the recent postnational phase of globalization, to the new world-
wide interactivity that has broken down (both globally and within
First World countries, especially the U.S.) previous notions of
space, place, and cultural identity. Following this pathway, one
would focus most upon the development of postcolonial, global-
cosmopolitan, and multicultural artistic forms and attend to the
debates on polyphonic representation and historiography these
have sponsored. On the other hand, one can focus, with Jameson,
on postmodernism as a new (and much more complete) stage in
the capitalist narrative and place avant-garde First World art in
different media under the microscope in order to determine recur-
ring aesthetic features. As a living, white, male nature poet who

had located himself in the American pastoral and epic traditions, Ammons, in reacting to the polycultural, urbanist antifoundationalism of the 1980s, had difficult new centers with which to renegotiate his creative peripherality.

Ammons's response to both streams of the postmodern was a combination of interest and resistance. To the new interests sparked by postnational globalization, Ammons has responded by giving a number of his longer poems—most notably *Sphere,* but also sections of *Garbage*—a global scope: thus, the conclusion to *Sphere* preaches a "united poem, a united, capable mind, a united capable / nation, and a united nations! capable, flexible, yielding, / accomodating, seeking the good of all in each." The poem ends this vision of inclusion and universality under difference with a celebratory vision of the globe floating through space and time, a moment in which each is returned to his/her own identity, "we're clear: we're ourselves: we're sailing" (S, 79). At the same time, this passage indicates how traditional Ammons's commitments also remain: the very terms the vision is couched in (inclusion, universality, self-identity) are, in fact, targets of poststructural-multicultural polemics. [12]

In *Garbage,* we see Ammons negotiating even more loaded, because concrete, terrain with his comic focus on the "priestly director behind the / black-chuffing dozer" (G, 20), the "garbage spreader" who dreams at times of his fat wife Minnie ("so fat, fat people / like to be near her") and who loves "every bit of her, every bite (bit) round enough to get / to: and wherever his dinky won't reach, he finds / something else that will" (G, 37). Coupled with one of the playful self-images Ammons adopts in the course of his protean (and postmodern) display of personae and parody, that of a "hole puncher or hole plugger: stick a finger / in the dame (*dam,* damn, dike), hold back the issue / of creativity's flood," these lines do a lot to offend the decorums of contemporary political correctness. At the same time, however, Ammons comically transforms the dozer man from redneck to high priest of the Delphic oracle of the landfill (at the landfill's peak, a transfiguring fire burns) and a hero of Homeric ancestry: he stares into the fire "as into / eternity, the burning edge of beginning and / ending," all thoughts "of his paycheck and beerbelly" fall away, and, finally, he gets "back up on his bulldozer / and shaking his"—Homeric— "locks backs the bulldozer up" (G, 32–34). Indirectly, yet aggressively, taking on the pieties of the day, Ammons establishes his antithetical figure (Southern, white, male, beerbelly) as a representative icon for the contemporary age in as gently humorous and ironic a fashion as he had evoked Odysseus as a model in *Tape for the Turn of the Year.*

What is the upshot of these hidden polemics? The answer lies, I believe, in Ammons's continuing sense of himself as a marginal figure, something that lasts into the time of his fame and the time when marginality has been claimed aggressively by multiculturalism and feminism. Perhaps in the spirit of, but also certainly against these new marginalities, Ammons creates a fat white Southerner who ploughs garbage on a landfill as a representative figure for our new world of environmental crisis, even as he recrafts a new, more extreme version of his own identity. In *Tape*, the speaker's marginality/peripherality was part and parcel of his isolation in provincial New Jersey and his precarious position in the poetry world; more importantly, it was part of the humility of the voice of the poem:

> I believe that man is
> small
> & of short duration in the
> great, incomprehensible,
> & eternal: I believe
> it's necessary to do
> good
> as we can best define it:
> I believe we must
> discover & accept the
> terms
> that best testify:
> I'm on the side of
> whatever the reasons are
> we are here:

(T, 98)

The version of Judeo-Christian humility—the sense of awe and human smallness in proximity to magnitude—evoked here runs throughout the whole poem, reinforced as it is by much of the Christmas atmosphere. The poem's play of tones thus touches, at what seem particularly deep and exalted times, on a well of pietistic feeling, even as *Tape* utterly resists a theistic focus (and, in fact, omits Christmas altogether from its record). In *Garbage*, by contrast, the marginality of the speaker is more austere, less consoling. *Garbage* contains, in both slapstick-comic and serious form, some of Ammons's most spare and lucid appraisals of having neared the edge of nothingness—of being old, of being deceived by hope, of suddenly realizing "I'm merely an old person: whose mother is dead, / whose father is gone and many of whose / friends and associates have wended away to the / ground" (G, 22). As inhabitant of the edge of chaos, as one who conceived of lifeform, institution, psyche, idea, and poem as constructions of and from process, as an imaginative ecocentrist who continually displaced human centrality in the web of natural relationships, Ammons always was one to whom the postmodern notion of decentering the self was not alien; this awareness has increased in *Garbage*, where the speaker's self-conscious marginality has fewer consolations. In *Garbage*, the dominant metaphor for the processes of selfhood is recycling; thus, "we're trash" (G, 46), material going through transformations, and "tears / when we are helpless are our only joy" (G, 39). At extreme moments in the poem, Ammons writes from a severely posthuman perspective.

As with Tom Wolfe's *Bonfire of the Vanities*, there may be, in *Garbage*, some covert attempt to trump the "others" at their own game. But the game is not exactly the same in both cases. As I have been arguing, Ammons's extreme marginality is, in *Garbage*, ecologically based; as such, according to the terms of Arran Gare's *Postmodernism and the Environmental Crisis*, Ammons would supposedly be postmodern, for "postmodernism is 'eco-centric'." But when Gare goes on to write, Ammons's reservations become clear:

> It is associated with respect for non-Western societies and cultures, for the previously suppressed ideas of minorities, for nature worship and Eastern religions and for non-human forms of life.[13]

For Ammons, though he claims Lao-Tsu and the *Tao Te Ching* as major influences on his work, does not pit the wisdom of non-Western societies and minorities against that of the Western tradition in his formulation of ecocentric views. As Ammons states overtly in *Garbage*, his poem is "about the pre-socratic idea of the / dispositional axis from stone to wind, wind / to stone (with my elaborations, if any . . .)" (G, 20): the Western tradition, in particular the pre-Socratic nature philosophers whose influence is marked throughout Ammons's work, hold the seeds for Ammons's ecocentric decentering of the self.

The real heart of the matter is that Gare was stretching to make the statement he did. Environmentalism has been often seen, as Andrew Ross shows in *The Chicago Gangster Theory of Life*, not as keeping the company Gare evokes, but as antiprogressive, anti-libertarian, antimodernist, white-Western-male, and conservative, an oppositional movement separate from other minority activisms.[14] Still more crucial is the fact that the new scholarship in literary and cultural studies has, in many ways, heightened the potential gap between ecocentrism and other progressive movements: as ecocritic Lawrence Buell has maintained in the course of trying to bridge this very gap, "revisionary scholarship on race and gender has shown [that] nature has historically been not only directly exploited, but also the sign under which women and non-whites have been grouped in the process of themselves being exploited" and that it stresses "nature's function as an ideological theater for acting out desires that have very little to do with bonding to nature as such."[15] Environmentalism as a social and intellectual movement, in short, displays much of the same ambivalence in its relationships with other new activisms as Ammons does with contemporary postmodern theory.

Thus Ammons's continuing gendering of nature, along with his sexualized humor, signal a subversion of recent theory—which is, of course, much given to styling itself as subversive.[16] More crucial still for our present purposes is the fact that Ammons's environmental imagination not only does not repudiate Western (and, as we saw in *Tape,* American) poetic and intellectual traditions, but it also sees selves constructed and unmade, provisional centers formed and dissolved primarily as a result of—or in the image of—natural and creative-imaginative processes, not social ones. Once again, having absorbed much from metropolitan theory, Ammons draws a line in the sand. Ammons is well aware of the self as a fiction, and he loves to play with different personae, often with parodic fecundity. At the same time, it would be impossible to say that *social* constructionism, in its most popular poststructuralist/postmodern forms, is really one of his concerns. Though Ammons readily acknowledges the force of the uncertainty principle in his imaginative relations with nature, he does not use its unsettling ontological critique to foreground human power relationships. Ammons does not share the historical or sociological interests that have been expressed in the poststructuralist description of the self as, in fact, a compilation of subject positions out of a variety of different social and intellectual discourses, which are in turn constructions of power. As a man whose years make him increasingly conscious of death, as one who lives on the border between society and natural process, and as a poet-subversive who picks the outrageous topic of garbage (not a topic for much canonized poetry), Ammons's often self-parodic depiction of his marginality in *Gar-*

bage seeks to escape the lens of social constructionism in the name of exploring more fatal, foundational systems, rather than examine itself through that lens. Ammons thus would eschew the radical position in the present "science wars" of the journal *Social Text,* even as he would repudiate simplistic positivism. The work of science, like the idea of "nature," is not, for him, reducible to politically-interested social constructions. In *Garbage,* then, Ammons's position is simultaneously critical of and responsive to a crucial strain of new theory: indeed, the poem, I would argue, is written in part out of an aggressively peripheral relationship to it.

What has happened to "nature" in the new dispensation brings me to my second area of concern, namely Ammons's similar response to what I have singled out as a second strain of postmodern theory to examine—namely, postmodernism as the cultural dominant of late capitalism, postmodernism considered as a First-World, urban phenomenon. In responding to this strain of postmodern theory, Ammons is even more overtly constructing an aggressively peripheral response to a new kind of metropolitanism, for, in this approach to the postmodern, metropolitan influence is determinative, the theory's central focus.

Just a few comments from Fredric Jameson will make clear what the stakes are. As Jameson puts it in one of his most memorable statements:

> I have already pointed out that Mandel's intervention in the postindustrial debate involves the proposition that late or multinational or consumer capitalism, far from being inconsistent with Marx's great nineteenth-century analysis, constitutes, on the contrary, the purest form of capital yet to have emerged, a prodigious expansion of capital into hitherto uncommodified areas. This purer capitalism of our own time thus eliminates the enclaves of precapitalist organization it had hitherto tolerated and exploited in a tributary way. One is tempted to speak in this connection of a new and historically original penetration and colonization of Nature and the Unconscious; that is, destruction of precapitalist Third World agriculture by the Green Revolution, and the rise of the media and advertising industry.[17]

The result of this elimination of the last of what Jameson calls the "precapitalist enclaves" is that "nature" is in effect done away with, and the "autonomous sphere of culture" has, in an explosion, expanded "throughout the social realm, to the point at which everything in our social life—from economic value and state power to practices and to the very structure of the psyche itself—can be said to have become "cultural" in some original and yet untheo-rized sense."[18] Jameson goes on to explain:

> in modernism . . . some residual zones of "nature" or "being," of the old, the older, the archaic, still subsist; culture can still do something to that nature and work at transforming that "referent." Postmodernism is what you have when the modernization process is complete and nature is gone for good. It is a more fully human world than the older one, but one in which "culture" has become a veritable "second nature."[19]

Clearly, such a proclamation of the end of nature as a physical and imaginative enclave and focus on an art form no longer with critical distance from, but in fact fused with the techniques and spirit of marketing and commodity culture generally would be anathema to most poets writing in the American nature tradition. Indeed, such developments—along with the metropolitanization of recent theory generally—have been criticized at length by Law-rence Buell, in his attempt to expose and then bridge the current gulf between environmental concerns and contemporary theory. In *Garbage,* Ammons's reactions are characteristically ambivalent: Ammons simultaneously incorporates and criticizes, as he con-structs again an aggressively peripheral position toward this new metropolitanism.

In the opening five sections, *Garbage* lives up to the shock value of its title: Ammons evokes the Florida landfill that gives him the most narrative segment of his poem with fulsome attention to the mess, the "toxic waste, poison air, beach goo" (G, 24), the "flies intermediating between orange peel / and buzzing blur"(G, 30), the "morsel, gobbet, trace of maple syrop, fat / worm" (G, 31). Poet of old age and wasted earth, he is not just lying down (with theatrical heroics) in the rag and bone shop of his heart; he is facing the devastation of nature. Nature has been (to use both Ammons's and Jameson's sexualized language) thoroughly penetrated here; no en-claves are left. In the course of the poem, Ammons provocatively asserts that people are garbage (G, 46), truth is garbage (G, 99), argument is garbage (G, 68), and poetry is garbage (G, 75) as well. Into all possible intellectual/psychological enclaves, then, the same commodification and spoilage seem to have seeped: Ammons is writing, in short, a poem that takes on the darkest side of the new metropolitanism directly.

True, the poem suggests some possibilities for amelioration of the situation. It toys, on one occasion, with the notion of fusion as a solution to our environmental woes ("that there / could be a straightaway from the toxic past into / the fusion-lit reaches of a coming time!" [G, 28–29]) and genetic engineering as a similar way out ("what about genetically engineered microorganisms / and a bright future: where's your faith, man:" [G, 108]). It also, in sections on the languages that animals speak, evokes ecocentrism (G, 50–51) as a viable way of thought. But, for the most part, what dominates is the absence of environmentalist solutions: it is as if Ammons (reflecting the society around him) is showing the fulfillment of his prophecy in "Extremes and Moderations," his assertion that "this seems to me the last poem written to the world / before its freshness capsizes and sinks into the slush" (CP, 116). Thus, when Ammons recollects a trip to Wheeling, the morning fog smokes away to reveal "mammoth standings / of steam, way out of size, too solid to vanish" that "oozed / up from the nuclear craters" of the plant ahead, and he ends the section with the unrelieved picture of "the freeway of / refineries, chemical streams, the gross companies / toughening the banks down by the banks of the O-hi-o" (G, 44). No human solutions are proposed; in more extreme moments, Ammons imagines that "the planet is going to / be fine, as soon as the people get off" and asks "why bother with carcinogenic residues—one / solar flare (nova) will recall all to light" (G, 109). Given statements like these, Ammons seems indeed to be no longer a nature, but a postnature poet.

But as Ammons has recently said, "I no longer weep for the earth. I can weep for us—but I now believe there is a freshness of dynamics of the center of what can happen on this planet that will restore the earth. All we have to do is change our ways or disappear, and the earth would be a splendid planet again."[20] Thus, once again, Ammons looks the new metropolitanism face to face and then proceeds to counter it by reinventing the nature tradition nonetheless. Perhaps the best way of putting the challenge he takes on is to say that, though he seeks to write nature poetry that is, at its severest, post-human, post-environmentalist, and post-pastoral, his poetry is decidedly not post-natural. Nature survives in Ammons's work, even as he writes poetry that has jettisoned all sure faith in the effectiveness of remedial activism and the existence of pastoral enclaves. His poem about the "pre-socratic idea of the / dispositional axis from stone to wind, wind / to stone" (G, 20) is just that: a formulation of a nature that is indeed posthuman. In it, all things are subject to the most extreme metamorphoses, recycling is the elemental and universal model for natural process, true for language, truth, and poetry as well as bodies, and a mystical or visionary awareness of the operation of the system as a whole is still possible, opening, despite Jameson, imaginative and spiritual vistas. Thus, when Ammons writes, "we're trash," he follows it immediately with "mostly radiant" (G, 46). And nature is still man's other in *Garbage;* the world has not dissolved into text, and representation does have a role still to play. At the peak of our metamorphoses (both physical and imaginative) we are able (Ammons resonantly states) to "know the other" (G, 22), the nature that made us; for we are not socially-constructed, but "we are natural: nature, not / we gave rise to us" (G, 21). There is, Ammons asserts in one of the many almost Augustinian moments of the poem, an "it" out there: "the it is the indifference of all the / differences, the nothingness of all the poised / somethings, the finest issue of energy in which / boulders and dead stars float" (G, 27) and this "it" is something that is imaginatively redemptive to approach in a moment of poetic vision.

As this faith surfaces in *Garbage*—in the post-environmentalist, post-pastoral, post-humanist landscape of the poem—Ammons also rehabilitates the rhetoric of natural supernaturalism, the romantic language of freshness, vision, regeneration, and celebration that he supposedly left behind with "Extremes and Moderations." Ammons rehabilitates it in a persistently comic mode, but it is a comedy that reanimates the very radiances it has such irreverent fun with. To start with, Ammons comically reclaims originality from intertextuality for his poem by narrating how it came into existence: going to research his topic, he punched

> out Garbage at the library and four titles
> swept the screen, only one, Garbage Feed,
>
> seeming worth going on to; and that was about
> feeding swine right: so I punched Garbage Disposal
>
> and the screen came blank—nothing! all those
> titles, row on row, of western goodies, mostly
>
> worse than junk, but not a word on Disposal: I
> should have looked, I suppose, under Waste Disposal
>
> but, who cares, I already got the point: I
> know garbage is being "disposed" of—but what
>
> I wanted I had gotten, a clear space and pure
> freedom to dump whatever, and this means most

of the catalog must go, so much that what is
left will need no computer to keep track of:

(G, 49)

A kind of open space for originality is left even in the penetrated
world of *Garbage,* and, though the poet comically dumps whatever
he wants into it, rather than plants it with organic forms, Ammons
still finds his old sense of imaginative autonomy and freedom in
doing so. Similarly, still more outrageously, Ammons, in describing
the trash heap itself, continually transmutes it via a comic version
of high romantic rhetoric: the fire on the top of the pile is a Delphic
oracle, even as the garbage is raked out by a man of Homeric
proportions, a figure (in this guise) resonant with freshness and
dawn. The trash heap is where "the consummations gather . . . :
here is the gateway to beginning, here the portal / of renewing
change, the birdshit, even, melding / enrichingly in with debris, a
loam for the roots / of placenta" (G, 28); and even if this is not a
revelation at the top of Mt. Snowdon, it is the next best thing for
Jameson's world, for something of romantic apocalypse is still
alive, within all the comedy. One of the most telling of these comic-
romantic transmutations of garbage is where Ammons reads the
landfill as a site of regeneration and renewal, poetic and spiritual
as well as physical: it is the place where "dead language is hauled /
off to and burned down on" and where the spirit is renewed. For

> where but in the very asshole of comedown is
> redemption: as where but brought low, where
>
> but in the grief of failure, loss, error, do we
> discern the savage afflictions that turn us around

(G, 21)

Stylistically, also, *Garbage* represents simultaneous absorption
of and resistance to contemporary postmodernism. *Garbage,* much
more than *Tape for the Turn of the Year,* embodies many of the
features of postmodernist textuality, even as it—stamped as it is
with the personality and personalized style of its creator—remains
more of a modernist "work" than a postmodernist "text." It is
important in this connection to remember Ammons's long interest
in John Ashbery's poetry, poetry that has challenged Ammons to
stretch his experimentation with the long, spontaneous, improvisa-
tional poem as far as possible. Compared to *Tape, Garbage* adver-
tises itself much less insistently to the reader as an experimentalist
genre, as a poetic project resonant with its creator's personality;

also, save for the first five sections, it leaves behind almost completely *Tape*'s narrative elements, its focus on poet-quester, its styling its task as a quest, and its use of classical echoes. If *Garbage* is post-pastoral, it is also post-epic; *Garbage* is much more chaotic, aleatory, and open in its structure than *Tape* was, something that is clearly marked by its free invention of multiple personae and its utter lack of closure at the end compared to the resonances of *Tape*'s final "so long." *Garbage* can, much more than *Tape* ever could, be read as a kind of hypertext, in which the colon juxtaposes series of separate minisections, ones that don't have to come in where they do, but could come in anywhere, in different orders at the click of a reader's mouse. As a result, *Garbage* displays almost none of the temporality of *Tape,* where the colons were copulas that helped propel the poem forward in a spontaneous, but finally linear rush of time. As with Heraclitus's image of the stream, there was, in *Tape,* everywhere the sense that there was a channel all the language was flowing within—the channel of the individual poet's private life—and the use of the journal format for the poem reinforced this sensation strongly. By contrast, in *Garbage,* where Ammons writes of the "pre-socratic idea" of the poem, he adds that it "(with my elaborations, if any) / is complete before it begins, so I needn't / myself hurry into brevity" (G, 20). *Garbage* is thus, unlike *Tape,* spatialized, so that everything in it is simultaneous (and therefore capable of hypertextual reshuffling): its form, in short, echoes Jameson's description of postmodernism as a pastiche of heterogenous material, post-historicist, and synchronic in temporality. The pitch at which Ammons writes also echoes Jameson's description of the postmodern replacement for the sublime as euphoria. In *Tape*'s contemplation of the greatness of things compared to human smallness, literary representation fails before extraliterary grandeur, and the traditional sublime is evoked. *Garbage,* by contrast, elaborates an always-already completeness, presenting us with a Jamesonian "impossible totality" that (even if the totality is nature's rather than multinational capitalism's) we are impossibly-simultaneously trying to experience and catch.

Of course, *Garbage*'s stylistic postmodernity, though striking, is not thoroughgoing. *Garbage* is very much the voice of an author stamping the poem with both biographical information and anecdote and a sense of personality; its rush is vocal, something that stems more from a particular Southern oral form (identified by the poet as "carrying on") than it does from postmodern textuality. Nor is the heterogeneity of the poem—filled as it is with Ammons's parodic, protean variety of personae, attitudes, illuminations, and ideas—quite pastiche, which Jameson describes as something different than ordinary parody, as "blank parody, a statue with blind eyeballs."[21] And, most fundamentally, the poem has, as we have seen, a definite subject matter, a sense of the extra-poetic that it seeks to represent. Thus, it does not, to cite several postmodern possibilities, move about depthlessly through simulacra, or interminably traverse the indeterminacies of Ashberyesque periphrasis, or seek, by focusing on the materiality of language, to create a series of unrelated sentences and fragments in order to undermine the referential notion of language, language as a window upon experience. Once again, then, stylistically as well as thematically, Ammons does not simply absorb metropolitan influence but instead cultivates an aggressively peripheral response to it, thereby resisting what he references.

Being clear about the continuities and differences between *Tape* and *Garbage* is crucial, I believe, for three reasons. First, it is important to a full appreciation of the continuing experimentation that marks Ammons's poetic career and of the force that drives that experimentation, Ammons's cultivation of aggressive peripherality. Ammons's attainment is so complete so early and his poetic personality is so distinctive and marked, it may be a temptation to see his career (after *Ommateum* [1955]) as a continuum, marked by gradual changes in emphasis, theme, and technique, all of which would be further elaboration of features already present at the time of *Expressions of Sea Level* (1964), *Tape for the Turn of the Year* (1965), and *Corsons Inlet* (1965). A closer look at the contrasts between *Tape* and *Garbage* thus help prevent homogenization of Ammons's oeuvre. Second, describing Ammons's work as I have done is crucial to resisting the temptation to see it, in a too-undifferentiated a way, as falling within existing traditions (or enclaves) of American romanticism or American nature writing. To yield to such a temptation would be to lose, I think, a sense of just how fully Ammons's work interacts with the contemporary literary and historical world and to forget just how worldly it is, just how much it is a barometer of the cultural disputes and historical circumstances of the last thirty years. Finally, investigating the ways Ammons's work interacts with recent cultural history shows vividly how *Garbage* is not just a high, late point in a major American poet's career, but also a significant opening for the future. *Garbage* is this for a number of different reasons: because it takes the nature tradition past the pastoral and into a thoroughly penetrated, postmodern world; because it faces the limits that even "postmodern" environmentalism places upon conceptions of nature and faces up to post-humanism as possibly the completest ecocentrism; and because it engages metropolitan theories and influences in order to show them in a new light, denying them the monolithic hegemony they seem now to many to have. *Garbage* anticipates new changes and opens new horizons for nature poets in a post-pastoral, penetrated world, a world in which the visible and audible has been twisted out of all old recognition by scientific abstraction, a world of environmental crisis and crisis for environmentalism.

NOTES

1. Quotations from A. R. Ammons's work are cited in the text with the abbreviations listed below.

T: *Tape for the Turn of the Year* (Ithaca: Cornell University Press, 1965).
CP: *Collected Poems 1951–1971* (New York, W. W. Norton, 1972).
S: *Sphere: The Form of a Motion* (New York, W. W. Norton, 1974).
G: *Garbage* (New York, W. W. Norton), 1993.)

2. Perry Miller, *Errand into the Wilderness* (New York: Harper and Row, 1956), vii–viii.
3. Jane Tompkins, "'Indians'; Textualism, Morality, and the Problem of History," *Critical Inquiry* 13, no. 1 (1986): 101–19.
4. Roger Lewin, *Complexity: Life at the Edge of Chaos* (New York: Collier Books, 1992).
5. Ibid., 12.
6. Ibid., 50.
7. Steven P. Schneider, *A. R. Ammons and the Poetics of Widening Scope* (Madison, N. J.: Fairleigh Dickinson University Press, 1994), 84.
8. Quoted in Schneider, *Ammons*, 20.
9. Fredric Jameson, *Postmodernism, or, The Cultural Logic of Late Capitalism* (Durham, N.C.: Duke University Press, 1991), xiii.
10. Ibid., ix.
11. Frederick Buell, *National Culture and the New Global System* (Baltimore: The Johns Hopkins University Press, 1994).
12. For example, Homi Bhabha writes a highly theoretical polemic against inclusion as a way of defanging cultural difference in his introduction to *Nation and Narration* (New York: Routledge, 1990); and the notions of universalism and self-identiy, familiar targets of a wide variety of multiculturalist-poststructuralist polemics, are repudiated with scathing force by scholars like Houston Baker (see, for example, "Caliban's Triple Play" in *Critical Inquiry* 13, no. 1 (1986): 182–96) and more temperately-theoretically by Lisa Lowe in her "Heterogeneity, Hybridity, Multiplicity: Marking Asian-American Differences" in *Diaspora* 1, no. 1 (1991): 24–44. For a more comprehensive discussion of these topics, see Frederick Buell, *National Culture and the New Global System* (Baltimore: The Johns Hopkins University Press, 1994), chapters 6–9.

13. Arran E. Gare, *Postmodernism and the Environmental Crisis* (London: Routledge, 1995).

14. Andrew Ross, *The Chicago Gangster Theory of Life* (London: Verso, 1994), 17–18.

15. Lawrence Buell, *The Environmental Imagination: Thoreau, Nature Writing, and the Formation of American Culture* (Cambridge: Harvard University Press, 1995), 21, 35.

16. Terry Eagleton relates this tendency as a reaction to the "blend of euphoria and disillusionment, carnival and catastrophe, which was 1968. Unable to break the structures of state power, post-structuralism found it possible instead to subvert the structures of language." *Literary Theory: An Introduction* (Minneapolis: University of Minnesota Press, 1983), 142.

17. Jameson, *Postmodernism*, 36.

18. Ibid., 48–49.

19. Ibid., ix.

20. Quoted in Jon Gertner, "A Walk With A. R. Ammons," *Audobon Magazine* September-October (1996): 82.

21. Jameson, *Postmodernism*, 17.

Dwelling on "The Ridge Farm": Action, Motion, and A. R. Ammons's Moral Landscape

MIRIAM MARTY CLARK

From a moment very early on, when the nomadic verges into the perambulatory and the radically unsheltered voices of *Ommateum* begin to claim habitation—the marsh, the shallows of the wind-rows, then a "lonely house," finally a porch, a driveway, a point of going out and coming in—A. R. Ammons is deeply interested in dwelling. "Dwell" and "dwelling" appear, often in clusters, in his poems: late in *Tape for the Turn of the Year;* early in *The Snow Poems;* late in *Sphere,* where Ammons distinguishes between a bodily dwelling ("in the flow of shapes"), subject to change and decay, and an imaginative dwelling (in "memory or imagined memory") not subject to such transformations. In "The Ridge Farm" this distinction takes the terms of drama in Kenneth Burke's sense of the word; throughout Ammons's sustained and formally difficult meditation on the ridge, "dwelling" defines the encounter of symbolic action—human agency and institutions from property to poetry—with the nonsymbolic realm of sheer matter and inarticulate nature.

The idea of dwelling emerges first in the play of language. "Dwelling," functioning as noun and verb, signifies both a structure and a state of mind. To dwell *with* is to linger awhile, "going ashore / to rest, regard the leaves / or talk with birds and / shore weeds" ("Visit").[1] Such lingering—going back to German and Old English *dwellan,* to remain, to delay, even to hinder—is part of what Ammons's punctuation sustains.[2] To dwell *on* is a practice of the mind, the practice of poetry; in nature—and, for Ammons, by analogy with thought—dwelling *on* is symbiotic, inhabiting and drawing sustenance from a host; it is also Ammons's most emotionally reso-nant mode, a way of holding on to the past and speaking of it in a poem like "Easter Morning." To dwell *in* is the homeliest prac-

239

tice—of ownership and habitation—but it is also the language of immanence, of radiance.

Immanence brings into the foreground *dwell's* biblical resonances. Three occurrences seem particularly significant for Ammons's verse. The first, Psalm 23's confident, "I shall dwell in the house of the Lord forever,"³ defines a relation between temporal and eternal and lodges against the promise of permanent residence a compelling vision of pastoral homelessness and vital temporality. This tension is played out brilliantly as *telos* and *nostos* in *Tape for the Turn of the Year* and again as shape and flow in *Sphere;* generally it is settled on the side of flow and motion.⁴ The second echo, of Isaiah's peaceable kingdom in which "the wolf shall dwell with the lamb," addresses relations within the natural order. Although his attentiveness to nature leads him away from Isaiah's utopia, Ammons's interest in kingdoms and interdependencies— maggots to jaguars—is evident everywhere. The third significant "dwelling" comes in John's incisive theology of the incarnation, "The Word became flesh and dwelt among us." This statement defines a relation of immanence and transcendence which is ground to virtually everything else that happens in Ammons and home to every high drama the poems present.

By the end of the twentieth century, however, "dwelling" is also Heidegger's term. Heidegger's *Bauen* comprises structure itself, the work of structuring or building, and simple habitation; in addition, he elaborates a fourth kind of dwelling that cultivates, spares, and tends to the earth where technology would ravage and exploit it.⁵ Together these four ways of dwelling neatly inscribe Ammons's characteristic concern with structures and measures; his sense of language as a house to be occupied in familiar, domestic, caretaking ways; his mindfulness toward things in their nature and in relation to the universe, also in their readiness-to-hand; his sense of dwelling (in, on, with) as the site of disclosure out of hiddenness; even his ecological turn.⁶

"Poetic dwelling," however, entails a higher and more specific vocation. "In the destitute time of the twentieth century," Heidegger writes in "What are Poets For?" "not only have the gods and the god fled, but the divine radiance has become extinguished in the world." In such a world the poet's work is to "attend, singing, to the traces of the fugitive gods"; it is to reach into the abyss, to discern the radiance, if only as absent or concealed.⁷ From the earliest "Hymns" through more recent lyrics like "Singing and Doubling Together," Ammons's approach to transcendent Otherness—often simply "You"—is one of attending, singing, tracing.

Although the balance of absence and presence, of concealment and revelation, varies from lyric to lyric, this mode of fugue and pursuit will be very familiar to readers of Ammons. Again and again, in Ammons as in Heidegger, "presence" is signified by "radiance"; but in Ammons the radiance is sometimes unsnuffed, abundant, pouring "without selection into every / nook and cranny not over-hung or hidden," as it does in "The City Limits" (CP, 320).

Unextinguished and to some extent unsought, radiance breaks out again in the penultimate section of "The Ridge Farm," in a luminous rereading of the first chapter of John:

> In the beginning was the Word, and the Word was with God, and the Word was God. The same was in the beginning with God. All things were made by him; and without him was not any thing made that was made. In him was life; and the life was the light of men. And the light shineth in darkness and the darkness comprehended it not.

De-theologizing the event, removing both God and Word, Ammons begins section 50,

> A light catches somewhere, finds human
> spirit to burn on, shows its magic's
> glint lines, attracts, grows, rolls
> back space and dark, stands dominant
> high in the midsphere, and reality
> goes into concordance or opposition, the
> light already dealing with darkness
> designating it darkness, opposition by
> naming, and the intensity of the source
> blinds out other light: reason
> sings the rightness but can do nothing
> to oppose the brilliance: it dwells:
> it dwells and dwells:[8]

Ammons elides "In the Beginning," bringing into a single tense (present) what had comprised two and narrowing the gap John's account opens between *was* (signifying both eternal standing and temporal priority) and *is,* between *being* and *becoming.* At the same time, he preserves some of the connection to Genesis through imagery suggesting command of the void, the organization of the world into light and dark. More important, he preserves the brilliant liminality of John's prologue, which Frank Kermode calls, aptly, a "threshold poem."

Such liminality "stands for the condition of the eternal at the threshold of that which is not eternal but *becomes,*" Kermode writes, "the eternal on the point of an unheard-of participation in that which cannot be eternal because it is created."[9] While Ammons's lines echo and draw on these terms, they do not reproduce the orthodox dialectic. Kenneth Burke's notion of "pontification" or *terministic bridging,* however, provides a way to think about the non-theological (but not desacralized) dialectic of the "Ridge Farm" passage. Burke describes this "priestly" function that builds a bridge between disparate realms, so that things here and now may be "treated in terms of a 'beyond' and so infused with new meaning."[10] Section 50 of Ammons's poem does something very much like this, treating the realm of "human spirit," "human concern," "reality," "what is," even "reason" in terms of a "beyond" expressed in terms of the nonhuman or supernatural, magic, dominance, source, brilliance, light. The terministic bridge is poetic inspiration, poetic dwelling itself. "The light," Ammons writes, "tendance, neglect / is human concern working with / what is" (SV, 40).

But there is more at stake than the threshold poem in thinking of Ammons's lines alongside John's. Like the three synoptic gospels, John's first chapter entails its source in the prophetic passages of Deutero-Isaiah (Isaiah 40–55). As the gospel narrative opens, John the Baptist claims the prophetic voice—I *am* the one—and points readers back to Isaiah 40:

> The voice of him that crieth in the wilderness, Prepare ye the way of the Lord, make straight in the desert a highway for our God.
> Every valley shall be exalted, and every mountain and hill shall be made low: and the crooked shall be made straight and the rough places plain.

The liminal moment near the end of "The Ridge Farm" entails (though less explicitly and less bindingly) the same prophetic source. Ammons's sustained experimentation with the prophetic voice provides a general warrant for such a claim. But here I begin more particularly, with a verbal echo that unfolds into a shared image of what it means to be a truth-bearer in a world of forms, poetic or natural. "My business," he writes,

>   is to make
> room for the truth, to bust the couplet,
> warp the quatrain, explode the sonnet,
> tear down the curvatures of the lengthy:
> the truth is commodious, abundant:

>   (SV, 30–31)

Like the Isaiah writer, Ammons addresses himself in these lines
to truth or meaning in excess of what sensible forms will sustain.
This excess leads both to the metaphoric obliteration of forms
(sonnets, curvatures, valleys, hills) and to their ironic reinscrip-
tion; what voice—poetic, prophetic, pontifical—conveys both vio-
lently ruptures existing forms and charges them with meaning. In
this moment of terministic bridging the poem receives in several
ways the overflow of meaning: by its absorption into an altered
symbolic landscape; its transformation into the unattainable of a
Kantian sublime; its manifestation as what Herbert Marks calls
"prophetic stammer" beginning in "the impression of sheer accu-
mulation, of forbidding non-sequential abundance."[11]

A second warrant emerges in the language of the poem, particu-
larly a cluster of key words: voice, wilderness, highway (and the
related word "macadam," which appears importantly in another
American long poem, Hart Crane's *The Bridge*)[12], ridge and sum-
mit (mountain words), and revelation. This vocabulary situates
Ammons in a landscape that is, in multiple ways, post-prophetic.
A highway has been laid in the wilderness, for good and for ill,
bringing cars and civilization. The wilderness pools and "open
rivers in high places" (Isaiah 41:18) have been dammed and pol-
luted but they have also become the materials of "nature poetry";
the mountains, worn to ridges, can be bought and sold as property
but also form the visionary landscape of the poem; the voice in
the wilderness hardens into the willed and the individuated but it
remains audible.

Balancing revelation against idolatry, which it proscribes vigor-
ously, even satirically, the Isaiah text seems to ask, what can na-
ture be made to stand for? For Ammons, this isn't merely a
question of how much the natural world will bear of pollution,
technology, and exploitation but also what real investment of
meaning and feeling its nonhuman otherness will sustain. Put in
this way, the question establishes a new dialectic for the poem,
one *not* founded in relations between natural and supernatural
realms, the temporal and the eternal, the representative and the
unpresentable. Instead it situates the poem in the encounter be-
tween motion and action, as Burke defines them, that is, between
the nonsymbolic realm of nature and the realm of symbolic action
which comprises not only language but the sociopolitical order and
in it such categories as reason, abstraction, law, institutions,
money, and property.

Burke's influence is abundantly evident in the lyric poems of
the third section of *Sumerian Vistas*, one of which—"Information

Density"—is dedicated to him. Two aspects of Burke's thought converge in especially productive ways with Ammons's own in these lyrics. The first is his interest in "scope and reduction" and its Socratic partner, "merger and division." Burke's proposition subsequently takes many different forms. "Every circumference, no matter how far-reaching its references, is a reduction," he writes, early in *A Grammar of Motives,*

> any terminology of motives reduces the vast complexity of life by re-
> duction to principles, laws, sequences, classifications, correlations, in
> brief, abstractions or generalizations of one sort or another. And any
> generalization is necessarily a reduction in that it selects a *group* of
> them as a single entity. Thus, the general concept of "man" neglects
> an infinite number of particular differences in order to stress certain
> properties which many distinct individual entities have in common. To
> note any order whatever is to "reduce."[13]

Implicit even in this succinct account is a strong sense of the mobil-
ity of thought and attentiveness—their widening-and-narrowing
range, their dynamic of neglect and selection, of inclusions and
exclusion. Ammons's interest in scope, in the vital tension between
amplitude and abstraction, is evident at every turn; in "Information
Density" he makes an explicit connection to Burke. "Generaliza-
tion scans the contours or terrain," he begins,

> for the spot to take on concretion in,
> the way a squirrel, having floated through
>
> arches, zigzagged digs for a nut, pear core,
> or pats one in: generalization acquaints us
> with the wider forms of disposition, airily
>
> leaves out a lot in order to be cursory and
> carries little substance so as to move big:

(SV, 71)

Ammons then shifts his attention to a hawk, whose roving "con-
nects dots into nearing curvatures"; then—in a final, deft counter-
poise—he observes a jay lighting "right into what he wants" just
as "the eagle wheels up in rigorous quiet, higher / and higher to
find the right piece of ground" (SV, 71). In their ascending and
descending movements, these lines advance a dialectic—they
seek ground.

  Ammons's use of the word "motion" in nine of these lyrics and
in the section's title, "Motions' Holdings," also suggests a debt to

Burke. Here Ammons observes Burke's crucial distinction between "action"—"any verb, no matter how specific or how general, that has connotations of consciousness or purpose" (GM, 14)— and "motion," by which he refers to events in the nonverbal, nonsymbolic realm of sheer matter. Ammons invests some play in "motion" all along, using it to signify the body's turns and gestures—from dancing to dying—or punning (in the subtitle of *Sphere*) on its parliamentary sense. Increasingly, though, he uses it as Burke does to signify the dividedness of the world into language and matter, idea and brute physical fact. In "Motion Which Disestablishes Organizes Everything," reprinted in the prose collection significantly titled *Set in Motion*,[14] motion represents physical deterioration—crumpling knees, irregular bowels, crooked teeth, things undone by time and gravity; against these forces language and ideas offer only temporary, misleading consolation.

In *Sumerian Vistas,* he uses the term similarly to designate a nonverbal realm and to speculate on its relation to language. In "Trivial Means," for example, he writes:

> We don't want to be just
> the narrows or shambles through which
> great motions make their way:
>
> we want to know why or how
> the motions stirred first
> and whether their moves are
>
> prefigured or moment-to-moment
> providentiality and surprise:
>
> (SV, 120)

Against "motion" he then sets some forms of motivated and free human action: "discerning outline," "recognizing and measuring true," pondering the "necessity" that governs motion, even reckoning the duality that makes man only part the symbol user, part still "[servant] to the flesh" (SV, 120).

"The Ridge Farm," however, begins in a landscape momentarily devoid of human presence. His mode is a familiar, benign irony about this: nature's very existence in the poem depends on human language and its figures, its tropes. We understand the motions of trees in wind and snow through the idea of "average" or "balance": "The cedars nod to / an average under gusts and blusters" (SV, 3). The squirrel with "no aerial rail to catch" finds a different route (SV, 6); the rabbits who settled "out of the air" at dusk to eat dandelion stems nibble them up "like drunk drinking straws" (SV, 39); sweeps of space, unpopulated, nevertheless "haunt" and "starve" (SV, 37). By these gestures Ammons combines a certain sense of inevitability (language is inescapably metaphoric) with a pervasive self-consciousness about language's address to inarticulate nature.

But because human presence—especially in its collective, historicized form as "culture"—is represented as troublesome (exploitative, encroaching, merciless, unyielding) the poem returns to a vision of nature purged of human presence, including language. If nature could speak, he thinks early in the poem,

> nature would say,
> be still, that is to say, indifferent
> like me, only to say so would
> motion difference:
> probably this is why nature says nothing—
> it has nothing to say

(SV, 5)

Still, the poem does not fall silent at this point, nor does it turn entirely on the irony by which the poet undertakes to "give voice" to nature. Instead it embarks on a sustained exploration of the rugged interface between action and motion, culture and nature, language and the nonlinguistic world.

For Ammons, as for Burke, this distinction involves much more than an acknowledgement (comic or rueful in tone) of the poem's unbridgeable distance from its subject. In Burke's logology—on which, I suggest, "The Ridge Farm" turns elaborately—it implies a unity that is both temporally and logically prior, even "proto-Edenic." "Logologically, there is a 'fall' from a prior state of unity," Burke writes, "whenever some one term is broken into two or more terms, so that we have the 'divisiveness' of 'classification' where we formerly had a 'vision of perfect oneness'."[15] The division of Creation into "action" and "motion" (or "nature" and "culture," which are key terms in the poem) thus signifies the fallenness of the world and defines the space in which a drama of sin and redemption, rituals of rebirth or purification, will be played out.

These terms also prefigure an accumulation of guilt and sin words in the second half of the poem: justice, horror, lust, mercilessness, eros, error, guilt, strictures, arraignment, courts, jails, hell, and many others. These belong to a large cluster associated with "the negative" as Burke defines it, which is to say with a moral rather than a semantic function (GM, 296), hortatory rather than propositional in nature. For Burke, the negative—grounded in the Decalogue with its "Thou shalt nots"—is a human invention and forms the basis for human moral agency. Through language and symbolic action, amoral nature is infused with its terms and strictures. Burke's most succinct definition of the negative forms both a list and a cycle in a postscript to *Language as Symbolic Action*. He begins with (1) Property, which he associates with the social order; (2) The Negative, surveys and "reinforces" property with its assertion, "no trespassing." It also leads—importantly for Ammons, as I will argue later—to (3) Mortification and its variants, "self-visited upon those who would exhort themselves not to transgress beyond necessity upon the property of others," and to (4) No-no imagery, in which "sensory positives"—including "rot, death, offal, associations with such privacy as characterizes the privy parts"—are infused "with the genius of moral negatives." The drama of the negative is further enacted in (5) Victimage, "purification by sacrifice, by *vicarious atonement,* unburdening of guilt within by transference to chosen vessels without" and (6) Completion, and the transformation of local problems of order into "grandly Universal replicas—supernatural, metaphysical, or naturalistic—all heading in the Norms of Justice." As the list ends, the dramatic cycle of guilt and purification is renewed; signifying this, Burke adds (7) *Da Capo* (LSA, 478).

I want to postpone, briefly, discussion of the broadly proscriptive and hortatory elements of "The Ridge Farm" and turn first to the categories of taboo ("No-no imagery") and mortification, in part because that is where the negative is most visible and where its significance is first established. In ways that will be very familiar to Ammons's readers, this poem operates with a potent sense of linguistic taboo, experimenting with forbidden words: fuck, shit, assholes, coonyus. As in some earlier poems like "Shit List," he takes on the subject of excrement with loving and lavish attention. "Shit sticks," he writes,

> its fragrance in the old
> days confirmed the caveman he was coming
> home: a man's shit (or tribe's) reflects
> (nasally) the physical makeup of the man
> and the physiologies of those others
> present, plus what they have gathered
> from the environment
> to pass through themselves

> the odor of shit is like language,
> an unmistakable assimilation of a
> use, tone, flavor, accent hard to
> fake: enemy shit smells like the enemy:
> everything is more nearly incredible
> than you thought at first
>
> (SV, 12)

Here shit's power to signify tribe and territory momentarily deflects attention from it as an expression of the negative. But the very equation shit = language betrays the extent to which language infuses nature and invests it with symbolic (and, by definition, moral) value; as soon as shit is brought into language it becomes an expression of the negative. In a later section of the poem Ammons considers even more directly the infusion of nature with moral negatives, this time having to do with sex. "How / our forefathers hated woods and sex," he writes, "so much of both to deal with / cut down or back." Even in the present, though its practical consequences have been "tamed" by the pill, sexuality is read under the hortatory No as "irresponsibility," moral wilderness, transgression:

> the sperm
> rage, such a wilderness, shot wild,
> why we can horse deeply in with
> irresponsibility's ease (SV, 37)

"I'm afraid," he concludes, imparting with the moral order a moral economy as well, "nature's going to send the bill: it usually does."

Like Burke and Freud before him, Ammons understands the cloacal as intimately related to transcendence, not only by inversion but through an equational structure that associates it with other aspects of individual life and culture—including money, which is recurrently important in the poem—under the signs of privacy, shame, mystic secrecy, and purification. It would be quite possible, I think, though it isn't my plan here, to use Burke's reasoning about the operations of the "demonic trinity"—the three principles of the erotic, the urinary, and the excremental (GM, 302)—to generate a reading of "The Ridge Farm" from beginning, where shrubs clunk like "chunk money" against the house, to the end, with its lean, flowing brook and its final "mishmashes of tinkling circlets" (SV, 41). To do so would make purposive sense, given the poem's profound concern with pollution, both (as I will argue) of an individual, moral and spiritual kind and with the pollution of earth by a culture of consumers. And it makes a particularly

tempting kind of sense of the final stanza, where the image of
the brook accomplishes a double purification, carrying away the
dishwater (itself both cleansing and polluting) and providing a
"transcendent image of release as fundamentally conceived in
terms of urination" (GM, 303).

Another kind of "No-no imagery"—rot and offal—verges into
mortification with the unflinching consideration of rot and bodily
decay. Lodged between two visions of eternity—one in which God
figures as a satellite transmitter, sending arbitrary signals and pick-
ing them up; another a comically retributive "heaven" in which
animals gobble up humans—Sections 16, 17, and 20 are intensely
occupied with the breakdown of the body by old age and death.
Ammons considers first the way "the structures of the mouth /
crack down to incontinent corners / moist, the eyes weeping / air's
mere burn" (SV, 12). Then he turns, almost without pause, to the
body's physical fate after death:

> we live again in the bellies
> of worms, fly again (?) with
> winged worms: we come sponging
> back to the tables of our children
> to be swatted: since this
> is one place,
> going is coming, ending beginning,
> individual shape shed
> like exoskeletons of spiritual flies.
>
> (SV, 14–15)

Finally he contemplates the skeleton itself, noting that "When the
hand falls apart it makes / a handful of bones," he writes,

> a spill or smallest cairn: no matter
> how much the hand taught
> of love or how many times it flew
> upward to catch the raiments of heads
> of hair or how busy it seemed in water
> quick fish or how it was the strongest
> shoal many a death could reach.
>
> (SV, 16)

Soon he pushes the bones closer but at the same time backs up
from real mortification by lightening his tone and calling the object
a "collection" rather than a "hand":

> here it is now, a fact, neutral,
> plain, open for inspection, the cutest
> collection, a peak white as a
> peak tip, take some into your hands
>
> (SV, 16–17)

This consideration of human mortality is followed by other medita-
tions on death and decay, occasioned by the discovery of a dead
mole in a watering can and by the appearance of a dead squirrel
by the roadside. These sections (24, 25, 31, 38, 41) have, as Burke
predicts, a potent sensory dimension; "Something really smelled,"
Ammons writes of his discovery of the mole in the watering can's
brown juice, "I'd just had / lunch: squooshy ice cream, I nearly /
unhad it" (SV, 19–20).

How these "sensory positives," as Burke calls them, are "in-
fused with the genius of moral negatives" is an interesting process
and one that emerges only in the larger context of the poem. On the
one hand, Ammons treats decay as a natural mechanism situated
squarely within the nonsymbolic and nonethical world of motion.
Writing of an elm stump, he observes how,

> the meat
> mush-sodden feeds mushrooms, big
> whiteheaded, and brackets respond
> vigorously to the softening:
> various mechanisms appropriate,
> necessary, useful, even beautiful
> will do away with it in time and then
> the mechanisms will find other work,
> earth's supply of dutch elm stumps run out
>
> (SV, 8)

As soon as this mechanism enters the language as metaphor, how-
ever, the poem addresses itself to the realm of action. Rather than
comparing the "play of the mind" to wind ruffling the water on
creeks or streams, he proposes,

> or even runlets developed in
> gravel by macadamways, why not
> dwell the mind on mushrooms till the several
> kinds define themselves, select their habitats,
> go through a few life cycles, and reach their
> roots into where they come from and
> of what and how they go and get
> back from there: attend to mushrooms and

all other things will answer up:
while if you flick off (leaping like light)
all the scallops of a broad scape to keep it
noted and active, you may not in your own
summaries add much up

(SV, 8–9)

In substituting a metaphor of symbiosis for metaphors of poetic inspiration (wind and light), Ammons wishfully reconceives poetry in terms of motion and natural process rather than of action (play, notation, summary). Such poetry would participate in a natural economy of consumption without waste tantamount to dwelling without exploitation or mastery. No longer characterized by freedom, inspiration, individuality, and immortality, poetic voice is mortified through a humbling association with necessity and decay.

The logic of guilt and mortification is critically important in "The Ridge Farm." Burke's genealogy—or logology—of guilt provides a useful gloss and sheds light on some of the poem's most difficult passages. "Logologically, one could identify the principle of personality with the ability to master symbol-systems," Burke writes. "Intrinsic to such a personality is the 'moral sense,' that is, the sense of 'yes and no' that goes with the thou-shalt-not's of Order" (RR, 209). In "The Ridge Farm" the mastery of symbol-systems, marking a state of fallenness in the divide between nature and culture, is the fundamental source of guilt. It generates multiple responses and small dramas, among them the mortifying impulse to merge wordlessly into natural processes.

But mortification implies appetite or drive. In "The Ridge Farm" that drive takes several, related forms: toward an enduring individual voice; toward a durable "self"; toward culture with its symbols, forms, and objects; and toward abstractions and hierarchies. In addition to being the "inventor of the negative," Burke's man is "goaded by a spirit of hierarchy," that is, he is driven and entranced by higher and higher forms of abstraction. In "The Ridge Farm," this hierarchical motive is visible again and again. It is there in the outward "spiel" of knowledge and thought into "the looser peripheries" (SV, 9). It is represented in the ridge—in the contemplation of it from far away "showless, summary beyond the trappings / of coming and going" and, metaphorically, in the ascent to it. It is there in the poem's several ventures in the direction of a godhead and in its embrace of the "beautiful / high suasions of language, / celestial swales, hungering the earth up into heaven" (SV, 16).

The hierarchical motive is always in tension with the mortifying impulse to enter wholly into natural processes and mechanisms; in this it echoes the tension between scope and reduction, merger and division that is played out in the lyrics of *Sumerian Vistas*. The hierarchical spirit takes a number of key terms in Ammons— "knowledge," "perception," "reason," "summary," "sweep"; none is more important in this poem than "imagination," which signifies not only the power of making in language but the drive to read upward and forward from the natural order to the verbal one. Section 35 provides perhaps the best examples of what I mean. In these lines Ammons again longs to pass from culture and "action"—represented by mortality's "net," "responsibility's strictures," poetic forms, also by courts and jails, arguments and sophistry—into nature and "motion," signified by free verse, song, rivers, branches, brooks, and "nothing." "I stick to / nothing," he writes,

> I will not hear the terms of arraignment
> or appear in the marble courts
> I will not bear the sophistry,
> subtle ramification, of the arguments
> for and against:
> yet the guilt sharp as jails has gotten through:
>
> (SV, 29)

The lines that follow establish a source for his guilt in hierarchical motives and in the distinction between motion and action. "The air dissolves and absorbs," he writes,

> oceans dissolve and absorb
> the imagination changes things
> whose change, the hell of things, comforts me
>
> (SV, 29)

Imagination is no natural process; it acts. It "changes things" and in doing so produces guilt, even hell. Again in the couplets of Section 41 Ammons writes of giving up on "creativity" but always coming back to it, noting "how painful beauty is that gets away / full and unbesmirched" (SV, 35), untouched by creative doodle, the actions of poetry, and the strivings of imagination.

Thus the poem internalizes both the drives and the proscriptions that produce guilt and its expression as mortification. Ammons accomplishes this partly by allegorizing them as dramas of property. For Burke "property" represents a primary category of the negative, and invokes not only the social order with its symbolic categories of money, law, and rights but also the essential hortatory "NO"—"No Trespassing." In one section of the poem Ammons offers a very brief vision of an afterlife in which—natural and social orders no longer fallen and divided—there is no category of trespass:

> everyone knows
> that when we die we wake up
> elsewhere from the dream life into
> life, hop over a fence and
> walk off across nobody's pasture

> (SV, 22)

Working in the tradition of Emerson and Frost, Ammons is radically suspicious of land ownership, arguing that what is really valuable cannot be possessed in any durable, complete, or exclusive way. The first time the ridge comes into view, which it does not do until Section 13, it appears simultaneously as property and not-property:

> I like the ridge, its rolls my fixed ocean:
> not *my,* I don't own an inch of it:
> and not theirs, either, the ones who
> do own it, for they don't see it or
> their part in it:

> (SV, 10)

In a later section of the poem he writes again about property. Recounting a trip "to see the high farm out by Mecklenberg," he interrupts his description of the place to remark:

> I would buy a whole 130-acre farm
> for one hermit lark, his song,
> especially his song at evening by a
> pond:

> (SV, 27)

A few lines later he adds ruefully, "it's got so the only place you / can appreciate won't appreciate" (SV, 27).

At the same time, this section of the poem inscribes an act of trespass. Despite his knowledge of the climb, the place, its animal inhabitants, he does not own the property he walks on. If it is the same ridge he describes in Section 13, he has revealed early in the poem that he doesn't "own an inch of it"; moreover, he says that he "would buy" a farm for the hermit lark's song and he notes that the dog's master is "not around" (SV, 27).

In fact, the ridge farm seems almost Edenic in its proportions. For all its oldness and shabbiness, it is idyllic, populated by animals roaming and singing freely. Nature is in spring leaf, and there is an (unforbidden) "apple tree a hundred / years old." Once the climbers have ascended the ridge, there is no further labor; "you don't have to sweat once you're there," he writes. The verbal and sociopolitical order and their categories of law (trespass), money and property (appreciation), even art with its cultivated forms (this is, though verse, no *Georgic*) are suspended. Finally language itself is suspended as silence becomes "ineluctable." "Noise is motion," he observes; silence is non-motion, represented as depth. Symbolic action virtually disappears from the landscape. As in the meditation on mushrooms, the speaker aligns himself wishfully with the nonsymbolic world, listening and going deep.

And yet with each of these suspensions Ammons reasserts the dividedness and the fallenness of the world. This Edenic scene lacks what Burke calls the "proto-Edenic simplicity of absolute unity" (RR, 174). The section contains dozens of large and small markers of the divide between culture and nature, symbolic and nonsymbolic realms: the place name ("by Mecklenberg"); the measurement of land in acres; the inaccessibility of the farm (to "hassling lumbermen" and nearly to the climbers); the adjective "wild" applied to "turkey"; the presence of the house; the absence of the "master"; the prominence of the pun; even the oxymoron of ridge and farm, of rugged nature cultivated and then neglected.

We "symbol-using animals" have a stake in both realms. "The Ridge Farm" examines, largely through its explorations of the negative, the way individuals approach not only a divided world but a divided self, whose very divisions signify fallenness and disunity. One approach, as I have suggested, is characterized by a desire—unattainable in language and irreconcilable with the hierarchical motives fundamental to being human—to leave the symboled world of culture and words and to enter wholly into nature and its mechanisms. Particularly when they are associated with the processes of decay, these moves constitute not only a symbolic mortification of the physical body but an attempt to obliterate or mortify poetic voice. This impulse is audible as early as the third section of the poem, where Ammons describes poetic voice as not "distinctive" but "assimilated from the many tones and sources"; paradoxically, the word "assimilates" both signifies and precipitates the breakdown of one voice into many, of writing and speaking into "predominant and subsidiary motions" (SV, 4).

A second approach, which ultimately encompasses the first in "The Ridge Farm," is to dramatize and interrogate crossings between the two realms, articulating as fully as possible the way the two orders infuse each other. This includes not only the way sociopolitical orders infuse the natural, so that nature can be said, for instance, to "send the bill" for human recklessness (SV, 37), but also the way natural orders (rot, predation) can be read into the social. These infusions open a space of linguistic play and instability to which Ammons has long been attentive. But the infusion of nature with the negative, a purely human and linguistic phenomenon, is of singular importance here because it constitutes what Burke calls "the dramatistic starting point." As the basis of human agency, the negative establishes the action-motion dialectic and initiates the drama (or dramas) of guilt and redemption that Burke finds at the heart of all of the varieties of symbolic action.

Ammons's poem does a nimble two-step, then, first infusing nature with the negative, rendering it "property" even (crucially) where it is not-property; this enables him to dramatize as trespass every action in or on nature, every encroachment of technology, every venture of reason, language, institution (including universities and writing programs), or culture. The importance of trespass is established scenically—not only in this poem but very widely in the lyrics, particularly those of *Brink Road*[16]—in Ammons's attentiveness to boundaries and lines of demarcation: the wall of the house, the window glass, the jutting ridge, the highway or macadam that separates civilization from wilderness and provides a route between. This latter is especially interesting not only because he uses it recurrently but because it draws together an image of the macadam as the route of human incursion and the image of the highway into the wilderness as a sacred way of revelation. In short, the poem provides symbolic lodgings right at the edge of culture, within walking distance of nature.

Moreover, the poem invests virtually all of its anecdotal resources in trespass narratives. The anecdote of the climb to the high farm, with its implicit act of trespass, is closely preceded by two accounts of a reverse kind of "trespass" in which nature crosses over into culture. The first is of the mole that accidentally gets into a watering can in the garage and dies there, later to be discovered and thrown out where,

>   the crows will come
> and peck it up, up, and away, the way

> they do squirrels killed on the
> streets: pulling at the long, small
> intestines and getting a toehold on
> small limbs to tear off the big flesh

                                                    (SV, 20)

The second tells of a squirrel dead by the roadside,

> his legs spraddled stiff into space
> the high eye full of the morning sun
> the other
> scrinching wide open on the grainy macadam
>
> oh, me, I said, myself affected, cars
> are our worst predators

                                                    (SV, 25)

These stories operate analogically, narrating trespass and pursuing "guilt" further than the account of human trespass can or will, all the way to symbolic "victimage" or sacrificial death in the evisceration of the mole, elaborately envisioned, and in the eleven-day display of the squirrel's deteriorating body. Symbolic trespassers, the mole and the squirrel fulfill the penalty, as a scapegoat might, for an *act* of trespass. In the more sustained narrative of the squirrel, this victimage is public: it happens on the roadway, is observed by others including passing bicyclists and perhaps a "cop," and is kept in view "by a man cutting his lawn" who chucks it back onto the roadway after it gets "chucked off" (SV, 35). Moreover, the squirrel's death is a consequence of less of an individual act than of a collective incursion of civilization into nature. Burke notes in passing in one of his essays that because animals cannot read road signs, they are exposed to such fates in the symboled world.

These trespass anecdotes, I suggest, perform an illustrative rather than a transformative function. For all the horror and fascination they induce in the speaker, the dead mole and the rotting squirrel do not supply tragic pleasure, catharsis, or release. Nor do they provide symbolic expiation or purification, although the squirrel's story concludes in a kind of transcendence—the squirrel ending at last in (wished-for) worms (Section 41) and "worms ending in song" as the loud oriole sings overhead (Section 47). For all of its considerations, "The Ridge Farm" simply does not advance with the purposiveness of a single lyric or drama in which an audience or a speaker moves through such victimage to a final state of unity or purity. Rather Ammons uses these little dramas of trespass and victimage as one way of exploring the circumstances of the symbol-using animal. Through them he marks as inevitable but also as morally and ethically perilous the encounter of culture and human agency with nature, the real and symbolic actions of the one upon the other.

The final two sections of the poem likewise serve an illustrative and exploratory rather than a dramatic purpose. Here I want to consider them not successively, as the culmination of a sustained drama or lyric process, but side by side as representations of how the dividedness of creation into symbolic and nonsymbolic realms—action and motion—might be symbolically resolved. Like the trespass narratives, and in ways that relate closely to them, these concluding stanzas provide a retrospective way to read Ammons's difficult, even recalcitrant poem. There are a number of productive ways to talk about what happens in these two strophes—one representing a purification by fire, the other by water; one working a resolution into unity, the other into stasis; each taking up in turn the prophetic impulse of the poem and the purgative.

To talk about the first of these two sections as a "purification by fire," it will be helpful to return to a much earlier passage in which Ammons first contemplates bodily decay. "The waste in a woods gives off the best heat and brightest / illumination," he writes in a parenthetical meditation,

> all growing is
> gourd green: but the fallen
> lie about dry and light, lightwood,
> ready at a click of fire to
> rage response, its fast undoing its
> best revelation

(SV, 12)

In a literal sense he refers here to fallen limbs and dead wood; but this section has already defined human beings not only as *part* of nature but as fatally subject to it, put together and taken apart by natural processes, so that "the fallen" logically includes "us." "Fallen" also signifies, again, the division of the world into distinct orders, unity into diversity and One into many. In the lines that follow this interruption, Ammons articulates at length the human situation at the intersection of the natural order—its processes and necessities—with the elusive supernatural or "sacred" order, and the verbal or symbolic order which comprises attention, reason, exploration, consideration, acceptance, poetry itself; to be human is to lodge, sometimes unsteadily, between the "sacred" and "the giving way under us" which is natural process. But this very condition of fallenness is necessary for revelation, the penetration of both natural and symbolic orders by the sacred. More prosaically, the fact that it is "waste" that burns suggests an analogy between the natural "waste" of the woods and the moral pollution brought about by human agency (in the invention of the negative) and expressed as human actions in and on nature.

The light that finally breaks out, near the end of the poem, in the fallenness and waste of this landscape purifies in several clear ways. First, it burns away the vestiges of "true" and "distinctive" voice, which is the hallmark of human agency and symbol-mastery and as such is a rich source of guilt and ambivalence. Transpersonal, the light simply "finds human / spirit to burn on"; when it dies out in one place, it "moves / to find a place to break out elsewhere" (SV, 40). Second, it unifies the dividedness of the world, subsuming into its brilliance both nature and language, freedom (represented as human spirit, reason, tendance, dedication) and necessity; in doing so it radically redefines poetic dwelling. At the same time, it completes or perfects a cycle, simultaneously fulfilling creation (by association with John's incarnational passage), consuming it in a final blaze, and returning to its first moment, in which the world is divided anew. At the point of completion or perfection, here is Burke's *Da Capo:* "the / light already dealing with darkness / designating it darkness, opposition by / naming" (SV, 40).

The last section of the poem enacts, on the other hand, a purification by water. There is more at stake here than the drama of urinary release, though this is a subject of recurrent interest for both Burke and Ammons. In bearing away pollution (and ablution, by way of the dishwater) the brook provides both literal and symbolic purification. As the "real" brook is burdened and imperiled by the real products of consumer culture, the poetic brook carries off the moral pollution that is the product of human agency and, in the end, of poetry itself. "I like nature poetry," Ammons writes,

> where the brooks are never dammed up or
> damned to hauling dishwater or
> scorched out of their bottoms by acids:
> the deep en-leafing has now come and
> the real brook in certain bends dwells

(SV, 41)

Not coincidentally, the scene that follows has some of the elements of a baptism; there is the water, of course, and a descending bird:

> yesterday I
> looked upbrook from the highway and
> there flew down midbend a catbird to
> the skinny dip, found a secure
> underwater brookstone and began, in a
> dawnlike conclave of tranquility, to
> ruffle and flutter, dipping into and
> breaking the reflective surfaces with
> mishmashes of tinkling circlets.

(SV, 41)

There is, by way of the poet, a voice in the wilderness and—in his thought of damming and damning—some call to repentance, sustaining to the end the moral energies of the poem. Only the voice from above is missing.

This final stanza also achieves a kind of stasis, bringing nature and poetry into a single term, finding in it both ground and dwelling. That we should be, in this moment, right where highway and wilderness meet—looking "upbrook from the highway"—is a measure less of the poem's steady unfolding than of its remarkable, unforeseen coherence.

NOTES

William R. Harmon provided generous, insightful help with the final version of this essay. I am grateful for his careful reading and suggestions.

1. A. R. Ammons, *Collected Poems 1951–1971* (New York: Norton, 1972), 129; hereafter cited in the text as CP.

2. This is perhaps what Richard Howard refers to when he writes of "the paradox of poetry as process and yet impediment to process" in Ammons. "The Spent Seer Consigns Order to the Vehicle of Change," *A. R. Ammons,* ed. Harold Bloom (New York: Chelsea House, 1986), 34.

3. All references are to the King James Bible; hereafter cited by book and chapter.

4. Helen Vendler suggests that in Ammons, "The temporality and temporariness of any dwelling makes it alive." *The Music of What Happens* (Cambridge: Harvard University Press, 1988), 316.

5. Martin Heidegger, *Poetry, Language, Thought,* trans. Albert Hofstadter (New York: Harper & Row, 1971).

6. "Ecology is my word: tag / me with that," he writes in *Tape.* As in Heidegger, this claim entails a dwelling—through the Greek *oikos,* a house—so he adds an invitation, "come in there" *Poetry, Language, Thought,* (112).

7. Heidegger, *Poetry, Language, Thought,* 91–93.

8. A. R. Ammons, *Sumerian Vistas* (New York: Norton, 1987), 40; hereafter cited in the text as SV.

9. Frank Kermode, "John," *The Literary Guide to the Bible*, ed. Robert Alter and Frank Kermode (Cambridge: Harvard University Press, 1987), 445.

10. Kenneth Burke, *Language as Symbolic Action* (Berkeley: University of California Press, 1966), 189–90; hereafter cited in the text as LSA.

11. Herbert Marks, "On Prophetic Stammering," *The Book and the Text,* edited by Regina Schwartz (Cambridge: Harvard University Press, 1990), 60.

12. "Macadam," a road surface made of compacted broken stone held together by tar or asphalt, appears as the first word of an early draft of *The Bridge.* John Unterecker cites a 1923 letter in which Crane quotes this opening verse to Allen Tate:

> Macadam, gun grey as the tunny's pelt,
> Leaps from Far Rockaway to Golden Gate,
> For first it was the road, the road only
> We heeded in joint piracy and pushed.

He was never to lose the theme announced in these lines—or the first two lines themselves," Unterecker points out in *Voyager: A Life of Hart Crane* (New York: Farrar, Straus and Giroux, 1969), 279. In the final version of *The Bridge* the lines appear, in very slightly modified form, as the opening of the "Van Winkle" section of "Powhatan's Daughter."

13. Kenneth Burke, *A Grammar of Motives* (Berkeley: University of California Press, 1969), 96; hereafter cited as GM.

14. A. R. Ammons, *Set in Motion: Essays, Interviews, and Dialogues,* ed. Zofia Burr (Ann Arbor: University of Michigan Press, 1996), 113–15.

15. Kenneth Burke, *The Rhetoric of Religion* (Boston: Beacon, 1961), 174–74; hereafter cited in the text as RR.

16. A. R. Ammons, *Brink Road* (New York: Norton, 1996).

"Pray Without Ceasing" and the Postmodern Canon

Stephen Cushman

As the number of years until the millennium dwindles, the number of awards, prizes, and grants to Ammons's name grows. Forecasts risk embarrassing the forecaster, but anyone who wagered that Ammons's readership will wax into the first quarter of the new century would not get long odds from Lloyd's. If the North Carolinian from Ithaca still had to depend solely on the promotional zeal of Harold Bloom, who first called serious attention to him in the 1970s, one might feel less confident in making this wager. But admiration has passed to a new generation of poets, critics, and readers, as the proliferating imitations and dissertations make clear. Furthermore, Ammons manages not only to win awards, prizes, and grants but also to bring his books back into print, and to draw enthusiastic crowds to the public readings he rarely used to give, at a time when no critical trend makes him particularly eligible or attractive for special consideration.

Nevertheless, despite the feat of consolidating his fame against the grain of fashion, one sector of the poetry market remains unimpressed: the anthologizers of poetry that labels itself "postmodern." In both *The Postmoderns: The New American Poetry Revised* (1982), edited by Donald Allen and George F. Butterick, and *Postmodern American Poetry* (1994), edited by Paul Hoover and published by Ammons's own publisher, the textbook giant Norton, Ammons's name and work stand conspicuously absent.[1] Of course they do, many will argue. Partisans of the avant-garde will contend that Ammons's work resists insufficiently what Hoover calls "mainstream ideology" (xxv), whereas partisans of the Emersonian lineage Bloom claims for Ammons will contend that his work identifies itself too fully with the sublime tradition of the transcendental signified to keep such disreputable company. But whether one backs the poetry of opposition or the poetry of accommodation, as Robert Von Hallberg names the two sides, one appears to have little choice but to acquiesce in Ammons's exclusion from anthologized representations of postmodernism.[2]

Since Ammons flourishes despite this exclusion, it would seem not to matter much. But it does matter; it matters because anthologies reflect how we describe to ourselves not only our collectively varied tastes and needs but also our varied senses of literary history. As Ammons observes in *Sphere* (1974), "the anthology is the moving, changing definition of the / imaginative life of the people, the repository and source, / genetic."[3] In the pages that follow, I want to argue that if we acquiesce in the exclusion of Ammons from anthologies of postmodern poetry, whether we read him with pleasure or not, then we have got something about postmodernism or something about Ammons, if not both, badly wrong.

In making this argument, I will begin by trying to make sense of the early long poem "Pray Without Ceasing," partly because it has received little critical attention and partly because of its unusual publication history. Apparently composed during 1967, the poem did not appear in print until the Autumn 1973 number of the *Hudson Review* or in a book until *Diversifications* (1975). The eight-year gap between composition and book publication is significant because it includes the publication of Ammons's first *Selected Poems* (1968) and his *Collected Poems* (1972), as well as his winning of the National Book Award (1973) and the Bollingen Prize (for 1973–74). In other words, by concentrating on "Pray Without Ceasing," we can isolate an aspect of Ammons's work that is present from early in his career but not fully represented in the published work that brings him the first wave of national acclaim. When that aspect surfaces again in *The Snow Poems* (1977), it gets severely rebuked by reviewers and submerges, although it remains always present.

Faced with the difficulties of "Pray Without Ceasing," many a reader may sympathize with Pound's confession in Canto 116: "I cannot make it cohere."[4] But readers who hunger for coherence, especially those who have cut their teeth on the shards and fragments of the *Cantos, The Waste Land,* or *Paterson,* can make the poem cohere reasonably well. To begin with, anyone inclined toward historicist readings will find "Pray Without Ceasing" more congenial than most of Ammons's work, since late-twentieth-century history stamps the poem explicitly. Both internal evidence (Ammons's reference to "a 41-year-old man") and the placement of the poem in the chronologically arranged *Selected Longer Poems* (1980) point to a composition date of 1967.[5] For an American writing in 1967, the landscape of awareness necessarily includes Vietnam, and the war makes several graphic appearances in "Pray Without Ceasing."

But merely saying that Ammons alludes to events and conditions in Vietnam does little to make the poem cohere. After all, the twenty years of American involvement in Vietnam, beginning with the agreement to train the South Vietnamese army in 1955 and ending with the fall of Saigon in 1975, cover many different phases. Comprehension of Ammons's war passages deepens when we consult the historical record and begin to understand the timing of his poem. Written somewhere around April Fools' Day 1967 (5), "Pray Without Ceasing" coincides with the third phase of Rolling Thunder, code name for the sustained bombing of North Vietnam. Phase III of Rolling Thunder dramatically escalated the air war, as both the number of sorties flown and the tonnage of aerial munitions dropped nearly doubled the rates of 1966.[6] Against this intensifying background, Ammons's images of the incendiary napalm and its disfiguring effects emerge as remarkable understatements rather than sensational indulgences:

> you heal back from napalm: the
> flame-scars pull chin to chest,
> the fingers stick:
>
> (SLP, 3)

> a child sits in explosion's
> clutter, homeless, his small
> driftwood legs, his eyes inventing
> an equal rage & dark, white smears
> of burn
> the mask
> his face must lift:
>
> (SLP, 3)

These restrained passages, carved mostly of monosyllables and concrete diction, appear early in "Pray Without Ceasing" and introduce not only the war motif but also the motif of fire:

> the Buddhist nun burns for the peace
> her ashes will achieve:
>
> the village woman coming home finds
> her shack afire, her
> son & husband shot:
>
> (SLP, 13)

ent STEPHEN CUSHMAN

Ammons's image of the burning Buddhist nun recalls a three-week period during May 1966 when at least ten Buddhist monks and nuns assumed the lotus position, had themselves doused with gasoline, and burst into flame after lighting matches.[7] His enjambment ("burns for the peace / her ashes will achieve") tempts the unsuspecting or historically forgetful into reading "burns" figuratively, as though Ammons were describing the nun's strong emotion, and even though the all too literal sense quickly corrects this reading, the syntactic completion cannot erase all traces of that emotion, which continues to hover in a generalized form throughout the poem.

In fact, the expression and containment of strong emotion become thematic in "Pray Without Ceasing." Although the Buddhist monks and nuns immolated themselves in protest against American support of the Saigon regime, giving media audiences in the United States their first palpable images of antiwar protests, Ammons's own rhetoric tends not toward protest but toward elegy. Here it helps to remember that as of April 1967 the antiwar movement in the United States had not yet gained the widespread strength it gathered after the Tet offensive (31 January 1968), the emergence of Eugene McCarthy and Robert Kennedy as candidates for the Democratic presidential nomination, and the many civic disruptions of that election year. Instead, at the moment Ammons is writing, "the flood of American power that arose after World War II," along with national confidence in that power, is cresting.[8]

Anticipating the wider public response yet to come, Ammons's elegiac focus on civilian casualties expresses strong emotion in distinctly personal terms:

> my mouth, become eyes, weeps
> words: words spill
> into
> hyacinths: for my acquaintance
> with grief is
> intimate, lost voices my credentials:
> singing's been sung: the same
> body is crying:
>
> (SLP, 3)

In this passage, which follows the one about the child sitting in "explosion's / clutter," Ammons nods to classical elegy (the hyacinth) and echoes Isaiah 53:3 ("a man of sorrows, and acquainted with grief") before he connects his grieving to autobiographical losses. In the final two lines Ammons reveals the logic of his elegy, as he contemplates the convergence of his losses with all losses. He depicts himself as someone whose personal sorrows make him susceptible to the sorrows of strangers, a man who hears something falling at the opening of his poem, perhaps rain or the hailstones he discovers at the end of the poem, and cannot help thinking of what else is falling on others: "napalm isn't falling here" (7). In a move reminiscent of Whitman's declaration in "Crossing Brooklyn Ferry" that "I too had receiv'd identity by my body," Ammons identifies himself with his weeping body and then identifies the weeping he has done in the past—for two brothers, mother, father, as we learn elsewhere in his poems—with the verbal weeping he does now for the boy with the burned face or the bereaved woman whose "left arm like a sickle reaps at the / air / for the harvest / already taken" (13).

One way to make "Pray Without Ceasing" cohere, then, is to read it as elegy and to ask the question that Freud enables us to ask of elegies: Does it work through mourning to consolation or does it become arrested in melancholia?[9] Or, to rephrase the question in the language of the poem, do the hailstones that Ammons finds in the grass and puts in his mouth at the end of the poem really heal the burnings of grief or do they only briefly numb the aching tongue? But like *The Waste Land,* another poem that many read as elegy, "Pray Without Ceasing" also confronts a reader with different voices that strain the coherence of this elegiac reading. In much the same way that Eliot quotes, echoes, and alludes, Ammons weaves together Hermes Trismegistus, the nursery rhyme about Dapple Gray, instructions from a laundromat, and various instances of wordplay. Ammons may be confirming this similarity and acknowledging the technique of *The Waste Land,* which also moves through fire toward prayer, when he shapes the line "O Egypt I sometimes hear the" to resemble Eliot's "O City, I can sometimes hear," which in turn recapitulates two earlier lines that echo Marvell.

How can readers of Ammons make these other voices cohere, especially with no Eliotic endnotes to lead or mislead them? Actually, with a little library work they can do so without much difficulty. In the case of Hermes Trismegistus, for instance, we discover that the passage Ammons quotes comes out of the third part of the *Asclepius,* a dialogue between Trismegistus and Asclepius originally composed in Greek between 268 and 273 A.D. but now available to us only in Latin:

"O Aegypte,
Aegypte, of thy religious rites nought
will survive but tales
which thy children's children
will not believe;
nought
will survive but words graven upon
stones that tell of thy piety."

(SLP, 2)

This passage appears in a section of the *Asclepius* that Walter Scott calls "the Prophecy."[10] In this section "Hermes predicts the extinction of the national religion of Egypt" and "laments the impending abandonment of the old cults . . . in the face of Christian hostility."[11] With his warnings of profound, impending changes, Hermes Trismegistus serves Ammons as Tiresias serves Eliot, providing him with a prophetic, even an apocalyptic, voice that merges easily with the historical context of 1967.

A nearby passage in the *Asclepius* shows that this prophecy contemplates the same kind of annihilation through violence that Ammons witnesses in southeast Asia: "In that day will our most holy land, this land of shrines and temples, be filled with funerals and corpses. To thee, most holy Nile, I cry, to thee I foretell that which shall be; swollen with torrents of blood, thou wilt rise to the level of thy banks, and thy sacred waves will be not only stained, but utterly fouled with gore."[12] One can argue about whether Ammons wants us to substitute for "Aegypte" the name "Vietnam," in which case the destruction of an indigenous culture threatened by the spread of Christianity becomes an instance of historical repetition, or the name "America," in which case the prophecy becomes a jeremiad warning Ammons's own country of the eventual consequences that its invasive belligerence will bring down on it: "And in that day men will be weary of life, and they will cease to think the universe worthy of reverent wonder and of worship."[13] But either way, the rhetoric of prophecy functions intelligibly throughout "Pray Without Ceasing" and complements the rhetoric of elegy.

If we want to, we can also make sense of the Dapple Gray rhyme or the laundromat directions. In the case of the latter (8–9), Ammons may be having a little fun with an instance of found art, as with a straight face he whittles the humorless directions into lines of comically different lengths:

> (2) if rotary knob type meter—
> turn knob:
> tub
> will start filling not later than 1/2
> minute after operating coin slide:
>
> (SLP, 9)

But he also may be contrasting this example of American labor-saving machinery, and the cultural ethos it reflects, with events in Vietnam, where material excess characterized the American presence: "By 1967, a million tons of supplies a month were pouring into Vietnam to sustain the U. S. force—an average of a hundred pounds a day for every American there." Furthermore, these supplies were not all military, as "Westmoreland and his logistical experts inundated Vietnam with the luxuries that have become necessities for U. S. forces far from home,"[14] luxuries such as washing machines that long ago became necessities for people in a country that consumes most of the energy in the world. In the grotesque contrast between the American washing machine and the Vietnamese woman's burning shack, we recognize another instance of jeremiadic prophecy.

In the case of the truncated rhyme about Dapple Gray, Ammons again reminds us of *The Waste Land* and its use of children's verse: "London Bridge is falling down falling down falling down." But in "Pray Without Ceasing" the nursery rhyme, which appears twice (4, 7), functions not as a fragment shored hopefully or nostalgically against ruin but as another image of brutality. The whole rhyme goes this way:

> I had a little pony,
>   His name was Dapple Gray;
> I lent him to a lady
>   To ride a mile away.
> She whipped him, she slashed him,
>   She rode him through the mire;
> I would not lend my pony now,
>   For all the lady's hire.[15]

In alluding to the betrayal of childish trust by the abusive lady, Ammons reinforces our sense that the speaker of his poem feels deeply wounded, even betrayed, by the operations of violence he can neither stand nor ignore. But like the speaker of the nursery rhyme, Ammons also describes with unnerving understatement the physical punishment inflicted on the innocent.

If we want to tie together the voices that thread their way through
"Pray Without Ceasing," a passage that follows the description of
the woman coming home to her burning shack becomes key:

> how can I know I
> am not
> trying to know my way into feeling
> as
>
> feeling
> tries to feel its way into knowing:
>
> (13)

In this artfully structured chiasmus, Ammons points to the ques-
tion that haunts his poem: What are the limits of sympathy? Yes,
"the woman flutters, / her grief absolute and / not a mystery" (13)
and, yes, Ammons has had his share of griefs, too. But does his
knowledge of her situation, a knowledge gleaned from newspapers
or television, authorize him to identify his grief with hers? To
return to the earlier discussion of the elegiac logic of "Pray Without
Ceasing," is all grief really identical? Do his own lost voices give
Ammons the "credentials" (3) to mourn adequately for Vietnamese
civilians? In exploring these questions, Ammons finds himself in
much the same predicament that confronts Whitman in what be-
came the long thirty-third section of "Song of Myself." Speeding
his way through glimpses of the 1854 wreck of the *San Francisco,*
the hounded slave, the mashed fireman, the old artillerist, and the
massacre of those who surrendered at Goliad in March 1836, Whit-
man has the temerity to announce, "All these I feel or am." For
some, his declaration "I am the man. . . . I suffered. . . . I was
there" rings with the scriptural authority and sublime pathos of
Lamentations 3:1: "I am the man who has seen affliction"; for
others, it collapses into pious, deluded cant. Although Ammons
takes some of the same risks Whitman does, he differs from Whit-
man by making his sense of those risks explicit.

At this point I could continue my reading of "Pray Without Ceas-
ing" by evaluating the success of Ammons's attempts at sympa-
thetic identification, but instead I want to examine the nature of
my own procedure so far. In trying to make the poem cohere, I
have been assuming that the poem represents the operations of a
single consciousness or subjectivity. Given this assumption, I am
free to read anything that Ammons throws at us as something that

points, no matter how obliquely, to some underlying truth or meaning or concern or question. Like the psychoanalyst who reads a patient by means of that patient's slips, lapses, evasions, digressions, asides, and non sequiturs, I have been reading the apparent incongruities of "Pray Without Ceasing" as clues, traces, or symptoms of Ammons's anxiety that the personal griefs and pleasures of "a 41-year-old man living on dandelion leaves / from the cool edges of junkyards," vivid as they may be to him, cannot connect that man to people caught in a war twelve time zones away. In turn, this anxiety threatens Ammons with a realization of how trivial and irrelevant his work can feel in wartime, the same realization we see Stevens fending off in the unconvincing epilogue to *Notes Toward a Supreme Fiction* ("Soldier, there is a war between the mind / And sky").

In reading the poem this way, I have not been merely stuffing a dummy for the purpose of destroying it now. I have to admit that I find my own arguments persuasive, within their limits, and I have no desire to embarrass anyone else who does, too. But I also have to admit that whereas my reading probably justifies excluding "Pray Without Ceasing" from any anthology of postmodern poetry, another kind of reading, or anti-reading, justifies—even demands— its inclusion. To make this point, I will focus on the descriptions of postmodern poetry laid out by Hoover in his introduction and return to moments in "Pray Without Ceasing" I ignored before, moments such as this one:

> stock in trade
> gunstock
> stockings
> stocks & bonds & good
> stock
> put no stock in that
> a stock case
> in stock
> stock the soup

(SLP, 1)

What? Did this passage slip off the pages of a book published by Sun & Moon, Burning Deck, Hanging Loose, or Roof? No, it crops up a mere nine lines into "Pray Without Ceasing" and is the first of three such passages scattered throughout the poem, the second and third taking "pop" and "cock" as their central words respectively.

In the first paragraph of his introduction, Hoover tells us that in his anthology "postmodern" means "the historical period following World War II" and suggests "an experimental approach to composition, as well as a worldview that sets itself apart from mainstream culture and the narcissism, sentimentality, and self-expressiveness of its life in writing" (xxv). Some may want to respond with Stevens's aphorism in "Adagia" that "All poetry is experimental poetry," but let us grant that some poems assert themselves as more experimental than others. Having done so, we find that Ammons's "stock" passage shows a much greater tendency towards experimentalism than, say, Charles Bukowski's "my old man," which appears in Hoover's anthology. Bukowski's poem uses a simple narrative line, complete sentences, and plenty of subordinating conjunctions to make sure that we follow the father-son encounter. In case we miss the significance of that encounter, the end of the poem determines it for us: "I guess that's / as close / as we ever got" (61). Bukowski's poem may be effective and moving, but its approach is hardly experimental, if by "experimental" we mean that it attempts to push beyond familiar free verse techniques, representational conventions, and rhetorical strategies.

By contrast, Ammons's passage gives us none of the reassuringly familiar features of Bukowski's poem. Instead it gives us a quick tour through the many parts of speech "stock" can play in English, along with its functions in idioms or compound words. Where does such a tour show deference to "mainstream culture"? Can anyone argue convincingly for the presence of sentimentality or self-expressiveness here? Can one even decide whether this passage emanates from the same consciousness or subjectivity represented elsewhere in the poem? One might charge Ammons with narcissism, since showing that he can think of several uses of "stock" perhaps reflects a total absorption in his own engagement with language, but if such engagement constitutes narcissism, then most of the material in Hoover's anthology must plead guilty, too.

I could try to exert my interpretive will over this passage, to tame its disruptiveness by arguing that Ammons is dramatizing his flight from the pressures of contemporary historical reality into the safe haven of relatively empty signs. But why should I? What happens if I compare this passage to statements about language poetry that Hoover makes:

> . . . the language poet builds up a mosaic structure by means of seemingly unrelated sentences and sentence fragments. This progression of non sequiturs frustrates the reader's expectation for linear develop-

ment at the same time that it opens a more complete world of reference. The emphasis in language poetry is placed on production rather than packaging (beginning, middle, end) and ease of consumption. (xxxvi)

What a useful description not only of the "stock" passage but also of the rest of "Pray Without Ceasing." As its readers can testify, it builds up a mosaic structure of seemingly unrelated fragments, frustrates their expectations of linear development, and opens a more complete world of reference. Furthermore, it originally did so when most of the more famous language poets were still in their late teens or early twenties.

To discuss "Pray Without Ceasing" adequately, let alone to appreciate it, sooner or later we have to discuss indeterminacy, a concept central to Hoover's representation of postmodernism. Calling it "the period's most important theme," Hoover describes indeterminacy this way: "Indeterminacy means the conditionality of truth, as well as a compositional tendency away from finality and closure; the text is in a state of unrest or undecidability" (xxxi).[16] This description feels sound enough, and it gives us another way of approaching not only "Pray Without Ceasing" but also many moments in Ammons's work, especially *The Snow Poems*. In the case of "Pray Without Ceasing," we recognize immediately the compositional tendency away from finality and closure. Has Ammons resolved anything by the end of the poem? Maybe, maybe not. My attempt to make the poem cohere could not decide, for example, whether or not Ammons's grieving leads to consolation or whether or not he answers satisfactorily the question that begins, "how can I know I / am not / trying to know my way into feeling." And I cannot now with any conviction decide how to make the "stock," "pop," and "cock" passages cohere. Following Alan Holder's lead, I could try to discover in their relative placement some sort of metonymic logic that I might be able to incorporate into my reading, or I could point out the purely auditory coherence of the triad, as these three passages show the poem metaphorically projecting the principle of phonemic equivalence (here assonance and rhyme) along what Roman Jakobson would call the axis of substitution.[17] In other words, perhaps an impulse towards nondiscursive, indeterminate wordplay determines not only the associations within each of the three passages, but also the links among the three passages.

In our thinking about indeterminacy, Ammons helps us by making it the basis of a compressed *ars poetica* near the middle of "Pray Without Ceasing":

to those busy making themselves
great, with grave music and
solemn looks, a thorough using up and
setting forth of language's materials,
I send
empty statements, slip-shodiness,
incredible breeziness and such:
the wind we go to
understands everything:
I sing, though, in a way, the best I can,
for I may be understood
where I do not understand:

(8)

This confession anticipates much in Hoover's introduction. In particular, Ammons's admission that some of his statements are "empty" connects directly to Hoover's assertion that the "empty sign" is one means by which postmodern poets resist "centrist values of unity, significance, linearity, expressiveness, and a heightened, even heroic, portrayal of the bourgeois self and its concerns" (xxvii). Many might argue that Ammons, with his endowed professorship and domestic life in the suburbs, does nothing to resist and everything to foster heightened, heroic portrayals of the American bourgeois self, but on those who did argue this way would fall the burden of explaining away Ammons's withering caricature of that self and its pathetic frailty:

little artery, couple inches long,
branching into cardiac muscle: it pops
and you give up philosophy and
ultimate concern, car payments, son and wife,
you give up the majors & minors,
the way you like your egg cooked, your
class ring, lawn,
sparrows nesting in the garage, the
four crocus bulbs (maybe more next
year), toenails and fillings:

(SLP, 10)

Even if we ignore Ammons's implicit dissent from American foreign policy in Vietnam before that dissent became popular, the ironies tingeing this detached, skeptical self-portrait disqualify it as a credible affirmation of what Hoover calls "mainstream ideology."

In dogging these descriptions of postmodernism and comparing them to "Pray Without Ceasing," what do I want? Will I be happy if I get a letter from Paul Hoover telling me that I have convinced him to include "Pray Without Ceasing" in the second edition of his anthology or from Hayden Carruth thanking me for teaching him how to read Ammons as a postmodern and retracting his negative review of *The Snow Poems* in the *New York Times*? No, I would not, although I might begin to feel that we had a fuller and more accurate picture of Ammons than many people have now. No, I would still be unhappy because I would have succeeded only in getting Ammons absorbed by a critical fiction that his poetry challenges and, in my judgment, discredits.

That critical fiction is the one that promotes "indeterminacy" as a criterion for anything, especially as a criterion for judgments about the history of American poetry. How useful is it to say that postmodernism means the period following World War II and then proceed to identify as definitively postmodern a characteristic feature of Emily Dickinson's poetry? And even if it were useful, how honest is it to call a poem "indeterminate," when to use this adjective is necessarily to determine that certain kinds of readings of that poem are appropriate and others are not? For that matter, how indeterminate are poems that can only be read as indeterminate? Far more deeply and truly and revealingly indeterminate is a poem like "Pray Without Ceasing," a poem that leaves a reader suspended between the possibilities of reading for coherence and reading against coherence. A poem or a book or an anthology that denies reading for coherence necessarily takes charge of its readers and rules out certain options for them. But with "Pray Without Ceasing" readers do not have to decide, for example, what the ending means so much as they have to decide whether to read for meaning at all. If they do, they discover certain things; if they do not, they discover others.[18] This burden represents a profound challenge, one that makes much of Ammons's work, especially in the long poems, more authentically experimental than much of what gets called "postmodern."

No verbal sign can empty itself completely. To set out to build a poem of mostly empty signs that require readers to fill them in whatever idiosyncratic or contrived ways they might choose is not a great task. A great task is to manage the ratio of partial fullness to partial emptiness, so that even the moments of apparent emptiness brim with the possibility of fullness, a fullness that readers cannot attribute solely to a source either wholly within them or wholly without. Ammons manages this ratio as well as anyone, and this skillful management turns us toward one last aspect of "Pray Without Ceasing" I have not yet mentioned: prayer.

Ammons's title comes from the King James translation of Paul's first letter to the Thessalonians (5:17). At this moment in the letter, Paul is taking his leave and delivering his final exhortations to the church at Thessalonica:

> Now we exhort you, brethren, warn them that are unruly, comfort the feebleminded, support the weak, be patient toward all men. See that none render evil for evil unto any man; but ever follow that which is good, both among yourselves, and to all men. Rejoice evermore. Pray without ceasing. In everything give thanks: for this is the will of God in Christ Jesus concerning you. Quench not the Spirit. Despise not prophesyings. Prove all things; hold fast that which is good. Abstain from all appearance of evil. (5:14–22)

Paul's string of imperatives aims both to instruct and to reassure within a larger theological context that may or may not illuminate Ammons's poem.[19] But although attempts to coerce "Pray Without Ceasing," or any of Ammons's work, towards Protestant Christian orthodoxy can distort as much as they reveal, we cannot dismiss the reappearance of Paul's injunction near the end of the poem as merely ironic (15). Instead, as I want to suggest in closing, Ammons offers us that injunction as a figure for the appropriate activity of both poet and reader.

On the one hand, Hoover and others could contend that of all activities prayer reflects and reinforces notions of authority, whether we call that authority tradition or convention or orthodoxy or mainstream ideology. This line of argument could continue that prayer solidifies the relative positions of the one praying and the one prayed to, as well as what Hoover and others call the phallocentric syntax employed by a male-dominant hierarchy (xxxiv–xxxv). No doubt, many, many people pray in ways that justify this argument. But on the other hand, people can also pray in ways that disrupt and subvert and suspend many of the cognitive and cultural operations that most of Hoover's poets would like to see disrupted, subverted, and suspended. In a wry moment late in *Sphere*, for example, Ammons muses, "I wonder if one / can pay too much attention, as one can pray too much and / forget to shop for dinner."[20] Shopping for dinner, as opposed to stealing it, growing it, killing it, going without it, or hiring someone else to shop for it, epitomizes the condition of what Hoover would call the bourgeois self; yet here Ammons shows that self suddenly disoriented, and the smooth operations of mainstream culture suddenly threatened, by prayer.

One could think of other examples of the connection between prayer and disruption, such as the Buddhist nun in Ammons's poem, or Christopher Smart making a public nuisance of himself by kneeling down in parks and streets, or the figure of Amos in Elizabeth Bishop's poem "The Moose": "When Amos began to pray / even in the store and / finally the family had / to put him away." Perhaps these examples signify nothing more than the irrational excesses of mania or madness and so cannot teach us anything useful about prayer practiced in moderation by responsible citizens. But Emerson's definition of prayer in "Self-Reliance" suggests why prayer, even in moderate doses, cannot help but involve indeterminacy: "Prayer is the contemplation of the facts of life from the highest point of view." Since the highest point of view is not the point of view that my limitations and the contingencies of my life allow me, and since those limitations and contingencies determine my point of view, contemplating from, or even toward, the highest point of view necessarily means un-determining my own point of view. In other words, for a determinate self prayer inevitably means indeterminacy, along with all the collisions, contradictions, shiftings, incongruities, disjunctions, gaps, and blanks that accompany it.

Yes, someone might counter, but when you speak of there being a highest point of view, you posit something determinate at the other end of all the indeterminacy, and so you differ from Hoover's postmodernists, who would claim that there is nothing determinate beyond indeterminacy. In response to this objection, I would point out that ultimate indeterminacy has been a prominent feature of Christian orthodoxy since at least the fourth century, when that orthodoxy was debated and formulated in documents such as the *Quicunque Vult*, commonly called the Creed of Saint Athanasius, which contains the line "The Father incomprehensible, the Son incomprehensible, and the Holy Ghost incomprehensible." In the mystical theology of the Eastern Church, this ultimate incomprehensibility led to negative or "apophatic" theology, which proceeds by denying any kind of thinking or statement that affirms God is one thing as opposed to another.[21] As this reminder should make clear, people have been preoccupied by indeterminacy, particularly by trying to talk about it without violating it, much longer than since World War II.

What consequences does incomprehensibility, whether immediate or ultimate, have for reading "Pray Without Ceasing," as well as for writing a literary history that includes it? Readers who want to make the poem cohere will have to spend time thinking about whether Ammons directs the imperative "pray without ceasing" to himself or to us or to both—as though saying, Unless one prays without ceasing, one cannot hope to withstand the debilitating consequences of grief. These readers may debate whether the poem itself constitutes a prayer, a representation of prayer, or a prelude to prayer. Meanwhile, readers who do not insist on making the poem cohere may hear in Ammons's quotation of Paul a command for how to read his poem, and beyond it Ammons's other poems, and beyond Ammons much of what people write, whether anthologizers call them "postmodern" or not. In this context, "pray without ceasing" means something like "honor indeterminacy." If we hear the command this way, we stand a better chance of enlarging our reading and realizing the emancipating effects of indeterminacy without trivializing it into the dogma of those whose attitudes towards particular values are anything but indeterminate. Among these emancipating effects, we may discover that, as Ammons hopes, we understand him where he does not understand, precisely because he does not understand what is not understandable. But even if we do not discover any such thing, honoring indeterminacy in many forms and at many moments will free us, poets, readers, anthologizers, critics, and literary historians alike, from the vanity of imagining that in the indeterminate we have found something new.

NOTES

1. *The Postmoderns: The New American Poetry Revised* was published by Grove Press in New York. The first edition of the anthology, *The New American Poetry,* appeared in 1960, or after Ammons's privately printed *Ommateum* (Philadelphia: Dorrance, 1955) but before his first published volume, *Expressions of Sea Level* (Columbus: Ohio State University Press, 1964). Other recent anthologies that omit Ammons are Douglas Messerli's *From the Other Side of the Century: A New American Poetry, 1960–1990* (Los Angeles: Sun and Moon, 1994) and Eliot Weinberger's *American Poetry Since 1950: Innovators and Outsiders* (New York: Marsilio, 1993). Meanwhile, recent literary history has treated Ammons no better, as he does not appear in Robert Von Hallberg's description of "Poetry Since 1945" in volume 8 of the *Cambridge History of American Literature* (New York: Cambridge University Press, 1994). Since I will be referring to the Hoover anthology frequently, page references will appear parenthetically in the text.

2. Robert Von Hallberg, *American Poetry and Culture 1945–1980* (Cambridge: Harvard University Press, 1985), 228.

3. A. R. Ammons, *Sphere: The Form of a Motion* (New York: Norton, 1974), 17.

4. Alan Holder introduces his brief remarks on "Pray Without Ceasing" with the assessment that "the work does seem to go one step beyond Stevens' prescription that a poem should resist the intelligence almost successfully" (*A. R. Ammons* [Boston: Twayne, 1978], 132). Compare R. W. Flint's disclaimer that begins "It's too early to say much about 'Pray Without Ceasing,' a phantasmagoria of verbal happening . . ." ("The Natural Man" in *A. R. Ammons,* ed. Harold Bloom [New York: Chelsea House, 1986], 183).

5. For the text of "Pray Without Ceasing," I will use *Selected Longer Poems* (New York: Norton, 1980) on the assumption that more people can find it easily than either the Autumn 1973 *Hudson Review* or *Diversifications*. Ammons's reference to his age appears on page 14 and the chronology of poems on the acknowledgments page. Subsequent page references to this edition will appear parenthetically in the text.

6. See Raphael Littauer and Norman Uphoff, eds., *The Air War in Indochina,* rev. ed. (Boston: Beacon, 1972), 37, 268, 279; as well as James Clay Thompson, *Rolling Thunder: Understanding Policy and Program Failure* (Chapel Hill: University of North Carolina Press, 1980), 42.

7. Stanley Karnow, *Vietnam: A History* (New York: Viking, 1983), 449.

8. Thompson, *Rolling Thunder,* 3.

9. For an excellent study of modern elegy, see Jahan Ramazani's *Poetry of Mourning: The Modern Elegy from Hardy to Heaney* (Chicago: University of Chicago Press, 1994).

10. "O Aegypte, Aegypte, religionum tuarum solae supererunt fabulae, eaeque incredibiles posteris tuis, solaque supererunt verba lapidibus incisa tua pia facta narrantibus" (trans. Walter Scott, in *Hermetica: The Ancient Greek and Latin Teachings Ascribed to Hermes Trismegistus* [Oxford: Clarendon, 1924], 1:342). The dating is Scott's (*Hermetica* 1:76).

11. Ibid., 1:58, 59.

12. Ibid., 1:341.

13. Ibid., 1:343.

14. Karnow, *Vietnam,* 436, 437–38.

15. Iona and Peter Opie, eds., *Oxford Book of Nursery Rhymes* (London: Oxford University Press, 1975), 143.

16. In *The Poetics of Indeterminacy: Rimbaud to Cage* (Princeton: Princeton University Press, 1981), Marjorie Perloff anticipates Hoover's formulation and acknowledges her own borrowing of the term "undecidability" from Tzvetan Todorov (4). See also Perloff's distinction between her use of "indeterminacy" and Derridean theory: "'Indeterminacy,' as I use that term in this book, is taken to be the quality of particular art works in a particular period of history rather than as the central characteristic of all texts at all times" (17). Meanwhile, in *The Cosmic Web: Scientific Field Models and Literary Strategies in the Twentieth Century* (Ithaca: Cornell University Press, 1984), N. Katherine Hayles considers literary indeterminacy in the context of the Heisenberg Uncertainty Relation: "The observer and the system, or as Heisenberg occasionally said, the subject and object, are thus seen as an inseparable whole that cannot be subdivided without introducing the indeterminacy specified by the Uncertainty Relation" (51). Since Hoover's sweeping use of "indeterminacy" excludes Ammons, my argument is with him rather than with Perloff and Hayles, who use the term in more careful, limited ways.

17. Holder connects the "cock" passage to other passages about sex in the poem and the "pop" passage to the one about the cardiac artery that "pops," which I shall consider later in another context. He then concludes that the "sequence that started with the suggestion of sex ends with death" (*Ammons*, 135). This reading would help tame the disruptiveness of the "cock" and "pop" passages, but it would not necessarily ease the critical anxiety Holder himself acknowledges as he begins his discussion of the poem: "One hopes that one's discoveries of relationships among its parts are not merely factitious, the results of a kind of critical gerrymandering" (*Ammons*, 132). With respect to the triadic configuration of the "stock," "pop," and "cock" passages, consider Ammons's suggestive invocations of "3, the mystical figure" (*Ammons*, 1) and "the triadic Hegel" (*Ammons*, 4).

18. Compare Hayles's formulation: "To switch to that new viewpoint will render indistinct and hence indeterminate aspects that may have been clear in the former viewpoint" (*Cosmic Web*, 53).

19. Although he does not mention "Pray Without Ceasing," Frank J. Lepkowski has led the way into an important conversation about Ammons's relation to Christianity. See "'How are we to find holiness?': The Religious Vision of A. R. Ammons" in *Twentieth Century Literature* 40, no. 4 (Winter 1994): 477–98. Lepkowski concludes persuasively that "we may see Ammons more fruitfully not as our Emerson, but rather our Herbert, not Romantic so much as truly Metaphysical" (497).

20. *Sphere*, 70.

21. Vladimir Lossky, *The Mystical Theology of the Eastern Church,* trans. by members of the Fellowship of St. Alban and St. Sergius (Crestwood, N.Y.: St. Vladimir's Seminary Press, 1976), 25, 42.

"Essay on Poetics": The Serious Playfulness of A. R. Ammons

James S. Hans

The poetry of A. R. Ammons has always been most ably defined in terms of its playfulness: it has regularly sought to work through its own "one:many mechanism" in order to unfold the rhythmical dynamic of the universe from Ammons's place within it. In so doing, Ammons has provided us with poems whose range of interests include all the things that come into his purview. Like Williams, he finds ways of stuffing into his work everything from quotations from other texts to accounts of playing with his son to descriptions of trees in his backyard. "Essay on Poetics" has always been the definitive Ammons poem for me because it demonstrates so well the confluence of energies that are at work in his playfulness while also reflecting his full awareness of the seriousness of his play. Ammons regularly reverts to frivolity in the poem and often seeks to disarm us by casual gestures designed to undermine his own seriousness, but in the end the poem is devoted to the grandest quest of all: an attempt to measure the dynamics of the universe through the divining rod of the poetic line.

"Essay on Poetics" suggests in a variety of ways the breadth of Ammons's vision even as it points out the limitations of his perspective. Nowhere are these features more deliberately on display than in Ammons's assertion of his goal:

> I am seeking the
> mechanisms physical, physiological, epistemological, electrical,
>
> chemical, esthetic, social, religious by which many, kept
> discrete as many, expresses itself into the
> manageable rafters of salience, lofts to comprehension, breaks
>
> out in hard, highly informed suasions, the "gathering
> in the sky" so to speak, the trove of mind, tested
> experience, the only place there is to stay, where the saints

are known to share accord and wine, and magical humor floats
upon the ambient sorrow. . . .[1]

This is a bold statement for a poet, declaring as it does that Am-
mons is in effect looking for the philosopher's stone. Such ambi-
tions hardly seem appropriate for a writer any more, whose work
ought to be devoted to lesser tasks like playing with the emotional
intensities of words. At the same time, Ammons's great goal is
modulated through a rather prosy utterance, one that comes close
to sounding bureaucratic in nature. "I am seeking the / mechanisms
physical, physiological, epistemological, electrical, / chemical, es-
thetic, social, religious" is quite a mouthful. After the simple and
straightforward "I am seeking," we find ourselves in the midst of
an unusual and somewhat uninformative term—"mechanisms"—an
inversion that places "mechanisms" in front of the words that mod-
ify it, a series of abstract terms presented to us in a list, and a list
that comes forth with no apparent order to it. It doesn't move from
large to small, from physical to mental, from natural to social, or
in any other way that would suggest a kind of hierarchy. Is the
order a function of rhythm, or does it take on the shape it does
simply because this is the way it came out? We don't know, but
we can see that the features of these lines both establish a grand
theme and undercut it at the same time by the nondescript display.
   The other side of these lines has another kind of leveling effect.
We are presented with a series of clauses designed to suggest the
great importance of the theme, and the repeated attempts to nail
it down suggest how elusive that theme finally is. But isn't it enough
to establish that the poet wants to show how the one:many mecha-
nism "expresses itself into the / manageable rafters of salience"?
This statement accomplishes most of what is necessary here. First
it tells us that the theme is lofty, then it encourages us toward
conviction by being elusive at the same time. What, after all, are
the "manageable rafters of salience"? Sounds powerful, striking,
essential, and poetically suggestive at the same time. Likewise, we
have one of the strengths of Ammons's work on display here: he
doesn't say that *he* has done much of anything at all. He is merely
the "seeker." He hasn't produced the "manageable rafters of sa-
lience"; he has merely created a context through which the one:
many mechanism "expresses itself." Ammons is the site through
which this expression appears—and thus essential for the break-
through—but he doesn't make it happen by creating a fiction
through which the mechanism displays itself. He simply provides
a place—the long poem—for the mechanism to unfold. Given such

clarity of purpose, Ammons doesn't need the other descriptions of the effects of the one:many mechanism. He hit the target the first time out, and the rest of the clauses are largely for display purposes. Why, then, might Ammons feel compelled to produce a series of assertions rather than settling for just one?

Each of the lyrical flights in these lines is undercut by being squished together into the series of which it is a part. How does "lofts to comprehension" add something that isn't found in the manageable rafters of salience? Why should "breaks / out in hard, highly informed suasions" be necessary after these remarks, only to be followed by the "gathering / in the sky," which in turn leads to three more stabs at description? By the time we arrive at "where the saints / are known to share accord and wine," has our sense of Ammons's mission developed in significant ways? Clearly yes in some respects, for each of these locutions plays the double role of suggesting the impossibility of stating once and for all what the one:many mechanism is all about, even as it lyrically attempts to evoke its potential. In this context the separate statements accumulate greater force through addition. Each grabs part of the essence of the mechanism and thus helps us to elaborate a better sense of what it is.

Even better, the various assertions manage to provide a context through which the one:many mechanism shows itself to be the most commonplace of human interactions with the world, and the most glorious. In some respects our moments of comprehension are nothing more than an expression of this mechanism, those occasions on which the world makes sense to us for at least a moment. In others, the "hard, highly informed suasions" convey both the curve of insight and the persuasiveness of its power: we arrive at certain convictions precisely because they seem obvious, necessary, and appropriate all at once. The "trove of mind" and "tested experience" in turn push the mechanism into the regions of everyday life where our sense of the world is reinforced by its appearance within the larger mechanism that generated it in the first place. Now we know the import of tested experience: it is that repository of knowledge within us that convinces us there is a one:many mechanism of which we are a part; it is the divining rod that allows us to locate ourselves within the patterns of the mechanism as we move through life. Each further insight into the mechanism confirms all the others and thus becomes part of the treasure trove of wisdom we accumulate that makes our patterns in life seem fitting to us. We regularly come back with conviction to our sense of things, realizing that it is "the only place there is to stay," precisely because each approach to the gist of the one:many mechanism confirms all the others.

The pragmatic effects of our encounters with the world are finally blended with the religious elements to which they are attached, the high powers of the "gathering in the sky" and the sublimity of that place "where the saints / are known to share accord and wine." The one:many mechanism does more than produce the patterns of the universe: it provides us with multiple points of access to them through which their powers become apparent to us. For Ammons the place where the saints share their communion, where all the world's glories come together, is the most compelling expression of a mechanism that reveals itself in countless small ways every day. Through this insight Ammons hopes to tinge the everyday with that touch of aesthetic glory to which it is entitled, even though we tend not to look for it there. And by demonstrating the omnipresent, powerful, transformative effects of the one:many mechanism through his various evocations of it, Ammons also provides us with the means through which to see a world in which "magical humor floats / upon the ambient sorrow." The woes of life remain a defining element of who we are, always encircling us. But we can arrive at an understanding of the "ambient sorrow" through which we make sense of ourselves that also allows for the "magical humor" of the playfulness of life to float on top of the negativity that never goes away.

Here again Ammons demonstrates his understanding of the playfulness of the universe by asserting its connection to the sorrows of life in a way that makes it much more than a palliative that provides a temporary escape from our woes. Aesthetic pleasure is not that which offers a state of oblivion, blocking out the sorrow of life. Instead, it hefts those woes up to the point where magical humor is allowed to float on top of them, defined and expressed by those woes while also offering each of us a larger sense of how our sorrows fit into the overall patterns of life. Sorrow isn't overcome, abandoned, or transformed in Ammons's aesthetic. It is put in its place, in the midst of which we can also find the magical humor that makes life worth living, that keeps us afloat in a sea of woes that often seems about to overwhelm us.

Once one establishes the ways in which Ammons's statement functions to provide a full account of his sense of the one:many mechanism, though, one comes back to the other side of this poetic utterance, its leveling tendencies. To begin at the end of the statement, we can say that it makes perfect sense for Ammons to try to broaden our understanding of the one:many mechanism by the clauses that link it to everything from the trove of the mind and tested experience to the accord of the saints. We can also recognize how these utterances have their own appropriateness and beauty. But they are presented in the text as part of the "run-on" effect of the poem as a whole: it is as though Ammons gets started and then chooses to run with the poem as far as it will go. Like much of Ammons's poetry, "Essay on Poetics" is notable for its lack of definitive stops, preferring colons to periods or other more insistent forms of punctuation. It just keeps going, and we are meant to think that there is no reason why it couldn't keep unfolding for an indefinite time. When Ammons glibly brings the poem to an end by declaring "well, my essay is finished" (52), we have to wonder why he chose that point to end it, for there seems no necessary reason why things come to a close there. Ammons satisfies our curiosity on this point by informing us that the ending was arbitrary, just as the beginning was. Writing the poem helped him "to get through the snowstorm" (52) that forced him to remain at home. As he does in other long poems, Ammons acknowledges that "having a project is useful especially during natural suspensions." So the poem helped him fill up his time, but the snow has stopped and life is returning to normal. The project has served its purpose and Ammons can bring it to an end.

Ammons once again deliberately undermines the seriousness of his effort in the poem in an attempt to get us to revise our overly dramatic sense of why and how poems are written. Sometimes they come about because the poet has time to kill. Also to his credit, Ammons points out one of the central elements of poetic composition: one makes up a project, establishes various parameters for it, and then sees where it takes one. When it seems to have filled itself out, one lets it go. If Ammons makes the arbitrariness of the ending (and the beginning) seem a bit more capricious than most poets do, that is because he deliberately exaggerates the quality he wants to call our attention to so that he can show yet another of poetry's uses for the writer and the reader: it helps us get through periods in which there seems to be little else for us to do. There is nothing wrong with that, and there is nothing in that context that would keep us from achieving a profound sense of the world at the same time that we are also filling up time. The sublime and the banal often dwell in the same place in everyday life, and they most certainly have the same residence in Ammons's poetry.

Nevertheless, when it comes to lyrical abundance, to the expression of sublimity, a paratactic mode of thought—there is this, and then this, and this, and this, and so on until the poet decides he is done—tends to even out the emotional intensity of the poem. It is hard for the saints to share accord and wine for very long when the poem quickly moves on to something else, so the regions with the most impressive rhetorical flourishes end up losing some of their power. The listmaking tendency in the poem has the same effect: it is difficult to heft something up "out of the miry circumstance" (47) when it is part of a series whose whole point is to keep all the troops in line. Ammons's word choice contributes further to the leveling of tone. It is not that one should avoid using language that comes from a wide range of social interests, but lines like "mechanisms physical, physiological, epistemological, electrical," tend to dissipate the energy of the poem through their abstraction and through the polysyllabic mouthful in their middle that threatens to lose the reader's interest. Ammons may only be showing the expansiveness of his ambition here, but more likely—and more typically—he is making large claims on our attention while deliberately undercutting them at the same time, disarming us by putting such a glob of words on the page all at once.

The leveling tendencies in the poem are equally reflected in Ammons's definition of his poetry. He sees it as a "one:many mechanism, internally irrelevant to scope, / but from the outside circumscribed into scope" (31). This is a perfect formulation of what drives Ammons's work—and the world. One couldn't ask for a more informed statement about the approach to knowledge in our age. It is based on patterns, on fields, on flows of energy, on movement back and forth between what Ammons calls "the high levels of oneness and the / numerous subordinations and divisions of diversity" (49). No poet of our time better understands this dynamic. No poet knows so well how poetry works by expressing precisely this rhythm, which is the rhythm of everything there is. Ammons's genius is located in his awareness of the elaboration of the one:many mechanism and in his understanding of the sway back and forth between those high levels of oneness and the numerous subordinations and divisions of diversity. If one can complain about the tendency of his poem to keep moving whatever the cost, it does so of necessity: it must push forward to wend its way through the pattern of oneness and manyness. As Ammons knowingly remarks: "stop on any word and language gives way" (32). For poetry to exemplify and express the unfolding patterns of the universe, it must always be moving on, and this rhythm is deliberately and incessantly on view in "Essay on Poetics" and all of Ammons's longer poems. "Gotta keep moving" is their motto.

At times, however, the movement seems to be for movement's sake. It is as though we are too intimately in the midst of the process of composition because Ammons hasn't edited out those stanzas where he uses certain lines to take him to a place where he knows better what he is up to. Ammons no doubt does this on purpose. In the midst of his early discussion on how much he could learn from tracing the patterns of his imaginary thousand cows, for example, he swerves off somewhere else:

> anyway, there's a time when loose speech has to give in,
>
> come up to the corral, run through the planked alleys,
> accept the brand, the medication, surrender to the
> identity of age, sex, weight, and bear its relationship
>
> to the market: there's no market for most speech, specially
> good, and none for loose: that's why I don't care
> how far I wander off. . . .
>
> (SLP, 32)

The "anyway" that begins this brief section reflects Ammons's tendency to display the places where his material lacks ready transitions. He needs to get from his specific discussion of cows and cowpatterning to the next part of the poem. He knows his poetry is based on tossing out an idea and seeing how far it goes, then coming back around and tossing out another idea in the hope that finally all the ideas reflect the patterning on which the poem is based. Consequently, he insists on leaving the loose ends loose: he's done with the cows and wants to move on to something else— a series of remarks on the nature of oneness—so he tells us that his attention has extended itself as far as it can when it comes to the cows and must now move elsewhere. Again, the honesty and integrity of Ammons's poems are based on his willingness to let them reflect the way he thinks the patterns of mind (and universe) actually work. This is part of the poet's charm and his disarming nature.

Nevertheless, the risk Ammons takes is reflected in the lines I just quoted: a poet who leaves the processes of his mechanism on display for all to see also gives the reader an opportunity to question the ratio between good speech and loose speech. There is nothing wrong with demotic language itself: Williams was a master at using everyday experiences and discourse to produce poems of great power. Nor is there a problem with demonstrating the patterns to which one's poetry is devoted, even if those patterns undercut our traditional notions of seamless thought and poetic constructions. Nor, finally, is it inappropriate to create a poem with a dynamic that has low and high points. How else is the reader going to recognize eloquence unless there is a crescendo toward which things build? But Ammons is not just casual. The "anyway" in these lines is colloquial, offhand, and it reflects a willingness to have one's weak links clearly on display, but it is followed by speech that is deliberately "loose." Loose speech does indeed have to "give in" and "come up to the corral, run through the planked alleys, / accept the brand, the medication," and it must finally "surrender to the / identity of age, sex, weight, and bear its relationship / to the market" if the poet is going to have any chance of getting an audience.

Ammons's poetry derives its strength from a one:many mechanism of great power, but at the same time it is based on a phrase in which the crucial word is "mechanism." What are we to make of that? A mechanism, Webster tells us, can be a piece of machinery or "a process or technique for achieving a result." It can be a "mechanical operation or action," or it can reflect "a doctrine that holds natural processes (as of life) to be mechanically determined and capable of complete explanation by the laws of physics and chemistry." Finally, the word can refer to "the fundamental physical or chemical processes involved in or responsible for an action, reaction, or other natural phenomenon (as organic evolution)."[2] All of these definitions apply to Ammons's use of the term. Throughout his career Ammons has demonstrated a commitment to the sciences, and his poetry reflects the best wisdom science can offer us. One of the strengths of his work is his awareness of science, just as the genius of his poems is based on his knowledge of the rhythmical sway between oneness and manyness that is the fundamental process of everything in the universe. No one makes better use of his scientific knowledge than Ammons—particularly early in his career when such links were rather rare—and we see him deliberately calling attention to the parallels between his own work and the latest scientific discoveries toward the end of "Essay on Poetics," when he blithely throws into the "mix" of his poem three quotations from scientific treatises that reflect his points about one:many.

A poem based on an idea of the mechanism, though, risks becoming a "piece of machinery," which has among its characteristics a tendency to be mechanical in nature. A piece of machinery that is devoted to "a process or technique for achieving a result" can be so insistent on the result that it strips the technique of that which would give it flavor. In a way, Ammons compensates for the potentially mechanical nature of his mechanism by elaborating a device—the stanzaic structures through which his words pour out in measured cadences—that embraces the manyness of the world. Because it does so, it bears along with its sway the richness of accident: who knows what will come up next? Did those cows at the beginning of the poem just pop into Ammons's head at that moment of the composition, or were they an element he had anticipated beforehand? To what extent are his lines based on expectation or surprise? To what degree are they always marching toward a more or less predetermined end?

The virtue of Ammons's mechanism is that it begins by acknowledging accident and surprise, making them central to the entire enterprise. The mechanical nature of the stanzas is overcome because it opens the poet up to experiences that might not otherwise come his way. The mechanism allows the poet a great freedom: "I get lost for fun, / because there's no chance of getting lost" (34). If there is a tendency in the poem for loose speech to get carried away, right around the corner there is always a redeeming moment when everyday speech takes Ammons to the center of something highly important. And here he tells us one of the great strengths of his "mechanical" view of the universe and the composition of poetry: unlike most people—who are afraid of getting lost—Ammons knows there is no way that he *can* get lost. The one:many mechanism is so thoroughly written into the processes of life that it is bound to take him back to a familiar place. Therefore, he can risk opening himself up to what comes next without worrying about losing himself. His knowledge of the mechanism gives him the confidence to forego the usual self-conscious assertion of control in poetic and everyday situations.

This willingness to get lost in the knowledge that there is no way to get lost expresses another fundamental element of Ammons's work: the poet never declares that his poetry is devoted to *self-expression*. He isn't interested in expressing a self, doesn't devote his attention to the hum of subjectivity. He doesn't tell us much about Ammons throughout his career because he realizes that none of that material really matters. His poetry is largely devoted to seeking out the mechanisms of the universe, and there is nothing subjective about that quest. Ammons's poetry is as good as it is because he realizes that the best poetry has little to do with selfhood, even if it may use elements of the poet's life to express the manyness of the poetic context. Ammons can give up the self-centeredness of so much contemporary poetry because he has confidence in the mechanisms of the universe to take him where he needs to go. The great strength of any significant poet is found in the confidence that lets the universe tell the poet where to go. It may go against current fashion to make such a statement, but Ammons's career begins and ends with that self-assurance, and he is right to have it.

Ammons's understanding of the one:many mechanism allows him to give himself over to the process of the machine, to the composition of the poem, without worrying about whether the rhythms of the process will lead him astray. He believes in the rhythms that drive his poem, and he will follow them where they take him. His mechanism is thus truly "a process or technique for achieving a result": the completed poem. Further, the mechanism at the center of Ammons's poetry embraces "a doctrine that holds natural processes (as of life) to be mechanically determined and capable of complete explanation by the laws of physics and chemistry."[3] The word "complete" in this statement is a bit shaky—both in general and for Ammons—but Ammons's confidence as a poet comes from his firm belief that his poetry expresses the mechanisms at the center of all natural processes. If he doesn't submit to the notion that physics and chemistry can explain everything, that is at least in part because poetry does a much better job with the mechanisms of the universe when it comes to their rhythm than anything science could hope to do.

In tune with Ammons's conviction that things sway both backward and forward, though, one returns to the question of whether the great strength of the poetry—its commitment to and confidence in the one:many mechanism at its center—isn't also its weakness—a tendency to be too mechanical, to move at times into locutions that are repetitious, loose, ill-fitting, and unqualified as proper expressions of the mechanism that produced them in the first place. The unrelenting pace of the longer poems, their willingness to go on and on, reflects perhaps too much confidence in the mechanism. It can produce everything Ammons thinks it is capable of generating, but perhaps in the end the most difficult of distinctions—between loose and everyday speech—isn't achieved as often as one might hope for it to be. At times one feels caught in the midst of a machine whose only goal is to keep moving, to push one along, and although the reader always has the option to stop and think, to pause or put the poem down, still there is a push in the longer poems that works against their own interests at times. At best it undermines those occasions when the poem approaches its most eloquent reaches; at worst it wallows too much in contexts that don't offer us much in the way of either interest or understanding.

The distinction between loose and everyday speech also needs to be made at the level of the details that are included in a poem. Everydayness is as crucial to Ammons's work as it is to our lives, and it is one of the poet's great strengths. Most often the everydayness of the poetry is highly effective: Ammons's small poem-within-a-poem on the elm tree in his backyard (37–40) is at once playfully amusing and compelling testimony of his commitment to measuring the world and to his conviction that "much is nearly stable" (34) in our world. The poem unfolds with precision, and yet the poet willingly learns how to accept some fundamental limitations: it is hard—perhaps impossible—to locate anything precisely in our world, but because so many things are at least nearly stable, one can make responsible attempts to be as precise as possible: "I am just going to take it for granted / that the tree is in the backyard" (39). Ammons tells us after he makes this assumption that "it's necessary to be quiet in the hands of the marvelous," hitting the right note of humor and wonder at the same time. His everyday attempt to understand his elm tree has to acknowledge its limits—he will assume the perspectival view that the tree is in his backyard rather than attempting to achieve an absurdly over-precise "scientific" demarcation of it—even as it shows us how we build lives (and poems) out of such judgments every day. Because much *is* stable in our world, we don't have to achieve the precision that scientific instruments make available to us, at least not most of the time. We can provisionally accept the fact that the tree is in the backyard and move on with our judgments of it. This bit of everydayness in the poem works at several levels, moving along the process of the poem and elaborating it in a variety of interesting ways, even if it is only a tree in Ammons's backyard.

Every time one moves toward the loose speech in the poem, one is pulled back toward the powerful understanding of the mechanisms that drive the world and the poem to an ever-richer understanding of the dynamics of life. If Ammons begins by stating his goal of seeking the fundamental mechanisms of the universe, he ends by making equally large claims for poetry itself. He declares his sense of poetic value toward the end of his "essay" by quoting from two scientific treatises that speak to the intricacy and fragility of life, and then he asserts that

> poems are verbal
> symbols for these organizations: they imprint upon the mind
> examples of integration in which the energy flows with maximum

effect and economy between the high levels of oneness and the
numerous subordinations and divisions of diversity: it is simply
good to have the mind exposed to and reflected by such examples:

it firms the mind, organizes its energy, and lets the controlled
flows occur: that is simple good in itself: I can't stress that
enough: it is not good for something else—although of course

it is good for infinite things else. . . .

(SLP, 49, 50)

This is a precise and compelling delineation of the nature of poetry
that avoids all the lapses and sloppinesses of our contemporary
views of what the art is all about. Instead of being an expression
of something subjective or personal—though obviously poems can
be based on these elements as well—the poem is a symbolic mani-
festation of the intricate processes of the most complex organiza-
tions in the world. Regardless of thematic content or emotional
orientation, poems manage to provide "examples of integration in
which the energy flows with maximum // effect between the high
levels of oneness and the / numerous subordinations and divisions
of diversity." To the extent that poetry accomplishes this task, it
manages to express the fundamental process of the universe: the
flow through a grid of integration that reflects the order of an orga-
nization of materials. Poems evoke and exemplify this grid of inte-
gration through their form and pattern and manifest the flow by
the movement of the words through the grid: stop on any word
and language gives way. A poem needs to keep moving precisely
because it is movement through an organized system that makes
it what it is and that allows it to be part of the energy flows of the
universe. It is a specific modulation of the energy of existence,
whose integration allows us to attend to the complex relations of
the organizations through which our lives are played out.

If Ammons's poetry is intrinsically playful, that is because it
reflects the basic play of the universe, the modulation of specific
energies through particular forms of order that allow pattern and
relation to display themselves with as much intricacy as the local
organization can support. Thus, the more intricate the poetic
structure, the better able it is to provide a richer flow of materials
through its integrating mechanisms. The manyness it brings to at-
tentive order better reflects the oneness of which it is finally a
part. This playful flow of energies within fields is that which most
distinguishes Ammons's poetry from his contemporaries. His
awareness of these fields of play makes his work even more strik-

ing. Ammons declares the significance of poetry while he manages to demonstrate the manner in which the flows of the universe are essentially aesthetic in nature. Poetry is so important for us because it reveals the constant flow of energy through pattern that constitutes the nature of our lives.

Ammons can make such large claims for poetry because the "mechanisms physical, physiological, epistemological, electrical, / chemical, esthetic, social, religious" through which we comprehend existence are all based on the same flow between oneness and manyness that is the chief focus of all poetry, whether it knows it or not. As our own age has repeatedly emphasized, poetry works through "motion and artificiality (the impositional remove from reality)" (32), but for Ammons this artificiality doesn't lead to a cynical assertion of power dynamics within society. It may be true that "language heightens by dismissing reality" (32), but it does so in order to reflect another more fundamental reality: the playful flow of energy through an integrated grid. That is as real as things get, even if poetry achieves its manifestation of that flow by dismissing reality in its specific words. Poetry both "has a hold on reality and suppresses / it" in order to provide us with the sense of flow within pattern, of modulating rhythms through which the mechanisms of the universe make themselves apparent to us. This is why poems cannot "violate the bit, event, percept, / fact—the concrete" (32) on the basis of which they display themselves, for such a violation creates "the separation that means / the death of language." Instead of employing the artificiality of language and poetry to demonstrate his own social power over the word, Ammons uses it to show the forces to which any serious poet must submit: the inevitable and totally real modulation of energy through which all that lives presents itself in the world, regardless of whether the organization is chemical, religious, physiological, or any of the other specific forms of organization we have developed to measure the flows of the universe.

It is worth emphasizing the key word in Ammons's assertion about the examples of integration poetry provides: he says they *imprint* these examples on the mind, an idea that suggests our need for a process whereby the repetition of information and structure gradually allows us to achieve a coherent sense of the patterns through which our lives are ordered. We first move into the pattern because it is comfortable to us, and then through repeated imprintings we become aware of its effects and their uses in our lives. The rhythms that are imprinted on us through the poem exist extrinsic of the social world, but the social world—through the life of the poem—provides us with a means through which to achieve an understanding of the rhythms on the basis of which we make sense of life, bring pleasure to it, and provide some meaning for it, both individually and culturally. The poem brings us to self-awareness about these processes—a crucial and relatively recent step in the course of human history—by revealing the pattern of pattern, by imprinting on us the fact that the various modulations of energy in the universe are all reflections of the movement from manyness to oneness and back again, the rhythm of the saints, the place in our lives where much is "nearly stable" precisely because these patterns are intrinsic to the universe and not merely arbitrary impositions of a social order onto an unruly world that resists such intrusions.

Practical man that he is, Ammons doesn't stop with his description of what poetry does. He shows us its pragmatic effects as well when he tells us that "it is simply / good to have the mind exposed to and reflected by such examples." It is both a simple matter and a good one because the imprinting that poems provide "firms the mind, organizes its energy, and lets the controlled / flows occur." One can look far and wide for a clearer depiction of what poetry does: it disciplines the mind by organizing its energies and need do nothing more. It allows the controlled flows of our minds to occur in well-ordered ways even as it lets us know that pattern and rhythm are the essence of knowledge rather than something imposed on it. As humans, we are constituted through the controlled flows of our minds and of the life around us, but without a discipline through which to manage these flows, they—and we—are less capable of modulating the processes of the universe. Poetry is thus the discipline of disciplines: its entire point is to firm the mind in order to allow the controlled flows to occur. Other disciplines—social, religious, scientific—are based on the same processes, but they are not in themselves necessarily devoted to enhancing our ability to modulate the rhythms of life. At their best they do so, but more or less unconsciously. Part of the firming of the mind that poetry provides is based on the fact that it shows us what it is doing. It both disciplines our energies and calls attention to the rhythms out of which life itself is constituted, flowing back and forth within its grid in order to exemplify and express the patterning of existence as a whole.

Ammons tells us that in the beginning there was rhythm and pattern: the world is first and foremost an aesthetic place. Poetry doesn't impose an aesthetic grid on life in order to make it more appealing to us. It draws the aesthetic patterns of life out for us so that we may observe them more clearly. In a world divided up by rational, linear, analytic tools, pattern seems to disappear altogether. The knowledge that we are pattern-making and pattern-discerning creatures is lost in the reduction of understanding to information. Only an aesthetic mode of knowledge can call attention to the fact that the specific "bits" we discern in the world are by themselves nothing at all. Only the relation of those bits in a pattern, in a dynamic flow, gives them any meaning. Ammons's poetic universe is a relational one from the ground up. There are no isolated bits here even if it is also true that "every point in spacetimematter's // a center" (33). For Ammons there is "nothing but centers: centers of galaxies, systems, planets, asteroids, / moons, drifts, atoms, electrons" (33) and so on for every organization that we are capable of delineating. But this doesn't mean that these centers are autonomous bits extrinsic of the processes around them. On the contrary: each of the centers takes on meaning in relation to the other bits in the midst of which it finds itself. The flows of the universe are modulated through specific densities or centers that organize the universe's energy, but the energy that flows through the specific densities—regardless of whether we are talking about atoms, human beings, or poems—doesn't "belong" to the specific density. It is part of the flow of life that coalesces for a period of time around and through the discipline or order that integrates it, again regardless of whether one thinks of atoms, human beings, or poems. This is the simple process on the basis of which Ammons builds his understanding of the world and the place of poetry within it.

That poetry is a discipline through which the energies of our mind are organized in richer, more complex ways is in some respects not as striking as it first appears. People have often thought that poems bring a discipline to the mind in one way or another, and Ammons's statement doesn't stand out for that reason. It is striking because of the perfect fit it impresses on the matter: it doesn't make poetry into an arbitrary subjection of reality to an artificial discipline that is designed to remove us from reality, nor does it turn poetry into the "objective" expression of the principles of the universe. Patterns are always implicated in the world—and we are always implicated in them—in such a way that our knowledge of them can never be arrived at objectively. Pattern only produces itself through a flow that modulates the energies in the first place, and the rhythm is always contingent on the specific flow of which it is a part. Poetry needs the "bits" of life to give reality to its flow, for as pure abstraction pattern has no effects whatso-

ever. Only by bringing us to the concrete bits of everyday exis-
tence, only by allowing pattern to assert itself through them, can
the poem evolve a rhythm that is adequate to its means.

Ammons is quite specific about what he is up to and how it
differs from our ordinary ideas of the poetic act: "the way I think
is / I think what I see: the designs are there: I use // words to draw
them out" (32). The poet doesn't make things up as he goes along
any more than he allows his subjectivity to run wild. He thinks
what he sees, notices designs in the world of which he is a part
and uses words "to draw them out" so that they are available to
us as well. In this way writing poetry is as much a "firming" process
as reading it is. Poetry works only to the degree that it manages
to allow the controlled flows of life to occur, only to the extent
that it draws out the patterns that are intrinsic to the rhythms of
language and of life as a whole.

Ammons has thus taken a twentieth-century insight—poetry
makes nothing happen—and reinforced it, while providing it with
a more important series of links. It is true, Ammons tells us, that
poetry makes nothing happen. It works by firming the mind, by
organizing its energies, by allowing the controlled flows to modu-
late themselves in ways that are consonant with our understanding
of the world. That is all poetry is designed to do and all it needs
to do. Ammons insists that "that is simple good in itself: I can't
stress that / enough: it is not good for something else." There is no
need to turn to "extrinsic" activities to find a purpose for poetry. It
is good—both aesthetically and ethically—for poems to accom-
plish these tasks, and they suffice in and of themselves. *Of course*
poetry makes nothing happen: it is a happening itself, and a self-
aware happening at that. But Ammons also undercuts the neutrality
of "Poetry makes nothing happen" by arguing that the rhythms of
a poem involve the good in life as well: we become better people
through our increased understanding of the patterns of life. Am-
mons's ethic is implicit rather than explicit, assuming that the more
we know about the modulation of energy in the world—and our
own specific manifestations of it—the better able we are to make
fitting use of those energies through which our lives unfold.

Ammons also asserts that poems are "good for infinite things
else." We take our understanding of the controlled flows of a poem
and apply it to the situations in our life, again more often than not
without specifically thinking about the transfer between poetry and
life. One might suggest that the poetic firming of the mind gives us
greater insight into the controlled flows of existence, which in turn
allows us to express those flows in accord with the dynamic of

which they are a part. Poetry doesn't exist in its own discrete space without any contact with the other forms of organization in the world. It both expresses those forms and leads back to them. It thus retains its non-instrumental character, even as it has as many instrumental applications as humans can imagine for it.

Having come this far into Ammons's sense of poetic mission, we need to remark on his belief that he should have such a mission. We live at a time when poets are highly circumspect in their assertions of the importance of their work, yet Ammons insists that poetry reveals the most fundamental processes of the universe and provides us with the most profound wisdom we shall ever possess. How is he able to hold on to such beliefs in our highly skeptical age? What allows him to sustain himself on such a basis without succumbing to the onslaughts of doubt that must beset any writer in a time not hospitable to writing? I would argue that it is precisely his noncentered orientation toward life and writing that allows Ammons to have such confidence. Any poet who can say "I get lost for fun, / because there's no chance of getting lost" realizes that patterns will assert their presence regardless of his desire for them and knows that they have little to do with any self-interested quest for the nature of things. Ammons draws the designs out because that is what humans are constituted to do. As a poet, he simply does this better than most and is also able to call attention to what he is doing. Knowing that the patterns exist extrinsic of his desire for them allows Ammons to recognize how closely linked all patterns are, how relational the universe is from ground up. Thus, there is no reason to be afraid to make assertions based on the patterns one has been able to draw out of one's experiences in the world.

Likewise, any poet who can declare that "much is nearly stable there" is a writer whose convictions derive from an aesthetic sense of the world. The easiest poetic strategy is either to assert that one has noted the stabilities in the world or to admit that no stability exists. Traditionally, we label these the objective and subjective viewpoints. Ammons realizes that he is working out of neither perspective but is instead relying on an aesthetic awareness of the world that recognizes the stability of pattern: it is *nearly* stable because patterns change in accord with the flows that are modulated through them, but it is still relatively stable inasmuch as patterns remain consistent and notable for long periods of time. The easier road in our day is to insist that all patterns are arbitrary designs we impose on the world. But Ammons knows that poets have always devoted their attention to delineating the nearly stable patterns through which life constitutes itself. That awareness allows him the kind of conviction that is not possible from a subjective stance and provides him with the confidence to reassert the centrality of poetry for the development of our understanding of the world and for the coherent organization of our minds and our attitudes about the nature of things.

At the same time, it is worth noting that Ammons grounds his work in the playful dynamic of the world, even as he mixes it with the more typical kind of playfulness in order to distance himself from the emotional affects of the patterns he discerns. The humor of the poem, the acute self-awareness that regularly bends the poem back on itself, and the almost eager willingness to undercut the most profound moments of the work deliberately undercut the emotional intensity of the poem and suggest an unwillingness to follow through in the affective domain with the consequences of the playful mode. I am not arguing that Ammons needs to eliminate humor or avoid wordplay that undercuts the buildup of emotional intensity in the poem, for these can be essential elements of the work as much as anything else can be. As Ammons declares:

> one thing
> always to keep in mind is that there are a number of possibilities:
>
> whatever sways forward implies a backward sway and the mind must
> either go all the way around and come back or it must be prepared
> to fall back and deal with the lost sway. . . .
>
> (SLP, 43)

The essential sway of the poem requires the poet to circle back, sometimes with a new awareness, sometimes with an ironic attitude toward where he has been, sometimes with the declaration that he has followed a particular strand of the pattern as far as it can go.

There are indeed a number of possibilities, and the playful dynamic of the poem has more than enough room for humor, for word play, for the undercutting effects of a poet who wants to remain firmly linked to the everyday world's grittier language:

> I believe in fun:
>
> "superior amusement" is a little shitty: fun is nice: it's what
> our society is built on: fun in the enterprise: I believe in it:
> I have no faith in the scoffers: they are party poopers who are

afraid they ought to believe in history or logical positivism and
don't have any real desire to do so: they are scarcely worth a
haircut: organisms, I can tell you, build up under the thrust to

joy and nothing else can lift them out of the miry
circumstance. . . .

(SLP, 47)

Having fun here, Ammons delights in employing words like "shitty"
and "party poopers"; they allow him to embrace a wider range of
language, and he is happy for the opportunity to do so. And there
is surely no reason why "Essay on Poetics" or any other poem
can't be devoted to fun. But "fun" is a word that undermines its
own playful heritage: however much fun depends on playfulness,
playfulness is much larger than fun. It sways from the littlest jokes
about "party poopers" to the most profound assertions of pattern
of which humans are capable.

It may be true that our society is built on "fun in the enterprise,"
just as it may also be true that "fun is nice," but what does "fun
is nice" mean? It signifies only a kind of deliberately limited en-
gagement with the playful energies of the poem as a whole. The
poem itself is not "nice." It wears no happy face when it confronts
the world. It may have funny bits in it, disarming humor that helps
the poet cover his shyness, and rhetorical strategies that allow him
to swerve away from the emotional engagements the poem leads
him to even as he regularly resists them, but it certainly is not *just*
a tool for fun. It is a playful mechanism that has the lightness of
humor in it, but it also moves regularly through its rhythms toward
the fundamental patterns of the world. Ammons is well aware of
this, informing us that "organisms . . . build up under the thrust
to / joy and nothing else can lift them out of the miry circum-
stance." "Essay on Poetics" too builds up under the thrust to joy,
but every time it approaches it, it quickly moves away, embar-
rassed by its own powers. Likewise, every time the drift moves
the poem toward the ambient sorrow of our lives, it swerves off
on an another excursion into pattern itself.

Although it is not poetically necessary for Ammons to clip the
affective range of his poem every time it approaches joy or sorrow,
he seems inclined to do exactly that. It is as though joy and sorrow
are too *personal* to be expressed in a poem devoted to a lucid *non-
personal* display of poetic energies. This is why the poem goes out
of its way to include the pieces of everyday life—talk of Christmas
presents and playing with son John, remarks about walks out for
food in the high snows—but always manages to strip these links

to Ammons's life of any emotional connection. There is no power
in these sections because Ammons refuses to give us access to the
affective links that should naturally evolve in the poem. He sways
away from them, uses the mechanism of the poem to distance
himself from that which he inevitably moves toward. He too builds
up under the thrust to joy (and sorrow), and uses that thrust to
energize his poem. In the end, though, he pulls back, leaving the
dynamic without the emotional intensity that should also be a part
of it.

Even if Ammons deliberately limits the emotional range of "Es-
say on Poetics," he provides us with the means through which to
embrace those intensities in our own lives. The evocation of the
one:many mechanism lays bare the patterning processes of the
world that engage all elements of our being. The poem thus encour-
ages us to lift ourselves out of the miry circumstance of life, to
thrust toward our own kinds of joy, both through the poem and
through an understanding and deployment of the mechanism that
allows us to move into the patterns through which our lives unfold.
It also prompts us to recognize and accept that the "magical humor
floats / upon the ambient sorrow." The play of the poem insists
that poetry isn't an escape from sorrow but a means to allow the
magical ambience of life to float on top of the sorrow that is also
an inevitable, daily part of our existence. The relationship between
the magical humor and ambient sorrow of our lives is presented
to us with stark honesty throughout the poem.

We are told that "poems are arresting in two ways: they attract
attention with / glistery astonishment and they hold it: stasis: they
gather and / stay" (44). "Essay on Poetics" certainly lives up to
that formula, regularly providing the "glistery astonishment" of
recognition as Ammons repeatedly brings us to the point where
we see the centrality of the one:many mechanism to all the pro-
cesses of our lives. The repetition of the pattern, the circling
around that brings us back again and again to the one:many inter-
play in the poem and life, helps both to "gather and / stay." One
time around the circuit and we might forget the dynamic of which
we are a part. The repetitions help convince us of the probity of
the patterns we discern, allow us to develop confidence in their
ability to make sense of our lives, provide us with the means to
acknowledge the fundamentally poetic nature of existence. No
other poet of our time manages to develop this playful reach with
such power. No other writer understands so well that the poetic
mission today is the same as it was in ancient times: to seek out
and evoke the playful rhythms through which the universe is con-

stituted, to declare the centrality of those rhythms to our own lives, and to encourage us to embrace the patterns through which the ambient sorrow and the thrust to joy produce the richness and diversity of everything that lives.

NOTES

1. A. R. Ammons, *Selected Longer Poems* (New York: Norton, 1980), 34. Subsequent quotations are from this edition and will be noted parenthetically with page numbers in the text.
2. *Webster's New Collegiate Dictionary* (Springfield, MA: Merriam, 1975), 713.
3. Ibid.

"How Does One Come Home": A. R. Ammons's *Tape for the Turn of the Year*

WILLIAM HARMON

A. R. Ammons, who was born in 1926 in Columbus County, North Carolina, reached an early summit of his career when his big *Collected Poems: 1951–1971* was lauded with admiration and prizes, including the 1973 National Book Award for poetry. One work, however, which had been published in 1965, was presumably too long to be included in the *Collected Poems:* the omission of *Tape for the Turn of the Year,* however understandable, could have unjustly drawn attention away from a unique poem that has remained one of Ammons's finest and most distinctive achievements. I judge that the *Tape,* the earliest of his many long poems and still one of the very best among them, belongs among the select company of large poems genuinely American and genuinely great.

A good deal of Ammons's triumph in the *Tape* is a function of his choice of limits: how to start and stop; how much parochial matter to include, and how much ecumenical; how to use a local language in ways that can admit universal subjects without surrendering a personal voice; how to maintain epic pace and scope without sacrificing attention to minute detail. The format—among the silliest-seeming of limits—at first appears to be merely a gimmick, like Jack Kerouac's widely advertised use of rolls of teletype paper to facilitate the unbroken delivery of spontaneous prose. And Ammons virtually confesses as much:

> it was natural for
> me (in the House &
>   Garden store one
> night a couple weeks
> ago) to contemplate
>   this roll of
> adding-machine tape, so
> narrow, long,
> unbroken, and to penetrate

300

                into some
                fool use for it: I
                thought of the poem
                then,
                but not seriously:[1]

In time, the reader can calculate that the night in question, a
fortnight or so before 6 December 1963, would fall very close to
the day—was perhaps the very day (22 November 1963)—of the
assassination of President Kennedy, an occasion nowhere distinctly
visible in Ammons's poem but, all the same, necessary and un-
avoidable in its extrinsic context of loss and sorrow:

                            now,
                two weeks
                have gone by, and
                    the Muse hasn't
                rejected it,
                seems caught up in the
                    serious novelty:
                                            (T, 3)

In the later book-length poem *Sphere: The Form of a Motion*,
Ammons suggests the general circumstances of the selection of
such a tape to help stave off confusion:

  when anxiety rises words too start to stir rising into schools,

  moving into sayings (a recourse, though delusional) like winds
  making up before a mild May-evening thunderstorm, the winds
  spilling across the trees, then like surf sucking back in a

  growing tug: at such times, I pick up a tape, stick the end
  into my typewriter, and give everything a course, mostly
  because in a storm course is crucial and in proportion to the

  storm must be fought for, insisted on.
                                            (S, 52)

    The tape, evidently about a hundred feet long and three inches
wide, becomes the first home of a poem in thirty-three parts in the
form of a journal running from 6 December 1963 (a Friday) through
10 January 1964 (another Friday),[2] with entries of various lengths
(between 27 and 474 lines, all short) for every day except 24, 25,
and 29 December (that is, Christmas Eve, Christmas, and the fol-

lowing Sunday). The prevailing analogues are a serial-cyclical form like that of *In Memoriam* (a "sad mechanic exercise"[3] to spend time mourning the premature death of an heroic figure) and the general contour of the *Odyssey* (the paradigmatic poem of homecoming):

> my story is how
> a man comes home
> from haunted
> lands and transformations:
>
> (T, 9)

Let me qualify my ascription of a memorial purpose to Ammons's *Tape* by repeating that the specific event and occasion are nowhere explicit. True, the White House is mentioned (T, 28), and certain passages are meditatively elegiac (e.g., T, 153 and 179); but nothing in this long poem strikes quite the same note of collective sorrow as Ammons's modest "Belief: *for JFK*," written at about the same time as the *Tape* and first published in 1964:

> drums gather and humble us beyond escape,
> propound the single, falling fact:
> time, suspended between memory and present,
> hangs unmeasured, empty
>
> . . . .
> if we could break free
> and run this knowledge out,
> burst this energy of grief
> through a hundred countrysides!
> if bleak through the black night
> we could outrun
> this knowledge into a different morning!
>
> (CP, 180–81)

We cannot adequately locate the *Tape* in history without realizing the terror of the public setting, even though the "single, falling fact" itself is never propounded outright. No poem written at that time could ignore the assassination, and any poem that seems to do so must be deploying a deliberate strategy of sublimation, reluctance, compensation, or denial. Ammons copes by controlling his immediate local and temporal materials, connected to a single voice and person, gathered around a hollow core of shock—the gift of emptiness that the poet, at the end of the *Tape*, says he has delivered to the sympathy of the reader:[4]

> I've given
> you my
> emptiness: it may
> not be unlike
>   your emptiness:
> in voyages, there
> are wide reaches
> of water
> with no islands:

(T, 204)

No authentic modern odyssey can follow the tidy rhumb line or great-circle routes of past journeys.[5] In the final extension of relativism, you certainly cannot go home again; but the uncertain journey, where motion and mutation are necessary, becomes itself a new home. Ammons, who served aboard a U.S. Navy warship during World War II, would be familiar with a vehicle that is also a home. Many Americans could sing today, "Be it ever so mobile. . . ."

As it happens, Ammons's ostensibly random journey repeats in some detail the pattern of earlier homecomings, even to the degree of including, mutatis mutandis, a trip to the Underworld. For Gilgamesh, Odysseus, and Aeneas, such excursions provide honor to the dead and prophecy for the quick. In Ammons's re-enactment, as in Leopold Bloom's parallel experience in *Ulysses,* the outright ritual, which takes the form of attending a memorial service for William Carlos Williams (who had died in March 1963), marks the low point of the journey. Here, in the twenty-second entry (30 December), a dead poet is remembered and the virtual terminus of the dying year is observed with a pessimism that recalls the evacuated landscape of Hardy's "The Darkling Thrush." The service is placed in a setting of loss and descent, with a bus ride akin to dying and a big city akin to Hell:

> the dump swarms with
> gulls & smoke:
>
> yesterday I gave
> to the memory of
>
> William Carlos Williams
>
>   (reception in NY
> for Mrs. Williams)

```
        sat in the back of
        the bus up
     & the motor ground my
     head to dust (gray,
            graphitic)
        & a man fell
     in a fit
     in the bus station: three
     men held him till
     he jerked still:
        a crowd circled &
        watched:

     (we're monkeys, scratching,
     our heads
     & asses &
     dumb with joy & tragedy)

        so many people
     with bodies only:
```
                                             (T, 129)

Home from this hell—recalling the surprise of Dante in Hell and
Eliot in hellish London that death had undone "so many"—the
poet relaxes ("how good to be back"—T, 130) and, with nowhere
to go but up, makes room for certain pleasures that promise what-
ever it is that serves as salvation and safety in a floating world.
With a clarity of vision and voice, as though with faculties purified
by the experience of an infernal region, the poet-celebrant attends
to a comfortable amalgamation of the domestic and the sacred:

```
        I hear the
        porkchops frying!
        ah,
     there's the sweet, burnt
     smell!
        sounds in the kitchen,
        pots lifted
        with empty
     hushing ring,
     the plunger of the icebox
        door
        snapping loose: the
        sizzling roil of
        porkchops turned:
        protest, response:
```

                    flashes of aluminum
            light
                    as the pots work, the
                    glint of tines
                        as the table
                        dresses: the
                        holy
                        slow
                        lifting & turning
            in the spinach pot:
            rituals, hungers,

                        motions over
                        fire,
                        the stance &
                        tending:

                                    (T, 132–33)

Suspended astonishingly between these brilliant images of the
preparation of the dinner (smells, sounds, sights) and the actual
realization and consumption of the food (tastes, textures, the kines-
thetic pleasure of being on "the outside edge of / painfully full"),
comes a unique passage that stays in my memory as the still point
of the turning poem. At 6:08 p.m., Monday, 30 December 1963,
the poet hears the voice of his wife, Phyllis:

                    .   "You
                        can
                        come
                        sit
                        down
                        now
                        if
                        you
                        want
                        to."

                                    (T, 133)

She speaks nowhere else in the poem; almost nobody, in fact,
speaks in the poem, unless you count the poet himself and various
reports of short conversations rendered in indirect discourse. And
nowhere else in the poem is a sentence period used. But here,
in an extraordinary column of ten ordinary monosyllables wholly
faithful to the American idiom (and probably transcribed verbatim)
and yet deftly articulated by rhythmic and harmonic linkages, the

lost poet, fresh from the multiple horrors of hell and death-in-life, hears the welcome words inviting him to share the multiple joys of sharing a meal with his wife. "You can come sit down now if you want to": we all have heard it. But not until Ammons has fixed it on his tape, delicately centered, shrewdly prepared, have any of us been put quite so close to the radiant comforts of our own immediate routines and our own daily speech.

The ground bass of the vertical array is the reverberation of monosyllables, each spaced as though to have democratically equal weight; as the ear hears them, the syllables gather in tentative patterns, loosely trochaic. On closer inspection, the words display an uncommonly high degree of coherence, stability, and acoustic symmetry. The "down" and "now" at the middle of the line share consonant as well as vowel sounds. Branching from this center, the halves of the line seem to be subtle, complex reflections of each other. "Down" and "now" we have looked at; "sit" and "if" share a vowel; "come" and "you" are more faintly linked than "can" and "want," but are linked nevertheless; and the two outer syllables, "you" and "to," rhyme perfectly.

In the succeeding entry—31 December—Ammons looks ahead:

> after this,
> this long poem, I hope I
> can do short rich hard
> lyrics: lines
> that can incubate
> slowly
> then fall into
> symmetrical tangles:
> lines that can be
> gone over (and over)
> till they sing with
> pre-established rightness:

(T, 143)

Ammons's best short poems satisfy these requirements perfectly—none better, I think, than "Small Song":

> The reeds give
> way to the
>
> wind and give
> the wind away

(CP, 222)

In "Reflective"—

> I found a
> weed
> that had a
>
> mirror in it
> and that
> mirror
>
> looked in at
> a mirror
> in
>
> me that
> had a
> weed in it

(CP, 170)

—as in "Glass," "Mirrorment," and several other short poems, Ammons may recollect Heidegger's curious *ereignenden Spiegel-Spiel,* the "coming-to-pass interplay of mirrors" that constitutes our total world.[6]

Among the atomic and subatomic particles of language where Ammons loves to dwell, we find the commonest words—"You can come sit down now if you want to"—and those tricky monosyllables (*let, still, fast, quite*) that are so ordinary they often project antithetical meanings that mirror and reverse each other.) Having noted the vitreous aspect of some of Ammons's poetry, we can pause to note two of his poems that graphically demonstrate the reflective nature of poetry. In both, the medial gap allows the small words to move in two directions—call them priapic and ethical—that the bilateral symmetry suggests and (being yonic) displays:

Chasm

> Put   your
> self   out
> and   you're
> not   quite
> up   to
> it   or
> all   in

(CP, 229)

Cleavage

Soon   as
you   stop
having trouble
getting down
to   earth
you   start
having trouble
getting off
the   ground

(CP, 322)

But back to the *Tape.* Beyond the pole of what I have called the
still point of the turning poem, a good deal of tape—time and space
yet to be taken—remains. The homecoming motif recurs explicitly:

(if you were
sitting on a
distant strand,
longing for home,
you'd have to
conjure up things to
occupy the time,
too)

(T, 136)

and then gives way to a sustained meditation on the occasion of
the loss of home, the national catastrophe that may have effected
the *dépaysement* in the first place:

screens
between us & memories
we can't bear:
what unmentionables
of guilt & terror!
go back & see
terror as fantasy,
guilt as innocence?

but we've
purposely lost
the road back:

. . . .
let's accept this
provided & open

>   possibility & go
>   ahead:
>   we may redeem ourselves:

                                        (T, 136–37)

Beyond this point, where a measure of reconciliation and repose is achieved, the pace of the poem slackens somewhat, although the presence of the remaining tape to be filled exerts a compulsion of its own. The twenty-third entry (31 December), one of the longest and most varied, ruminates:

>   last day of the year:
>   I've been at this
>   25 days—this
>   idle tendance
>   of typewriter & Muse—
>   nearly a month of Sundays:
>   I'll miss the
>   hovering over time,
>   the watchfulness—

>   . . . .
>   I anticipate: the
>   empty tape is still
>   imposing,
>   frightening:

                                        (T, 144–45)

On the first day of the new year, the pluralist poet settles into something like acceptance that even promises affirmation:

>   beside the terror-ridden
>   homeless man
>   wandering through
>   a universe of horror
>   dwells
>   the man at ease
>   in a universe
>   of light:

>   let's tend our
>   feelings &
>   leave the Lord
>   His problems
>   (if any): He
>   got us this far on His own:
>   & millions have come

                        & gone in joy
                        (predominantly):

                                                    (T, 155)

   The first word of the *Tape*, "today," works as the musical tonic
of the whole poem, which is almost all in the key of "today minor";
of the twenty-three December entries, ten begin outright with "to-
day" and four others strike that note very near the beginning. Of
the ten January entries, "today" is the first word of eight and the
second word of yet another. In this long coda, then, the tonic is
asserted most strongly as the note toward which the homecoming
must aim. The poet attends to the weather of the day and, from
that center, launches casual excursions into ethics and aesthetics.
The parenthetical "if any" and "predominantly" in the passage just
quoted leave a margin for exploration and questions:

                        what of the evil man?
                        is he evil because he
                        realized himself
                        or because he didn't?

                                                    (T, 158)

                        see the roads I've
                        traveled
                        to come to you:
                        monsters I've engaged:

                        have I earned the grace
                            of your touch?

                                                    (T, 159–60)

   Even Odysseus knew, from Tiresias's prophecy, that his return
was impermanent; in any event, however, Penelope would remain
the true wife and, in Ammons's variation, the moving center that
generates the complex series of shifting peripheries:

                        a man's center is his
                        woman,
                        the dark, warm hole
                            to which he brings
                        his meaning . . .
                        you been lookin for a
                        center to the universe?
                        's it:

                                                    (T, 188)

But, despite the confidence of that colloquial, monosyllabic affirmation of the certain center, a radiating circumference of salient questions still remains:

> reader, we've been thru
> a lot together:
>> who are you?
>> where will you go
> now?

(T, 200)

> how do the hopeless
> get some fun out of
> life?

(T, 201)

> have our minds taken us too
> far, out of nature, out of
> complete acceptance?

(T, 202)

And, in a passage very near the end of the tape, the means of homecoming are pondered in phrases stated (though not punctuated) as a question:

> coming home:
>> how does one come
>> home:
>
>> self-acceptance
>> reconciliation,
> a way of
> going along with this
> world as it is:

(T, 203)

Yet another question toward the end of the poem seems to be in a different key:

> what
> must I do
> to reach
> the top?

(T, 183)

The ordinary journey of return follows the trace of a horizontal homing, and that dimension dominates Ammons's poem; but there is also a vertical impulse, as though upward to the top of the ziggurat of the literary life with its own temptresses, whirlpools, and gigantic one-eyed monsters. In a peculiar way, one goal of this movement is Ithaca: not Odysseus's island kingdom but the town in New York, where, in fact, Ammons was to go in September 1964 to teach at Cornell. The horizontal homing is foolish in a most serious way; the ambition to climb the poetic-academic mountain, spoken honestly by an honestly idiosyncratic poet, reaches beyond earnest folly into burlesque. The first adumbration of the politics of avarice is straight enough:

> I know you,
> man:
>   am grateful to the
> order, however imperfect,
> that restrains you,
>   fierce, avaricious: the
> Top: Olympus,
> the White House, the Register:
>
>   (T, 28)

But, before a page is turned, Odysseus is analyzed and the spirit of Avarice animates two further incarnations, one vulgar and one most tender:

> Odysseus screwed a lot but
> never got screwed: or
> if he did, he screwed back
>   harder, first
>   chance he got: he never
>
> "took nothing lying down":
>
>   (T, 29)

Whereupon the Odyssean poet regards himself in Homeric singing robes:

> my song's now
> long enough to screw a
> right good-sized article
> with:
> flexible to vault me
> to the Top:

> I hope it will lift me into
> your affections:
> that's what I need:
> the top I've chosen,
> the mt I wd climb:

(T, 29)

Through six thousand or so line-feed and carriage-return opera-
tions, the progress of the tape represents a homecoming in one
dimension and a mountain-climbing in another.

In yet a third dimension, the poem moves toward its own lan-
guage, a mother tongue clearly analogous to a mother country.
"Language," says Heidegger, "is the house of being"; and Gary
Snyder says, "My language is home."[7] Any such house or home
can come to mean the place you start from and also the unaccount-
able origin to which you try to return. The search for a lost or
missing language has preoccupied American poets from the begin-
ning, and none has found a thoroughly accommodating idiom with-
out some sacrifice. The vernacular may exclude certain necessary
ranges of dignity, but the high style may preclude certain necessary
ranges of practical detail.

Not too far along the midway of his circus, the modest Ammons,
having just called his growing tape "accomplished florescence,"
favors his own spacious idiom:

> empty places
> make room
> for
> silence to
> gather:
> high-falutin
> language does not
> rest on the
> cold water
> all night
> by
> the luminous
> birches:

(T, 131)

> poetry has
> one subject, impermanence,
> which it presents
> with as much permanence as
> possible:

. . . .
    only the lively use of
        language lives:
        can live
        on dead words
          & falsehood: the
    truths poetry creates
        die with
        their language:
          stir any old
    language up,
    feel the fire in it &
    its truths come true
        again:
        the resource, the
    creation, and the end of
        poetry is
        language:

. . . .
poetry is art & is
    artificial: but it
realizes reality's
potentials:

                    (T, 145, 176–77)

"I've been looking," he says , "for a level of language—

    that could take in all
        kinds of matter
    & move easily with
        light or heavy burden:

                    (T, 144)

The reader who has been confronted with unambiguous examples of such a level of language should not really need assurance of this sort, but few poets seem willing to forfeit the occasion for putting in their two cents' worth. Ammons assembles a series of examples of the most assured use of the widest range of American idioms, and throughout the poem he adds asides to justify his practices:

    I've hated at times the
self-conscious POEM:
    I've wanted to bend
    more, burrowing
with flexible path
into the common life

& commonplace:

. . . .
poetry has no use, except
the entertaining play:
   passion is
   vulgar when not swept up
into the cool control
of syllables:

. . . .
unity & diversity: how
to have both: must:
   it's Coleridge's
   definition of a poem:

                            (T, 144, 178–79, 185)

(Unexpectedly, with a reference to *Biographia Literaria*, Ammons here may be echoing the end of Philip Larkin's "Toads," first published in 1955:

   I don't say, one bodies the other
     One's spiritual truth;
   But I do say it's hard to lose either,
     When you have both.)[8]

Mundane aesthetic meditations do serve one good purpose in the *Tape*. They furnish a range of territory somewhat in the middle distance, a "mesocosm," so to speak, between the terminal extremes of epic macrocosm and lyric microcosm. In Ammons, these poles are as far apart as in any poet since Tennyson. We have come to assume that the traditional cosmological dimension of epic is no longer available to poets because of the great and specialized complexity natural science, which has moved, in education and in daily life, to a zone far removed from the arts. Ammons, however, at one time or another a major in "pre-med, biology, chemistry, general science," a bachelor of science from Wake Forest College, and a regular reader of *Scientific American,* [9] can manage the hard words and long numbers with a graceful authority unmatched by any contemporary, with the possible exception of the late George Starbuck. The details of the immediate day—weather, meals, stray memories—would shrivel into unredeemable triviality without a macrocosmic perspective, just as the general cosmology would vaporize into unredeemable gaseousness without the mundane, pedestrian, diurnal detail:

10,000 yrs

>Troy
>burned since then:
>but the earth's been
>"resting"—entering
>a warm
>cycle: the Sumerians
>had not, that long ago,
>compiled
>their
>holy bundle of
>the elements of civil-
>   ization, nor
>had one city-state stolen
>it from another:

(T, 6–7)[10]

>the 200–inch glass
>shows a
>billion-billion galaxies:
>what is God
>   to this grain of sand:

(T, 201)

Toward the end of the *Tape,* in the thirty-first and thirty-second entries (8 and 9 January), the poem, momentarily threatened with a flattening of imagination, takes two surprising turns that introduce further dimensions of experience and language. Having committed himself, early on, to work on the "crusty / hard-clear surface" (T, 6), the poet stays away from things deep and dark; even his own childhood memories deal with sensations of surfaces, ordinarily cold and austere. Against the "black night" of "Belief: *for JFK,*" the poet early in the *Tape* proposes a morning that is not a mourning:

>may this song be plain as
>day, exact and bright!
>no moonlight to loosen
>   shrubs into
>shapes that
>never were: no dark
>   nights to dissolve
>   woods into one black
>   depthless dimension:
>may this song leave

> darkness alone, deal
> with what
> light can win into clarity:
>
> (T, 4)

But, as the poem nears its completion, the determination to avoid the dark depths is weakened:

> deep down inside are
> fireworks
> & a whole mess of rivers:
>
> (T, 186)

And what follows is a large vista, recalling panoramic symbolic paintings by Bosch or Chagall, of human figures acting out a range of activities and attitudes: solicitude, anger, song, lechery, suffering, squabbling, disappointment, love; but, after a sketch of the "very interesting / country," the poet stops:

> I'm afraid to visit:
>   wd take another tape to
> get there:
>
> (T, 187)[11]

And, returning to affairs of his own place and moment, he tells about a visit to a refuge for wild birds. Here, with images of Canada geese slipping and skidding on a melting edge of a lake, the poet's language similarly begins to slip and slide:

> two bald iggles
>   been sighted out
>   there:
>   tell me:
>   can you beat that?
>   I looked for any but
> couldn't find some:
>
> (T,188–89)

The thirty-second entry (9 January), which follows immediately after this passage of lexical dissolution, presents the images of a rainy day in Katzenjammerese:

> today ben
>   der clouds
> downwashen

        die rainingdroppes
        und
    tickleticklen
    der puddlepoolens

                                        (T, 189)

In this penultimate entry of the *Tape,* the orbits of idiom and refer-
ence both reach their greatest scope. At the beginning and end,
English dissolves into a mud-luscious effigy of language, as though
the poet were digging into the very bottom of his old bin of verbal
resources. At the same time, between these Germanic boundaries,
he seems to lift his idiom to its most sublime height. In virtually
the only episode in the poem that qualifies as mysterious, the poet
addresses a familiar compound Other whose characteristics de-
mand a range of imagery that calls up, all at once, the elemental
universes of Buddhism, Christianity, and pre-Socratic atomism:

        the tenderspoken
        assurer: the gentle
            enlightener &,
        till enlightened,
            protector: arrive:
            say you're
            going on a journey
        & need one to teach:
        teach me,
        father:
            behold one whose
            fears
            are the harnessed
            mares of his going!
        fiery delights,
            pounding hoof
            & crystal eye:
            where before
            dread
            & plug-mule
                plodded:
        clod:
        mere earth:

        . . . .
        unto a clod, how unlike:
        dance!
            throw in:
            throw yourself
                into the river

of going:
where the banks also flow:

(T,190–91)

Since universal flux works here both as subject and context, it is
a good place to comment briefly on the colon, which is the pre-
dominant punctuation of the *Tape*. There is only one sentence pe-
riod in the whole work, at the end of the speech of Wisdom-
Penelope-Phyllis that I have called the still point of the turning
poem; even the last word of the poem is followed by a colon.
Earlier, I had judged that Archibald MacLeish, overusing the colon
for one monotonous didactic effect—sanctimonious inconclu-
siveness—had made it into a gimmick and worn it out. Ammons,
however, has given new life to the colon. It is not just a question
of preference (Ammons has said, "I like the action of the colon)"[12];
the suggestion of flowing seems necessary in long works. Pound's
Canto I—beginning "And" and ending "So that:"—foreshadows
C. S. Lewis's argument in favor of the style of *Paradise Lost:*
"Continuity is an essential of the epic style. If the mere printed
page is to affect us like the voice of a bard chanting in a hall, then
the chant must *go on* . . . . We must not be allowed to settle down
at the end of each sentence." Lewis then persuasively demon-
strates how "Milton avoids discontinuity by avoidance of what
grammarians call the simple sentence."[13] In Ammons's case, a cer-
tain readjustment is necessary, but it need not be radical or large.
His diminished epic avoids discontinuity by avoiding what gram-
marians call the period.

In the final entry (the thirty-third, 10 January), with the end of
the tape of the *Tape* in sight, the Odyssean poet achieves a sat-
isfying—if not final and terminal—consummation of his complex
voyage. The model homecoming finds accomplishment in an eco-
nomical summary of the odyssey, a bright salute to the world, and
a courteous *nunc dimittis:*

          old castles, carnivals,
          ditchbanks,
               bridges, ponds,
                    steel mills,
                    cities: so many
          interesting tours:

          the roll has lifted
          from the floor &
          our journey is done:

thank you
for coming: thank
you for coming along:

the sun's bright:
the wind rocks the
    naked trees:
    so long:

(T,205)

"So Long!"—a lovely, enigmatic expression that gives the title
to the valedictory poem of *Leaves of Grass*—adds Ammons to the
roll of American poets who have attempted the highest flights.
Whitman used *So long!* as a striking refrain, novel but durable. "A
salutation of departure, greatly used among sailors, sports, and
prostitutes," runs the definition Whitman gave William Sloane
Kennedy. "The sense of it is 'Til we meet again,'—conveying an
inference that somehow they will doubtless so meet, sooner or
later."[14] In his own poem, Whitman could be describing Ammons's
enterprise. "Enough O deed impromptu and secret," he says;
"Enough O gliding present—enough O summ'd-up past. . . ."
Compared with Ammons's conclusion, Whitman's sounds
melodramatic:

Remember my words, I may again return,
I love you, I depart from materials,
I am as one disembodied, triumphant, dead.

But we have room for both poets. One, in 1860, found affectionate
words for his blessing on the reader. The other, as 1963 turned into
1964, found, by a miracle of fortune and genius, the unrepeatable
conjunction of occasion and voice to add another grand long poem
to the national treasury.

NOTES

1. *Tape for the Turn of the Year* (Ithaca: Cornell University Press, 1965), 2–3;
hereafter cited in the text as T.
2. Nothing internal specifies the years, but the dustjacket gives 1963–1964. In
the poem, 13 December is a Friday, as was the case in 1963. Richard Howard is
wrong in locating the setting as December–January 1964–1965. Misconstruing the
date, Howard then mistakes the prevailing attitudes: "Mooning around the house
and waiting for *Expressions of Sea Level* to come of the press in December of
1964, the poet produced, in a two-month period, and with a determination to
reach an end that became more than obsessive, became self-destructive, 'a long

thin poem' written on a huge roll of adding-machine tape run through the typewriter to its conclusion. . . ." *Alone with America: Essays on the Art of Poetry in the United States Since 1950* (New York: Athenaeum, 1971), 9. A similar dismissal marks Helen Vendler's complaint about the "merely fussy" in Ammons's work: "There is a fair amount of this sort of thing, especially in the rather willed long poem *Tape for the Turn of the Year* (you buy a roll of adding-machine tape and type on it for a couple of weeks until the tape is all typed and then you have finished your poem)." "New Books in Review," *Yale Review,* 62 (1972–1973), 421. Even Harold Bloom, one of Ammons's earliest and most vocal champions, concludes that the *Tape* is "a heroic failure that is Ammons's most original and surprising invention"; faint praise could hardly be so damning. *The Ringers in the Tower: Studies in Romantic Tradition* (Chicago: University of Chicago Press, 1971), 280.

3. *In Memoriam,* V. "A use in measured language lies," Tennyson says in this stanza. The edges of the tape serve Ammons as just such a measure. Ammons discusses margins and indentations in "The Limit," *Collected Poems: 1951–1971* (New York: Norton, 1972), 266–67; hereafter cited in the text as CP.

4. Such breakdowns occur in Hopkins's "The Wreck of the Deutschland" (stanza 28), Pound's *Cantos* (particularly LXXIV), Williams's *Paterson* (Book III), and Eliot's "East Coker."

5. Pound's Canto LXXIV suggests the progress of the modern *commedia:* "By no means an orderly Dantescan rising / but as the winds veer."

6. See Thomas Langan, *The Meaning of Heidegger: A Critical Study of an Existentialist Phenomenology* (New York: Columbia University Press, 1959), 121. This kind of mirrorment is clearly related to the Lacanian emphasis on the *stade du miroir* in human development.

7. See Langan, *Heidegger,* 108–12, and Gary Snyder, *Regarding Wave* (New York: New Directions, 1970), 42.

8. Philip Larkin, *Collected Poems,* ed. Anthony Thwaie (London: Marvell, 1988), 90.

9. See autobiographical statement, *Diacritics* 3 (Winter 1973), 2; and CP, 314–17.

10. Typically and consistently the sophisticated primitivist, Ammons works on peripheries, surfaces, margins, edges, beaches, and origins. In the eighth entry (13 December, T, 56) the poet buys the complete plays of Aristophanes. Subsequently, Ammons refers to The Thesmophoriazusae (T, 57) and The Ecclesiazusae (T, 90). But, while these references are witty and incidental, Ammons's preoccupation with Sumer—perhaps the oldest civilization of which we know—is steadfast. "The holy / bundle of elements" appears in "Discoverer" (CP, 137); later, "Essay on Poetics" includes the passage, "the holy bundle of / the elements of civilization, the Sumerians said" (CP, 300). Man of Ammons's earliest poems refer to Sumer, and *Sphere: The Form of a Motion* mentions the Sumerian divinity Enlil (S, 71). In time, Ammons was to entitle a volume *Sumerian Vistas.* Among the me's, the scores of elements of Sumerian civilization, of which about sixty have survived in myths, we find the usual institutions (godship, kingship, lordship, crafts) and some not so usual: sexual intercourse and prostitution, descent into the nether world and ascent from it, fear and outcry, weariness, and the troubled heart. See S. N. Kramer, *Sumerian Mythology* (New York: Harper, 1961), 66.

11. In time, Ammons wrote two other long poems—*Garbage* and *Glare*—on rolls of tape, but they were wider than that used for the original *Tape.* The illustrations accompanying a magazine article published in 1996 show Ammons's old

typewriter with a tape fed into it, and the text mentions that Ammons is at work on a tape. Jon Gertner, "A Walk with A. R. Ammons," *Audubon* 98, no. 5: 74–82; illustrations by James McMullan.

12. In conversation, July 1973.

13. C. S. Lewis, *A Preface to Paradise Lost* (1942; reprinted New York: Oxford University Press, 1961), 45. Cf. Coleridge: "The reader should be carried forward, not merely or chiefly by the mechanical impulse of curiosity, or by a restless desire to arrive at the final solution; but by the pleasurable activity of mind excited by the attractions of the journey itself. Like the motion of a serpent, which the Egyptians made the emblem of intellectual power; or like the path of sound through the air; at every step he pauses and half recedes, and from the retrogressive movement collects the force which again carries him onward." *Biographia Literaria,* ch. XIV.

14. See *Leaves of Grass,* ed. Harold W. Blodgett and Sculley Bradley (New York: Norton, 1965), 503–6.

Part IV
From the Wind to the Earth: An
Interview with A. R. Ammons

From The Wind to the Earth: An Interview with A.R. Ammons

STEVEN P. SCHNEIDER

Schneider: What gives *Garbage* its jazzy improvisational feeling?

Ammons: It was entirely improvisational. It was not premeditated nor was it ever revised. It is exactly the way it was written the first time, except for perhaps a word revision here or there. As you will see when you see the tape, it is the way it was written just spontaneously on sitting down at the typewriter. I wasn't thinking of publication; I rarely think of an audience when I'm working. School had ended in the spring of 1989, and I usually have some trouble with not having a structure. It's often at times like that that I write something, actually for my own engagement and entertainment.

Schneider: How long did it take you to write *Garbage?*

Ammons: It was over a period of two or three months. I wrote entirely without thinking I was writing a book and completely unaware of an audience. I think it came in eighteen parts, or something like that. It was actually just eighteen strips of paper, some of them one foot long, some of them three feet long, whatever. And then I would just tear a strip off and put it there and then that was the book. Nothing else was ever done.

Schneider: Is there movement in *Garbage* between an underlying theme and improvisational variations, as there often is in jazz?

Ammons: I had this basic image of the garbage mound, which looked like a ziggurat for me and became the controlling symbol. With that anchor as the central concern in the first part of the poem, presenting it in the first part of the poem and watching it go away in the rest, you couldn't get lost so you feel free. You just keep on writing because the poem has centered.

Schneider: When did you first see that mound of garbage?

Ammons: A couple of years prior to writing the poem.

Schneider: How did you settle on the unrhymed couplets in *Garbage?*

Ammons: The poem just began that way. There is one place where I have three lines. I must have just decided to do that. I've done long poems in three lines and four lines, and maybe I just decided I would try two lines. It turned out to be a very limber way to do it. If you have a stanza of four lines, and you later revise and take something out, you have to find exactly the same length of thing to put back in, which is a great trouble. Somehow this felt more open and limber to me.

Schneider: In the poem you suggest that the mound of garbage is the "sacred image of our time." I'm reminded of an earlier lyric "The City Limits," where you talk of the "radiance" that does not withhold itself from anything, even what can be found in the city dump. What is the source of this vision for you, of seeing the sacred in the lowly, in the profane?

Ammons: When forms have used themselves up, and by that I mean people or language or any other kind of construct, and it's worn out and jaded and thrown away . . . On the planet nothing is dumped off, so it has to be regenerated and transfigured and to become the new thing. It seems to me that this is among the greatest concerns of sacred literature—the transfiguration from death and decay and degeneration into the spirit or the new world or the coming back of things as in the vegetation myth. There is this passage through the lowest before there is another cycle that could possibly attain the highest. This seems to me one of the most frequently contemplated subjects in mythology and religion.

Schneider: I know that in American poetry this was a preoccupation of Whitman's. You also find a good deal of discussion of regeneration in wisdom texts of the East.

Ammons: There's also a kind of deep satisfaction in having the lowliest meet the highest, rather than separate things in the world into categories such as the secular and the sacred, the pure and the bad. And to realize that there is an interpenetration in all these things and a use and discovery of energy that can take the worst and transform it.

Schneider: Is the source of this vision for you personal experience or immersion in those myths and texts you have encountered? Is it something you have cultivated over a lifetime?

Ammons: Yes, of course. But seeing that garbage heap, which was very high and impressive, and then connecting it very quickly with sacred images—Mayan temples, ziggurats of Sumeria, and pyramids of Egypt, as being centralizing images for whole cultures—brought together for me the sacred and the profane.

Schneider: It turns out to be a wonderful image because garbage is one of the central problems of our time.

Ammons: Sure. It's usually in trying to deal with the problems of one's time that one creates the sacred images.

Schneider: I'm thinking that perhaps that's one reason for its popular appeal. Somehow in that poem you struck a popular chord.

Ammons: I did. I'm surprised. It struck me, that's why I guess it strikes others. I had it in mind for a couple of years and in fact a year earlier I had sat down and tried to start the poem but somehow it didn't go and so I just put it aside. I must have thought about it for a year without knowing it, just meditating on it. But the second time when I sat down it seemed to get going.

Schneider: Were you surprised by the success of the poem?

Ammons: Absolutely. Totally taken by surprise. I had not even proofread it, so among the "Garbage" there are several typos, missing words and things.

Schneider: But those must have eventually gotten cleaned up.

Ammons: No they didn't. They're in the poem. I didn't proofread it. I thought it would be interesting to have some clutter of that kind. That wasn't the reason I didn't proofread it. I didn't reread it because I just couldn't face reading it again. You can be so afraid that something isn't good that you can't stand to find out one way or the other.

Schneider: Let me ask you about the material on which you compose some of your long poems—these rolls of tape. Why? Why not just sit down at the typewriter and write on standard typewriter paper?

Ammons: I did write *Sphere* that way. But I had had a longstanding problem with this. You may notice that almost all my early poems are about thirty to thirty-five lines long. I was unable in those days to take the paper out of the typewriter and start again with a blank sheet and continue of course. So I wrote all the poems on one page.

Schneider: When you say "unable"?

Ammons: Nothing would happen. I just couldn't go on. So the poem naturally became one page long. I had this problem. How do you get beyond one page? Ten years later when I was living in South Jersey I saw a roll of adding machine tape on the shelf of a garden store and since I was already concerned about free verse and the possibility that a free verse poem could be considered as traveling down the page as much as across the page . . . I found that here was a tape that allowed you just to go on down, down, down the page without ever having to take it out or break your attention. So I just simply took it home and stuck one in the type-writer and typed to the other end.

Schneider: You had that insight while you were in the garden store?

Ammons: Yes. Of course, I had the problem for twenty years. I did learn how to go beyond one page later.

Schneider: In the 1950s and early 1960s you had the desire to write a longer poem but hadn't yet solved the problem.

Ammons: Yes. I finally did when I started to write a longer poem in 1959. I started a series of poems which I was going to call Cantos. Somehow these enabled me to write two to three page poems. Then I abandoned that project and gave those poems indi-vidual names. They became the poems in *Expressions of Sea Level,* so I had begun to solve the problem. *Tape* still offered me the opportunity to think of a poem as a kind of juggling in which the poem is up in the air and the two sides of it are being walled in and are having to ricochet off each other as it goes down. You have some important events on the left hand side of the line as well as on the right hand side, whereas for example in a heroic couplet it's a kind of heavy ending—right side where the rhyme is.

Schneider: The idea of writing on two sides of the page really shows up in *The Snow Poems.*

Ammons: But I mean the two ends of the line—not necessarily with two passages of poems as I have in *The Snow Poems.* You make as much use of each end of the line as you can—the front and the other end. The whole motion is down the page because that way you build up a tension between the horizontal movement of the line and its need to break and go down the page. It's a cross-reference. I think in the *Tape* it slows the motion down. It's like a recording . . . there are passages which you can just slow down to the point that it just barely moves and I just love that.

Schneider: How wide was the tape you composed *Tape for the Turn of the Year* on?

Ammons: About an inch and three-quarters. It's a very narrow one. The later ones are three inches.

Schneider: When you look back and compare the wider line length of the tape used to compose *Garbage* with that of *Tape,* what do you discover?

Ammons: It gives you a very different feel because the rhythm has to adjust to the line length. I complain about that in the section "Strip" of my newest long poem, *Glare,* about being confined. In fact, that is the only subject of the poem, how hellish it is to be writing these lines.

Schneider: But there must be some compensation.

Ammons: Oh yes, any kind of problems are our best procedures. Any kind of problem like that is great to work with. But as I told you, *Sphere* was done on regular sheets of paper. Little gimmicks and tricks like that roll of tape have always enabled me to get started. They just take the pretension out of writing.

Schneider: Is the material of the tape itself less daunting to work with than typewriter paper, and does it allow for a kind of spontaneity and openness that you find in those long poems?

Ammons: Very early on when we were in Berkeley in the early 1950s I never wrote on regular sheets of paper. My wife would bring home mimeographed paper that had been used on one side and I would use the other side.

Schneider: Even back then you were environmentally conscious?

Ammons: No. It just seemed like I wasn't doing anything important. I was just working on trash paper and it enabled me somehow to work. It's like in my drafts I almost always begin with a small letter.

Schneider: That's what you mean by a gimmick?

Ammons: To take the pretension out of it. I always found that very useful.

Schneider: One of the things that strikes me about *Garbage* is the way that it swings from the sublime to the mundane, from the high to the low, for instance, from the contemplation of the significance of the stars to a consideration of the cost of soybeans or an anecdote about the chipmunk and the tabby. Is this the curvature of your experience of being in the world?

Ammons: Of inclusiveness. Everything is all here. The chipmunk is here, the stars are here, and all these actions take place. They are part of the reality, and I like to include what's here. I have a poem in *Brink Road* entitled "Picking Up Equations." It's about when the wind storm comes through it breaks off stuff from trees: bark, bunches of limbs, and they land in accordance with how heavy they are and how hard the wind is blowing. But at some point there is an item that goes farther than any other. And so it's an arc including everything. I didn't know what that meant. But it means to me now that there are actions and views, political or otherwise, that have their own standing and so forth. But I am interested in the one that includes them all. I don't feel represented by one of the smaller actions, although I don't know why that's true, but I don't. I feel very great composure and satisfaction in thinking that I know what those lesser positions are, but that I also know the curve that includes everything.

Schneider: What is the source of this "inclusiveness" for you? I know Emerson and Whitman have been important to you, but it sounds like you have worked out this position for yourself.

Ammons: I have. One absorbs so many influences from so many places that you can't really identify. This is a version of the one: many problem which I had such a problem resolving for myself before I discovered that someone else, such as Plotinus, had already done this 2,500 years ago. But I didn't know that so I worked through it myself to the point where I could abandon it. *Sphere* finally realized that, concretized that whole problem—that we're on one earth which has a great many things of diverse action going on. The planet we live on is the reconciliation of the one: many problem.

Schneider: I remember your using the image of the earth itself, with its variegated surface and its common lode center.

Ammons: That's what the whole "sphere thing" refers to.

Schneider: This image suggests there has to be an equilibrium or balance between the one and the many.

Ammons: Which doesn't mean you depreciate the concrete particulars at all. They're all here, but also there's just one situation, which is the planet itself.

Schneider: Do you see your poetry as making correspondences between the dynamics of nature and the dynamics of perception?

Ammons: If my poetry can't appeal to that, I don't have any poetry. Most people are reading me as some kind of nature poet and they are not hearing the concerns. I'm talking now about the shorter poems. They don't analogize and allegorize in a way that I enjoy. So many people have bought into the myth of concretion now that the only way you can write is about a particular thing. I appreciate that very greatly. Without a particular world we don't have one at all. Concretion is a myth, however. Look into any so-called "solid object" and it breaks down into this, that and the other until finally there may be nothing going on there but motion or spirit or energy. There's nothing there.

Schneider: We live in a culture and a time which values materialism, the surface value of objects.

Ammons: But the spirit can blow right through it.

Schneider: That's where religion and twentieth-century physics sometimes meet.

Ammons: When I say "spirit," I mean something like twentieth-century physics. I mean energy and things like that.

Schneider: Finer levels of energy?

Ammons: By spirit, I mean motion.

Schneider: One of the issues that you are grappling with in *Garbage* is the meaning of growing older. What served as the catalyst for your concern with aging and death in this poem?

Ammons: It's hard to pick out anything in particular. Death is a concern for everyone and I think particularly for the very young, for people who are nineteen and twenty and twenty-five, because they haven't had their life and yet there is a possibility, even though there is a probability that they will have a long life, there is a possibility at all times that they could lose it through an accident. Then they would have lost the opportunity to have a life. When you get to be my age—I'm seventy years old—you've had a life. Nobody can take it away from you. Although you are approaching death, you have had your life and I suppose that the main thing is that as you get to be seventy years old you look back over that life that you do have to look back over and you see what's missing now, who has gone on, who is not here. You see the windings of the way that brought you where you are, and I think you try to make some kind of story out of that that will give the many many events some sort of salience, suggest a meaning or a value. This would be your own history of things which means it would be highly selective and personalized and would only represent your view of things. I guess everybody has the right to try to construct their life and themselves in that way.

Schneider: At one point in *Garbage* you say "I can't believe / I'm merely an old person / . . . many of whose / friends and associates have wended away to the / ground." Is that because you now have a greater awareness of time?

Ammons: Well, that, and the fact that you come into the world and it's all here. You don't know any world where there is someone missing. But as you get older you are constantly confronted with this difference between being alive in a limited time period and this vast expanse of nothingness that people disappear into, including yourself, never as far as I'm concerned to return. And so great meaning, in my opinion, then begins to apply to that person, who was here and now is not. And it remains something I cannot take in. I can't take that in . . . how we could be here concerned about what kind of clothes we are wearing, what color to paint the kitchen, and whether to get shoelaces for the kids today or tomorrow. Those concerns occupy our few years here, and then we were never here before and we will never be here again. It doesn't compute. I think that's why there are so many inventions about what becomes of us after we're dead. It's very hard to imagine that nothing happens. And yet I'm quite convinced that that's the situation, that the universe as far as I can see has no dynamic need for a batch of leftover souls.

Schneider: Your lyric "Clarity" has always been a touchstone for me. It's about a rock slide, which seems solid and stable yet it is undermined and in the process of forming a different configuration reveals new "knowledge." It's that flux and instability of experience which as a poet you strive for and are open to.

Ammons: Very good. That's what that poem means. I think it means some kind of twist or knot of energy that gets in us and we don't know what it is. But somehow if it can express itself and resolve itself then somehow you have all this new "terrain" to read in which you learn what that tension was, what that problem was.

Schneider: The longer poems present to you the opportunity to resolve a number of "knots." Is that your attraction to writing these longer poems?

Ammons: I think the attraction is having something to do. You need something to do. But at the same time you do that you do everything else that goes on in your mind and your feelings. That's what doing something is. You're a poet and you may know what I have experienced, which is sometimes your ear is not connected with the world and you just don't write anything. There seems to be nothing, absolutely anything to write. At other times the connection is constant. Everything is translating itself into words. Isn't that right?

Schneider: Yes it is.

Ammons: I prefer to live that way than the way where I'm disconnected. So I go in and I start something and then whether I'm at the typewriter or downtown, my ear is engaged. I'm listening, I'm looking, I'm alive. I'm thinking of word combinations and things like that. I may not remember them when I get back to the typewriter but I remember something similar, something else. And I would much rather live that way than the other way. It's a way of living.

Schneider: A way of being in the world . . .

Ammons: Exactly!

Schneider: . . . In which you feel more connected.

Ammons: More alive. Of course, in being alive you are concerned about certain things and that gets in there but you don't write the poem in order to *do* anything.

Schneider: I remember in one of the longer poems you talked about it allowing you to work things out.

Ammons: To be involved. To jump in and start going with it.

Schneider: It's interesting to see the pattern, over the course of your career, of long poems often following on the heels of a collection of shorter lyrics. What might this pattern indicate?

Ammons: I think it must indicate in me an inability to live anywhere except in an extreme. You live in one extreme and then the only way to correct that is to go to the other extreme. It may be something like that.

Schneider: It would also speak to a desire not to be constrained by any particular form.

Ammons: Not to be identified to any particular form as well. To be able to include all the arcs if possible.

Schneider: Let's talk about *Tape for the Turn of the Year*. Did you think when you wrote it that the long poem would become so important to you?

Ammons: I would have had no such contemplation. I just wrote it for the same reason I write now. I was between jobs then, just before coming to Cornell University. I had read here [in Ithaca, New York] in July 1963, and in about December 1963 I started this poem which I finished in January 1964. Then I came to Cornell in the fall of 1964. So this tape was written in South Jersey. I think part of the reason I got a job here was that David Ray, who was teaching at Cornell at the time, asked to see a copy of the poem, and I sent it to him in manuscript. He wrote me back a very nice letter saying it was "an interesting sort of electrocardiogram." I was pleased by that. I did have a point with the poem. I wanted it to be possible to have an arbitrary beginning where the tape begins and an arbitrary end of the tape which would at the same time, however, be organic. That is to say, if you begin with me as the person who has to fill up this tape and take this trip then it would be similar to a hero in a novel who begins something and then gets into deeper and deeper complications as one feels trying to fill up a tape that long. Either you come out of it or you don't. If you do come out, getting to the end was the reason for taking the trip. When you get to the end, you have completed the organic structure. So many critics have asked, "how can you just end the poem where the end of the tape is." If the enterprise was to reach the end of the tape, then that's how I can do it. What it was filled up with from beginning to end was less important at that point than the formal concerns for me. Anything that you would put in there to promote the journey would be like life . . . sometimes you're in a hell of a mess and you have to keep going anyhow, and then you have a good stretch. There's a lot of stuff in there that I didn't think of at that time and don't now think very much of as poetry.

But it filled up the space it had to fill and every now and then it had these sort of lyrical resolutions which would slow down to just the most beautiful pause and silence. Then it would pick up and go on with something else. Lots of interesting things in it happened for me without my being able to regard it as anything special as a poem.

Schneider: Critics have commented on the innovativeness of the form. At the time there wasn't anything quite like it.

Ammons: But they never seemed to have gotten that it could be like a novel, with a beginning, a middle, and an end.

Schneider: You mention the notion of a journey. Is this the Ulysses theme you are referring to, the sense of coming home?

Ammons: Yes. I think so.

Schneider: But what is home then? Is it a journey back to North Carolina? That seems too literal.

Ammons: It's an emotional or spiritual condition that you might reach. It's a reconciliation or resolution of some kind.

Schneider: One of the benefits of the tape on which you composed and the long poem as a form is that you have the amplitude and the space to work through a wide range of motions and counter-motions within yourself.

Ammons: Yes. Those things happen without being finalized in any way. The most common metaphor is that life is a journey. *Tape* then becomes a mini-life.

Schneider: Were you reading any of the modernists' longer poems, such as Williams's *Paterson* or Pound's *Cantos* prior to your composing *Tape for the Turn of the Year?*

Ammons: I had been familiar with the *Cantos* since Berkeley in 1950. The draft of 30 Cantos was an astonishment to me, and I was very interested in it. I have never cared that much about the content of William Carlos Williams's own writing, although I have borrowed so much from him in terms of form. I never could get through *Paterson* to tell you the truth. He used to tell it to me when I would visit him.

Schneider: In *Tape* you describe going to New York.

Ammons: Yes, that was a visit after his funeral when Mrs. Williams was given a reception in New York. But I had been up to see him three or four times at the insistence of Josephine Miles. I had taken him for drives in the country because he couldn't drive then. He would take me to all these places that are described in *Paterson* and show me the Falls and tell me all the stories that were already in *Paterson,* for example, about the boy jumping in the waterfalls. He would hold on to my arm and walk right up to the edge of the Falls and look down.

Schneider: In Dana Gioia's book *Can Poetry Matter,* he has a chapter on the long poem entitled "The Dilemma of the Long Poem." He writes there that "it is not surprising that one finds no incontestable masterpieces among the major long poems of this century but only a group of more or less interesting failures." He includes Pound's *Cantos,* Williams's *Paterson,* and Berryman's *Dream Songs.* Do you agree with him?

Ammons: I don't think so. But I agree in a sense with what he said that they are all failures. However, there is a sense in which a "failure" is not a failure. The very symbol of the twentieth century is more nearly included by Pound's *Cantos* than anything else I know of. Fragmentation. Multiplicity. Insanity. And everything else of this century is pretty well represented there, along with some undesirable things one wishes were not true. Speaking formally, I think it's a very very interesting "failure."

Schneider: What do you mean by "failures" that are not always failures?

Ammons: In a nearly similar sense that an unfinished symphony gains interest sometimes because it is not finished. It's wonderful the way the *Cantos* peter off into fragments. What represents the twentieth century any better than that? Would a flawlessly put together beautiful thing do it for us? A century of such vast torment, warfare, misery, genocide as this century. We've lived in perhaps the most barbaric one that was ever invented. Who the hell needs a "success" in such circumstances?

Schneider: One of the devices that you use in *Tape for the Turn of the Year* is the daily journal entry.

Ammons: Yes. The reason that it starts with "today" is that was what the poem was going to be called at one time. I thought it was going to be called *Today* because it was going to be the surface of things as they occur—from day to day to day. Later on I changed the name of the poem to *Tape for the Turn of the Year.*

Schneider: Much of the poem is the recording of those surface observations.

Ammons: That is what it is all the way through, yes.

Schneider: That seems to be a very journalistic impulse, presenting the news of today.

Ammons: Emerson said something that has affected me more deeply than anything he ever said. That was some casual remark, I think in the "Nature" essay: "Let me record from day to day my honest thought without prospect or retrospect. . . . I have no doubt it will be found to have been symmetrical." Your honest thought today may be one thing and it may be different tomorrow. He says you have to be honest day to day. Put down exactly what you think even though it contradicts something and without regard to the future or the past, but just today. And then, that will cause possibly to emerge from the depth of your mind or your experience, this alignment which is symmetrical and harmonious and you learn from that something that you could never have gotten to head on.

Schneider: This notion of recording the walks, recording the weather, your daily observations . . .

Ammons: That's right, you are just getting into it.

Schneider: That's an Emersonian orientation, day to day.

Ammons: From that something may emerge.

Schneider: In a sense that was the psychology behind *Tape for the Turn of the Year.*

Ammons: I think so. I think in most of my long poems it has been. That was the key around which anything else would have to develop—the surface from day to day.

Schneider: I remember your talking about your poem "Cascadilla Falls" in terms of this journalistic impulse. You go out, observe, and see what happens and begin recording it and that takes you to someplace, often times a discovery.

Ammons: The walk is a symbol for that, too, in which you just begin to walk but you don't know what you will encounter or how you will return. What's important are the incidentals.

Schneider: The impressions of the walk itself. This sounds similar to the "pop psychology" which espoused "Be Here Now."

Ammons: Yes. That's okay. I like pop psychology, also other kinds.

Schneider: The profound source for this attentiveness to daily experience can be found in Lao-Tsu, who, of course, Emerson read.

Ammons: And so did I.

Schneider: When did you read Lao-Tsu?

Ammons: I read him after I read Emerson. He leads you himself to his Oriental sources. He tells you about them, and I followed.

Schneider: Do those continue to be important to you?

Ammons: Absolutely, very much so.

Schneider: The *Tao Te Ching.* And what other texts?

Ammons: That's the center for me—Lao-Tsu.

Schneider: Is your interest in flow in part a consequence of reading the *Tao Te Ching?*

Ammons: Yes. But I think what is at stake in Lao-Tsu is a difference between wholeness and silence and the fragmentariness of thought and speech. I've always been interested in that.

Schneider: Let's switch topics for a moment. What is it about geology that you find particularly interesting?

Ammons: It must be the compression of so much history into something that lasts so long like a rock. You have a piece of granite that is a hundred million years old and it's somewhat daunting.

Schneider: You write in *Tape:*" How strange / we are here, / raw, new, how ephemeral our/ lives and cultures, / how unrelated / to the honing out of / caves and canyons." One of the feelings that I've always gotten from passages like this is that you are trying to contrast the relatively short time period of human history with natural history.

Ammons: It throws into perspective the ephemerality of our days.

Schneider: I argue in my book about your work [*A.R. Ammons and the Poetics of Widening Scope*] that this is the intention of your poetry—to widen our scope.

Ammons: Yes you do. Yes.

Schneider: Often, we have a kind of a tunnel vision and get very caught up in our narrow concerns. Is geology a way of breaking down that?

Ammons: Well, I think it certainly has that result.

Schneider: How about the plate tectonic theory, which explains that when there are shifts in the earth's surface there is both creation and destruction, simultaneously? You mentioned that this is an analogy for your sense of process in these long poems. Can you elaborate on that just a little bit?

Ammons: You know that one of the most terrifying laws that we have is that for every action there is an equal and opposite reaction. This means that you can't just have something happen on the earth without something else having to give way or some compensation because there is nowhere for it to go. So, we never have these pure drives of any kind unless we set up artificial situations because on this planet for every action, there's an equal and opposite reaction. If you take a drug, you have side effects. If you move here, then something is displaced there.

Schneider: It's called karma.

Ammons: And in Emersonian terms it would be "economy." Every move is economically trained out into itself by these other forces and presences that are there.

Schneider: In terms of the composition of the poem, what is the connection that can be made?

Ammons: It would mean mostly that you would be kind of stupid to come up with any very pure train of thought or very pure movement of things, without at the same time, taking into account the downside or whatever else is present there. Otherwise, you would be simplistic and foolish.

Schneider: So, if you make a move towards . . .

Ammons: If you make a move, somebody else is going to lose one or some compensating action must take place.

Schneider: You strive to be cognizant of that within the poem itself.

Ammons: Without those opposing forces, you don't have the tension of a severe description of things governed by a total circumstance rather than just overriding something with some platitudinous declarations.

Schneider: That would account for the swings in emotion and the swings in subject matter . . .

Ammons: It could be—about piling the extremes into the middle, into a mixture in the middle.

Schneider: Isn't that easier to accomplish in a longer poem?

Ammons: I think there is more room for it usually. A long poem gives you a chance to amass.

Schneider: Kerouac had this theory of improvisational prose and talked about the undisturbed flow from the mind. Does that seem to be an apt description of the composition of *Tape for the Turn of the Year?*

Ammons: Well, you know, it's a rhetoric. Everything is a rhetoric. And as part of this rhetoric you pretend that you are creating a "spontaneous flow" that imitates the mind. Actually, it is nothing like what is going on in the mind. It is far from being the same thing as what is going on in the mind. But, it imitates what the mind would be like operating on a spontaneous basis.

Schneider: Are you suggesting there's some censorship or editorializing?

Ammons: All the time, and so much more is going on in flashes and images that you don't put into the poem. The stream of consciousness is a made thing just like a sonnet is.

Schneider: It's a construction.

Ammons: It's a construction. It's a construction. It is a rhetoric. It is a means of expression.

Schneider: It would be naive to think that *Tape* or any other of your long poems is a spontaneous flow?

Ammons: Of course. I would compose maybe two to three pages in a day, but you would think a million words in a day. So, obviously something selective has been filtered out and so on. But it can still be spontaneous, I think, in a sense that you're going about your daily work and something occurs to you and just unrolls itself. You put it in the poem. It's spontaneous. You didn't try to work at getting it and you don't revise it. It is just something to say comes to mind and you go put it down.

Schneider: How much did you revise *Tape?*

Ammons: Some, but very little of the parts that remain. Most of the revisions were cuts. I just cut out passages.

Schneider: So you took out passages, but what is there is not revised very much?

Ammons: Hardly at all.

Schneider: In the December 12th entry of *Tape for the Turn of the Year* you describe the physical mechanisms of the body and conclude:" if you have condemned the / body, you have / condemned a miraculous / residence—/ temple / we should try to keep / the right spirit in."

Ammons: I thought that was interesting. The temple is the body and is sort of preferred there to the spirit. We should try to make the spirit accommodate it, to be at least worthy of the temple it's in rather than what it is usually thought of the other way—the spirit is what is valuable and the body is just corruption.

Schneider: Part of the way that you worked toward that vision is through a very detailed biological description of physiological processes and the intricacy of the body's structure.

Ammons: Right. How marvelous it really is.

Schneider: As a structure?

Ammons: Yes.

Schneider: You write: "specialized tissues / bind us to the bones: an / outer cage / protects softer organs: / lovely / loose mesenteries—/ permitting digestion's / roil & change." What is the source of scientific discourse in your poems?

Ammons: It's just what I knew. I was just using the language of my own thinking, and I was interested in that. I was filled with a wonder at the attitude that some people would take toward the body and toward the spirit and feeling the way I thought about it was different from a lot of people.

Schneider: Do you mean from a Christian point of view that the body is depraved?

Ammons: Yes, that's what I mean. And I was trying to reverse that.

Schneider: So, you were working against that?

Ammons: Yes.

Schneider: To redeem the body?

Ammons: It is true that the body's only as good for as long as it can be. But, it sure is incredible while it's there. The more you know about the body, the more astonishing it becomes. To just have it dismissed by somebody as being a piece of corruption compared to some incorporeal, everlasting spirit always made me somewhat ill.

Schneider: Where did you learn your knowledge of the body? Did you take anatomy in college?

Ammons: I had taken comparative anatomy. In college we had studied a cat. I had walked around with a cat strung over my shoulder for weeks at a time. I knew every muscle, artery, and nerve in the cat's body. But, I was just generally interested in these matters. I think that where my poems differ from other peoples' is that I have just always been attracted to how things work. I was never very much at emotional evaluations of things or personal relationships, but I was fascinated by what made things work and how they did work.

Schneider: From an early age?

Ammons: Yes. As a kid I was fascinated by what made things work. I did all those things like trying to build little ponds with mud banks and sitting around fishing tiger fly larvae out of little holes, or watching ants make nests. Things like that.

Schneider: You were fascinated by this?

Ammons: Oh yes, total absorption.

Schneider: Which would explain your majoring in science?

Ammons: I wish I would have stuck with science. I would have been a terrific scientist, I suppose.

Schneider: Is your fascination in the weather also indicative of this interest in the way things work?

Ammons: Yes, because another interest I've had is not to be responsible for anything—feeling guilty and scared about being responsible for saying something about this, that, and the other. The weather is almost completely innocent territory. You could write about that forever and feel as if you're writing about nothing. That's been another prospect for me, writing about something that doesn't matter—if it's not taken seriously or if it's almost so far on the periphery it's like the weather. Actually, you know, the weather is an atmospheric equivalent of our moods and impressions of things. In writing about the weather, you just about hit the emotional tone of the time. There's storms, there are blank highs, there are troublesome lows, there's precipitation. If you look at the way human beings feel, it will analogize into states of the weather without any trouble. In fact, so much so that one wonders if we don't get our changes of mood somehow from that very source. You know how we complain when it gets gray, how we feel brighter when it's bright, scared when a storm is coming, afraid of high winds. Stuff like that. That's how I became interested in the weather as being a tonal thing that you can write about. It introduces as much subject matter as anything else, even though you're just talking about the weather. And nobody is going to come and get you on account of that, or shoot you up against the wall or something like that.

Schneider: Do you think that your interest in the weather extends from your upbringing on a farm where the weather is so important?

Ammons: Absolutely, it's so crucial. You live or die by the weather. But, also, it is always something there—something to write about. If you have nothing to write about, you can just look out the window and say it's 50 degrees today.

Schneider: And that kind of gets you going.

Ammons: Yes, it's going to get down to 32. *(laughing)*

Schneider: The Snow Poems are very much about the weather, aren't they?

Ammons: Exactly. That is what they are supposed to be altogether. It starts with the first snows in the fall and goes through to the end in the spring. The whole purpose there again was to write about nothing. I had originally meant to write a thousand pages in which I was going to show that you could go on inexhaustibly about nothing. I thought that by the time I got to page 300 and something that I had more than proved that, so I didn't do the thousand pages. I regret it now and wish I had gone ahead and just made a colossally unreadable book about nothing.

Schneider: There is something inside you that is very iconoclastic, that wants to tear down precious models.

Ammons: You can say that.

Schneider: By making a statement about nothing, in a sense, it's an iconoclastic gesture about those who invest so much importance in experience.

Ammons: It's something like that. I remember saying somewhere once that until the Parthenon goes, we don't have a chance.

Schneider: While we're on the topic of weather, I'm sure you've heard about the Butterfly Effect in chaos theory, that the flap of a butterfly's wings in Brazil sets off a tornado in Texas.

Ammons: I don't believe it. I think it's interesting to think about, but I don't believe it for a minute. There are too many opposing actions that neutralize a butterfly's wings within three minutes after he started for the air. Forty-five other things change it back.

Schneider: But the butterfly is a metaphor for disturbance, for the effects of perturbations in one part of the universe.

Ammons: But, I don't believe for a minute that it starts that way, do you?

Schneider: Well, I think it's an interesting theory.

Ammons: I do too. I've had people write to me saying that I had partly anticipated the theory. One person wrote to me that when she came across in "Corsons Inlet" the line "rule as the sum of rulelessness," that she had come to where she had wanted to be.

Schneider: Did she say that those lines are an anticipation of a concept in chaos theory?

Ammons: I was thinking the same thing, but I just don't believe that it really happens that easily, that the butterfly sets off the tornado in Texas.

Schneider: I connect that concept with what we were talking about earlier in terms of creation and destruction, that by making a move in one place, it has a ripple effect in another place.

Ammons: Yes, but it is not a ceaselessly augmentative effect.

Schneider: Maybe it's oversimplified.

Ammons: I do think it's a theory of a possibility that's imposed on a very complex set of circumstances and without any dependable straight lead from the beginning to the results. How would you ever account for the placidity of a day like today?

Schneider: Some would argue that it's a temporary pause in an ongoing process.

Ammons: The cause of it is so complex. Every leaf on every tree has something to do with the results: the wind, the absorption of sunlight, the amount of shade, the use of water that is lifted from the ground into the leaf, the amount of oxygen that is generated, the carbon dioxide that is used up. I just don't believe it, although I think that it is very interesting.

Schneider: What do you think of the parallels that some people have talked about between chaos theory and your own work?

Ammons: I think that it's true that there are.

Schneider: Mandelbrot said he is not so much interested in the directionality of a lightning bolt as he is in the zigs and zags. He suggests that it's the odd shapes in the world that carry meaning, that its pits and tangles are the keys to the essence of our existence. And, rather than seeing them as blemishes, he sees them as the keys to meaning. Isn't this very interesting insight echoed in *Sphere?*

Ammons: I think my work agrees completely with that concept as a whole.

Schneider: Let's talk about some of the ways it does agree. Let's talk about the form of *Sphere.* You say in section 138, "I'm sick of good poems, all those little rondures / splendidly brought off, painted gourds on a shelf."

Ammons: That really gets to it, doesn't it?

Schneider: Yes. Are you talking about the sonnet there? How does the long poem work against that?

Ammons: It would just dissolve such a small, little perfect configuration of things, painted and artificial, dead. The underground flow and process of the long poem would just float something like that along.

Schneider: The flow or motion is the dynamic joining of form and motion. In conjunction with this, a number of critics have talked about the colons in your work. In *Sphere* there are no end stops, which allows for a dynamic flow through the poem. Does that make sense to you?

Ammons: Yes, there's one sentence and one world!

Schneider: And the sphere itself is at the heart of the poem?

Ammons: It's the contour that resolves all the action. Everything happens on this circle, in this sphere.

Schneider: Which is the earth itself?

Ammons: Yes, I'm saying that our minds have identified, have grown into dynamics that are similar to the ones on earth itself. So then our minds, when we make allowance for one thing we make allowance for the other. We take into consideration say both sides of something, or if something that goes forward, something is displaced in front of it and will have to find another place to go.

Schneider: Is the parallel between human consciousness and the way the earth works what you are exploring throughout *Sphere?*

Ammons: Yes, absolutely.

Schneider: How does the motion of the poem lead the mind to the experience of "no-motion," to the experience of silence? You write in Section 67 of *Sphere,* "The purpose of the motion of a poem is to bring the focused, / awakened mind to no-motion, to a still contemplation of the / whole motion, all the motions, of the poem." In the next section you write, "To be lowered down the ladder of structured motions to the / refreshing energies of the deeper self." What's your sense of how a poem works to create that experience for a reader?

Ammons: I was at Mount Holly one time. I gave a reading with two other people and then we were asked to participate in a panel discussion and one of the professors in the audience says, "What is the single most necessary thing to a poem?" And, nobody said anything for a while, and then I said "reticence." He wondered why that was. I said, well, you have two things: you have the exposition of the poem and then its disposition. The exposition begins with movement and language, picking up images and rhythms and it winds its way until it stops. When it stops, it's no longer an exposition. It stops, but it has become a disposition. You can remember back now the way it came to be as if it were standing there like a piece of sculpture. Being composed itself and still— what used to be moving and full of sound. It now becomes still and silent. Now, at that point, as with a piece of sculpture, you can look at it from this side and see one journey of life going down the side. You go to other side and there's another way of looking at this sculpture. Go again and there's another way of looking at it. There's an infinite number of ways of looking at it and the poem achieves that same quality when its exposition is over and you now think of the whole poem. You are thinking of it as if it were a piece of sculpture. And it can be approached from any number of angles. So, that's what I mean by having achieved silence and disposition.

Schneider: This silence or disposition is the experience of the wholeness of the piece, not the different parts?

Ammons: That's right. Not when it's still talking, but when all the parts have talked their way into the thing, but now it's all present in an instance.

Schneider: Poetry in our culture is not valued very much, but we're desperately in need of this kind of experience.

Ammons: Absolutely. If people in this world, in this country, knew what they were missing in poetry, it would be astonishing 'cause there's just simply so many things going on in a poem that nobody suspects are there, and yet they are being represented and defined and opened up and shown. People don't even know how to look for it.

Schneider: Could that experience of silence be one of the things that many people are missing?

Ammons: Yes, and once you have it, it puts you in such a relation to the people that don't because you know it instantly and you hear all these wild people carrying on about this, that, and the other thing. All you want to do is weep or laugh because they are so out of it that they don't even know it. Poets are the ones who are supposed to be out of it, but believe me, this may not be the case. *(laughter)*

Schneider: I intended to ask you about your typewriter, your Underwood here. How long have you had it now?

Ammons: Well, I bought it in Berkeley in 1951 I think, and I had a standard upright before that, that had really worn out completely and I traded it in for this one. This one was, of course, a used typewriter, and I told you I had it welded up some. But, I've just simply typed on it ever since.

Schneider: Have you ever thought of getting rid of it and getting an electric typewriter?

Ammons: I have not really thought of that. An electric typewriter always worries me to death because the ribbon cah't be used again. You can't reuse the ribbon. It just wastes away.

Schneider: What about the computer?

Ammons: I don't like the computer because on medium length and short poems, I like to retype the whole thing if I change a word, then I like to retype the entire poem.

Schneider: Why's that?

Ammons: To see how it would look. Also, you don't need to have easy access to your poem. If you change a word, you need to reconsider the entire poem that this has become a part of. So, that is what I always did. Also, I notice that when you introduce a new word into a poem you sort of disturb every other word to some extent, so by going over it again, you sometimes see something else that should be changed because of the word you just introduced. You think maybe some significant revision could take place just in the process of retyping the poem. With a computer, you could change a word and walk off. So, I've retyped some of my poems many, many, many times. I thought it would be useful. What I like about a typewriter like that is the simplicity. You know if you have a computer, you have to turn the thing on, don't you, and it's on whether you are typing or not. Well, I don't like that.

Schneider: So, you don't like the noise and the vibration feeling and the radiation?

Ammons: Right.

Schneider: So this typewriter just sits there quietly?

Ammons: Absolutely never says anything. *(laughter)* You don't have to plug it in. I remember one time Richard Howard was here and he tried to write a letter on it. He just couldn't and gave up. My fingers are adjusted to those keys and I can do very well with it.

Schneider: The impulse to get back to our more natural origins is something consistent throughout the body of your work. You encourage a move beyond the confines of the city in both "Extremes and Moderations" and *Sphere.*

Ammons: As a country person I have always felt astonished by people in New York City living in all those glassy buildings with concrete and nothing else. The organic basis of life is missing there and human artifice has tried to replace everything, and it seems to me that a person who dwells in such a situation is bound to be crazy. I know that's not true, but it's just so far away from the natural origins of things.

Schneider: I'm wondering now at this point in your career if you still hold to those feelings about the country versus the city?

Ammons: I used to be so full of anxiety when I'd go to the city because there was so much going on that I couldn't wait to get out. But now I can go to the city and be perfectly calm and I enjoy it consequently much more. I've even considered getting an apartment and retiring somewhere to the city and to have that whole other side of life that I know nothing about. But, I discover on visiting the city for a few days, that unless you have something to do there, pretty soon there is nothing to do. You can go to the museums and things like that, but you need to be engaged in something. Otherwise, it can be just as boring as sitting up here some weekends in Ithaca.

Schneider: It seems to me that you've discovered much entertainment in the natural world. I mean literally that it is a show.

Ammons: It is a show all the time. You can walk outside and look up at the clouds and you think supposing a movie producer had to produce that, how much would it cost? Things like that. Or you've got a stream coming down and all this water. Where do you get the water? How would you put on this show?

Schneider: And your poetry is in a sense a record of the myriad displays of intelligence and creativity in the natural world.

Ammons: Some of them so small and insignificant, apparently insignificant, and yet inquired into they have their place.

Schneider: And, of course, if you were to move to the city that entertainment . . .

Ammons: Would be gone. You would have to be just focused on people and contemporary culture, I think, to get the most out of the city. But, I have always been kind of a dislocated observer and I don't see how it would do me very much good to spend a lot of time in the city. Now, I am energized by all that activity for awhile.

Schneider: When you say "dislocated observer," what do you mean?

Ammons: Just kind of wondering around in the peripheries of nothingness and not engaged in the big social business of the world.

Schneider: I want to ask you about the structure of *Sphere* and some of your other mid-career long poems. There are central metaphors that come to mind that critics have used and you yourself have used to describe them. In *Sphere,* for instance, you talk about the poem as a "mesh" which can widen to let everything breeze through. In "Extremes and Moderations" you talk about the "lattice work" which will let the world breeze through unobstructed.

Ammons: I think it's a network of metaphysical consideration that stands for the world, and whatever thought and motion can breeze through—these apprehensions and comprehensions.

Schneider: Both a mesh and a latticework have openings.

Ammons: It's a complex weaving of some kind that has openings. I mean you wouldn't want to build something like a glass tower that obstructs motion. Everything has to go around it. In nature, you have these configurations that are interwoven and yet permit, sometimes I suppose encourage, circulation.

Schneider: What is the source of your "ecological consciousness"?

Ammons: It started on the farm when I was a farmer. It was also developed through my reading of *Scientific American.* What you refer to as "ecological consciousness" began to appear in *Tape* and in earlier poems before the *Tape* there was a lot of stuff like that. I didn't come to Cornell until about half of *Collected Poems* had been composed.

Schneider: The poem "Fall Creek" on page 188 is the dividing point. It marks the first Ithaca poem.

Ammons: Yes. All the rest of the poems in *Collected Poems* that appear after that were written in Ithaca. It was just by accident that this dividing point came in the exact middle of the book. The poem "Kind," written prior to "Fall Creek," expresses an ecological interest in that it speaks up for the smaller things in creation. It's actually criticizing people who are more interested in these big displays like sequoias than they are in some tiny little blossom down by the roadside.

Schneider: It's stating that the very small and insignificant is as important in its own way.

Ammons: In fact, it is more important there because the sequoia can't produce the flower like the little plant can.

Schneider: In "Extremes of Moderations," you say at one point "This seems to me the last poem to the world." Were you feeling an acute sense of the possible destruction of the planet?

Ammons: I was thinking that we had probably passed the margins where the earth could be recognizable as the dynamics of the earth itself. We had introduced so many changes to it.

Schneider: Do you still feel similarly, or do you think we've gotten through that environmental crisis?

Ammons: No. I think we've gone into the artificial and there is no return. I really feel that the only hope we have now is to continue to try to educate ourselves from the natural processes that remain available to us so that we can duplicate these artificially and sustain ourselves wherever we are on Mars or outer space or wherever we go, that we just about have done in the earth. Not that the earth is damaged. If we would get off, it would recover itself beautifully in 25,000 years. All the streams would be pure. The air would be absolutely clean. You know you could drink water from any place out there all right, most anywhere. In other words, there is no reason to be worried about the planet. It can recover, but what we've done to it may cause us to eliminate ourselves. I'm not hysterical about that because we at this point understand so little about this total complex, that is the climate and the possibility of the earth. It would be foolish for us to say definitively. We might even be doing some good and not know it. We may be stalling off the next ice age by raising the temperature a half a degree. Who knows? We don't know. But it does seem to me that our interference now with the natural world has passed the line where you can say this is "natural." If you go to a lake up in the Adirondack Mountains and there is not a single fish in it, you know that that's not natural but that these smokestacks somewhere have killed the fish with the acid rain, and things of that nature. Also, when you look up at the sky, such a simple thing that you won't note it because you never saw the sky in any other way, but it used to be true when you looked up what you saw were clouds, and now what you used to have maybe thought was a mare's tail cloud is some vapor trail from a jet that has gone through. You see, you don't even get to look at the sky anymore.

Schneider: So you don't have much hope for reversing this trend?

Ammons: No, I don't think that you can go back at all. I think that the only way to go is forward.

Schneider: And to recreate in artificial terms?

Ammons: A natural world. We're doing it already. This prospect is being studied all over the world.

Schneider: If you look back at the group of your long poems over the last thirty-five years, which ones have been particularly significant in terms of your development. Do you have any favorites?

Ammons: I don't really like to say what my favorites are if it disposes somebody else to think that they ought to think similarly, because my experience is that often what I like differs from other people and often what I like is inferior to some other form because of some circumstance in the writing, like a child who is crippled more than one that is perfectly adequate to take care of themselves. I do recall having written "Hibernaculum" at a very important time to me, and I still like *Sphere* a whole lot, perhaps because it cost me so much in terms of effort to put it together. *Garbage* was just a complete surprise to me. I was just really writing for myself and maybe that's why I was able to open up in that in some ways that people say I had not before because I was not even thinking of poems. I was writing something that interested me and kept me going.

Schneider: What larger patterns or rhythms of nature do you see in your work?

Ammons: We were talking yesterday about how you go from day to day, but then later you may realize something that puts things together. It seems to me that there has been a tendency in my work that the chief presence in the early poems is the wind. Somewhere along the way it becomes water. Years of brooks and things like that. And then it becomes mineral or earth, and it seems to me that my own forms of anxiety, or hysteria, or whatever, have grown closer and closer to the ground through the years. First it was wind—very substanceless. The poems are far projected, highly assimilated, mythological, distanced, and in the wind. And then very gradually it comes closer and closer to where we are.

Schneider: Until finally it gets transfigured into garbage.

Ammons: And you're in the earth, right. It is really kind of an astonishing pilgrimage from the wind to the earth.

Chronology

Chronology of A. R. Ammons's Long Poems by date of publication in a book of his poetry. Please note that several of these long poems originally were published in journals, sometimes years prior to their appearance in a published volume of Ammons's poetry.

Tape for the Turn of the Year (1965)
Briefings: Poems Small and Easy (1971)*
"Summer Session," published in *Collected Poems 1951–1971* (1972)
"Essay on Poetics," published in *Collected Poems 1951–1971* (1972)
"Extremes and Moderations," published in *Collected Poems 1951–1971* (1972)
"Hibernaculum," published in *Collected Poems 1951–1971* (1972)
Sphere: The Form of A Motion (1974)
"Pray Without Ceasing" (composed in 1967, first published in *Hudson Review,* Autumn 1973), published in *Diversifications* (1975)
The Snow Poems (1977)
"The Ridge Farm," published in *Sumerian Vistas* (1987)
"Tombstones," published in *Sumerian Vistas* (1987)
Garbage (1993)
"Summer Place" (*Hudson Review,* Summer 1977), published in *Brink Road* (1996)
Glare (1997)

---

*Marjorie Perloff in her essay for this volume claims *Briefings* as a previously undiscovered long poem by A.R. Ammons, suggesting that it be considered as a sixth book-length long poem.

Notes on Contributors

ALEX ALBRIGHT is associate professor of English at East Carolina University. Professor Albright is the editor of the *North Carolina Poems* by A. R. Ammons (1994). His many articles have appeared in *The Southern Quarterly, North Carolina Humanities,* and *American Film.*

FREDERICK BUELL is professor of English at Queens College, where he directs the American Studies Program. He has published two books of poetry and two books of criticism: *W. H. Auden as a Social Poet* (1973) and *National Culture and the New Global System* (1994).

MIRIAM MARTY CLARK is associate professor and director of the Great Books Program at Auburn University, where she teaches courses in poetry, the short story, and twentieth century literature. Her articles have appeared in *Contemporary Literature, South Atlantic Review, Modern Fiction Studies, Mosaic,* and *Twentieth Century Literature.*

STEPHEN CUSHMAN is Professor of English at the University of Virginia. He is the author of *William Carlos Williams and the Meanings of Measure* (1985), *Fictions of Form in American Poetry* (1993), and *Blue Pajamas* (1998), a book of poems.

ROGER GILBERT is associate professor of English at Cornell University. He is the author of *Walks in the World: Representation and Experience in Modern American Poetry* (1991). Professor Gilbert's reviews and articles have appeared in *Contemporary Literature, Southwest Review, Western Humanities Review, New England Quarterly,* and *The Oxford Companion to Twentieth-Century Poetry.*

JAMES S. HANS is a professor of English at Wake Forest University, where he has taught since 1982. He is a specialist in twentieth

351

century poetry and his books include *The Value(s) of Literature* (1990), *Contextual Authority and Aesthetic Truth* (1992), *The Mysteries of Attention* (1993), and *The Site of Our Lives: The Self and the Subject from Emerson to Foucault* (1995).

WILLIAM HARMON is James Gordon Hanes Professor of English at the University of North Carolina—Chapel Hill. He is the author of the critical study *Time in Ezra Pound's Work*. Professor Harmon has published several books of poetry, including *Treasury Holiday*, winner of the Lamont Award of the Academy of American Poets, and *Mutatis Mutandis*, winner of the William Carlos Williams Award of the Poetry Society of America.

ROBERT P. HARRISON is a professor in the Department of French and Italian at Stanford and is the author of *Forests: The Shadow of Civilization* (1992), *Body of Beatrice* (1989), and *Rome, by Pluie* (1994).

MARJORIE PERLOFF is Sadie Dernham Patek Professor of Humanities at Stanford University. She is the author of *Radical Artifice: Writing Poetry in the Age of Media* (1994), *Poetic License: Essays on Modernist and Postmodernist Lyric* (1990), and *Poetics of Indeterminacy: Rimbaud to Cage* (1981). Her most recent books include *Wittgenstein's Ladder: Poetic Language and the Strangeness of the Ordinary* (1996) and *Poetry On and Off the Page: Essays for Emergent Occasions* (1998).

STEVEN P. SCHNEIDER is associate professor in the Department of English at the University of Nebraska at Kearney where he directs the graduate program in English. Professor Schneider is the author of *A. R. Ammons and the Poetics of Widening Scope* (1994). His poems and articles have appeared in *The Literary Review*, *The Iowa Review*, *Prairie Schooner*, *The Wordsworth Circle*, and *The North Carolina Literary Review*.

WILLARD SPIEGELMAN is Hughes Professor of English at Southern Methodist University. His books include a critical study of contemporary American poetry entitled *The Didactic Muse: Scenes of Instruction in Contemporary American Poetry* (1989) and a more recent study of English romantic poetry entitled *Majestic Indolence: English Romantic Poetry and the Work of Art* (1995). Professor Spiegelman is the editor of *The Southwest Review*.

DANIEL TOBIN is associate professor of English at Carthage College. He is the author of *Passage to the Center: Imagination and the Sacred in the Poetry of Seamus Heaney* (1998). His poems and articles have appeared in the *Yeats/Eliot Review, The Southern Humanities Review, The American Scholar, Poetry, The Paris Review,* and *Doubletake.*

HELEN VENDLER is A. Kingsley Porter University Professor in the Department of English and American Literature and Language at Harvard University. She has published many books on modern and contemporary American poetry, including *On Extended Wings: The Longer Poems of Wallace Stevens* (1969), *Part of Nature, Part of Us: Modern American Poets* (1980), *The Music of What Happens: Essays on Poetry and Criticism* (1988), *The Given and the Made: Lowell, Berryman, Dove, Graham* (1995), *The Breaking of Style: Hopkins, Heaney, Graham* (1995), and *The Art of Shakespeare's Sonnets* (1997). Professor Vendler is also poetry critic for *The New Yorker.*

Index of Names

Index of Works by A. R. Ammons and Others

WORKS BY A. R. AMMONS

WORKS BY OTHERS